WILLIAM PLOMER

William Plomer

A BIOGRAPHY

PETER F. ALEXANDER

Oxford   New York

OXFORD UNIVERSITY PRESS

1990

Oxford University Press, Walton Street, Oxford OX2 6DP

Oxford New York Toronto
Delhi Bombay Calcutta Madras Karachi
Petaling Jaya Singapore Hong Kong Tokyo
Nairobi Dar es Salaam Cape Town
Melbourne Auckland

and associated companies in
Berlin Ibadan

Oxford is a trade mark of Oxford University Press

British Library Cataloguing in Publication Data

Alexander, Peter (Peter F.)
William Plomer: a biography. (Oxford lives).
1. English literature. Plomer, William, 1903–1973
I. Title
828′91209
ISBN 0–19–282731–6

Library of Congress Cataloging in Publication Data

Alexander, Peter (Peter F.)
William Plomer: a biography / Peter F. Alexander.
p. cm.
Includes bibliographical references.
1. Plomer, William, 1903–1973—Biography. 2. Authors,
English—20th century—Biography. I. Title.
828′.91209—dc20 [PR6031.L7Z525 1990] [B] 90-7082
ISBN 0–19–28273–6

Printed in Great Britain by
Clays Ltd.
Bungay, Suffolk

*For Christine, Rebecca
and Roland*

Acknowledgements

WILLIAM PLOMER had the extraordinary gift of inspiring not just affection, but love, in many of those who knew him well, and one of the signs of this was the eagerness with which his friends pressed forward to help me in the writing of this book. Plomer's good judgement was nowhere shown more clearly than in his choice of Sir Rupert Hart-Davis as his literary executor, and it is to Sir Rupert that I and every other Plomer scholar owe the greatest debt. He and his wife June welcomed me to their home with unmatched hospitality, and he spent days answering my hundreds of questions, gave me permission to use all Plomer's writing, allowed me to photocopy the thousands of letters in his possession, and supplied me with dozens of addresses of other people who could help me. His name opened doors to me everywhere. He generously read my manuscript, proving to be the most accurate of proof-readers and the most experienced of advisers.

Sir Laurens van der Post, Plomer's oldest friend, welcomed me repeatedly to his homes in Aldeburgh and London, spent day after day talking into my tape recorder, patiently endured my questioning and supplied me with hundreds of letters which he had received from Plomer over the years. Without the opportunity to draw on his extraordinary memory, I would have been obliged to leave many areas of Plomer's early life in obscurity.

Mr Charles Erdmann, Plomer's faithful companion for nearly thirty years, entertained me royally, shared his memories with me, and presented me with one of the photographs reproduced in this book.

The family of Plomer's brother James, especially his wife Frances and his niece Wilhelmina (Billie), gave me invaluable information, and supplied copies of hundreds of Plomer's letters. They have been consistently supportive of the work that went into this book, and I am deeply grateful to them.

Mr Graham C. Greene, of Jonathan Cape Ltd., kindly gave me permission to look at the material held in the Cape archives in Reading University Library, patiently answered questions about Plomer's long association with his firm, and generously supplied me with relevant books.

Mr Michael Herbert, most sensitive and penetrating of Plomer's critics, kindly allowed me to read his unpublished thesis on Plomer and answered many questions, and I gratefully acknowledge my debt to his work and to him.

Professor James Kirkup kindly allowed me to read relevant sections of his unpublished memoirs, as did Mr William Oxley. The headmaster of Rugby School, Mr B. Rees, entertained me graciously and allowed me access to the school archives. Mr David Hindmarsh of Cambridge supplied important legal advice bearing on the interpretation of Plomer's will. Mr James Stern generously provided me with copies of many of Plomer's letters to himself.

Professor Wallace Robson, of the University of Edinburgh, and Dr Carl Baron, of St Catharine's College, Cambridge, have been unfailingly supportive during the course of this work and have put me on the track of much information I might otherwise have missed.

Miss Rosamund Strode, of the Britten–Pears Library, kindly gave me access to the large Plomer collection there, and painstakingly guided me through it. She also shared with me her memories of Plomer and Britten, and of their work together.

Others who agreed to interviews, who supplied me with copies of their correspondence with Plomer, or who provided vital information, include Jill Balcon (Mrs C. Day-Lewis), Sir John Betjeman, Mr Ronald Blythe, Miss Frances Boland, Mrs Mary Campbell, Mr Charles Causley, The Dowager Marchioness of Cholmondeley, Mr Mervyn Cooke, Dr Nigel Fortune, Mr P. N. Furbank, Ingaret Giffard (Lady Van der Post), Nadine Gordimer, Miss Muriel M. Green, Mrs Philippa Harrison of Michael Joseph Ltd., Lady Hart-Davis, Professor Ryuichi Kajiki, Mr John Lehmann, Miss Rosamond Lehmann, Mr David Machin of The Bodley Head, Ms Jane Miller, Dr Donald Mitchell, Captain Katsue Mori, Mr Simon Nowell-Smith, Mr Peter Parker, Mr Alan Paton, Sir Peter Pears, HM The Queen Mother, Mr Alan Ross, Sir Stephen Spender, Miss Rita Spurdle of Chatto & Windus, Ms Catherine Storr, Mr Shiomi Taro, Mr John Thompson, and Mrs Marjorie van der Post.

The bursar of Collingwood College, Durham, Mr C. D. Coombe, generously found me a flat during the early part of 1987, and thereby made my stay in Durham much more pleasant and comfortable than it might otherwise have been. I owe both him and the Fellows of Collingwood College a debt of gratitude.

I am grateful to the staffs of the following libraries for extensive help in the course of my research: Written Archives Centre of the British Broadcasting Corporation; the Britten Archives and the Trustees of the Britten Estate; Durham University Library; National English Language Museum, Grahamstown (and in particular Ms Jill Ainslie); the New Zealand National Library (incorporating the Alexander Turnbull Library, Wellington); Reading University Library, keepers of the archives of Jonathan Cape Ltd.; Rhodes University Library; the Library of Rugby School, and its librarian, Mrs Jennifer Macrory; the South African National Library, Cape Town; and the Special Collections of the University of Newcastle upon Tyne Library, especially Miss L. Gordon.

I pay particular tribute to Mr David Burnett, of the manuscripts section of Durham University Library, who did more than any librarian should be called upon to do to make my repeated visits to that institution not just productive, but delightful. His efficiency, patience, and extraordinary kindness overcame many obstacles that might otherwise have daunted me, and from his own wide-ranging scholarship he was able to supply information on subjects as diverse as graphology and palmistry. To him, best thanks.

I gratefully acknowledge permission from Sir Rupert Hart-Davis to quote all the Plomer material in this book, from the editors of *Music & Letters* to quote material previously published there, from Fransisco Campbell Custodio and Ad. Donker (Pty) Ltd. to quote from letters of Roy Campbell, from the Trustees of the Frank Sargeson Trust for permission to quote from letters of Frank Sargeson, and from Mr Harry Oppenheimer to quote the letters from Plomer to Van der Post in his private collection.

For financial help with the research that went into this book, I gratefully acknowledge generous grants from the Australian Research Grants Scheme, the Australian Academy of the Humanities, and the Arts Faculty of the University of New South Wales.

To my dedicated research assistant, Miss Meryl Potter, I owe special thanks for her patience; her methodical and painstaking labours have been an example to me. Miss Nola Potter accurately transcribed and typed tape-recorded interviews which were often almost incomprehensible. Mrs Effie Kallimanis kindly typed two sections of this book.

To those who gave me help, but whose names I may inadvertently have omitted, I offer sincere apologies.

P.F.A.

Contents

Illustrations

Charles and Edythe Plomer (*Photos: R. C. E. Nissen and Martin Jacolette. Durham University Library*

Edythe, William, and John Plomer, *c.*1907 (*Durham University Library*)

William Plomer as a schoolboy (*Durham University Library*)

Roy Campbell, Mary Campbell, and Laurens van der Post, 1926 (*Durham University Library*)

William Plomer, 1929 (*Photo: Ker-Seymer. Durham University Library*)

William Plomer relaxing at Glyphada, near Athens, 1930 (*Durham University Library*)

Bernard Bayes (*Durham University Library*)

William Plomer, Lilian Bowes-Lyon, and Marjorie Van der Post (*Durham University Library*)

William Plomer and Virginia Woolf at Monks House, August 1934 (*Durham University Library*)

William Plomer's birthday card to Rupert Hart-Davis (*Sir Rupert Hart-Davis*)

Joe Ackerley (*Photo: Kenneth N. Collins. Durham University Library*)

Stephen Spender (*Durham University Library*)

Rupert Hart-Davis and daughter Bridget, 1935 (*Durham University Library*)

Charles Erdmann, *c.*1940 (*Durham University Library*)

Charles Erdmann, Richard Rumbold, and William Plomer, 1957 (*Durham University Library*)

W. H. Auden and William Plomer, 1960 (*Photo: Mark Gerson. Durham University Library*)

Introduction

My whole [literary] output I regard as closely related to my life and myself.

Plomer to John Lehmann, 27 November 1955

To follow the life of William Plomer (his surname rhymes with 'rumour') is not just to follow the career of one of the most remarkable writers of the twentieth century; it is also to get a clear view of a whole circle of major writers, or rather of a series of circles. For years he moved at the centre of English writing and publishing, counting among his close friends Leonard and Virginia Woolf, Edith and Osbert Sitwell, E. M. Forster, Roy Campbell, Laurens van der Post, Stephen Spender, Christopher Isherwood, Edmund Blunden, John Lehmann, and many others. It was no ordinary man who could hold, over the course of so many years, the affectionate regard of individuals as varied and as distinguished as these. In addition, Plomer is without peer in the second half of the twentieth century as a discoverer of new talent. He recognized very early in their careers the gifts of writers as different as Ian Fleming, Arthur Koestler, Ted Hughes, Stevie Smith, John Betjeman, Vladimir Nabokov, John Fowles, and Alan Paton, and was instrumental in bringing many of them to public attention. He also discovered and introduced to the world one of the greatest of English diarists, the Victorian clergyman Francis Kilvert. Some of these 'discoveries' he came to know well and to regard as friends, and the comments he makes on them in his private correspondence are often very illuminating.

Plomer's own reputation has suffered something of a decline since his death in 1973, a decline from which it is only now beginning to emerge. He seems likely to shake off obscurity rapidly, in part because of the breadth and the diversity of his achievement, and in part because of the central position he occupied in the world of English letters. His poetic output was large and varied (he produced ten volumes of verse over the course of forty-six years), and he had the rare distinction among modern poets of having originated a new form of the ballad—wry, cynical, and sometimes cruel. It was a form that seemed to many readers to encapsulate something of the spirit of the twentieth century, the century of Buchenwald and Hiroshima, and it had a major and direct influence on the writing of poets as different as W. H. Auden, Frank Sargeson, and Charles Causley.

Plomer came to prominence initially as a novelist and short-story writer, and the first of his five novels, _Turbott Wolfe_, begun when he was only nineteen, established one of the two major themes that have dominated writing in English in the land of his birth, South Africa, ever since: that of miscegenation. Plomer's treatment of the issue of racism in terms of love, rather than hatred, was revolutionary, and in that important sense he may justly be called the father of South African prose writing. The other dominant theme in African literature, the impact of technology and the city on tribalized Africans, was also established by Plomer, in his seminal story 'Ula Masondo', and since then it has been elaborated by African writers, both black and white, almost endlessly.

In the 1950s he embarked on a series of collaborations with the outstanding English composer of the twentieth century, Benjamin Britten, for whom he wrote four libretti. Their first collaborative work was _Gloriana_, written in 1952 to celebrate Queen Elizabeth's coronation, and they went on during the 1960s to produce three 'parables for church performance': _Curlew River, The Burning Fiery Furnace_, and _The Prodigal Son_.

Another aspect of Plomer's achievement flowed from his residence in Japan during his impressionable early manhood. The novel in which he successfully incorporated the influence of modern Japanese writing, _Sado_, has been referred to by the leading scholar of the influence of Japanese literature on English writing as an important pioneering work, and as the first realistic novel with a Japanese setting.[1]

Plomer's life is also interesting in that he was an important artist who found himself ham-strung by an inability to accept, and to use in his work, a vital part of his own being—his sexuality. Plomer was a homosexual, and he found that fact almost intolerably painful, never losing his desire to escape from it. The consequences of his homosexuality were slow to come home to him, but they had a major and near disastrous effect on his work.

His writing can be distinguished as falling into three general periods in terms of output. From 1924, when he began writing, until 1929, when he first settled in England, he turned out a stream of stories and poems of a brilliant precocity, which analysed and attacked the societies in which he found himself. During the 1930s, however, he entered a period of agonized wrestling with his sexual identity. He longed to write about the central issue that dominated his thoughts, but found himself unable to publish what he wrote. Thus he abandoned novel after novel and his output of poetry slowed to a trickle. Then during the war, following a crisis in 1943, when he narrowly avoided serious trouble with the law, he entered a period of stability and self-acceptance. During this third period his productivity increased steadily. He abandoned novel-writing, and concentrated on the precise, beautiful verse on which his reputation now chiefly rests.

It is his sexual torment that in large part explains why Plomer wrote what he did, and (almost as important) why he did not write more. Yet he dodged this central issue entirely in his published autobiographies, and no critic has attempted to deal with it. 'You're quite right to suggest that homosexual overtones or undertones are present in my writings,' he told a friend towards the end of his life, 'and I hasten to say that any general view of my writings—and my life—should take notice of them.'[2] In writing this book I have kept this hint in mind, and have attempted to lift the mask Plomer so consistently presented to the world, and to show the true features of the extraordinary man and artist who wore it.

1. *Origins and Childhood*
1903–1914

WILLIAM CHARLES FRANKLYN[1] PLOMER was born in Pietersburg, South Africa, on 10 December 1903. The birth, which took
place about midday in the northern Transvaal's choking sub-
tropical heat, was a hard one, and the anxious father was told that
mother and child were likely to die.[2] They did not, but with the
child at least it was touch and go for several months, for in addition
to the usual problems of the new-born, he was infected with malaria
shortly after his arrival, and his parents were warned that if he
were to reach his first birthday he would have to be taken to a
better climate. Pietersburg at this time was a mere village, little
more than a collection of flimsy tin-roofed structures placed rather
oddly and forlornly in the bushveld, a low scattered scrubland of
acacia and thorn-trees that stretched apparently limitlessly on all
sides into the distance. In winter the climate was delightfully dry
and warm; in summer the rains (if they came at all) roared down
in those spectacular thunderstorms that are the most dramatic
feature of the South African climate, and the heat and humidity
became stifling, so that January and February were known as 'the
suicide months'.

The Boer War had ended just eighteen months before and much
of the Transvaal was still garrisoned. The population of the village,
only a few hundred in number, was divided into three clearly
demarcated segments. There were the Boers who had founded the
place; as they were released from concentration- and prisoner-of-war
camps they trickled back to their ruined homes and denuded farms,
and submitted large claims for war-damage compensation from the
British. Then there were the Africans, who had themselves suffered
heavily during the war, having been forcibly conscripted by both
sides, but trusted by neither. And third, there was the so-called
English community, some of them in fact South African born,
consisting mostly of civil servants and soldiers of the regular British
Army. Such social life as there was among those who spoke English
revolved around the garrison, which organized the activities

common to such outposts all over the Empire: 'a whirl of dances and dinners, picnics and tennis tournaments, gymkhanas and polo matches, puns and practical jokes, charades and drawing-room ballads', as Plomer, calling on the memories of his mother, was to write years later.[3]

But life was by no means all picnics and gymkhanas. The tropical diseases of Africa took a heavy toll of the expatriates: malaria, black-water fever, trypanosomiasis (sleeping sickness), yellow fever, and bilharzia kept the town doctor busy; the fever allowance paid to civil servants was poor compensation for the repeated spells of shivering and debilitation. It was clearly no place for a sickly child, and Plomer's mother set off with him on the long trip back to her mother in England, leaving her husband to cope for eighteen months on his own.

Coping on his own was something Charles Plomer was well used to doing. He was, if not a black sheep, a darkish-grey one, whose family had been pleased to help him settle in what were then known as 'the colonies'. The Plomers (the name was at that time pronounced to rhyme with Homer) were an old and not undistinguished family that had established itself in Elizabethan times at Radwell near Baldock. One William Plomer, an ancestor of the writer, was knighted in 1616, probably for a financial contribution to the often shaky finances of James I. He was a man of considerable wealth, as his possession of a minor stately home, Radwell House, and his family monuments in Radwell Church attest. His famous descendant jokingly dubbed him William II, since an earlier ancestor[4] had also been named William. The family fortunes went into decline soon after William II's death, however; his son, William III, was sheriff of the county, but before his death was obliged to sell Radwell House, and died childless.

The brother of William III, Thomas, was an Anglican priest at Stone in Buckinghamshire; one of his sons, John, also a divine, was headmaster of Rugby 'from 1731, when the number of boys was low, until 1759, when it was lower still', as his descendant was to remark.[5] John Plomer's brother, yet another William (IV) in a family not noteworthy for its imaginative choice of names, produced a son, William V, who made a fortune as a merchant, was knighted, and became Lord Mayor of London; his son, William VI, in turn became sheriff of London and was knighted as his father had been.

His son, William VII, Deputy-Lieutenant for Edinburgh, married one Catherine Pagan in 1819; their third son, Alfred George, born in 1829, was the writer's grandfather. He enlisted in the Indian Army, saw action against the Persians in 1856–7, and helped to put down the Indian Mutiny. He eventually attained the rank of colonel, and, when he inherited his father's money, retired to live in considerable comfort in England. His grandson remembered him well, recording that he had a 'frizzy black beard like a Sikh's', and adding satirically that 'his nose was large, his eyes small, his heart kind, his politics Conservative, his manners and opinions rigidly conventional, and his temper placid; he had great strength of body, and measured 48 inches round the chest; and it pleased him at times to play *The Two Obadiahs*, a popular song of the period, on the flute'.[6]

Alfred Plomer had four children: William, who followed his father's military bent and became a reserved and rather stolid soldier, commanding at one time the Royal Irish Fusiliers; Laura, who married Emslie Horniman, scion of a Quaker family that had made a fortune from tea ('Horniman's Pure Tea'), the brother of Annie Horniman, W. B. Yeats's friend and the woman who financed the establishment of the Irish National Theatre; Durham, a cheerful handsome ne'er-do-well who was killed in the Boer War; and Charles Campbell Plomer, the writer's father, born in London on 16 January 1870.

Charles Plomer grew from an unwanted boy into a nervous, unstable man, prone to sudden, unreasonable fits of rage alternating with a great need for affection shown through hugs and kisses. His son, who resented these sudden alterations of mood, came to believe that their origin lay in Charles's feeling that his mother, Helen Plomer, had never loved him, and had in fact disliked all her children except the spoiled Durham. Helen Lucretia Plomer had a violent and uncontrollable—or at least uncontrolled—temper, which allowed her to rule her placid husband completely. She seems, to judge by the veiled hints found in the pages of her grandson's accounts of her,[7] to have had a long-standing affair with a man who had admired her before her marriage to Alfred Plomer, an affair her children were half-aware of and bitterly resented. She made little attempt to conceal from Charles and his sister Laura the fact that she disliked them, and she thwarted them in many small ways. Little Charles, for instance, was the favourite of an old apple-woman, who one day offered him an orange in exchange for a kiss. The child was about to oblige her when his mother intervened, forbidding him ever to speak to the old woman again, and he, who longed for the physical affection his mother denied him, thought this ban bitterly unjust. 'This was one of those incidents of childhood that mark a man for life,' his son was to write decades later.[8] Charles Plomer showed his unhappiness by making at least one childish attempt to run away from home, only to be brought back by a policeman and beaten by his stern and unimaginative father; on another occasion he climbed out of a nursery window on to the parapet of the family's four-storey house in Stanhope Street, Bayswater, an escapade that his son put down to a desire to escape from his surroundings.[9] His nervousness showed itself in the terrible eczema from which he suffered as a child, and in the asthma that gripped him at intervals for the rest of his life.

After a rather patchy education at half a dozen schools, ranging from Westward Ho! (of Kipling fame) to a small school in France, at Guînes in the Pas-de-Calais, Charles was apprenticed to a wool merchant in Bradford. When he got into debt as a result of gambling and an expensive affair with a gamekeeper's daughter, his angry father packed him off to South Africa with a letter of introduction to Cecil Rhodes. He arrived at the Cape in 1889,[10] a remittance man without a remittance. The letter to Rhodes produced an interview with the millionaire, who weighed Charles Plomer up and seems to have found him wanting; the ordeal produced nothing more substantial than advice that he join the Cape Mounted Rifles. This advice he followed, but the hardness of the military life and a recurrence of asthma made him buy himself out after a year, and after this he knocked about the country. He ran a café in Port Elizabeth until his partner decamped with all the funds; then he managed a sheep farm near Queenstown, ran a native trading station near Lady Frere, acted as tutor to a farmer's children, did some fencing and bridge building: in short, he did anything that came to hand as he tramped about the country carrying his possessions tied in a bundle on a stick.

After six years of this rolling-stone existence, Charles joined the Bechuanaland Border Police, and participated in Jameson's ill-fated raid into the Transvaal at the end of 1895. He was captured on 3 January 1896 and imprisoned with the other raiders in the

Pretoria race-track, before being expelled from the Transvaal and returning briefly to England.[11] Back in South Africa in 1897, he became a journalist on the staff of the Pretoria *Press*, and lodged in that city with an official of the Transvaal's High Court. In the course of his work he got to know the president, Paul Kruger, for the old man made himself readily available to almost anyone who cared to call on him. Occasionally he would let fall some snippet of news that Charles was able to print, though the young Englishman paid for these rare favours by serving as the butt of Kruger's notoriously unsophisticated sense of humour; he would, for instance, pinch Charles's leg suddenly when his attention was elsewhere, and then bellow with laughter at the young man's pained outcry. Charles, who was a fine swimmer, impressed the president by a display of his skill at the Pretoria baths, when he swam round the bath underwater, picking up twenty-four plates which he deposited at Kruger's feet. '*Machtig! De kêrel swimmt net als een visch!*' (Heavens! The fellow swims just like a fish!) exclaimed the old man naïvely.[12]

Charles also got to know Jan Smuts, then the Transvaal State Attorney, and Louis Botha, who like Smuts was to become known as one of the most daring Boer generals. When the war broke out, Botha offered Charles a permit to stay on in Pretoria if he wished, but Charles wisely chose to leave with the rest of the British community, and actually returned to England before being sent back by his irritated father, who thought he should be putting his training as a soldier to use and was amazed that he had chosen to flee a war. Certainly the British Army at this stage was desperately in need of men with exactly Charles's experience of local conditions and of the local languages.

Charles had no interest in fighting, however, and he worked as a civilian transport rider, convoying oxen and supplies from the Orange Free State to the Transvaal. In this traffic he managed to accumulate some money, and as soon as the war ended, returned to England and proposed to Edythe Mary Browne, who was distantly related to him,[13] and with whom he had what in those days was called 'an understanding'. They had met as children, and had gradually come to think that they loved each other.

Edythe, William Plomer's mother, was born in 1874, the daughter of Edward Waite Browne of Cotgrave Place, Nottinghamshire, a gentleman farmer who died young of consumption. She had been brought up, in comfort if not wealth, by her widowed mother at Southwell in Nottinghamshire, had been rather poorly educated by English and French governesses, and trained (according to her son)[14] to be decorative rather than useful, and with no idea of the value of money. With her wide-set grey eyes, red-brown hair and high colour, rather straight mouth, and a neck a little too thick to be elegant, she was not a beauty, but the quietly watchful air she showed even in girlhood developed with maturity into a natural dignity that gave her real distinction. The advantages conferred on her by her upbringing included a strong Christian faith, great conscientiousness and a sense of duty towards the less privileged, a readiness for self-sacrifice, natural good manners, and an infectious sense of fun. In her marriage to the handsome, unstable Charles Plomer, she was going to need them all.

Charles was very good-looking, with his dark eyes, dapper moustache, glossy black hair, upright carriage, and the swaggering air of a man who has been about in the world and knows how to look after himself. Photographs of him at this time, cockily wearing the slouch hat adopted by both sides in the South African conflict, his carefully cultivated moustache giving him the piratical and carefree air of a Spitfire pilot forty years too soon, convey something of the charm Edythe Browne must have sensed in him. He seemed to offer a breath of fresh air and the possibility of freedom. On the other hand, he had very little money and no immediate prospects other than a knowledge of the country that Sir Alfred Milner (the High Commissioner for South Africa) and his 'kindergarten' of clever young Englishmen were going to attempt to Anglicize as quickly as possible when the war was over. No doubt Charles was hopeful that he could get a job in the burgeoning civil service in South Africa simply by asking for it. It was true that he had one or two strings to pull, including the acquaintance of General Sir William Cameron, Acting Governor of the Cape and an old friend of his father, but clearly his prospects in Africa were far from brilliant, and Edythe Browne must have been very much in love to marry him. Perhaps the prospect of release from the constricted life of a cathedral town, in which everyone knew everyone else's business and every curate had been considered as a prospective suitor, played its part in her decision. She accepted Charles Plomer.

They were married in London on 1 June 1901 (their wedding present from his father was £500, then a considerable sum) and after a brief honeymoon at Brighton sailed for South Africa. Charles was thirty-one, Edythe twenty-seven. Edythe's health seems to have been indifferent from the start; in Durban she fell ill and had to have an operation, from which she took some time to recover. It was a poor beginning in Africa for her, and it proved to be a portent. She never forgot the kindness with which her doctor, Sam Campbell, a member of a famous pioneering Natal family, sent his carriage each day to take her out for drives while she was recuperating. Dr Campbell had newly returned to Durban after surviving the siege of Ladysmith, and his wife had recently given birth to a son, Roy, who was destined to become a famous poet. His kindness seemed to Edythe a quite atypical example of courtesy in a colonial society which she thought in general crude almost to the point of barbarism.

With considerable difficulty and inconvenience, because the railway line had been cut in many places by the Boers whose activities were only slowly being controlled by Kitchener's lines of blockhouses and barbed wire, the newly-weds made their way to Pretoria, where Charles was given a minor post in the Treasury and they set up house. Edythe quickly fell ill again, however, this time succumbing to a combination of malaria, dysentery, and peritonitis, and she was advised to return to England for the sake of her health. She left Charles to sell the house again and take a job in the northern Transvaal once the war ended, working for the Repatriation Commission that Milner had set up to restore the Boers to their farms.

For six months Charles toured the thinly populated tropical region, checking claims for compensation put in by freed prisoners, and (predictably enough) finding them often greatly exaggerated. No doubt he took the job because it paid better than his Treasury post; but no civil servant would have regarded it as a plum position, and though he rather liked trekking about through wild bushland (it was after all a return to his previous gypsy existence) the sight of thousands of pounds being paid out to the defeated enemy, when Charles himself had been denied compensation for some of his possessions looted by the British forces during the war, became a source of grievance with him. Tiring of this occupation, he took a post with the Department of Native Affairs at Pietersburg. Again it seems probable that he was able to secure this position in part at least because Pietersburg was a far from popular posting in the

colonial civil service. It was at Pietersburg that his wife rejoined
him early in 1903, and shortly thereafter found herself pregnant.

In later life William Plomer was often to feel that he was in some
sense an outsider, not really belonging anywhere. This sense was
undoubtedly due in part to the accident of his birth in tropical
Africa, but of English parents, and to the fact that from the start
he led an extraordinarily restless life. Having been taken to England
by his mother within a few months of his birth, he returned with
her to South Africa in June 1905 to rejoin Charles Plomer in
Pietersburg. They had been back in Africa less than a year before
Charles went down with malaria and was given six months' leave.
This time all three of them went back to England, staying with Mrs
Browne at Southwell; they also spent a brief period enjoying the
sea air at Scarborough.

A second son, John, was born in May 1907, shortly after their
return to Pietersburg; unlike his brother, he was healthy from the
start. Perhaps it was the sense that his family was gradually
adapting to Africa that gave Charles Plomer the confidence to move
them, in 1909, to a still hotter, more fever-stricken town than
Pietersburg, Louis Trichardt, a hundred kilometres away at the foot
of the Zoutpansberg. If Pietersburg had been small and its social
life limited, Louis Trichardt was smaller still and its social life all
but non-existent, most of its population having melted away during
the Boer War, so that many of the houses were derelict. The local
African tribe, the Bavenda, remained fiercely independent (and well
armed) until after the Boer War; wild animals had multiplied during
the war, and lions, giraffes, elephants, and a wide range of buck
were commonly encountered by travellers. Edythe Plomer made
the week-long journey from Pietersburg with two small children in
an ox-waggon through this fascinating but hostile landscape, and
her eldest son, who in later years vaguely remembered the journey,
recalled it as apparently endless. On arrival in the steaming hamlet
overlooked by the barren slopes of the Zoutpansberg, Edythe had
to make her home in a dilapidated shack with earthen walls, clay
floor, and corrugated iron roof, and she must often have thought
back to the daisied lawns of Southwell and wondered what she had
come to. Fortunately she can hardly have foreseen what she would
suffer in Louis Trichardt.

This was the home of which William Plomer retained his first

memories, and they were memories of a primitive Africa that was
even then rapidly retreating. At night, with the windows open for
a little cool air after the heat of the day, he would hear the distant
roaring of lions or the nearby howling of jackals, a sound he
thought sad and wonderful. A trip to the primitive earth toilet was
an adventure, for it stood at a distance from the house and sheltered
all manner of dangerous or merely alarming creatures, ranging
from tarantulas to big black hornets. The 'garden', a couple of
hectares in extent, showed little sign of cultivation when the
Plomers arrived, though it was watered by a natural stream which
meandered through. The grass of the veld, waist-high in the years
when the rains came, swept up almost to the house itself, and
Plomer remembered one veld-fire in which the flames had burned
all round the house, 'mounting higher and higher in raging
arabesques, while our servants tried to fend them off with branches:
then suddenly a man on horseback, who had come to see if we
were all right, burst magically through the curtains of flame'.[15] It
was here that he first began to exercise that peculiar clarity of
vision that marks all his writing, and which he believed was
cultivated in him by his mother:

My first memory of any significance is of a brilliant spring morning at
Louis Trichardt. It had rained in the night, but now the sky was cloudless
and the world of an incomparable freshness and fragrance, exhaled by the
sparkling green veld and wafted in the air. I strayed out of the garden and
standing on the bank of the stream suddenly saw on the opposite bank,
perhaps twelve feet away, two large birds, a kind of wild duck perhaps.
One was resting on the ground; the other stood beside it. Their plumage
gleamed like many-coloured enamel in the sun against a background of
reeds, their eyes glinted like jewels, and they showed no sign of alarm,
but watched me as I watched them. My feeling was partly one of delighted
discovery (almost comparable, perhaps, to that of a naturalist discovering
a rare species), partly of pure delight, both heightened into an ecstasy
which could not then and cannot now be put into words, but seemed to
have in it a kind of mutual understanding and joy, as if the birds and I
knew that we were part of the same life, and that life was splendid . . . I
[took] increasing pleasure in the visible world and was indeed trained to
do so by my mother, herself richly endowed with what may be called the
visual appetite.[16]

The Plomers employed several servants, male and female, inside
the house and in the garden; Plomer retained a memory of the

'touch of warm brown skins',[17] since he was cared for from the start in Louis Trichardt by a black nurse, Maud Dgami, a photograph of whom he kept all his life. His mother tended to treat these servants as she would have treated white servants in England (allowing for the differences imposed by culture and language barriers); she saw her position as imposing duties as well as privileges on her, and regarded her servants as human beings not fundamentally different from herself. This attitude her elder son was to adopt, with momentous results in later life.

Charles Plomer's work with the Department of Native Affairs brought him into constant contact with the local Africans, for his duties included the task of determining the boundaries of the native reserves that were being set out at this time, and also in collecting the large sums in gold that local commissioners received in payment of taxes from the Africans. At least once a month he made a long and leisurely trip around his vast district, travelling in a mule-cart escorted by mounted police whose job it was to guard the tax money. In June 1908 he was away on one of these trips when John Plomer, now a little more than a year old, fell ill; his mother recognized the familiar signs of malaria, but these were soon complicated by other disquieting symptoms. Edythe Plomer, facing this crisis on her own in a remote settlement where she had no friends and few acquaintances, nursed the small child as best she could and sent out urgent messages summoning her husband and a distant doctor. The doctor arrived first and diagnosed diphtheria; there was very little that could be done. The disease was then a common and very quick killer; continual infusions to keep the throat clear, and a tracheotomy *in extremis* were the only treatments.

Charles Plomer, having ridden day and night for thirty-six hours, arrived home to find his wife and the doctor exhausted by the struggle. He took over the nursing from Edythe and made her rest; William, not yet five, lay by her side, and years later remembered listening to her weeping, and seeing through the open window the moonlight glittering on the stream.[18] Before dawn on 8 June 1908, Charles noticed the child becoming increasingly restless and called the doctor who, seeing that a crisis had developed, decided that a tracheotomy was the only hope. 'The courage of women knows no bounds,' William Plomer wrote years later; 'my mother held the child in her arms while the doctor cut its throat.'[19] In vain: the little patient was dead before the tube could be inserted. Louis

Trichardt could provide no coffin, and John Plomer was nailed into a packing-case lined with cheap velveteen and laid in unconsecrated ground, for the village lacked even a cemetery.[20]

Africa had dealt cruelly with Edythe Plomer, and it is not surprising that she conceived a dislike of the continent and longed to escape from it permanently, as soon as their financial position would allow it. The extremity of her suffering is reflected in the fact that years later she told her eldest son that John's death had made her question her belief in God.[21] Certainly life in Louis Trichardt had become unbearable to her. Charles gathered their small savings and once more sent her and William to stay with her mother. Presently he fell ill himself, was given six months' compassionate leave, and followed them to England. Though they would return to Africa, they would never return to Louis Trichardt.

In London they visited grandfather Alfred Plomer, who, through a series of unwise investments, had lost the greater part of his fortune—he was said to have lost £20,000 in one day[22]—and who, recently widowed, had moved into a flat in Kensington, in 1908 an unusual, dashingly modern mode of living for a man of his class. His grandson vividly remembered him at this time striding along Kensington Gore on the way to his club, splendid in a top hat and beaver coat with an astrakhan collar, very much the Victorian gentleman comfortably stranded in Edwardian London. He made a great fuss of William, whom he regarded as his only grandchild, although his daughter Laura had several children; Colonel Plomer had disapproved of her engagement and had disowned her for marrying Emslie Horniman, a foolish and vindictive stand that he maintained until his death. Concerned by the death of John, he insisted that William be left in England to be educated when his parents returned to South Africa, and he seems to have provided the money to make this possible, for the younger Plomers presently engaged a governess for William, Miss de Montmorency, whose grand name left her young charge confused about her sex, because he heard 'Miss de Montmorency' as 'Mr Montmorency'.

From London the Plomers, with the governess in tow, went to spend the winter of 1908/9 with Edythe's mother, who had moved from Southwell to the chilly spa town of Buxton in Derbyshire. William developed an immediate love and respect for 'Granny Browne': 'I thought her wise and charming, and was always anxious to please her.'[23] The influence of women—his mother, grandmother, and aunts—was to operate powerfully and irreversibly on him throughout his formative years, and the reaction he experienced against his father and grandfather as he grew up never affected his feelings towards his female relations. The influence of women was about to become critical in his life, for he was nearly five, and he would soon begin life without his parents.

Part of the price the British Empire exacted of its white masters was the destruction of their family life. Young Rudyard Kipling, born like William Plomer in a distant, unhealthy corner of the Empire, carried all his life the psychological scars of having been left by his parents, unwarned and unprepared, in the care of a virtual stranger. Kipling suffered cruel treatment at the hands of Mrs Holloway; Plomer was much luckier. Unlike Kipling, he had no sister to share his loneliness; but he was left, not with a hireling and stranger, but with Aunt Hilda.

She was his mother's only sister, and while the Plomers were living in Louis Trichardt, she had married Telford Hayman, who kept a preparatory school at Spondon House, near Derby. Hayman was a pleasant, cultured man, son of an Anglican priest and grandson of Dr Brewer, compiler of the *Dictionary of Phrase and Fable*, and Aunt Hilda seems to have been kindly and indulgent. Plomer lived with them very happily, from the spring of 1909 until May 1911. Because he was so young, Aunt Hilda kept him apart from the other boys in the school, perhaps to ensure that he would not be bullied. As a result, he wrote years later, 'Being parted from my parents and without brothers and sisters I found myself in one of those isolated and somewhat anomalous situations which were often to recur in one form or another in my later life.'[24] In retrospect he seemed already to have set out on that apparently self-sufficient, loner's path that he was to follow with few deviations throughout his life. He saw himself as a passive observer rather than an actor, and while this role may have been forced on him by circumstances at first, he later came to claim it for his own, and to proclaim it, in Joycean fashion, as the right attitude for a writer to adopt. He was still only five when he announced to his startled aunt that he wanted to be an artist.[25] If a child of five means anything by such an announcement, it is probably that he wants to be a painter. And indeed the boy loved to draw and paint, and showed a precocious aptitude for it.

He had no memories of his earlier visit to England, and began to discover the country now for the first time. During these two years without his parents he came to love England as he had unconsciously loved South Africa because it was the place on which he first opened his eyes. He recognized England, he said, 'as a mirror recognizes a face'.[26] He wandered around, sometimes on his own, sometimes with his aunt, in Locks Park or at Dale Abbey, registering the beauty of England with the sensuous vividness of the very young, and he described it years later with the tongue of a poet:

I wandered between low hedges of the small-leaved, wholesome-smelling box and under lofty hedges of the ripple-fruited yew, inside which were caves of darkness, full of dead twigs furred and powdered with black dust. I noticed the first snowdrops, skeleton leaves, and the ivy on the wall. I loved the richness of early summer, its meadows lavish with rusty sorrel and silky fescue, and I touched the rosy heads of clover and the hard-faced, faintly fetid moon daisies. I rejoiced in autumn mornings, when, after a blustering night, yellow leaves had been beaten so flat on the asphalt pavements that they seemed to have been painted upon them, and varnished horse-chestnuts lay thick on the ground, waiting only to be picked up.[27]

He had small friends from outside the school's walls, but he learned quickly that they had to be chosen carefully. In Africa he had not played with black children, and his mother had rather looked down on the other white families in Pietersburg and Louis Trichardt.[28] In Spondon he soon found that 'the world was largely populated by beings called the lower or working classes, and that they were a race apart ... One stared in silence at "the working classes", without hostility, but aware of their difference and strangeness.'[29] He seems to have been fascinated by them: the drunkenness of a big labourer, the urchin energy of the children (one of whom ripped off his blue Conservative rosette at election time),[30] their jokes which he could not understand. Looking back on this time, he came to believe that he had from the start associated them with sex, vaguely apprehended in the way a housemaid let him romp with her, laughing and saying, 'Oh, aren't you artful!' when he pinched her breasts, more clearly guessed at when he was told to look away from a labourer exposing himself in an alley. 'The solitary labourer, the rosy maid, the playful dogs in the street—all these had something to do with the business of sex ...

which somehow seemed nearer the surface in the working class, who accordingly began to figure in the fantasies which came into my mind before I fell asleep.'[31]

He was already fantasizing in other ways. He had a recurrent experience in the course of which he believed he was aware of ghosts in the garden of some people he and his aunt visited occasionally.

In this garden I had the feeling of being *en rapport* with what I could later identify as the eighteenth century. I will not say I saw or imagined but rather that I got to know two distinct characters, a man and a woman with the dress and manners of that period ... It is possible that the place was haunted by some echo or vibration of a poignant and insoluble situation in the affairs of persons who had lived there long ago, and that this echo or vibration was perceptible to my unhardened sensibility.[32]

A less superstitious commentator might have thought that the powerful imagination of the inchoate artist was operating in Plomer as it operated in Blake when, as a child, he saw angels among the reapers. Plomer was already something of a non-conformist; he hated cricket and refused to play it, a rare heresy for a schoolboy of the period. His hobbies were solitary and largely botanical; taken to church, he once sang words of his own to a hymn, and his aunt, bending down to listen, found he was improvising a song about flowers.

His mother seems to have missed him more than he missed her during the two years he spent at Spondon. Charles Plomer had secured a job in Johannesburg on his return to South Africa in 1908, but though the climate of the highveld (Johannesburg lies nearly 2,000 metres above sea-level) was far healthier than that of Pietersburg or Louis Trichardt, Edythe Plomer continued to regard herself as an involuntary exile. When she discovered, early in 1911, that she was pregnant again, she persuaded her husband to let her go home for the birth, and arrived in Spondon in March 1911. Her son left no record of his meeting with her after this separation, and possibly it made little impact on him. She, however, made a disconcerting discovery about him soon after her arrival when she asked him the time and discovered that he could not see the hands, much less the figures, on her travelling clock on the other side of the room. She learned that Aunt Hilda had allowed him to read in bright light while he had measles, and to this (probably wrongly)[33] his mother attributed the fact that his eyesight was permanently weakened. From then on and for the rest of his life he wore thick-lensed spectacles to compensate for myopia. Relations between Edythe Plomer and her sister were soured by this discovery, and Edythe presently took her son and an Alsatian governess named Adèle off to a house named Lowicks, near Frensham Ponds in Surrey.

Lowicks was a magnificent country home, which Charles's sister Laura Horniman had lent the Plomers while she and her husband Emslie were touring one of the remoter parts of Europe in style in their chauffeur-driven Rolls-Royce. The house, designed by Voysey, seemed to young Plomer (and doubtless to his Africa-weary mother as well) the epitome of comfort and modernity:

Lowicks was ... idiosyncratic, partly because everything was very high or very low. The roof came down steeply, almost to the ground; the casement windows were wide and low, the window seats very low; but the latches on the doors were so high that to open them one had to make the gesture of someone proposing a toast to the architect. High-backed chairs ... were pierced with heart-shaped openings, and on high shelves near the ceiling stood vases of crafty green pottery filled with peacocks' feathers in defiance of the superstition that they shouldn't be brought indoors. Coal scuttles, hot-water cans, and electroliers [electric chandeliers] were made of beaten or hammered brass or copper. The house, so fresh and modern in design, was perfectly comfortable, light and warm.[34]

After nearly two months of luxuriating in the comfort of this quiet house, mother, son, and governess moved to Bexhill in June, and there in August 1911 Edythe gave birth to another boy, Peter.[35]

During the time that Plomer had spent with Aunt Hilda, both his remaining grandparents had died: Edythe's mother first, and then the colonel. This left Plomer's parents considerably better off, and it also meant that the colonel's insistence that William should be educated in England could now be ignored. In addition it is likely that the experience of living in Johannesburg had brought home to her the fact that the highveld climate is among the healthiest in the world. Moreover, Johannesburg, though only a quarter of a century old, already had some excellent schools. When Edythe Plomer left for South Africa again, in September 1911, both children went with her, and she also took an English nanny.

Perhaps she went hoping that her husband could be persuaded to return to England now that they had the money to make this possible; if so, she was to be disappointed. Charles Plomer was much too active to want to retire (he was in any case still only in his early forties), and he loved Africa. Rough manners and unpolished ways amused him; to the end of his life he liked to tell the story of a Boer farming family with whom he had stayed during his rolling-stone days, who had given him the roughest of fare and bedded him down for the night among their numerous and verminous children—though ensuring that he slept at some distance from the eldest girl. In the morning Charles had enquired about the toilet. 'Ag, it is all my land,' his host had said placidly, with a wide sweep of his arm at the magnificent landscape of veld and mountain, 'Shit where you like!'[36] Charles treasured the memory of this remark. His wife, by contrast, recalled with disgust her first meal at a boarding-house in Durban in 1901, when a young man had sat down at the table opposite her, taken a large clasp-knife out of his pocket, and proceeded to clean his nails with it. She longed to return to the ordered, complex, safe world of England, and made little secret of the fact that she thought everything South African inferior to what she had left behind, but her husband's will prevailed—for the moment.

Charles had taken a house in Koch street,[37] then a dusty, unpaved thoroughfare near Joubert Park, in Johannesburg, sharing it with an Anglo-Irish major, a friend from his days in the Bechuanaland Police. When Edythe, the two children, and the English nanny arrived in September 1911, the major moved out. Charles Plomer's job in the Department of Native Affairs now involved him in the administration of the pass system, under which each African forced to come to Johannesburg to work in the mines in order to pay the taxes imposed on him, was obliged to carry an identity document called a pass, containing his name, his tribe, the name of his chief, and details of his employment. Without a pass he was liable to arrest and imprisonment. The system thus allowed the authorities to control the movement of the huge population of blacks to the cities, and to keep an eye on them while they were there. Charles Plomer worked in the central pass office in Johannesburg, at the head of a large staff of black and white clerks, interpreters, and police, administering this cumbersome and, for the blacks, increasingly galling system. He seems to have enjoyed his work, though, according to his son,[38] he was regarded as too much of a negrophile ever to be given a position of real importance, and eventually he was to be forced out of the civil service by the movement to employ more South Africans and fewer expatriates.

William Plomer was now seven, and his parents enrolled him as a boarding pupil at St John's College in Johannesburg at the start of 1912. St John's, then as now one of the best and most expensive schools in southern Africa, had been founded as an Anglican church school in the 1890s by the Community of the Resurrection, a monastic order (itself an outgrowth of the Tractarian Movement) that had its base at Mirfield in West Yorkshire. The fathers of the community had focused their missionary efforts on southern Africa, where in addition to St John's College they had founded numerous schools for Africans in South Africa and what was then Rhodesia. In Johannesburg itself they had established a large priory in Rosettenville, and they had also founded a seminary for black priests in the town of Alice, in what is now the Transkei. The energies of the Community were now at their height, and Plomer in later years considered himself lucky to have come under their influence.

St John's College was commandingly placed on a hill to the north of the city centre. Growing up around it were the houses of the Johannesburg rich, for the northern suburbs were destined to become the dwelling site of choice for the numerous millionaires created by gold mining. The school buildings, nobly designed and built of rough blocks of the hard, polychrome local stone, were more beautiful than comfortable; in the harsh highveld winters the boys' dormitories were freezing, and the whole place had about it a spartan air designed no doubt to mould the characters of its little inmates. It seems curious that Plomer should have been sent as a boarder, for his parents' house in Joubert Park was within easy reach of the school. Did his mother, who nursed the odd ambition that he should eventually go into the Navy, think it would toughen him up? Or did she hope that he would there be insulated from the rougher elements in South African society, who were likely to be screened out by the cost of the school? However it was, he went as a boarder, and seems to have enjoyed the experience, judging from the account he wrote years later. He liked the masters, who, invariably wearing cassocks and birettas whether they were conducting a service in the school's fine chapel or leading the boys in the daily early morning sprint across the playing-fields, dispensed Anglo-Catholic doctrine and the virtues of the English public-school system in equal quantities. He found them well educated, indeed cultured, men, most of them products of Oxford or Cambridge, with liberal ideals of a kind rarely encountered in South Africa.

Here for the first time (and perhaps the last) he felt part of a community, and he made many friends. Living apart from his parents was nothing new to him, and though he saw them only once or twice a term (when a boy who had no blot against his name would be provided with an *exeat* allowing him to leave the school grounds for forty-eight hours),[39] this was more than he had seen of them during the years in England. No one obliged him to take part in cricket or football, from which in any case his weak eyesight excluded him; instead, in company with his schoolfellows, he spent pleasant afternoons and evenings scrambling over the rocky kopje near the school, now heavily built up but then almost as wild as it had been in the 1870s, before the discovery of gold. He loved the climate of Johannesburg, with its brilliant, sunny winters and its magnificent summer storms, whose arrival was heralded by incandescent lightning in a blue-black afternoon sky, followed by a rapidly approaching roar as a wall of hail came sweeping across the iron roofs of the city.

Far from being kept away from the other boys, as he had been at Spondon, he was encouraged to join in the activities of the school. In particular he acted in the Shakespearian play the school put on each year. During the Easter term of 1912 he took part in a performance of *Macbeth*, directed by one of the masters, J. O. Nash. In the *St John's College Letter*[40] for the Easter and Lent term, he is listed in the dramatis personae: 'Boy, Child of Macduff: W. Plomer', and the brief account of the performance singles him out for special commendation: 'The little eight-year-old[41] Billy Plomer (child of Macduff) played most prettily, and touched all mothers' hearts.' Since the part is small his achievement should not be overrated. That same year, however, the school, perhaps emboldened by his success in *Macbeth*, cast him in the more important role of Titania in *A Midsummer Night's Dream*. In later years he was to derive a good deal of amusement from the thought that he had played a fairy queen in public. Writing in the school *Letter*[42] afterwards, one of the parents remarked, 'A dainty Titania was little William Plomer,' while another said that 'Plomer's Titania was more than good for so young a boy,' and, while criticizing the costumes and make-up of the boys playing female roles, exempted only Titania, who it seems had appeared entirely charming in white crêpe-de-chine and spangles. This exemption may have surprised Plomer, for he had wet the front of his spangled robe while nervously relieving himself before the performance, and had had to be hastily dried in front of a stove behind the scenes.[43]

Towards the end of 1912 his parents, whose financial affairs had been steadily improving since the deaths of Colonel Plomer and Mrs Browne as the income from inherited investments began to come in, took a large and rather grand house on a hilltop near St John's, and from the beginning of 1913 Plomer became a day-boy. They now began to live in some style, entertaining often, and making good use of the colonel's silver plate to adorn their dinner table. Plomer was able to invite his schoolfellows home. The homosexuality so common at some English public schools of this period[44] seems scarcely to have existed at St John's, but Plomer was engaging enough to attract at least one admirer. This was Charles Pritchard, a senior, powerfully built boy of seventeen or eighteen who had played Bottom to Plomer's Titania in 1912, and whom Plomer in his autobiography *Double Lives* was to describe, ambiguously, as 'touchingly protective towards me', adding only a little less ambiguously, 'I think he would have pleased Walt Whitman.'[45] Pritchard, who later became a tram-driver, was among those friends Plomer invited home, but his parents seem not to have thought it odd that a boy ten years their son's senior should take such a close interest in him.

The improvement in their finances allowed the family to see a little more of South Africa. They visited Pretoria, where the fine new Parliament buildings were rising. At Vereeniging, then a small town innocent of industrialization, they rowed on the grey-brown swirling Vaal. Twice they took the long train journey across the arid plains of the Karroo, whose huge, limpid perspectives seem always to terminate in mountains, and down through the vine-filled valleys of the Cape to St James's, in 1913 still a very English settlement on False Bay. At the Cape there were picnics on the blindingly white sand of Muizenberg, visits to Cape Point, where the waters of two oceans meet and can be clearly distinguished before they mingle far out to sea, and hospitality at Simonstown, where Charles Plomer found he knew the commander of the Cape station, Admiral Bush. And there were shopping expeditions in

Adderley Street, to buy souvenirs of the Cape, before it was time for the long puffing journey back up to the highveld.

But the turbulence that seems never far beneath the surface of South African life showed itself vividly in May 1913, when a strike that quickly led to violence broke out in the gold-mines, ostensibly about working conditions in the New Kleinfontein mine, but actually over the issue of the recognition of trade unions. Johannesburg filled with a seething mass of angry miners, who overwhelmed the police force, so that for a time anarchy ruled and it became dangerous or impossible for ordinary people to go about their business in the city centre. By July things had become so serious that the government (in the person of General Smuts, then Minister of Defence) called out Imperial troops to open fire on the crowd, and many strikers were killed in cavalry charges and machine-gun attacks more characteristic of open war than of industrial conflict. 'I remember being taken by my father to see the smoking ruins of a newspaper office in the middle of the city,' Plomer was to write years later, during the Second World War; 'there were heaps of debris in the street, and people were standing about, staring with an air of vacant anxiety at the traces of destruction, as they do nowadays after an air raid.'[46]

The violence was succeeded by a sullen truce, rather than peace. The railway workers began a drumbeat of threats to strike in their turn. Since South Africa is without navigable rivers and canals, and lorries and aeroplanes were only slowly being introduced, a railway strike meant the stoppage of all mechanical transport, resulting in widespread hardship if it continued for any length of time. In December 1913 the coal-miners struck; the railway workers came out in sympathy on 8 January 1914, and it was obvious that the gold-miners would follow them before long. The country seemed on the verge of a revolution, and though Smuts regained control by the arrest and illegal deportation without trial of nine of the leaders, the situation remained unsettled until the outbreak of the First World War.

This background of unrest and violence seems to have persuaded Plomer's parents that it was time to leave South Africa. They were helped towards this decision by their now comfortable financial position; there seemed no reason why Charles Plomer should continue to work for the Department of Native Affairs in a country apparently drifting towards chaos when he could afford to retire pleasantly in England or perhaps somewhere on the Continent. He was still only forty-three, however, and perhaps even at this stage he hoped to resist his wife's determination to have done with South Africa for good. So instead of resigning, he took six months' leave. It was to prove a prudent step, for Europe, far from being the haven of peace Edythe Plomer imagined it to be, was moving quietly and steadily towards chaos on a grander scale than anything she had feared in South Africa.

2. *Adolescence*

1914–1919

THE Plomers travelled by train to Cape Town, and sailed from there to Liverpool in two groups, for reasons which in later years William Plomer had forgotten: perhaps Charles's work required him to stay on a little longer, and Edythe, always eager to get back to England, elected to go on ahead. However it was, she went first, with three-year-old Peter, in April 1914, followed by her husband and William, now eleven, a month later. Charles Plomer seems to have enjoyed the trip, and to have allowed his son to spend his time in any way he chose. 'It was an eventful voyage,' William was to write dryly later.[1] With a friend he made on the boat, he visited the crew's quarters, was made welcome there, and got into a good deal of mischief. A children's fancy-dress party had been organized, and the ship's carpenter had decided that young Plomer should be a Red Indian. By way of dressing him up, he undressed him in order to stain him from head to foot in red ochre. A young steward who assisted in this operation thereafter took a close interest in the boy, and went further than Charles Pritchard, Plomer's school friend, had done. It was on this voyage, with the young steward, that Plomer had what he considered to have been his first homosexual affair; the steward slipped into his cabin, having made sure that Charles Plomer was safely occupied elsewhere, and induced the boy to submit to intercourse with him. The effect of this experience on the eleven-year-old child is incalculable. Many years later he was to tell several of his homosexual friends in London about this initiation. He told Stephen Spender that he was 'profoundly grateful' to the steward in retrospect;[2] but in his first autobiography he merely comments, 'A peculiar interest was taken in me by a young steward, and I doubt if my father would have approved, but no harm was done.'[3]

When Plomer revised his autobiography shortly before his death, he removed the reference to his father's likely disapproval, and in fact it is by no means certain what Charles Plomer's reaction would have been. Charles himself, as a schoolboy in Victorian London, had been allowed to roam the streets, and had several times attracted the attention of strange men who wanted him to come back to their rooms with them. One of these men, an Australian millionaire, had been so smitten with the boy that he had introduced himself to Charles's parents and offered to adopt him.[4] His mother might well have accepted this chance to get rid of the unwanted child, but his father refused. William Plomer, who must have heard about this curious incident from his father's own lips, makes no mention of Charles's views on the matter. There are other hints in *Double Lives* of homosexual incidents in Charles's own life, when his son describes how Charles, during his wandering years in South Africa, was associated with one or another 'romantic young Dutchman',[5] and there is a more explicit passage telling how Charles travelled from the Transvaal to East London at the outbreak of the Boer War, in a cattle-truck with a boy of fifteen who had been entrusted to his care. William Plomer then comments carefully, 'Charles, who was still only in his twenties [he was in fact twenty-nine], evidently took not the slightest interest in the war, but he had taken a great fancy to the boy, and they spent some idyllic weeks together on the Buffalo river near East London, bathing, fishing and idling.'[6] What weight should be put on such passages is unclear, but it is plain that Charles Plomer was not greatly concerned about the company his son was keeping on the boat to England.

The first sight of Europe was the peak of Teneriffe, and young Plomer, awakened at dawn to see it, never forgot the excitement he felt that morning.[7] When they docked at Liverpool some days later, they saw, sailing in after them from the Atlantic, the *Lusitania*, which was to be sunk by the Germans in May 1915. Charles Plomer was in no hurry to find a home on the Continent. He and Edythe had been considering various spots in France, Holland, and Belgium, their only requirement being that trips to England should be easily accomplished: Dieppe, St Malo, or Scheveningen had been suggested. Instead of crossing the Channel at once, however, they hired a car and did a leisurely tour of southern England with their two children, visiting most of their relations *en route*.

Their next concern was to find a school for William, and, having been provided with a list of likely establishments, they visited the most promising of these, taking young Plomer with them so that he could express an opinion. Although Aunt Hilda and her husband were still running their highly successful preparatory school, it seems not to have been considered; Edythe was obviously persuaded, by the damage done to her eldest son's sight, that her sister was not to be trusted twice. This was a pity, for Plomer had been very happy at Spondon, and he was to be frankly miserable at the school his parents chose instead.

Beechmont School was housed in a rambling, imposing Victorian house on the North Downs near Knole, outside Sevenoaks in Kent. Edythe Plomer considered hilly situations important for schools— its ridge-top site had been a strong argument for St John's College in Johannesburg. Beechmont had a beautiful, extensive garden with sweeping lawns and great thickets of rhododendrons and mature trees, and beyond the gardens spread hectares of fields and woods belonging to the school. From the school buildings one could see for many kilometres across the Weald. The place seemed delightful, and Charles Plomer thought the headmaster, Clement Bode, a pleasant man, but, as his son was to remark acerbically later,[8] Charles Plomer was no judge of character. It was determined that William would become a boarder in the autumn term. There seems never to have been any thought that he should live with his parents and attend a school nearby, though such an arrangement would have been quite feasible, even if they had settled on the Continent: Charles Plomer himself, after all, had spent some time at school in France.

It was now the summer of 1914. Tensions in Europe had been rising steadily since the Agadir crisis of 1911, and both Britain and Germany had engaged in a massive programme to build the new dreadnoughts that were to revolutionize naval warfare, the British confident that they could outbuild the Germans decisively by 1920. The scale of the mobilizations now taking place in Europe was producing a vague disquiet in the British people, disquiet that they tended to focus on the possibility that the German navy might come to rival that of the British Empire if nothing were done to prevent it. Yet when Archduke Franz Ferdinand and his wife were murdered on 28 June 1914, and Austria, backed by Germany, seized the opportunity to declare war on Serbia on 28 July, relatively few in Britain recognized this as the spark that would ignite Europe.

The Plomers had put off their search for a home on the Continent because of the general air of uncertainty about the future, but they were taken by surprise when war broke out. In July 1914 they were staying with Charles's sister Laura, whose husband had sold Lowicks and had instead bought Burford Priory in Oxfordshire, a stately Elizabethan house that had been allowed to decay, but which he was lovingly restoring. After breakfast on 5 August the Plomers, with the Hornimans and Charles's elder brother William, sat out in the sun in the courtyard, where strawberry plants grew between the flagstones, and read *The Times*, as troubled and excited families were doing all over England. The contrast between the serene beauty of the setting, and the foreboding events in the news, struck young Plomer forcibly: 'Was it possible that the atmosphere of warmth and peace and hope and infinite leisure was not as eternal as it seemed? It was.'[9]

Plomer's Uncle William, a retired colonel, was soon to go to France on active service. Even his artistic Uncle Franklyn, his mother's only brother, joined the Navy.[10] Charles Plomer, however, elected to return to his civil service job in South Africa, followed after a month or so by his wife and the three-year-old Peter. Once more they set up house in Johannesburg, helping to enrol and transport large numbers of African non-combatants (drivers and carriers) for the campaign against the Germans in East Africa. In later years William Plomer was at some pains to explain away his father's tumbling back into this safe job:

My father offered his services to the War Office, where it was thought that his knowledge both of French and Afrikaans, which is akin to Flemish, might make him useful as an interpreter or liaison officer. Presently he was ordered to France, but it was suddenly discovered that he was a member of the South African civil service, so he was told to report to the High Commissioner, who said he must go back at once to South Africa, where his services were needed.[11]

This was a period when almost anyone who wanted to get to the front was accepted without question, and Charles Plomer's civil service experience would certainly have been less useful in Africa than his military training and command of languages would have been in Europe; he would have been given a commission very quickly (he was in fact made a captain on his return to Africa). His age was no obstacle; his brother William, after all, was nearly a decade older. It is hard to avoid the conclusion that Charles seized on this chance to return to the Africa he loved, and equally hard to forget that when the Boer War had broken out fifteen years earlier, he had been careful to stay at a safe distance from it, despite the scorn of his father.

Before Edythe followed her husband back to Africa, she settled the cheerful tow-headed eleven-year-old William at Beechmont, and so began what he was to look back on as three of the worst years of his life. Beechmont's headmaster, Clement William Louis Bode, had founded his school near Stafford in the 1890s, where he had worked up a good connection with the newly rich bourgeoisie of Liverpool, Manchester, and Birmingham. Just before the turn of the century, encouraged by this success, he had moved to the new site in Kent, where his school faced much stiffer competition, and the numbers of pupils fell to fewer than thirty.[12] He was now gradually building the school up again, with much higher fees than he had charged in Staffordshire. His approach to the challenge of education seems to have been that of a successful businessman, rather than of a dedicated teacher or cleric.

At St John's, in Johannesburg, the masters had seemed more like large cheery boys than pedagogues; at Beechmont, Plomer quickly found that Bode was 'sour, spiritually withered and unjust'.[13] Whereas at St John's Plomer had happily embraced Anglo-Catholicism without fearing that his schoolfellows might think him mawkishly pious, he found Bode's beliefs, communicated to the boys in joyless Sunday sermons, 'repulsively boring, colourless, and hypocritical, poisoning some boys with superfluous feelings of sin and guilt'.[14] The effects were to last for nearly half a century, turning Plomer against the Christianity of his mother until after her death, and he was far from being the only boy who felt the way he did about Bode and Beechmontism. When, thirty years later, Plomer published an account of his hatred of Beechmont in his first autobiography, *Double Lives*, he received a letter from an earlier pupil of Bode's, G. Leedham, who wrote of the repressions and thrashings 'which seem to be inevitable in an establishment of this kind', adding,

I can absolutely endorse all you say about the cult of Beechmontism. Looking back nearly 45 years I still shudder at the thought of it all and all it stood for ... I was able to develop, in some respects, as a rebel and I remember only too well how three of us used to escape into those woods around the slope of the Weald and be a terror to the gamekeepers by letting off traps etc.[15]

At St John's Plomer had not been forced to play ball games, and had enjoyed acting in the annual productions of Shakespeare; at Beechmont, games, cricket in particular, were not just compulsory, but were thought of as a central part of the education being instilled, while artistic activities of any kind (other than drearily regimented dancing classes) were sternly repressed. Whereas at St John's, boys were encouraged to roam freely over the nearby kopje, the beautiful grounds of Beechmont—an important factor in the Plomers' choice of the school—were permanently out of bounds, so that the more spirited and adventurous boys, Plomer among them, found themselves constantly breaking the rules and being punished by beatings, impositions, sarcastic public ridicule, and other petty persecutions which to a schoolboy are not negligible. The spirit of rebellion thus aroused soon found other outlets, in smoking and homosexuality; in later life Plomer was to feel that Bode's tinpot tyranny had inculcated in him a lasting subversiveness which was to show itself subtly in his writing, and less subtly, but more secretively, in his sexual life.[16]

The effects of sending a sensitive boy away to such a boarding-school were incalculable. As a child Plomer was scarcely able to articulate his reactions, but uppermost amongst them was a terrible sense of having been betrayed and abandoned by the parents he loved and trusted. This sense of abandonment permanently affected his feelings towards his parents; he would never be as close to them again. The separation was combined with the miserable realization of being deprived of the warmth and support of home at a time when it most mattered. In later life he was to quote against his father lines from Cowper's 'Tirocinium', about sending boys away to boarding-school:[17]

> Thou well deserv'st an alienated son
>
> . . . . . .
>
> Add too, that thus estranged, thou canst obtain
> By no kind art his confidence again.[18]

Against his mother, for reasons that remain obscure, he was to nurse no such resentment, perhaps feeling that since his father took all the important decisions in the family, he was chiefly to blame for subjecting his son to Beechmont.

The three years he spent in this 'prison-like routine', as he later described it,[19] were relieved by pleasant holidays, either with school friends or with one of his aunts, Hilda or Laura. One of his friends invited him to a lovely country house near Maidenwell in Lincolnshire, while with another, Robert Synge, he first visited Radnorshire in the Welsh border country. Bob Synge lived at Cwmbach, between Hay and Brecon, in a house overlooking the Wye, with the Black Mountains rising beyond. Plomer fell in love with the country at first sight; he and Bob Synge spent their days walking on the moors, lying in the bracken listening to the ceaseless cascade of lark-song, or swimming naked in the icy mountain pools. Bob Synge was the only intimate friend Plomer made at Beechmont; he was to die soon after he and Plomer left Beechmont for different public schools, and Plomer never visited Cwmbach again.

The war, at first scarcely noticed by a schoolboy in England, gradually obtruded itself on his consciousness. Plomer spent Christmas of 1914 with Aunt Laura in London in her huge house on the Chelsea Embankment. (Like Lowicks, the Hornimans' Chelsea house had been designed by Voysey, and boasted such rare refinements as an electric lift.) Aunt Laura, moved by patriotism as well as charitable impulses, held a musical party for some wounded soldiers. One of the men who sat listening to the guitarist fascinated young Plomer, for he had lost his arms and legs and was blind. The torso lay in a bath chair, smoking and smiling while the boy gazed, very impressed: 'It was as interesting as meeting a Royalty or a Red Indian,' he was to record.[20] Perhaps any boy would have stared, but not every boy would have thought the sight worth recording in such detail years later. Already it is possible to detect that interest in people set apart from others by personality, philosophy, gifts, or circumstance, that fascination with those who live on the fringes of society, whether by choice or not, that was to be such a feature of all his writing.

The Christmas of 1915 Plomer spent with Aunt Hilda near Canterbury. What had been Spondon House School had been moved to a beautiful Queen Anne house, Kenfield Hall, where it continued to thrive. Plomer enjoyed his stay there, wandering around the large grounds, and as he contemplated his approaching return, at the end of the holidays, to the custody of the man he called 'the odious Bode', he must have wished that his mother had left him in Aunt Hilda's care instead.

He saw a lot of Aunt Laura and Uncle Emslie, because he spent each summer with them at Burford Priory, a house which he came increasingly to love as if it were his home. He loved reading the history of the place, and devoured every book he could find with some bearing on it, so that he came to feel that he had seen, as if it were a play he could remember, some of the events the house had witnessed in the seventeenth century. Uncle Emslie, tall, scholarly, and benevolent, with a droopy moustache, spent much of each day in his study, emerging only at mealtimes to tell his nephew stories of his days as an art student in Antwerp, where he had known Van Gogh.[21] These talks were rare, for Uncle Emslie, who had once been Liberal MP for Chelsea, had a rather reticent manner which many people mistook for superciliousness. But there were also occasional visitors to the Priory, more or less literary or arty, for the boy to meet: the publisher John Lane, whose many mistresses earned him the nickname 'Petticoat Lane'; Michael Sadler,[22] the bibliographer and novelist, at this time only twenty-six and still little known; the famous literary scholar Sir Walter Raleigh,[23] who demonstrated his remarkable strength by lifting a massive stone ball off one of the garden terraces for Plomer's amusement; and the sculptor Sir Hamo Thorneycroft, who was the uncle of Siegfried Sassoon (at this time writing his first war poems in the trenches of Flanders), and whom Aunt Laura jokingly persuaded to show his skills by doing some topiary work. There was also a dandified young professor from the University of Brussels, Monsieur Bizet, a relation of the composer, who lived in Burford during the war, and Aunt Laura arranged for Plomer to study French with him. 'Toujours répondez par une phrase complète,' he would insist when Plomer tried to keep the conversation going with an occasional 'Oui' or 'Non'. This teaching paid dividends in Plomer's increased fluency in French and his love of French literature in later life, and it was a strong contrast to the dismal, ineffective, and often painful teaching methods he endured at Beechmont.

Towards the beginning of 1917, Plomer's mother and young brother returned to England, leaving his father in South Africa. Travel for civilians during the war was not only very difficult to arrange, but dangerous; Edythe Plomer must have had strong reasons for risking the U-boats and the German raiders, one of which, the *Moewe*, was in fact sighted *en route*. In his later writing Plomer was to give two reasons for her journey: the need to settle him at his public school, and the fact that his father had now been moved to Cape Town by his civil service job, so that the Johannesburg house had had to be sold.

Neither of these reasons stands up to examination. Plomer was not due to finish his term of imprisonment at Beechmont until the summer of 1917, and in any case he had two loving aunts who had mothered him for three years and who could plainly have seen him safely installed at a public school if they had been asked to do so. As for the move to the Cape, houses were as readily available in Cape Town as in Johannesburg; in any case Edythe Plomer, once she arrived in England, was apparently happy to settle herself in a boarding-house in Eastbourne. Why not a comfortable home in Rosebank, the leafy Cape Town suburb where her husband was now established?

Plomer was careful to say virtually nothing in his autobiographies about relations between his parents, but it seems plain that they were strained from a very early stage. Edythe seems to have known little about her husband's more difficult characteristics when they married. In sexual matters she was almost completely ignorant, and had only the vaguest notions of what to expect on her wedding night. And of Africa, her son was to record, she knew nothing except what Charles had told her.[24] The repeated illnesses that made it necessary for Edythe to leave her husband again and again in Africa, and, taking her child, go back to her mother in England, must have been both tedious for her and expensive for her husband, given his modest income. Her excuse for these journeys during the Pietersburg and Louis Trichardt years was the need for a healthier climate, but no climate on earth is healthier than that of the Cape, which she actually had to pass through on her way to England. The truth was that these costly voyages, though they reflect some real concern about her health, gave her opportunities to get back to her beloved country—and opportunities to get away from Charles.

The rough manners which her husband had picked up during his gypsy years must have grated painfully on her, particularly since she associated such lapses with what she saw as the crudities of South African society. She was a sensitive, sympathetic woman, perhaps a little over-sensitive as a result of her sheltered upbringing, whereas Charles, at least by his son's account, was selfish and unimaginative.[25] More significant, however, there is good evidence that she found his wild temper hard to endure. His outbursts of anger were sudden, unpredictable, and utterly unreasonable. In later years Plomer described how his father's voice would rise to a scream, and his normally cheerful face twist into a demonic snarl, with the whites of his eyes showing all round the irises. While it lasted, the display was terrifying, and though afterwards he would often behave as if nothing had happened, his wife and children were left exhausted by nervous strain. The strain was sometimes more than merely nervous, for when Charles Plomer was in a rage, he was violent. His son gives two instances of this violence: one when, as a boy, Charles had rushed at his older brother Durham and had bit his coat with such force that one of his own teeth was torn from its socket;[26] the other when, engaged in running a native store in South Africa, he had ordered a Xhosa who had irritated him out of the store, and when the man would not go, Charles had seized a hatchet and flown at him, only to be knocked out with one skilful blow of the African's knobkierie.[27] Edythe Plomer, exposed to such displays of rage but unable to defend herself, must on occasion have had rather a thin time of it. William Plomer quotes just one snatch of conversation following a bout of his father's rage, which he describes as 'insane':

I remember him saying complacently, after some violent scene he had made about some trivial matter, 'Of course I'm quick-tempered, like my mother.' He spoke as if drawing attention to an interesting trait.

'What you mean', said my own long-suffering and quiet-voiced mother, 'is that you have no self-control; you get into violent rages about nothing, and other people have to endure it, God knows why.'[28]

It seems very likely that Edythe had had enough of Charles by 1917, and thought the dangers and the expense of wartime travel worth risking to get back to England, though the Eastbourne boarding-house, in which Plomer spent his Christmas that year with her, suggests that the family's finances were none too good. The notion that Charles could retire comfortably, probably illusory even before the war and entertained mainly because of Edythe's longing to get away from South Africa, was now recognized as quite out of the question.

The boarding-house was full of the rather sad human jetsam which washes into such establishments the world over: elderly women perpetually at odds with one another who, though they lived under the same roof, communicated with each other by little

notes left on a piano, and a lonely, penniless old retired captain of
the Marines whose keep was paid for by his sisters, who allowed
him only sixpence a week as pocket-money. 'Never have I seen a
man more solitary and wretched,' Plomer was to remember years
later; 'he appeared quite friendless and without hope, but he never
complained, was dignified and courteous, and kept his short white
beard in trim and his nails clean.'²⁹ There was nothing remarkable
about this lonely old man; he was and is all too common a figure.
What is unusual is the fact that any boy of fourteen, an age at
which most adolescents are intensely self-concerned, should have
noticed him at all, and reacted to him with such sympathy that
the memory never faded. Plomer's compassion, which was to
become such a strongly marked, attractive feature of his personality
and the source of so much insight in his writing, was already
developing, under the guidance of his mother.

Plomer entered Rugby in September 1917. The school was at that
time divided into three classes, modern, classical or 'Greats', and
the Army class, and after some initial confusion Plomer was placed
in the modern class. After a term in Troy House, at that time used
as a 'waiting house' into which new boys went until they were
assigned a permanent place in the school, and where his tutor was
a master named Cole, he was assigned to School House, of which
the housemaster was the headmaster himself, Dr A. A. David. A
tall, dark, and strongly built man, Dr David was to go on to become
Bishop of Liverpool, and he could perhaps accurately have been
called a muscular Christian, but he was also liberal-minded, sensitive
to the needs of his pupils, and genuinely interested in seeing that
they acquired a good education. Plomer found him a striking and
welcome contrast to Clement Bode. Whereas the Beechmont system
had seemed to be aimed at turning boys into ciphers, Rugby under
Dr David treated them as individuals, even though the school in
1917 had nearly six hundred pupils. Symptomatic of his attitude
was the way he lent Plomer his own copies of Turgenev.³⁰

Some boys new to Rugby complained bitterly about the rules,
official and unofficial, that hedged the pupils in, about the constant
beatings and the bullying, and about the inadequacy of the diet,
which left them always hungry. Flogging was still the accepted
punishment for infringements of the rules: ' 'Tain't the hagony, it's
the disgrice,' the school porter used to tell prospective victims

as he prepared them for birching.[31] The system of fagging, by which
the senior boys shouted for a 'fag' and got the last small boy to
arrive to carry out some menial task, such as making toast, Plomer
largely avoided by the simple expedient of ignoring the call. Used
to the penal system of Beechmont, he found that the Rugby system
allowed him a dizzy freedom by comparison.[32] He was frankly
amazed when the French master, Mr Brigstocke, perhaps noticing
how lost the new boy seemed, gave a tea-party on 10 December
1917 to celebrate Plomer's fourteenth birthday, and invited three
or four of the cleverest boys to it.

One of these boys was Robert Birley, who was to become
headmaster of Eton, and in the last decades of his life a dedicated
worker for the abolition of apartheid. He and Plomer did not become
particularly close, but Plomer formed a lasting friendship with
another boy whom he met early in 1918. This was Darsie Rutherford
Gillie, son of a Presbyterian minister, who had one of the keenest
minds of his generation at Rugby. He was some months older than
Plomer and more widely read. Plomer admired him a good deal,
and because Gillie's French and German were fluent, he was able
to introduce his friend to works in those languages that Plomer
would otherwise have missed, perhaps for years. They became close
friends, and even after Plomer left Rugby and Gillie went on to
become a scholar at Balliol, they continued to correspond. There
were to be times when Plomer would think of this correspondence
as one of his few remaining links with civilization.

The war was now becoming more and more obtrusive. At
Beechmont, though the boys bending over their French verbs could
actually hear the ceaseless mutter of the guns on days when the
breeze was from the south, the war had impinged on their lives
very little. At the start of the war every classroom had its map
marked with little flags to show the positions of the front lines, but
as month succeeded dreary month and the front remained static,
interest in the maps and flags had ebbed. At Rugby, by contrast,
the war seemed ever present. For one thing the success of the
German U-boat campaign had made food scarce, and the boys' diet
had been so reduced that they were given an extra half an hour
in bed by way of compensation. Although he could avoid the games
that had been forced on him at Beechmont, Plomer soon found
himself in the large, very active Rugby Officers Training Corps. The
OTC was seen as direct preparation for death in the trenches, and

was taken seriously. In 1917 the official school magazine, *The Meteor*, under the headline 'In Memoriam', printed page after page of names of the Old Rugbeians who had died in action or of wounds, and more pages of those newly gone out to fill the gaps in Flanders.[33] The older boys would remember many of the newly dead as their cheerful inky schoolmates of perhaps just months before, and those leaving school must have wondered rather sombrely what their immediate futures held. Nor did one have to go to Flanders to see the direct effects of the war: the raids on London by Zeppelins, rapidly succeeded by less vulnerable bomber aeroplanes, were for the first time in centuries bringing death by enemy action home to British civilians.

Plomer's own chances of surviving the war had improved as his eyesight had worsened. He had been excused sport mainly because of his sight; his myopia was progressive, and each visit to the oculist revealed that his sight had weakened further. Perhaps the strains of puberty and malnutrition played their part in this process, but bookwork by artificial light was chiefly blamed, and he had to be excused some of his form work and encouraged to spend as much time as possible outdoors. He used at this time to take a bicycle and go for day-long rides, sometimes with Darsie Gillie, through the deserted countryside, quieter early in 1918 than it would ever be again. By the summer of that year, however, it was clear that since he could now do no bookwork at all, there was little point in his staying at the school. Perhaps, too, the high fees at Rugby were a burden his father was not sorry to lay down: the war, in which so many quick fortunes had been made, had not been kind to the Plomers' finances. Dr David wrote William a farewell letter, prophetically suggesting that he might be able to 'do something good in life which would not fit in with an ordinary career'.[34] And with that, his single year at Rugby ended.

When the war had broken out in August 1914, the confident, fatuous cry 'It'll be over by Christmas' had been heard everywhere. As the years passed and the front moved backwards and forwards only a few hundred metres, the struggle had come to seem everlasting. As late as the summer of 1918, when the British and the French began a series of sustained, massed tank attacks against the German lines, few could believe that the end was in sight at last. Edythe Plomer, faced with the need to find outdoor occupation for her elder son for the duration of what might prove to be a very long war indeed, hit on the idea of sending him to a farm. Farm labourers were urgently needed and 'landgirls' had everywhere replaced conscripted men, so there was no difficulty finding a farmer who would give Plomer, now nearly sixteen, employment.

He was sent to a farm at Boxford[35] in Berkshire, between Newbury and Lambourne, where the farmer treated him kindly. Plomer was, by his own account,[36] not much use as a farm worker, though he laboured manfully at threshing time, and once had the exhausting experience of driving two independently minded heifers all the way back to Boxford from Newbury market. He had the utmost difficulty in understanding the broad local speech of the old labourer he sometimes worked with, but he felt strongly attracted to working people, and came to hero-worship a local gamekeeper of about thirty, who befriended him, and of whom he was to write cryptically that 'he might have become an even more important influence in my life than he was, but suddenly the war came to an end'.[37]

Plomer watched the Armistice Day celebrations in Newbury, where he saw the Kaiser burnt in effigy. For Plomer peace brought a rapid change in prospects, climate, and scenery, because his mother, after the strains of the war and probably tired of years of living in a rather dreary boarding-house, decided to go back to her husband and to the sunshine and plentiful food of South Africa. The Spanish influenza outbreak, which took more lives than the war itself, was raging in London, and young Plomer went down with it, recovering only after being very ill for some weeks.[38] No doubt the thought that the Cape might provide the right climate for recuperation played its part in the decision. Edythe did not enjoy making decisions by herself, and she carefully set out the alternatives to her sixteen-year-old son. Life in England was likely to be hard after the war; South Africa, on the other hand, seemed a land of promise. 'After all,' Edythe Plomer said, 'if your eyes settle down in two or three years' time, there's no reason why you shouldn't come back and go to Oxford, or do whatever you want to do.' Whether or not she believed her own arguments, she convinced her son. Back to Africa and back to Plomer's half-remembered father they went.

3. *African Artist*

1919–1920

On the voyage back to South Africa early in 1919 the ship was crowded, as almost all shipping immediately after the war was, with people anxious to resume lives interrupted by the conflict. Young Plomer was separated from Edythe and his eight-year-old brother Peter, and shared a cabin with a landowner from St Helena. Yet it was during this voyage that he really began to get to know his mother. It is from this period that he first begins to record snatches of her conversation, most of them remarks that he obviously thought witty or merely accurate, as when she said of an over-dressed fellow passenger, 'Almost the only woman on this boat who dresses with any style, but it's a style too splendid for the boat.'[1]

Plomer admired his mother enormously, and gradually came to feel a real sense of intellectual and emotional kinship with her. They shared a highly developed sense of humour, and more particularly a sense of the ridiculous in human pretensions. Edythe Plomer was particularly adept at pouncing on self-importance in the behaviour of those around them, and holding it up for her son's amusement. 'Looking back, I count the influence of my mother as the chief part of my education,' he was to write. 'It was she who chiefly sharpened my curiosity, my sense of character, my powers of seeing, enjoying and discriminating, my beliefs and my scepticism, and my consciousness of the fate of the larger and more vulnerable part of mankind, unprotected by money or power.'[2] For his part, he was now beginning to hold up his end in conversation; already his mother's equal in education, he was soon able to match and then surpass her in keenness of observation and wit. She was perhaps beginning to realize that she now had an ally in her clashes with her husband, someone who, if not yet capable of protecting her from Charles's rages, would be a fellow sufferer and companion.

This voyage south was a much more decorous affair than the trip to England, with Charles Plomer as a negligent guardian, had been. All the same the rapidly developing youth enjoyed it thoroughly. The days warmed as the ship steamed out of a particularly grim English winter towards the tropics. After the strain of the war, with its gloom, its food shortages, and its sense of a long period of peace and plenty ending for ever, shipboard life seemed romantic and fascinating, with its opportunities to observe radically different people forced into temporary companionship, its quickly blossoming and fading love-affairs, and its alteration of the routines of life. Some of the passengers were rich or important enough to attract attention: a scattering of Johannesburg millionaires and their showy wives vied with Lady Buxton, wife of the Governor-General of South Africa. Young Plomer's interest, however, was caught and held by a Portuguese girl of his own age, who was returning to her wealthy family in the Cape after a period at a finishing school in England. He spent a good deal of time with her, much attracted by her dark eyes and primrose skin.[3] For him, as for many boys of his background, girls were an unfathomable mystery. There is no way of knowing how far things went; not very far, one suspects, for he was uncertain of himself, and a girl of her ethnic background and social standing is likely to have been carefully chaperoned, but it is clear that his sexual orientation was not yet fixed.

They stopped at Ascension Island, at that time a British naval base. It struck Plomer, thirsting for fresh impressions, as being 'like an old coloured print, with its rufous rocky foreground, a few white buildings, on one of which a magenta bougainvillaea had spread like a stain, and the Green Mountain towering in the background'.[4] At this stage, he saw himself as a potential painter when he thought of his future at all, and it is noticeable that he describes scenes largely in terms of line and colour, as an artist might. His childhood interest in drawing and painting had been maintained at school, and he continued to develop his considerable talents as a visual artist. Not for another decade would he abandon the notion of earning his living as a painter.[5]

When they reached St Helena some days later, the landowner whose cabin Plomer had shared was met by his carriage, and took the Plomers on a tour of the island.

It was not at all the horrid rock which history books had led one to imagine. There were flowers and pretty people everywhere: wisps of tropical mist ran past like long scarves of grey chiffon in mysterious levitation, and the sun came out on groups of peasants working without haste and without rest in a steeply sloping sisal-field; on the winding upland roads donkeys trotted past with loads of melons or brushwood on their backs; young girls offered for sale necklaces of dyed Job's-tears; at Longwood [the modest house in which Napoleon had lived out the last years of his exile, and in which he died] the fresh Atlantic breeze blew through the empty rooms with their austere remains of decoration in the Empire style, and glancing through the windows one could see rows of blue agapanthus lilies wagging and nodding like the heads of people in a crowd. A smell of wood-smoke from a hut in a ravine, flowering creepers, flying mists and steamy fragrance—a lovely place of exile, but not for a self-made militarist emperor.[6]

They arrived in Cape Town in midsummer heat to find Charles Plomer standing on the quay waving to them, tanned and trim in an elegant lightweight uniform of bleached khaki. He was now forty-nine, though with his slim figure and his boyish grin under a neat moustache, he looked much younger. His eldest son looked down at him from the ship's rail with a combination of antipathy and jealousy: antipathy because, like many young men, he seems to have regarded his father as an older rival to be toppled;[7] jealousy because this man, after all, had first claim on the affections of his mother. 'The sight of him gave me no sense of homecoming,' he was to record coldly.[8]

For his part, Charles Plomer seems to have found his pale, gangling fifteen-year-old son all too much under the influence of his wife's ideas on such matters as the importance of perfect table manners, the value of the finer things in life generally, and art in particular, the crudeness of colonials and the superiority of all things English, especially the public-school education of which William was so proud. Charles had had a very comfortable war in South Africa, and he showed no interest in his wife's and children's experiences in bleak, wartime England. Rather than ask about William's attack of Spanish flu, he told them in elaborate detail about the ravages of the disease in Cape Town. South Africa was his focus now, and for his family's good it had best become their focus too. The Plomers were going to have to make their way in South Africa, and in his view there was no point looking back at a way of life now left behind for good. South Africa was the land of opportunity and growth, and William, if he was tough and determined enough, could make his way in it as Charles himself had done when only a little older. Charles had farmed and run a trading store for blacks: why should William think of any other future?

With such unbridgeable gulfs between father and son, mis-understandings were bound to arise, and a clash was not long in coming. Charles Plomer had been living very pleasantly at the International Hotel for some time, and it was there that he took his family once they disembarked. It was a comfortable place built in the style which the British had imported from India: long low buildings with broad verandas. The new arrivals luxuriated in the sunshine, in the physical beauty of the city curled between mountain and sea, and in the abundant food; the miseries of war seemed no more than a dream in this idyllic place. Oddly enough, it was the food that precipitated the collision between father and son.

At lunch one day the family was served some of the grapes for which the Cape is justly famous. Young Plomer took some, and fastidiously washed them in his finger-bowl before eating them. At once, in the hotel dining-room, Charles Plomer flew into one of his terrible rages, his voice rising, his face demonic with fury. Washing grapes in a finger-bowl seemed to reveal exactly the kind of attitude that would make life in South Africa difficult for his son. It was a gesture that affirmed Edythe's values and rejected Charles's own, the sort of behaviour that would disqualify William from the life his father anticipated he would have to lead. The pressure on young Plomer to yield to his father in this situation, with waiters and other guests looking mutely on, must have been intense, but he would not give way. With the contempt that perhaps only a teenager can feel for a parent, he replied, 'I'm not going to eat dirty grapes to please you or anybody else,' and he then reached for some more and proceeded to wash them also, with infuriating deliberateness, before eating them.[9] Battle had been joined, and already there was no doubt as to who was victor. The incident was a trivial one in its details, but its deeper significance lay in the fact that young Plomer was clearly beginning to show that tendency to subvert authority that Beechmontism had provoked, and which a growing sense of his own powers and abilities allowed him to exercise now for the first time, confident in the knowledge that his mother was firmly behind him.

Simply being in the Cape was a physical delight that more than made up for the tensions in the family, and Plomer recalled the experience years later in words filled with remembered sensuous pleasure:

Drunk with warmth, like a bee in spring, I wandered in the streets or in the resinous stony pinewoods on the slopes of Table Mountain, or under the heavy-shadowed oaks planted in the seventeenth century by Simon van der Stel [an early Dutch governor of the Cape], or into the Michaelis gallery of minor Dutch masters—clean, cool pictures of an honest, domesticated civilization. Or we visited my father's friends . . . Presently we moved out to the salty air and white sands (as Kipling observed) of Muizenberg.[10]

Charles Plomer was taking some weeks of leave during this time before returning to his pre-war job with the Department of Native Affairs in Johannesburg, and the family spent some time in the beautiful, aptly named town of Ceres, located on a superbly fertile plateau surrounded by the smashed moonscape of the Skurweberg range, and until just before the war accessible only by that feat of nineteenth-century British engineering, the Michell's Pass road. Here they spent some days simply enjoying the peace and the abundant fruit, and Plomer spent his days on the banks of the Breë River, which runs through the town, painting the landscape in water-colours.[11] No doubt this artistic activity was also a source of irritation to his father, though Plomer was to comment judiciously, 'If he did nothing, at this or any time, to encourage my preferences, it was because they didn't interest him.'[12]

By March or April 1919 they were back in Johannesburg, where they resumed the lives they had been leading five years before, though with changes reflecting their reduced income. Instead of the very large house they had then rented near St John's College, they now moved into a comfortable boarding-house in Parktown. Plomer gives as a reason for this the fact that his mother 'was not physically strong enough to run a house',[13] but this is disingenuous: black domestic servants were plentiful and cheap, and all but the poorest white families at this period would have had at least one servant indoors and one to run the garden. Almost certainly the financial losses they had suffered through unwise investments just before the war are the explanation for this drop in their living standards. And perhaps, as Plomer himself was to speculate,[14] they had been living consistently beyond their means during the pre-war years: the large house, the frequent dinner parties, the expensive schools, the even more expensive, frequent trips to England and back, perhaps these had always been extravagances they could ill afford.

One outlay that could have been avoided Charles Plomer now insisted upon: William must go back to St John's to finish his schooling. This decision raises some curious questions. The reason for his leaving Rugby is given, both in his autobiographies and in the Rugby School records, as his failing sight. Yet nine months after leaving Rugby he was enrolled at St John's, and there coped with the bookwork well enough to be regarded as one of the school's star pupils by the next year. Progressive myopia could hardly have been arrested so quickly with no more elaborate treatment than a change of climate: was failing eyesight merely an excuse given to cover Plomer's embarrassment at having to leave Rugby because his father could no longer pay the fees? Perhaps this is what he was hinting at when he referred to the headmaster of Rugby's having given his 'special circumstances ... careful and sympathetic consideration'.[15]

St John's had grown bigger, both in the number of its pupils and in the number of its buildings; some, but not many, of the masters whom Plomer had known before the war were still there; his beloved kopje was rapidly being built over, and the pleasure of climbing it was gone. All in all, he found that the place had lost much of the charm it had previously held for him. The change, however, was not so much in the place as in himself. The iron had entered his soul at Beechmont, and having had to leave Rugby after only a year had confirmed him in his role as an outsider; he would never be as much a part of the life of St John's as he had been before. His reserved, watchful self-isolation was recognized, perhaps almost unconsciously, by the other boys from the first day: 'Look who's here, the Emperor of China!' jeered one of them on first seeing the pale youth with the round spectacles, and Plomer accepted the role at once by putting his hands into opposite sleeves and bowing like a mandarin.[16]

By his own account he did little work in 1919, when he was in the fourth form, the penultimate school year; he fooled about, idled and dreamed, and made no friends, being driven in upon himself. The pre-war days, when he was able to invite friends home to a big house and entertain them in style, seemed a dream now; he was not going to bring any of his wealthy schoolfellows back to the boarding-house. From his parents too he remained isolated, tending at times to observe them as if they were total strangers. This was perhaps natural with his father, but even his mother came in for some cold observation. With the priggishness of youth, he found her and his father much too ready to express their opinions and show their emotions; they were not sufficiently English and reserved for him.[17] He responded with increased secretiveness of his own; his brother Peter, eight years younger than himself, was never a confidant. William went through a year of drifting, which he later attributed in part to the fact that his future was obscure: should he be training himself as an artist, or was he to be a trader or a farmer as his father thought?

During the school holidays, with no encouragement from his parents, he began building up a circle of artistic acquaintances. He frequented the art galleries in Johannesburg, and during 1919 and 1920 came to know the relatively few painters in the city. Two of them became friends of his. A young Afrikaans landscape painter, Enslin du Plessis, a sensitive, generous, and amusing man, not only encouraged Plomer's own painting, but also lent him the first parts of Proust's *A la recherche du temps perdu*, which not only widened his understanding of how prose fiction could be written, but also constituted the first detailed discussion of homosexual love he had come across in literature. Very few people in South Africa at that time would even have heard of Proust; that a boy of sixteen was reading him is remarkable.[18] Plomer was to remain friendly with Du Plessis, who later moved to London, until the end of his life. The other friend he made in these years was a young Jewish painter named Edward Wolfe, who had a greater impact on Plomer's development than anyone except his mother.

Teddy Wolfe, as his friends called him, was a small intense man, with a face of markedly Jewish cast under a fringe of black hair.[19] Plomer, taking his cue from his mother in this as in other matters, tended to look down on almost everyone he met in Johannesburg as members of a society 'mostly boring and second-rate', as almost any cultured European would have done at this period.[20] Teddy Wolfe escaped this judgement in part because of his artistic gifts, but in part because he brought with him a breath of the wider world, and even a whiff of the Bloomsbury group. He had trained in England and worked with Roger Fry at the Omega Workshops, imbibing Fry's enthusiasm for French painting in general, and the Post-Impressionists in particular. He had been to Morocco and painted there, and had returned to his home in Johannesburg with the romance of distant places clinging to him, self-assured, wholly convinced that the artistic life was the only one worth living, and possessed of a wonderfully attractive gaiety and zest for living. He provided young Plomer, diffident and full of the undirected longings of the adolescent, with an ideal on which to model himself, an ideal quite different from that which either of his parents would have envisaged for him. Plomer came to admire Wolfe enormously, and was strongly influenced by him. He represented a light to steer by at a time when Plomer felt himself to be drifting in the dark: 'He was as good a friend to me as a nomad who brings one dates and water in a desert. His work and his talk and the vivid environment which, like a bower-bird, he had created for himself, refreshed my eyes and spirit and easily lured me away from the tennis parties and the coming-out dances.'[21] Wolfe's ability to 'lure' him from the dances and other opportunities for meeting young women that his mother was arranging for him at this time is significant, for Wolfe was an active homosexual, and in this too seems to have been a decisive influence. The uncertain flirtation with the pretty Portuguese on the ship back to South Africa was not repeated, and in his memoirs Plomer categorizes the young women of Johannesburg as freaks and frumps, listing among the types he had met at his mother's insistence, 'the dumb *ingénue*, the congenital tart, the tomboy, the clinging goose, the sinewy sports-girl, the prim prig, the maternally-inspired social climber fresh from a Swiss finishing-school, the calculating teaser, the nubile monkey, and even a nymphomaniac . . . And were there no nice, ordinary girls? Oh, yes. Aren't there always?'[22] Under Wolfe's influence he had decided that women bored him.

Teddy Wolfe's homosexuality had at least one enriching effect on Plomer, however: it opened his eyes to the beauty of Africans and made him realize that they could be fitting subjects for art. During 1920, when Plomer was in his last year at St John's, Wolfe set up a studio in an empty mine-compound building that had been used to house migrant black miners. Here, with the great stamp-batteries for crushing ore pounding in the background, he showed young Plomer drawing after drawing of naked black miners. They were studies for an oil painting he was doing, a magnificent flowing picture of a miner's back, which was eventually bought by Enslin du Plessis.[23] The painting, deeply erotic to Plomer,[24] was an artistic breakthrough in South Africa; the idea that an African could be a fitting subject for art of any kind, painting or literature, met with strong resistance. Not until 1926, for instance, was the Natal painter Edward Roworth persuaded to paint some half-naked Ndebele girls, and though he was delighted with the result, he refused ever to exhibit them for fear of the likely public reaction.[25] More than any other individual, Teddy Wolfe began the process of opening Plomer's eyes to the beauty and desirability of black people. This awakening, subversive and even revolutionary in the context of South Africa, was to have far-reaching implications for Plomer and for South African literature.

But those implications were slow to develop, for though Plomer was beginning to 'see, to feel and to think', as he put it later,[26] he was still only an isolated schoolboy, full of the torments of an unfocused sexuality and deeply unsure of his future. He was now desperately anxious to convince himself and others that he was destined to be an artist, but in what medium? He was reading voraciously (the trouble with his eyes apparently forgotten) and he joined the excellent Johannesburg Municipal Library, concentrating on English poetry from Chaucer to Eliot, Russian novels, and all the modern prose he could find, including the novels of D. H. Lawrence. He read without anyone to guide his choice or inform his taste, and he seems to have discussed his reading with no one, for he had already left his sympathetic but less well-educated mother behind. For the first time, too, he had begun to write during his last year at St John's, in 1920. Not far from his home was a forest of eucalyptus trees, originally planted to provide pit-props for the gold-mines of the Reef and known as the Sachsenwald (now long since cut down and built over). Here the tall, spectacled schoolboy would take refuge with notebook and pencil, and in the dry fragrant air would compose immature verses in the style of the poets he was reading, among them, to judge from the poems themselves, Keats and Whitman. For poetic details he transmuted the beautiful African scene around him into a memory of the garden of Burford Priory, the electric African air becoming moistly English, the eucalypts becoming elms. Nothing shows more clearly the extent to which he felt himself to be an outsider in South Africa at this time. For subject-matter, naturally enough, he chose his own inner turmoil, or what he called 'the pain of growth and travail'.

Evening in Oxfordshire

O aqueous evening skies
pavilioning the world with silken light,
you rest,
you seem to be at rest,
but, ah, the restlessness of these!

They lie so still, these fields, these trees,
these labour-weary peasants passionate,
they seem at peace:
their loveliness seems like peace . . .

These cows,
garlanded with shadow,
drowsing under the willows,
yielding their heavy, fertile movements to the meadows
with all the grace of lost illusions, these . . .

These elms,
so rich, gigantic in their richness,
these ponderous elms,
twisting themselves to forms
as proud as grief . . .

These thick monk's-rhubarb leaves,
already wet with night,
where the weary wind creeps in—
gently, gently—
creeps in,
and, like a wounded bird, beats out its broken heart . . .

Those sage-and-yellow fields
or rye and charlock on the hills,
caressed by the ancient sun,
now falling asleep so softly,
so softly falling asleep . . .

O quiet and distant skies,
for all you sleep so still,
and even that these fields be part of you,
yet, you serene,
yet they are mad with pain—
with pain of growth and travail,
and with pain of unfulfilment,
with long unchanging pain . . .

> O smooth and wicked skies,
> O would that you might break!
> Then in the clash of worlds
> this peace-illusion might be lost
> in unremitting pain,
> or peace . . .
>
> O skies!
> the pain of growth and travail . . .[27]

Another poem dating from 1920, 'Symphony', shows the same use of external details, finely observed, to convey internal turmoil:

> Green evening light shines in his face
> As he paces his balcony to and fro.
> All cognisance of time and space
> Are lost in the modulationary flow
> Of his perpetual meanderings to and fro.
>
> A green trout swimming in a tank
> Glassy-green, inclining his fins ribbed and slow,
> A green weed waving on a bank
> In a desultory wind, to and fro,
> Have the same subtle dignity
> As this man who walks a balcony, to and fro,
> Lost to fear and affection and malignity
> In a promenade mechanically slow.
>
> His being is absorbed in a green electric glow
> As he paces back and forward, to and fro.[28]

The third poem surviving from this time is an imagist fragment which Plomer entitled 'Epigram: to a profane but entertaining companion in a tent':

> Pray hang the night with wordy tapestries:
> And every time you swear, that word
> Among the leaves of talk shall seem a bird.

The last of the poems known to have been written in 1920 was a portent of the future, for it alone is set in a clearly African context. More strikingly it deals with Africans, and in this sense is an extreme rarity for its time: it is nothing short of astonishing that a sixteen-year-old boy should have produced it. The influence of Teddy Wolfe lay behind this breakthrough of the imagination; if Wolfe could paint the Africans, Plomer could write about them. He described the poem simply as 'At present a FRAGMENT', and though its view of the Africans is an alien one, its title rightly suggests that this was an approach that he was to develop, and with startling results.

> Where men are tawny like the earth,
> And women amorous as birds,
> The songs to which their throats give birth
> Are strings of inarticulate words
> Set to fountainous dark refrains,
> Whose cadences are harsh with mirth
> And loud with crude insatiate pains.

None of these poems suggested that he was going to set the Vaal on fire, but they are more than the mechanical exercises in verse that many schoolboys produce. At least they show that he had read widely and had thought about his reading; they also showed that he had a talent for writing to rival his talent for drawing and painting. This was the period when he really began to consider whether he should not be a writer rather than the painter he had dreamed of becoming.

But there was a more immediate decision to be taken. In his last year at St John's, 1920, he distinguished himself by carrying off two of the eight prizes awarded to the fifth form, those for Latin and French.[29] The family went off to the Natal coast for the Christmas holidays, and began to think seriously about what the newly matriculated seventeen-year-old should do with his life. This was young Plomer's first visit to the Natal coast which he would later come to know well. It was tropical, humid, and fertile, with an African landscape and vegetation quite different from the austere, dry crispness of the highveld, and when Plomer, strolling through an orange grove, met an Indian girl in a magenta sari, the liquid eye she rolled at him seemed to invite him to realms of experience of which Teddy Wolfe would scarcely have approved.

Charles Plomer's income had recovered only very slowly from the losses of the war; he certainly could not afford to keep his elder son while he tried to make his way as an artist. Had he been a rich man it would have been no different, in any case: he simply did not believe that art was a practical option. At best he considered it a harmless hobby. 'He did not regard writing either with hope or approval as an eventual means of my making a living, but he did not try to prevent me from preparing myself for it as best I could,' his son was to write.[30] He did believe in education, however, and he now offered William the chance to go to Oxford. The budding artist turned it down, partly from the knowledge that his parents really could not afford to keep him at Oxford, partly because he was doubtful of the value of more formal education. (He seems to have resented, after his return from Rugby, even his father's insistence that he spend two more years at St John's finishing his schooling.)[31] With his South African matriculation he would in any case have had no guarantee of acceptance by an Oxford college; he would first have had to study Greek for Responsions, probably under an Oxford tutor, and since his knowledge of Greek was minimal, this was no small barrier.

Because he was so uncertain of his own destiny, and because his mother had no better idea than that he should join the Navy, his father made the decision: William would become a farmer. Charles Plomer had the most cheerful memories of his own gypsy years in South Africa; it would do William no harm to knock about a little, he must have reasoned, to work with his hands and to get rid of the inflated ideas inculcated by his mother and his artistic friends.

It so happened that there had sprung up, during Plomer's last year at school, a body devoted to helping young Englishmen settle on the land in South Africa. In 1820 there had been a large-scale influx of British settlers, most of whom had been settled along the Eastern Cape border as a buffer between the Cape Colony and the threatening Xhosa tribe. A century later there was again reason for bringing in British settlers, at least in part to counterbalance the dominant and rapidly growing Afrikaner population, which had no great love of the British Empire. Afrikaner nationalism was at this period increasing rapidly in strength, one of its aims being to counteract the influence of British expatriates in the South African civil service: Charles Plomer had already begun to feel insecure in his own position. An organization called The 1820 Memorial Settlers' Association was founded to redress the balance in favour of British influence.

It advertised repeatedly in *The Times* and elsewhere, and its plan was to bring enterprising young Britons out, settle them for a year or two with an already established farmer to learn the rudiments of the business, and then advise them on buying their own farms. The host farmer, in return for his co-operation with this scheme and for providing board and lodging for the apprentice, would get the help of another pair of hands, free. There was no difficulty about enrolling young Plomer as an apprentice, for though he was already in South Africa (and had been born there), his parents were unquestionably English. A list of potential farming hosts was produced for Charles Plomer's inspection. William's own desire, so far as it ran to farming at all, was to produce fruit in the Cape peninsula,[32] but William was not making the decision. Charles, with memories of his own wanderings in the Eastern Cape, chose a farm near Molteno, the town where, thirty years before during his rolling-stone years, he had organized a banquet for a visiting British dignitary. Suitable strong farming clothing and items of equipment which Charles thought a young farmer might find useful were bought for William; his boxes were packed, and in the midwinter chill of a highveld morning in June 1921 he waved goodbye to his parents and his brother on a platform in Johannesburg's cavernous main station, and presently found himself clattering and swaying in the train making its way southwards out of the city.

The young man who settled down to watch the tawny, treeless vastness of the veld glide by under a brilliant winter sun was still only seventeen, but he was already two metres tall, broad-shouldered and strongly made. His hair was blond with a golden tinge; his eyes behind their rather donnish round-lensed spectacles were light grey; his features were handsome and clean-cut like his father's. He had, however, none of his father's excitability and febrile energy. Instead, already strongly developed in him, was his mother's quiet watchfulness and a catlike air of controlled energy all his own. Isolation, first at Beechmont and Rugby, and later even within his own family, had taught him the value of keeping his own counsel; he might have originated the saying 'Let not thy left hand know what thy right hand doeth'. Already he had begun to think of himself as an observer of life, rather than an actor. He believed, or at least longed to believe, that he had qualities that would mark him out from ordinary men, but he must have wondered what kind of beginning he could make in the artistic life on an isolated African sheep farm. He would find out.

4. *The Stormberg*

1921–1922

MOLTENO is a small town in the Eastern Cape, on the railway line which runs from the Orange Free State down to the coastal cities of Port Elizabeth and East London. The town, named after an obscure prime minister of the Cape Colony, exists solely as the centre of a not especially rich farming district; it was a backwater in 1921 and it remains a backwater today. Plomer arrived on the railway line whose opening his father had helped to celebrate with that banquet thirty years before. No doubt tired from his two days in a jolting, clanging train, he booked into the town's single hotel, having learned that 'his' farmer would come to fetch him at the end of the week, and went exploring. There was not much to discover in Molteno. In later years Plomer described it as

a one-horse town, with its main street, railway station, and police station, a few shops with chickens pecking about on the threshold, a Dutch Reformed church, a Wesleyan Methodist chapel and, much smaller, an Anglican church. The streets were few, wide, dusty, and drowsy. An occasional ox-waggon creaked past. Everybody knew everybody else's business, and small scandals took on large proportions. Europe seemed a conception as remote as heaven or hell.[1]

What was most striking to a traveller who knew the steamy Africa of Pietersburg or the Natal coast was the icy wind that blew through Molteno's streets. The town is flanked by a ruggedly impressive range of mountains, the Stormberg, which rises nearly 2,000 metres above sea-level, and is often covered in snow in winter; the weather is as wild and as unpredictable as that of Emily Brontë's moors. Plomer's small hotel bedroom was freezing, and he must have thought this a miserable beginning to his adventure. In search of company, he went along to the Anglican church and introduced himself to the priest, the Revd Mr Horseham,[2] the religion of his mother and of St John's College retaining its hold on his affections still. The old clergyman and his tiny wife, English expatriates, received him with kindness and a roaring fire, fed him well, and talked to him of an England they had not seen for many years, a Victorian England that Plomer knew had been swept away by the war. The conversation consisted mainly of monologues by the rector or his wife, constantly interrupted by flat contradictions from the other. Either in his memory or in notebooks, Plomer treasured some of their odder behaviour or remarks, and when he came to write his first novel, *Turbott Wolfe*, he transformed the Horsehams into the Reverend Justinian Fotheringhay and his wife:

'The doctor says I am ill,' he [Fotheringhay] assured me, 'but Mrs. Fotheringhay is much worse. She will not take care of herself. She slipped down on her back about a year ago and hurt herself very badly. She hasn't been out of the house for nine months. And then last March down she went again on a beastly slippery floor—'
'No, I didn't,' declared Mrs. Fotheringhay, suddenly appearing in a doorway, with a pile of house-linen balanced on her arm.
'But, my dear, you did,' her husband asserted.
'No, it was in April.'
'O, very well then, it was in April.'[3]

After some days of kicking his heels around Molteno, Plomer was collected by his farmer, Fred Pope, and presently found himself jogging off in a horse-drawn Cape-cart (a form of two-wheeled, leather-hooded buggy peculiar to South Africa), in the direction of the farm, twenty kilometres out of Molteno towards Dordrecht. This experience too was to go straight into *Turbott Wolfe*:

I found myself seated beside Soper [Fred Pope] in a tall and jolting Cape-cart one afternoon ... Soper was a short wiry fierce ungainly excitable man with a very red face; a man very heartily disliked because he worked harder and achieved more than his neighbours. As soon as I saw Soper I felt that however much I might find myself at variance with him yet he was at any rate honest. His eyes were of the same candid topaz-yellow as those of the sheep that brought him a living.[4]

Fred Pope, for all his red face and fierce manner, was not only a highly efficient farmer, he was also kind-hearted and understanding, and Plomer was very lucky to have found him. Pope had answered an advertisement in the *Farmer's Weekly*, and had volunteered to be part of the 1820 Memorial Settlers' Association scheme,[5] and he had not much more idea than Plomer of what to expect from his new apprentice. His thousand-hectare farm, Marsh Moor, had been established by his father, who had built it into a thriving concern; it was to go from strength to strength under Fred and his son, Stanley, who at this time was five years old.[6] It lay (and still lies) in an amphitheatre of treeless, rocky mountains, their apparently gentle slopes deceptive, for they are both rugged and steep. The farm buildings are perhaps a kilometre from the highroad and are approached across flat, stony fields, too dry in most years for cropping. This is sheep and cattle country, and Fred Pope ran red poll cattle and a merino sheep stud.[7]

The long, narrow farmhouse, built in the 1840s by a wandering Voortrekker, was a thatched, single-storey building in the Dutch style, with a large central living-room from which the three bedrooms and the kitchen opened. Plomer described it as being without a veranda, but photographs of the period show a narrow veranda at one end of the house.[8] The building was screened from the road by a stand of fine conifers, and was surrounded by extensive outbuildings. Between the conifers and the road were primitive huts in which the black labourers and their families lived. The farmhouse itself sheltered the Pope family and Plomer; one of the larger outbuildings accommodated visiting tradesmen who sometimes called at the farm for work, among them an English carpenter named Eddie Ruddle[9] and a picturesque old Scot named William Dunbar Macdowall, an itinerant blacksmith.

After a day or two wandering about the farm to get to know its extent (half of its thousand hectares were mountainous, and rounding up recalcitrant sheep in these upland pastures was no laughing matter), Plomer was set to work. It was the lambing season, and presently there was a blizzard and a heavy fall of snow; there was plenty to be done in getting the ewes under cover and attending to their labours. Most of the really heavy work was done by black shepherds, but the new apprentice found his hands full enough:

I at once began to learn the arts of midwifery among the ewes and the curious variations among them of the maternal instinct. Many an evening have I spent in stone sheds by lantern light, obliging a reluctant udder to accept the blind mouth of an unwanted lamb, or dressing a live lamb in the skin of a dead one in order to persuade the bereaved ewe to bring up the changeling as her own offspring—exercises in patience.[10]

As a worker whose role was largely undefined, Plomer was set to any task that needed doing—fencing, thatching, roofing with corrugated iron, sowing broadcast,[11] carpentering, baking, churning butter, and butchering. These tasks, given the social structure of the farm (and indeed of South African society as a whole), consisted as much of overseeing the black labourers as of doing the work himself. On one occasion he was sent up to a mountain pasture to count a huge flock of sheep: he stood on a rock in the hope of getting a better view of them as they were slowly urged past him by an old Xhosa shepherd. Plomer's command of mental arithmetic was never strong, and he made three attempts at the nightmarish task, arriving at three markedly different totals. The fact that the increasingly exasperated old shepherd spoke only Xhosa and Afrikaans, while Plomer had scarcely a word of either language, did not make things easier.[12]

In some respects this simple life agreed with him well enough. There was no electricity, no car, no radio. Lighting consisted of paraffin lamps and tallow candles, by which everyone rose early and went early to bed. The food was simple, abundant, and invariable: wholemeal wheat bread and wheat porridge grown and ground on the farm; mutton, milk, and butter from the same source; and coffee bought on Fred Pope's weekly trips to Molteno. Baths were taken once a week, in water heated on the stove in big paraffin tins. 'My chief joy at Marsh Moor was health,' Plomer was to write years later. 'The dry, temperate climate, the superb mountain air, the long days out of doors, the brilliant cloudless nights, the sweet sleep and wholesome food, youth, freedom from care—these were great advantages.'[13]

He soon gave up going into Molteno with Fred Pope; the place had too little to offer. By contriving to cut his own hair with a pair of clippers, he even avoided having to visit the town barber.[14] When he had a day off, he would walk up into the mountains, enjoying the complete isolation. One of the delights of the South African veld is the huge variety of wild flowers, many of them very spectacular, and Plomer, who had loved English wild flowers, revelled in his discoveries of tree heaths and the wild lilies in which that part of the Cape is so rich. In a cave on the farm he was shown bushman paintings,[15] those fading and melancholy memorials of a people hunted almost to extinction by black and white pastoralists alike.

What he lacked was stimulating human company, though he made occasional visits to the Popes' neighbours and acquaintances: to a farmer named Radford Hope, for instance, who was the Popes' nearest neighbour, and to a family named Stretton, who had a fine farm in the direction of Dordrecht,[16] and whose young white housekeeper, Marjorie Hunter, much impressed Plomer. These visits to neighbours were rare, and it was the people among whom he was living on Pope's farm who naturally affected him most directly. His first impressions of Fred Pope proved accurate, and he never ceased to respect and like the man. Pope for his part thought young Plomer a very odd fish, and not in the least likely to make a farmer, but he was greatly taken by his new apprentice's skill at drawing. Plomer made a few detailed pen-and-ink sketches of the landscape round the farm, and he also did some very fine English scenes in the same medium, presumably from memory, a visual equivalent of his 'Evening in Oxfordshire' poem of the previous year. But what impressed Pope still more was Plomer's ability to turn out caricatures of the Popes and their friends and acquaintances, satirical little sketches which in a few rapid lines not only caught likenesses that were instantly recognizable, but also managed to convey something of the personality of the subject. Most of these sketches Plomer would light-heartedly show to Fred Pope if he thought they would provide amusement, and he would then instantly tear them up or drop them into the fire. Pope was almost as impressed by this careless destruction as he was by the skill that had produced the drawings.[17]

Whenever he could persuade Plomer to give him one, he preserved it, and the collection he built up has survived intact.[18] It includes caricatures (in the style of *Punch* of that period) of such subjects as Pope opening a bottle of warm beer and exploding in a cloud of foam, or Elsie Pope (Fred's sister-in-law) singing lustily to an old gramophone. Some of these sketches have amusing snatches of dialogue, little written caricatures in their own right, and, like the drawings, they demonstrate Plomer's capacity to seize on and convey aspects of character. A detailed drawing, for instance, shows the Revd Mr Horseham sitting in his old car amidst a dense cloud of smoke, his broad clerical hat shading a face purple with the effort of starting the vehicle, as he expostulates, 'Oh really, these cors are *too* feawful when you hevn't a nace garawge to *Househam* in! Chechaw, you old tin can, gijima, gijima!! But wait—dear me, the dem thing's on fire! Chechaw, chechaw!!!'

Other drawings included designs for an entire pack of cards which Plomer made for Fred Pope's son Stanley; only one of these survives, a careful drawing of a man in the wig and stock of the late seventeenth century.[19] There was also an elaborate, high-spirited design for a coat of arms for the Pope family. A shield bearing a plump sheep is supported by a triple-crowned Pope and an African; the crests are a loaf of bread and a bottle of Fred Pope's energetic home-brewed beer; the motto is 'Ovis hovisque magnificus per arduis semper sunt', and Plomer added his description, couched in suitably heraldic terms:

Arms:—In a field lucerne vert, flory counter-flory purpure, a hamel [Afrikaans for a sheep], prime, amiable, woolled superbly with a fleece snowy, stapled long. Supporters:—Sinister, a pope, crowned and robed papal, booted sable; having in the dexter hand, a pastoral staff. Dexter, a moor sable, in a field marshy, vert; having in the sinister hand, shears, straight from Sheffield. Crests:—A flask of yeast, up, distinctly. A loaf, excellent, whole-meal. Motto: Untranslatable.'

This cheerful nonsense amused Fred Pope, as it was designed to do, and it impressed him that a boy of seventeen was capable of producing such sparks of humour at will.

Among the surviving drawings are a few of particular interest to students of Plomer's writing. There are two portrait sketches of William Dunbar Macdowall, the itinerant Scottish blacksmith who greatly impressed Plomer, a man who held views on the blacks that struck Plomer as enlightened, but which irritated Fred Pope. Macdowall was a large, dignified man whom Plomer came to think of as a benevolent uncle:

He was a fine figure of a man with flowing golden moustaches and a ruddy face, a cheerful, sceptical sensualist with wonderful stories of his earlier days, when the country was freer and wilder and fuller of odd characters comparable to himself. In spite of his rough life he had retained many of the little as well as the stronger prejudices of his class: 'I do wish they wouldn't say "serviettes," ' I remember him saying. While I kept the forge going for him he built up for me out of his past a world of legend . . . But he left abruptly after giving offence by exhibiting an entire lack of colour prejudice.[20]

For Plomer, Macdowall was much the most sympathetic character on the farm, if only for the reason that, like Plomer, he refused to see the Africans as innately inferior to whites. He is given an important place in *Turbott Wolfe*, where he appears as Frank d'Elvadere, and his offensive lack of colour prejudice takes the form of telling a story in which a white man unjustly tries to whip a black, but is overpowered and beaten himself.[21]

Another of Plomer's drawings from this period suggests that he often met Fred Pope head on in argument about colour prejudice, and gave as good as he got. Entitled 'Post prandial politics', it shows two men disputing at the dinner-table so violently that they smash plates and glasses, and even pull off the table-cloth as they scramble on to the table to face one another. On the verso is written 'Fred Pope and WP disputing', but what is striking about the drawing is that both contestants have the face of Fred Pope, with bristling moustache, small angry eyes, and pugnacious jaw. The sketch implies that Plomer was quite willing to reproduce the arguments of his host so as to turn them satirically against him.

He used exactly this technique in an ironic prose piece he wrote at Marsh Moor during 1921, in which he is plainly speaking with the voice of Fred Pope and his kind, though he no doubt exaggerates Pope's position to include strong prejudices against blacks, Asians, Jews, Afrikaners, and anyone who is not a deeply conservative, Anglophile farmer. Fred Pope was sufficiently good-humoured about this squib to preserve it with Plomer's drawings.

South Africa

South Africa is inhabited by black people. The technical name for them is Something Niggers. They are, however, sometimes spoken of in ecclesiastical circles as Our Black Brothers.

Other inhabitants are Jews and Coolies, who live on the proceeds of doing other people down; and International Socialists, who live in hopes of doing other people in.

Most South African towns are villages; and most of the villages are not villages, but happy hunting-grounds. For Jews, of course. Any townspeople who are not Jews are Profiteers. The latter spend their time trying to get rid of the unnecessaries of life at four times the price they gave for them.

In some towns (and villages) there are actually a few people of British extraction. They are generally parsons, whose duty is to look after the souls of the other townspeople, who, of course, have got no souls to be looked after. Or they are doctors, busy doing away, at exorbitant fees, with anybody unwise enough to consult them. Or last, they may be lawyers, or magistrates, or policemen, trying magnificently to keep other people in order when they can't manage it themselves.

Let us consider the country districts.

There are some people with rather dusty-looking beards living on the land, and quite down to their reputations. For some extraordinary reason they are known as Dutch Farmers. They are neither Dutch, nor are they farmers.

On the contrary, they are debased Huguenots; talking a corrupt and execrable Low German; and their occupation is not farming, but trying to keep pace with their debts. Their chief characteristic is that when they want to thank you for anything (which isn't often) they invariably tell you to buy a donkey [A pun on the Afrikaans 'Baie dankie' (thank you very much)].

It is sometimes well to bear in mind that South Africa is an English colony.

The little agriculture that is carried on is entirely due to Englishmen, but this is the only indication of the fact.

The government is run by some of the Huguenots that have run off the land into what they fondly imagine to be politics. Commerce, of course, belongs to the Jews. All that is left are the Industries. Here again, one draws blank as far as Englishmen are concerned.

Diamonds are stolen by native gentlemen, and bought by Jews. Gold is found by other native gentlemen in order to provide baronetcies for other Jews. Ostrich feathers are kindly grown by benevolent ostriches to adorn the wives of the said Jews. Wool and mohair are provided by sheep and goats respectively so that brokers can make a living. They are called brokers because they are out to break the farmers.

In spite of all this, Englishmen are the backbone of South Africa, (bow-wow), even though, like most vertebræ, they are practically invisible.

In conclusion, it may be of interest to know that the motto for the Union[22] is 'Ex unitate vires'. The translation of this, of course, is 'Scratch a South African, and it's fifty-seven-to-one you'll find a Jew.'

The motto may also be rendered 'While there's Life, there's Hope.'

This parody of Fred Pope's views makes a serious enough point, made also in the representation of the views of Soper in *Turbott Wolfe*: he looked with suspicion on almost everyone not of his immediate family, and was cordially disliked by many of his neighbours in consequence. It was a view that Plomer recognized easily enough, for it was very close to his own mother's attitude; in reacting against it in Fred Pope, he was asserting his independence from his own family, and acknowledging the increasing distance that lay between them.

Plomer would not have dared to hint to Fred Pope at the real nature of his own feelings on the 'colour bar'; it was enough that Pope knew him to be a negrophile. In truth, Plomer continued to take his lead from Teddy Wolfe, and his reaction to younger Africans at least was an erotic one; as they worked together in the wool-shed, for instance, the gleaming male nakedness of the labourers struck him as resembling 'heroic bronzes'.[23] He was reacting to them as Teddy Wolfe had reacted to the naked black miners. Had Pope ever come to realize that his apprentice was sexually attracted to the African labourers on the farm, his horrified reaction can readily be imagined; Plomer's response to the blacks broke a double taboo, against miscegenation and against homosexuality, and it would be difficult to say which was the stronger in South Africa at this period. Plomer must sometimes have shrunk within himself as he imagined how his host would react, and his imagination went to work on the scene, removing it from the homosexual context by a simple change of detail: the gender of the white who is attracted by African sexuality becomes female. In *Turbott Wolfe* Soper tells with grim relish the story of a white woman who is attracted to an African labourer and invites him to her bed; Soper and a neighbour, by way of retribution, tie the labourer up and castrate him. That Plomer could face this scene imaginatively only a year or so after leaving the Popes' farm, even with the protective change he makes to it, shows remarkable courage. It also shows the degree to which he felt alienated from the people among whom he lived. His secret life had already taken him a long way from South African society.

How little Pope knew about his smiling, watchful young apprentice is shown by the fact that he had no idea at the time that Plomer was writing. He had great respect for Plomer's ability to consume books, however; on one occasion Pope offered him a volume to read, recommending it enthusiastically, and when it was returned the same afternoon he supposed that Plomer had not liked it. 'Yes, it was very good,' Plomer had assured him. Pope refused to believe that Plomer had read it so quickly, so Plomer invited him to test his knowledge of it. Pope opened the book at random and was astonished to find that Plomer could give an account of any passage so detailed that it was close to a quotation, word for word.[24] This impressed the farmer as an almost miraculous feat of speed-reading and memory.

Marsh Moor, though it must have seemed to Plomer at the time a cultural desert, was not entirely lacking in literary connections. Mrs Pope's mother, Mrs Cawood, had been one of the children taught by Olive Schreiner at Ganna Hoek, the Karroo farm where she had been a governess in the 1870s.[25] Schreiner, whose remarkable work *The Story of an African Farm* was published in 1883, was at this period South Africa's best-known novelist. Her writing was noteworthy not only for its feminist message, but also for the revolutionary way in which it used the African landscape, which Schreiner lovingly described in print with greater subtlety and clearer vision than anyone before her. Curiously enough, she failed to do the same for the Africans, who, to judge from her writings, hardly entered her consciousness.

She had died in the Cape only the previous year, and had been buried under a hemispherical cairn on the top of a hill known as Buffel's Kop near Cradock, little more than a hundred kilometres from Molteno as the crow flies, so that Plomer felt spiritually close to her. 'Such is the power of the written word,' he was to remark, 'that she was in fact a closer companion to me than those beings with whom my life was passed.'[26] She had been in revolt against conventional Christianity and against established patterns of sexuality, as he was. He delighted in Mrs Cawood's story of how Schreiner had been sacked from her post as governess for replying to a homily from her employer with a scornful 'God, indeed!' Plomer was wiser, or at least more prudent, in dealing with his own hosts; he simply kept silent, transmuting his scorn into print later.

Schreiner was not his only companion through the power of the written word at this time. He corresponded regularly with his parents, though none of his letters to them has survived.[27] He also wrote to his beloved Aunt Laura and to Uncle Emslie, who at this time put on paper for him a vivid account of Van Gogh during their student days together.[28] Plomer's interest in Van Gogh had been increased by the fact that one of the books he had with him was an edition of Van Gogh's letters.[29] Other volumes in his small library included the poems of Blake and of Rimbaud. These, he was later to say, had been enough to sustain him: 'With such great examples before me, how could I fail in my small and obscure way to see that the world of imagination and of art was worth all one's loyalty?'[30] He exchanged regular letters with his old school friend from Rugby, Darsie Gillie, who was now a student in his first year at Balliol. Gillie continued to send him interesting fragments of his reading in French and German. One of these snippets was a poem by the German Johannes Kuhlemann, entitled 'Tristan d'Acunha', of which Gillie supplied a translation he had made himself of the first two stanzas.[31] The poem reached Plomer in March 1922, and he wrote back thanking Gillie for it, and saying that he had read it and a book Gillie had sent 'almost at a sitting—quite an accomplishment on a S. African farm belonging to someone else'.[32] This poem, which Plomer carefully preserved, was to bear magnificent and unexpected fruit a few years later.

Plomer's reference to reading under difficulties on a farm 'belonging to someone else' is perhaps a reflection more of his desire to keep his activities secret from the Popes than the result of too many farming chores. In later years he was to claim that 'at Marsh Moor there was scarcely any time for writing, but I once sent some verses to Harold Monro, the leading poetic impresario of his day. He wrote me an encouraging letter in reply.'[33] The truth is that though Plomer worked hard during the week, with only Sundays entirely free of chores, he found time to do a good deal of reading and writing at Marsh Moor, and he wrote to Harold Monro not once, but several times. The Popes, however, had no idea that he was writing anything but letters,[34] an early example of his life-long secretiveness and his tendency to keep different aspects of his life in quite separate compartments.

Harold Edward Monro[35] had in 1913 founded the Poetry Bookshop to publish poetry, to encourage its sale, and to promote poetry readings. He was also the publisher of Edward Marsh's series *Georgian Poetry*, which appeared between 1912 and 1922, and which gave a name to a whole period of English verse. In addition, from 1919 to 1925 he published a poetry magazine called the *Chapbook*, of which whole volumes were devoted to introducing new poets to the public. In choosing to write to Monro, Plomer was acting both boldly and shrewdly: an unknown youth on a remote African farm was making an appeal to one of the leading literary figures of the period, but one known to be sympathetic to new writers. He had actually written his first letter to Monro in April 1921, before leaving Johannesburg for Marsh Moor. At St John's College he had met an old schoolmaster named Simpkinson, who happened to have taught Monro at Radley, and who suggested that Plomer write to the great man. Plomer opened his letter to Monro by explaining this, and continued:

Knowing that I wrote poetry he [Simpkinson] was kind enough to offer me an introduction to you. Unfortunately the man has had a 'stroke', and is now trying to get well at the Cape, so I hope you won't think me saucy for writing to you on my own account. By the way, I am a child (17) and a public school boy (Rugby).

I do not dabble in verse for the sake of indulging sterile emotion, though I am still sufficiently adolescent for my outlook to be vague. (I am afraid this is a terrible letter, but most of what I write is disastrous.)

I am writing very little at present, not being in accord with my material surroundings, but I have presumed to enclose a few specimens of my work, and I should be far more than grateful for your opinion of them.

Not being old enough for certain Elizabethans I have read a little, or only the best, of the following: Drummond of Hawthornden, Peele, Crashaw, Carew, Herbert, Vaughan, Burns, Byron, Meredith, and Swinburne. I am intimate with the following: Herrick, Donne, Marvell, Blake, Wordsworth, Coleridge, Shelley, Keats. Tennyson was the first poet I read. I am familiar with all the 'moderns', except John Drinkwater, A. E. Housman, and a good many very minor people.

Is it necessary for me to read J.D., A.E.H., and the v. minor people?

Let me congratulate you on 'Milk for the Cat' and 'Suburb'.[36]

If you think my stuff hopeless, pray say so. I must apologise for being so long-winded, and, indeed, for writing at all.

Yours faithfully,
William Plomer[37]

He enclosed copies of 'Evening in Oxfordshire', 'Symphony', 'Epigram', and 'A Fragment', written, like the letter, in the beautiful italic script he had already adopted. Monro, who no doubt was constantly deluged with such letters from hopeful young writers, took months to reply, but he must have been touched by the naïve tone of Plomer's letter, with its combination of youthful confidence and youthful self-doubt. He replied very encouragingly on 31 July 1921, complimenting Plomer on his work and asking to see more of it before he expressed a firm opinion.

Plomer received this reply after his arrival at Marsh Moor, and he was utterly delighted by it; the ebullience of his response shows the extent to which Monro's letter had given him confidence. He began with his new long address at Molteno, and continued:

Having accomplished my address, dear sir, or dear Mr. Monro, or dear Harold Monro, I will proceed:-

First of all, I am so overjoyed with your letter that I am bound to write even more incoherently than usual. It seems to me almost incredible that you should even have read more than one of the things I sent, but that you should write a charming and sympathetic letter seems outside the bounds of possibility.

And really, can I believe that you want to see more? Oh heavens, if you only could imagine the value of your sympathy which is a thing as necessary to me as food or sleep.

But, as usual, I scrawl like a hysterical female instead of a discreet public school product. However.

You shall certainly have such MSS. as are fit to have, but out of what I write very little is of any value whatever, if that.

What an elegant sentence that was!

I hope within a few days to finish a poem which I have been working at for months, but as I am an embryo farmer, I have to compose as I work, and I only have a little time on Sundays for actual writing. But when this poem is fair-copied and complete, I will send it off at once, and I hope it will give you pleasure, though I doubt it.

Simpkinson is better.

I wonder if you would mind sending me a list of P.B.[38] publications, and can you give me any details of the next few Chapbooks? I have got most of the first lot.

Yours ecstatically
William Plomer

Your 'Underworld' is an admirable poem: have you got a Rhyme Sheet of it?

Please tell me whether to call you 'sir',

> or 'Harold Monro',
> or 'Mr. Monro',
> or anything else.

Please call me anything but 'sir.'

And to accompany this rather bumptious juvenile letter—he would never again be betrayed into anything so careless or revealing of his feelings—he enclosed the poem he had been working on, a development of his earlier 'Fragment', by now entitled 'Death':

> With half-smiles he went, with vague gestures of the head
> and valedictory movements of the hands:
> like distant clouds he saw, and then forgot,
> the meaningless faces of his executioners,
> he being shaken by a fabulous joy,
> knowing the ambulation and the laughter of savages—
> cruel, but careless, and as amorous as birds:
>   he hears the songs to which their throats give birth—

echoes of inarticulate words
set to fountainous dark refrains,
whose cadences are harsh with mirth
and loud with crude insatiate pains.
And chanting in their conical grass huts
those move familiarly, who know with him
the sky alive with stars,
the thrill of flowers that wound the sky with flames,
the vibrancy of dark viridian seas,
their foaming ice-green pools and fiery sands;
and singular trees adorned
with savourous strange-blooded fruits . . .
So death comes like a flower, seen suddenly.

The vivid African fragment from which this poem had grown has been lost amidst the vagueness of the imagery; the exotic confusion in which Africa is here depicted might have been read about rather than seen, and the speaker of the poem is apparently a white man being led out to death at the hands of black savages, rather than someone able to show real sympathy for them. Though he had begun to find his subject-matter, he had yet to discover how to deal with it, and it would have been understandable if Monro had been disappointed with this poem.

Yet the young poet's remarkable skill in handling words is evident in another poem he sent Monro under separate cover a few days later,[39] the lines he called 'Barges':

Never hearse, with slow cavalcade of horse,
Moving as in a trance by night with flares,
Had the profound abandonment of the barges
Continuing slowly along unechoing thoroughfares:
The sound of far deserted surges but enlarges
The infinite rippling of the tide along their course.

The beauty of the long slow lines is very striking, and though Plomer disparagingly wrote of the poem, 'I wonder if this is anything more than an exercise in onomatopoeia?' he was justly proud of this piece of work.

Monro did not reply to this letter, and it was not until 2 April 1922 that Plomer took up the correspondence again, this time sending him a strange poem sequence, of which he wrote,

I enclose a thing I have written.
I say a 'thing' because I can't feel justified in calling it a poem. It is, I

think, a sort of vaudeville landscape. I do not pretend even to myself that it can have any sort of value as literature. I flatter myself that it may show a sort of feeling for landscape, and a kind of sense of humour.

As I say, I only send it to you on your request, and because it is an honour to be asked to send you my work, such as it is, and because I value your opinion prodigiously.

I really wrote this thing quite against my will. I suppose my EGO or something else went and did it. Please remember that I am just eighteen;[40] and that I know I haven't written anything yet. But I hope to most fabulously. Do please write.[41]

The poem series is prefaced by a complicated and rather silly vaudeville story which is intended to set the tone for the whole:

The muffin-man had been in a cavalry regiment. He used to wear her stays and she said his calves were too square, but even so, it was too late. He got the living and she had twins. The groom gave notice and she gave up the 'cello and went off with a fishmonger called Schwerdt. He changed his name to Wrollough, and swallowed his false teeth. I think there was another man, who kept a circus. But she came back from Peru with a man called Alfresco and a wig. And now the muffin-man is dead . . .

The three poems that follow, entitled 'The Morning', 'The Afternoon', and 'The Night', are feebly surrealistic, with odd mysterious references to the Muffin-man, though here and there Plomer hit upon a fine image, showing, as he said, a feeling for landscape:

> I come upon the poplars as the sun goes down.
> Staccato, as the sun departs,
> The sharp dark trees
> Pierce the stark earth like darts.

Perhaps surprisingly, Monro wrote once more after receiving this rather unpromising material, again encouraging Plomer to keep writing.[42] Plomer did not get this letter until October 1922, and by then had grown discouraged by Monro's silence: 'I had leaped to the conclusion that you were sick of my incoherent versifying; and I had sadly decided to combine both performer and audience in my own person,' he wrote.[43] As he had done before in his letters to Monro, he complained of the lack of mental stimulus at Marsh Moor:

I hope the enclosed show a little advance, but I would have you remember that I am only just 19, and that by reason of environment I am a little numb as to my mind.

I can only remember having had one moderately intelligent conversation since I last wrote to you. It was with an amazing Swiss missionary. The tragedy is, I can only remember one thing he said. That was:

'Le cubisme—c'est le fin.' This may have been true, but it wasn't what you might call horribly constructive.

. . . Your letters are flowers in a desert.

The poems he now sent Monro showed a definite advance. One of them, 'The Visitor', though a mere imagistic fragment, conveys a powerful sense of the way Monro's own letters (flowers in a desert) could change Plomer's mood at Marsh Moor:

> The sun blazed in, after a long dull day,
> Upon the small square room where sick I lay.
>
> His light slid off the opening door.
>
> I hear a laugh; and at the threshold towers
> Familiar, one that flaunts a sheaf of flowers.
>
> Who could but be content once more?

Another, 'Famille Arlequin', shows his rapidly growing technical mastery. He wrote confidently of it, 'I believe you will like this. It exhibits my almost congenital love for any sort of vaudeville.'

> Nimble, with ease
>   The tumblers leap,
>   Stoop, spring, and creep.
>   Their tricks begin
> With coloured spheres, trapeze,
>   And discs of tin.
>
> Swift time they keep
>   With sudden vaults
>   And somersaults;
>   Juggle and spin.
> Their eyes seem half asleep,
>   Silken their skin . . .
>
> In sequin hats,
>   With poise and pout
>   Troop slowly out,
>   As they tripped in,
> His wife, his elfin brats,
>   And Harlequin.

And the lines which he had first written in 1920 and reworked as 'Death' (Monro had picked it out for particular comment in his second letter)[44] now took a much more successful form as 'Amanzimtoti':[45]

Here men are tawnier than the earth,
   And women amorous as birds,
Thrilling with songs to which soft throats give birth—
Fluent, echoing, inarticulate words
Set to fountainous refrains,
   Whose cadences get harsh with mirth
And loud with crude insatiate pains.

They may be heard through long warm nights
   (When shallow seas are vibrant, and the sands
Give up the ghost of noon's fierce burnings)
   Beating upon monotonous drums with their brown hands,
In tunes and dancing to submerge delights,
   Fears, sins, and sacraments, and swift sub-human yearnings.

Here, under flowers that wound the sky with flames,
They live; and, dead, are not so much as names.

The title of 'Amanzimtoti' was a portent. Amanzimtoti is a holiday resort not far from Durban, and the Plomers had spent the Christmas of 1920 there. Plomer's mind was turning back to the Natal coast at this time, because of a most unexpected proposal from his father.

Pope had been patient with his inept apprentice, but it had grown daily more obvious that Plomer's future did not lie in breeding sheep. The truth was that he not only disliked the animals; he actually feared them. Years later he was to write of them, with uncharacteristic seriousness:

Persons unfamiliar with the ways of sheep think of them as merely silly and timid and as being all alike ... there are as many variations of character among them as among horses, cats or dogs, and they are capable of exhibiting, among other qualities, affection, cunning and wilfulness. 'The rage of the sheep' is a ludicrous-sounding phrase, but it does not seem so when one has seen a man charged and knocked over by a full-grown Merino ram with great voluted horns, testicles like a bull's, and the light of battle in its eyes.[46]

Towards the middle of 1922, when Plomer had been with him for a year, Pope wrote to Charles Plomer and told him that his son would never make a sheep-farmer.[47] Plomer tries to disguise the fact in his autobiographies, saying that he was by the end of 1922 'quite seriously, though dispassionately, preparing to set myself up as a sheep-breeder there in the Stormberg',[48] adding two sentences later that he was also considering studying fruit farming in the Western Cape. In truth, he was never more completely a fish out of water than as an apprentice farmer.

It happened that by the end of 1922 Charles Plomer himself was contemplating a change. In January of that year the labour unrest never far below the surface of South African life erupted in the form of a violent revolutionary strike in Johannesburg. The immediate cause was a proposal by the South African Chamber of Mines (controlled by the mine-owners) to open semi-skilled work to black labour. Until then, all skilled work had by a legalized colour bar been reserved for whites. White miners saw this move as threatening their wage levels, since blacks were paid so much less, and the response of the white workers was a violent strike involving both gold-mines and coal-mines, rapidly leading to serious bloodshed in Johannesburg. Rioting made it very difficult and dangerous to move about in the city, and innocent passers-by were several times the victims of attacks by the rioters.

Edythe Plomer had used the excuse of very similar violence in 1914 to press her husband to leave South Africa; she did the same now. Once more Plomer's parents travelled to England, taking the eleven-year-old Peter with them, to see whether it would be feasible for them to retire there. As their train left Johannesburg station in January 1922 it came under fire, and they had to lie on the floor of their carriage as bullets snapped and zipped about them.[49] Once again, however, Edythe's hopes of leaving South Africa for good were defeated by the evident impossibility of their being able to afford to retire in comfort in England. After leaving Peter at boarding-school in England (thereby showing that they had learnt nothing from their elder son's experience at Beechmont), they returned to South Africa in June or July 1922, and Charles Plomer, still only fifty-two, resumed his job with the Department of Native Affairs, now looking after the 'welfare' of Africans working on the mines—in unskilled jobs, for the white rioters had won their point. Within a few months, however, he was retired with a very small pension, as the long-threatened process of replacing expatriates with South Africans (most of them Afrikaners) gathered pace.

This meant that just when Charles Plomer was told that William was wasting his time as an apprentice, he was himself at a loose end, and urgently in need of some way of making money if he was not to retire in penury. The strain of his situation seems to have weighed on his mind, and perhaps there were renewed pressures in his marriage, for, although his son was to permit no hint of such a thing to enter his autobiography, there is some evidence that Charles had a nervous breakdown at this time. It is even possible that the breakdown was the cause, not the result, of his leaving the civil service.[50] The scheme he hit on to support himself and his family at this time of crisis was to take over the running of a native trading station, popularly known as a 'Kaffir store', together with some land, so that he and his elder son could engage in what Charles hoped would be highly lucrative farming and trading. Enquiries he set in train with a friend in the civil service in Natal convinced him that Zululand was the very place for this madcap scheme.

It was in this way that young Plomer, increasingly out of place at Marsh Moor, got a letter from his father in September 1922, telling him that his future lay at one of the oldest trading posts in Zululand, a place called Entumeni. Lifting his eyes from the letter to the bare mountains surrounding Marsh Moor, now just beginning to green again after the bitter winter, Plomer had a sudden vision of a 'softer, warmer landscape of sub-tropical verdure'.[51] For him Zululand was a romantic name redolent of muscular warriors clashing assegais against oxhide shields, of beehive huts placed in circles on gentle green hillsides, of warm mist drifting through dense natural forest. Besides, he had begun to think that anything would be better than Marsh Moor; he wrote at once and with enthusiasm, agreeing to his father's proposal. He knew no Zulu, or the name Entumeni might have given him pause. It means 'The place of thorns'.

5. *Entumeni*
1922–1925

PLOMER had agreed to meet his father in Durban in December 1922, so that the two of them could visit Entumeni to look the place over before they committed themselves.[1] Charles Plomer travelled down from Johannesburg, and his son took the train through Queenstown to join him. From Durban the two of them took a slow train together through the cane fields of the richly fertile Natal coastal plain north-west to the Zulu capital, Eshowe. Here they spent the night in a hotel, and the sound of the continuous rain pattering among tropical verdure entranced young Plomer after the dry cold of Marsh Moor's bare mountains. The next morning they were collected by the son of the non-resident lessee of Entumeni in what Plomer called 'a rickety flivver', with chains on the wheels to cope with the hilly roads composed of thick red mud, and were driven out to inspect their prospective home.

To any tenants not powerfully predisposed to approve, it would have seemed a thoroughly unappealing place. Entumeni was isolated from any white neighbours and lay within a Zulu reserve, the inhabitants of which would be their customers. The store from which they hoped to make their living was barnlike, dilapidated, dark, and full of unsaleable rubbish. The house, of wood and iron, was equally run down, filthy, unpainted, and without a toilet. What was humorously termed 'the garden' was unfenced and innocent of cultivation, its crop of weeds inadequately kept under control by several half-wild donkeys. The fifty hectares of farmland that went with the establishment supported some skinny cattle, several chickens which tottered in and out of the house, light-headed from hunger, and an old horse. The outgoing sub-tenants were still in residence, and the place was being offered as a going concern— 'going downhill', as Plomer sardonically remarked, 'at a Gadarene pace'.[2]

The young Norwegian who showed them over the trading station must surely have been astonished when they professed themselves delighted with it. More than that, they were thoroughly excited at the idea of taking it over, and when they went back to Johannesburg together shortly before Christmas 1922 to tell Edythe Plomer about their discovery, someone named them 'the two enthusiasts'.³ The truth is that they would probably have taken anything they had been shown, for each of them had powerful reasons for wanting to make Entumeni a success. For Charles Plomer the alternative was to return to England and live out the remainder of his life in a rented house in some south-coast town, whereas Entumeni seemed to offer a continuation of the free and easy life he had enjoyed as a young man when he first came out to South Africa. For his son, almost anything seemed a pleasant alternative to what he called 'wool-gathering in the Stormberg'.⁴ With regard to this unlikely scheme, then, father and son were at one, and that in itself was a rarity.

Their united front took the wind out of Edythe's sails. She opposed their enthusiasm with a series of level-headed questions, and got very unsatisfactory answers. Was the road good? No. Was the house habitable? Barely. Had they seen the books? No; the sub-tenants had said that the books had been sent away for audit. (A wry smile from Edythe.) Did William think the land likely to be productive? Possibly, but it was completely different from the hardy, heathy country he was used to, and was certainly unfit for sheep breeding, the only branch of farming he knew. Was there any white society? They had heard that there was a mission station a mile or so away, and that a few white farmers had settled here and there outside the native reserve. Did they know what they were letting themselves in for? No, but if they couldn't make a success of it, it wouldn't be from want of trying.⁵

One cannot help feeling sorry for Edythe Plomer. In her longing for England she was continually frustrated, and her scorn for everything South African as colonial and second-rate was its own punishment, making her think of herself as a miserable exile. Like her husband, she was now in her fifties and might have been looking forward to a period of peace and comfort; instead, by all accounts, she was to be plunged once again into a situation like that at Louis Trichardt, of which she had such terrible memories. 'Some women might at this point have said, "My God, why on earth did I ever marry you? If only I had known what I was being let in for!" But she didn't say it—at least on this occasion.'⁶

Charles Plomer now compounded boldness with extravagance,

by using much of his remaining cash (probably a retirement payment from the Department of Native Affairs) to buy a large, new, shiny black Buick touring car for trips between Entumeni and Eshowe, though neither he nor his son knew how to drive. They hired a chauffeur to drive them to Entumeni by way of Durban at the end of January 1923,[7] and on the way William learnt to drive, though inexpertly; he disliked most machines, and never learnt to handle them well.

Between Durban and the Zululand border they came to a swollen stream across the road, the result of a heavy storm up in the hills, and after some debate decided to attempt to ford it. When they were in mid-stream the volume of water suddenly increased dramatically and, seeing that the car was in imminent danger of being swept away, the three men leapt out and heaved it into shallower water. Throughout this crisis, during which she had been in real danger of drowning, Edythe Plomer impressed her son by sitting 'as calmly as if at a tea-party'. For all that, her heart must have sunk within her: if this was the prelude to Entumeni, what would the performance be like?

They set about transforming the trading station, pouring in money and energy. As Plomer was to write,

We fenced the garden, we painted the house and built on to it a pillared concrete verandah, we improved the outbuildings and built new ones, we hacked away undergrowth and grubbed up rank and sinewy weeds, we provided proper quarters for the servants, who had in any case to be trained, we struggled with the store, with the house, and with the hundred acres.[8]

As with Plomer's work at Marsh Moor, one must remember to put these labours into an African context. The Plomers largely oversaw this work rather than actually doing it themselves. The reserve was heavily populated with Zulus who had no ready means of earning money other than by offering their labour, at astonishingly low rates of pay, to the Plomers and their few white neighbours. It would be a mistake, then, to think of Plomer or his father grubbing weeds out of the garden or splashing paint on to the house. In this they had the help of a skilful Zulu handyman, Mose Qwabe,[9] who directed a team of Zulu labourers. The Plomers' main work was in the store, which Charles Plomer organized, though even here they had help. In fact, to start with, since they knew so little about trading and knew no word of Zulu, they hired a white assistant to help run the store; finding him too expensive, they soon replaced him with an educated Zulu, Lucas Makoba, whom Plomer found to be an intelligent and interesting companion.[10]

The projected farming, which Charles had hoped his son would be responsible for, was soon given up entirely: no one had either time or inclination to ride the old horse; the donkeys sank into mud holes in nearby valleys and had to be heaved out with ropes; the cows contracted odd diseases or wandered into the Zulus' small fields to eat their crops; and the chickens grew strong enough with adequate feeding to deposit their eggs in the forest where no one could find them. They were clearly not going to make their fortunes on the land, at least not with William Plomer as manager of farming operations. He had now begun learning Zulu at nights with the aid of Bishop Colenso's dictionary of the language, and had discovered what 'Entumeni' meant. 'Thorny were those early days,' he commented later, 'as formidable in some ways as those at Louis Trichardt years before. My mother would have been justified in saying to my father what Hardy (of the comic duo) often used to say to Laurel, "And *now* look what a mess you've got us into!" '[11]

Yet Entumeni was not without its pleasures. One of the chief of these was the surrounding countryside. Zululand is one of the loveliest parts of a startlingly beautiful country, and even Edythe, with all her longing for green English hills, had to admit that the landscape and the climate of Zululand were delightful. Her son described it with evident love years after:

Open, fertile, and undulating, with clusters of dome-shaped native huts, groves and thickets and streams, and patches of cultivated land here and there, haunted by exotic birds like toucans, hoopoes and humming birds and by small mammals like the galago, and with a rich and varied flora, it invited inquisitive saunters which we were quite unable to take. From the very first we were pleased with the climate, which never ran to extremes, and particularly with the heavy but not wetting mist which in the summer, after a hot day, would often rush upon us from the south and steep everything in an opaque and silvery silence.[12]

Moreover, in spite of everything, and perhaps to Edythe's surprise, Charles Plomer was making rather a success of running the store. He genuinely liked the Africans who had after all been his life's work, and they were soon persuaded that he did not intend to exploit them. He gradually won their confidence, and whole families began using the store as a social club, having nothing much else to do with their days. Once William began picking up the language— and of all the southern African languages, Zulu is the easiest to learn—the customers felt even more at home. They could barter their produce—grain, chickens, eggs, or hides—for an astonishing variety of goods, ranging from snuff to glass beads and from gramophones to iron pots. The customers came to regard the store as a kind of treasure-house of the white man's technology, and many of them would walk kilometres for the pleasure of hearing a Zulu record played on a large-horned gramophone, or admiring themselves, perhaps for the first time in their lives, in a full-length mirror. In consequence the store, after running at a diminishing loss for a year, began to turn a useful profit.[13]

William Plomer's reaction to the Zulus was one of unaffected admiration: it was the reaction he had had to the labourers at Marsh Moor, the reaction of Teddy Wolfe to the Johannesburg miners:

Their physical beauty was conspicuous, for many of them went about all but stark-naked, and their mere presence was to me deeply and agreeably disturbing . . . The young bucks, descendants of Chaka's braves, ornamented with a few beads and little else, and moving with superb grace, erectness and ease, were often models of bodily perfection.[14]

They reminded him of Herman Melville's comparison of the Marquesan islanders with the inhabitants of New York: 'Stripped of the cunning artifices of the tailor, and standing forth in the garb of Eden—what a sorry set of round-shouldered, spindle-shanked, crane-necked varlets would civilized men appear!' Under the impetus of these feelings, he began putting Africans into his poems and into the prose he was writing at this time. An example is his striking poem 'The Black Christ', which he sent to Monro in May 1923:

> Shadow lies like a stain
> And light like milk on the thin
> Ebony face, with death subduing the fine
> Nerves receiving impacts of pain,
> Each like an instrument-string, tone within tone.
>
> Now the last agony is done.
> Taken down
> From the Rood, with tears of blood sown
> The twisted body lies prone.

Three days in the tomb,
And stark, the body rises again.
The black lips quiver, they frame
Words unknown:
The body the same,
But behind the eyes the brain
Pursues what is flown.

'The Black Christ' illustrates not just Plomer's interest in the Zulus, but also his renewed openness to Christian teaching, probably under the influence of his gentle, pious mother. Among the white neighbours whom they soon got to know, the nearby missionaries were the only people they cared to admit to their friendship. The Entumeni Mission was one of the oldest in Zululand, having been founded by Bishop Schroeder at the end of the nineteenth century. The chief missionary in 1923, a Norwegian named Astrup,[15] was a dignified old man, educated, courtly, and benevolent, and always dressed in a frock coat in spite of the warmth of the climate.[16] Plomer liked and admired him, in part because he was an interesting character, and in part because of his evident devotion to his Zulu flock. He treated them with a courtesy and a gentleness that were in striking contrast to the attitude of the white farmers who were the Plomers' only other neighbours. Two of these, English expatriates named Essery and Ward, not only oppressed the Zulus and treated them cruelly, but even boasted of it to each other—though not, after one attempt, to the Plomers.[17] By comparison with these ignoble whites, the Zulus seemed ever more attractive companions to Plomer.

He had tried to keep his correspondence with Monro going, though the last letter he had had in return had arrived in October 1922. In his reply to that he had written, 'I shall have no peace till you write again!' and perhaps Monro thought him too pressing and importunate. Plomer wrote again in November 1922, sending Monro a poem called 'There Is No Coming Back', and adding, 'I hope to hear from you very soon,' but silence had descended on Monro's side of the correspondence. By May 1923 Plomer was so discouraged that a note of formality began to replace his earlier exuberance:

Dear Mr. Monro,

It is *vital* to me that you write at your very earliest convenience. The Muse grows numb for want of applause or condemnation. Even a slightly amplified acknowledgement would keep her poor heart beating.

Your humble servant
W.P.

Monro did not reply, and Plomer's next letter, of 28 October 1923, enclosing a poem, 'The Ships of Love', in the style of Yeats's early love-dialogues,[18] was a single coldly dignified sentence:

Dear Mr. Monro,

Will you oblige me with an answer?

Yours faithfully
William Plomer.

And when even this drew no response from Monro, Plomer did not write again. With the end of the correspondence with Monro died his hope of having his work included in Edward Marsh's *Georgian Poetry* volumes or of being published in some form by Monro's Poetry Bookshop.

He was determined by now that he would be a writer, and with the tenuous link with Monro broken, he set about trying to build others. He had begun writing journalistic articles, on such subjects as Afrikaans place-names and Zulu life, and some of these were printed in the Johannesburg *Star* in 1923, but what he still chiefly longed for was the publication of his poetry. There were two major newspapers in Durban, but it was a publication even closer to Entumeni that attracted his attention: the Zulu paper *Ilanga lase Natal*, which had been founded by a remarkable Zulu priest, the Reverend John L. Dube. It is evidence of Plomer's widening interest in the Zulus that he initiated a correspondence with Dube during 1923, and soon began sending him poems, the first of which Dube published on 15 February 1924. This first of Plomer's verses to appear in print was signed 'PQR'; significantly, it concerned the need for whites and blacks in South Africa to move towards one another, and it predicted that peace could be achieved only if the races could live 'side by side'.

A Game of Chess

'Neither will win,' the watchers say
Now that the contest starts.

'For Black men move without their heads,
And White without their hearts.

'And if one shall advance,' they said,
'So much as one short pace,
His fellow-men will shun him then
A traitor to the race.

'You wooden men give up the game,
For what are all these squares
But black and white and black again,
The pattern of your cares?'

The Chessmen quiver into life,
For love has conquered pride,
Those that were angry face to face
Are quiet side by side.

On 7 March 1924, in the same paper, Plomer published another poem, 'Post Mortem', a neat but undistinguished satire on the pretensions of educated Zulus, and a week later *Ilanga lase Natal* printed what were described as 'Three Folk Poems' by 'PQR', in which Plomer wrote, from the point of view of a newly Christianized African, lines that must have pleased his mother, but that make his later claim to have rejected Christianity at this time[19] look like an imaginative reconstruction of the past:

A New Disciple

In beaded skins,
With sticks and shields,
The heathen roams
His native fields.

But if he yields
To Christ his sins,
He loses less
Than what he wins;

For hearts and homes
Our Lord will bless
Dissolving sins
In happiness.

He appended to this poem, and to the two printed with it (one of them reprinted in *Turbott Wolfe*),[20] a curious note, written so as to continue the fiction that the author was a Zulu:

It is my hope that these simple verses may help to serve an early movement towards our own literature. A national literature can only be built up of many parts, and with infinite pains, but if we can plainly express now some of the true feelings of our people, however simple, we may be able to lay a foundation. Here I attempt to give you the intense Christian joy of the newly-converted.

Nothing shows more plainly the extent to which he identified with the Zulus, and wished to dissociate himself from his unattractive white neighbours, Essery, Ward, and others. Because he wrote anonymously, these neighbours did not link him with the poems, but they unquestionably realized that the Plomer family's attitude towards the Africans was quite different from their own, and perhaps felt threatened by the fact.

Certainly the Plomers were much disliked in the area. This was partly because they maintained a standard of living higher than that of their neighbours (their shiny black Buick, in which Plomer used to roar about at a dangerous speed, and the smart new toilet which they had built behind the Entumeni house and referred to as 'the Pagoda', were particularly envied),[21] but it was also partly the result of a sense that the Plomers gave themselves airs. Edythe's attitude of aloof condescension was particularly noticed and resented, and it is symptomatic that the Plomers were known in the district as 'The Royal Family'.[22] Increasingly Edythe saw herself as an English exile, and even as the ambassadress of an England under attack; in her speech, her mannerisms, and even in her dress she became more English than she might have been had she never left home.[23] Her disdain for South Africans had certainly spread to her eldest son, and he had begun to think of rocking the complacency of white South Africa by his writing.

Early in 1924 he began a novel, and from the start he seems to have intended it to focus on the uneasy, potentially explosive racial situation in South Africa. Realizing that to make the African characters in it more convincing he needed to know more about their thinking, he encouraged his father's black assistant, Lucas Makoba, to put down in writing his thoughts on what could be done to advance South African blacks.[24] He also paid a visit to John Dube at Ohlange on the north coast of Natal, and spent a long evening talking to that pioneering intellectual Zulu. Dube's achievements, besides starting *Ilanga lase Natal*, included founding a school, the Ohlange Institute, one of whose graduates, Chief Albert Luthuli, was to win the Nobel Peace Prize for his work aimed at bringing about racial equality in South Africa, and Dube himself had been one of the founders of the African National Congress. Plomer found him a most impressive, serious, fatherly man, and, like many Zulus, a fascinating conversationalist.[25] He was the sort of African thinker whom most white South Africans did not even know existed.

The next morning, before Plomer started for home again, Dube took him to visit an Indian settlement nearby, one of several Tolstoyan colonies founded by Mahatma Gandhi, who had studied law in South Africa and settled in Johannesburg, where he had soon established himself as a brilliant and prosperous barrister. In 1907 he had come to national prominence when he led a campaign of passive resistance against a Transvaal ordinance requiring all Asians to register with the authorities and carry identification documents similar to African passes. Though this first campaign was largely unsuccessful, Gandhi had begun to explore the possibilities of non-violent protest, and when in 1913 a new Immigration Act controlling the movement of Asians was proposed, he began a campaign involving a march of thousands of Asians from Natal into the Transvaal. This time he was successful in forcing the South African government to negotiate with him. Shortly thereafter he left for India, to practise on a grand scale the techniques he had begun to perfect in Africa. His influence in South Africa lingered, however, and the Phoenix settlement near Ohlange, dedicated to keeping alive his ideals, was still run by his son Manilal, a youth of Plomer's age.

Dube and Plomer found Manilal Gandhi superintending the production of an Indian newspaper. The young Indian struck Plomer as graceful, gentle, mentally alert, and of finely bred appearance. The importance of the meeting at Phoenix was not apparent to any of the three at the time, but years later Plomer was to write of it as an event of great significance.

It was a strange meeting this, between the son of a great man who had been kicked, stoned and imprisoned for defending his own people in this harsh and radiant country, a representative of a recently barbaric race who was seeking to better his oppressed and disoriented people by helping to adapt them to a 'Western' civilization of a sort, and myself, a mere youth, but a member of ruling race who was there to show that he regarded it as a misruling race.[26]

Unquestionably his meeting with men such as these convinced him of the absurdity of a system that ruled out the possibility of any but whites contributing to the running of South Africa.

The novel which he was now writing rapidly, working in the evenings by lamplight, using a hard pencil on thin paper,[27] was in part a vigorous attack on white South Africans' right to rule. He called it *Turbott Wolfe*, and its eponymous hero is an English painter who settles in 'Lembuland'[28] at a trading station bearing a strong resemblance to Entumeni, and there sets about trying to undermine the colour bar by encouraging miscegenation. Plomer later wrote of it that 'it was a violent ejaculation, a protest, a nightmare, a phantasmagoria—which the dictionary defines as "a shifting scene of real or imagined figures" '.[29] Most of its characters were real rather than imagined; Plomer put many of the people he had come across in South Africa over the previous four years into the novel, and took the trouble to pencil into the margins of his own copy of the work the names of many of the originals.[30] From these notes, and from the vivid descriptions of many of the same figures in his autobiographies, it is possible to trace most of the characters' origins.

Among the principal characters, the white goddess Mabel van der Horst, whose marriage to Zachary Msomi precipitates the crisis in the novel, was based on Marjorie Hunter, the young woman who acted as housekeeper for the Stretton family (Dunford in the novel), and whom Plomer had known and admired while working on the Popes' farm in the Stormberg. Wolfe's black assistant, Caleb Msomi, was modelled on Lucas Makoba, Charles Plomer's Zulu assistant at Entumeni (Ovuzane in the novel). Zachary Msomi in the novel was Zephaniah Makoba, cousin of Lucas, in actuality. The Hlanzeni Mission, which with the missionary Karl Nordalsgaard plays an important part in the novel, was Entumeni Mission, founded by Bishop Schroeder (Klodquist in the novel) and run by Astrup; Nordalsgaard's housekeeper, named as Rosa Grundso in the novel, was Anna Steenberg in real life. Nordalsgaard's illegitimate son, Olaf Shaw, was based on Louis Elliot, illegitimate son of Astrup. Even such details as Astrup's having been a knight of the order of St Olav are preserved in the novel, where Nordalsgaard is at one point represented as wearing 'the Order of St Valborg'.

The unlikely sounding Bloodfield was based on the Plomers' neighbour Essery; Flesher on Ward. Even relatively minor characters had their originals: Cossie van Honk, the repulsive prostitute of 'Aucampstroom' (the nearest town to Ovuzane in the novel), had an original in a Mrs Venter, a Natal prostitute and midwife. The sinister Schwerdt, who in the novel carries on a mysterious traffic in unnamed, illegal, nauseating objects, was based on a Norwegian farmer near Entumeni.[31]

The details are worth stressing because they demonstrate how closely Plomer based his novel on the reality of South Africa as he had seen it. The plot, the arrangement of the characters, and above all the central themes of the book were his, but the characterization and description of Natal society were taken almost entirely from life rather than from his imagination. This makes the novel a peculiarly valuable document, not just as a seminal work of literature,[32] but also as a memorial of, and protest against, a social system that has endured far longer than Plomer believed it would, but that is now being swept away rapidly.

The most remarkable omission from the list of characters whose names Plomer gives in his notes, however, is the hero, Turbott Wolfe himself. Yet Wolfe, with his strange name, his talent as a painter, and his readiness to paint the Africans to whom he is sexually attracted, is clearly founded on Plomer's Johannesburg friend Teddy Wolfe. Nothing more plainly shows the remarkable influence of Teddy Wolfe on the young writer than this first novel. Yet it was an influence that Plomer in later years never acknowledged and took some pains to conceal. In his first volume of autobiography he did not even name Wolfe; only at the end of his life, when he was rewriting the autobiography, did he identify him, and then briefly and without linking him with the novel. Plomer's reasons for this omission are not far to seek, and they concern the true, but hidden motivation behind the writing of this remarkable first novel, which was to bring to the literary consciousness of white South Africa a theme that would dominate South African fiction for decades to come.

That motivation was the homosexual attraction Plomer felt so strongly for the Zulus around him each day. Just as Wolfe's paintings were in part an expression of the desire he felt for the gold-miners, and achieved their sensuous sweep of line precisely because of this, so *Turbott Wolfe* achieves much of its tension and power because it is the result of the frustrated sexuality of a young man who focuses his frustrations on the society that (to use Blake's words) binds up with briars his joys and desires. At the end of his life, Plomer hinted at the sexual motivation behind the novel, though even at that late stage his caution leaves the reader to deduce the nature of the intimacy he wanted with the Zulus:

I myself had been tenderly cared for in infancy by Africans, and as I grew up was conscious not only of feeling protective towards them but of warm admiration and affection for them. I wanted to be with them and to get to know them as fellow-beings ... Two things made this impossible. The first was the Berlin Wall of racial and social segregation which barred any but furtive or guilt-burdened intimacies. A feeling of guilt might arise, on the part of a white, from knowing that, presuming on his status, he was exercising, with impunity, some sort of *droit de seigneur*. The other obstacle was that earning one's livelihood in the Entumeni way made an almost whole-time demand on one's energies. Nevertheless, my strong flow of feeling had to shape something, if only a protest. The shape it took was on paper.[33]

In 1924 there was no law forbidding miscegenation in South Africa; there was strong social pressure against it, but a population of half a million people of mixed race showed how often this pressure was disregarded. There were, however, laws (modelled on those of Britain) making homosexuality a crime. Two other factors also prevented Plomer from achieving the intimacy of which he speaks: the fact that his mother would have reacted with horror to the breaking of this double taboo, and the fact that among tribal Africans homosexuality was rare.

Many central passages in *Turbott Wolfe* deal with miscegenation, and those in which Wolfe himself is attracted to the Zulu girl Nhliziyombi are outstanding for the delicacy and rightness of touch Plomer brings to them. One of the most remarkable is the scene in which Wolfe unexpectedly meets Nhliziyombi, whom he loves but has never told how he feels about her. It is one of the first inter-racial love scenes in South African literature, and it is handled with complete assurance:

'Greeting,' she said.
'Greeting,' I answered. 'Where are you going?'
'I am just going.'

These words were a formula, but my heart was in torment, and I could hardly keep my hands and lips from hers.

On a sudden impulse I took a gold pin that I wore in my tie, and pinned it to her clothing, where it gleamed in the sun.

'There you are,' I said. 'There's a present for you.'

'Are you giving it?' she asked incredulously.

'It is yours.'

She was alarmed at being favoured by a man she had come to know as Chastity, and exclaimed softly:

'O, white men!'

Then she ran down the path, checkered with shadows. Nor did she look back.[34]

In spite of the fact that the girl draws attention to the racial difference between them, she is perceived by Wolfe and the reader, not as a black woman, but simply as a woman who is alluring and has a paradoxical worldly innocence. No one in South African literature had written of a black woman in this way before Plomer made it possible with this finely realized scene.

Yet his real interest did not lie in black women. *Turbott Wolfe* does not contain any overtly homosexual love scenes. It does, however, contain a central and most interesting character, the white heroine Mabel van der Horst, who falls in love with an African, as Turbott Wolfe does, but who, unlike him, has the courage to marry. Mabel is described in terms that make it subtly clear that there is much about her that is unlike other women.[35] The male characters in the novel, white and black alike, are fascinated by her partly because of her beauty, but partly because her behaviour seems to them so extraordinary.

She is tall, narrow-hipped, and broad-shouldered,[36] and her most striking features, to Wolfe, are 'her fine legs and buttocks, and a royal back'.[37] She has an angularity of feature and an awkward bearing.[38] She smokes cigarettes with an unaffected ease. She talks in a way that seems strange to the men,[39] a hearty, straight-from-the-shoulder, hard-swearing delivery. 'What are we doing here? What the devil is all the mystery about, you bleeding parson?' she asks the uneasy missionary Friston when he has persuaded her to come into a romantic grove with him so that he can propose to her.[40] Having fallen in love with the Zulu Zachary Msomi (who is at first sight mistaken for a woman by Wolfe),[41] she pursues him aggressively, goes to bed with him, and demands that he marry her. In short, though no critic at the time or since has noticed it, she is designed by Plomer to be seen as devoid of the 'feminine' characteristics expected at this period of any woman in literature or in life. She is very like her creator, but in a dress, and she made it possible for him to turn his fantasies of intimacy with the handsome Zulus into literature, just as E. M. Forster was able to make *A Room With A View* socially acceptable by putting a boy lover (Lucy Honeychurch) into rather thin female disguise.[42] One of the few South African critics whose judgement on *Turbott Wolfe* Plomer accepted wrote of the novel that it was one 'of shattered perspectives and perverse stimuli, of lascivious gods and outer darkness'. Plomer agreed.[43] The triumph of *Turbott Wolfe* lay in the fact that Plomer had found a vehicle that allowed him to yoke his intense sexual frustration to a protest at South Africa's racial situation, to link an inner with an outer struggle. This was what gave the novel the force of a scream, and has kept it in print ever since its first publication.[44]

Plomer had actually written an early part of the novel while he was at Marsh Moor, in 1922. Like 'Famille Arlequin', one of his poems of that period, this earliest-written section of *Turbott Wolfe* shows his interest in vaudeville and fun-fairs, for it was the passage entitled 'Schönstein's Better Shows', vividly conveying the delights of a fun-fair.[45] It was not until the middle of 1924, however, that he was sure the book was going to be good; then he set about finding a publisher before it was even finished. Just as he had previously approached the leading poetical impresario of his day in writing to Harold Monro, he now cast about for the most enterprising publishers. His choice fell on Leonard and Virginia Woolf.

The Woolfs had founded their Hogarth Press in 1917, and by 1924 had built up a formidable reputation for publishing new, experimental work. Their list of authors was extremely distinguished, and they had shown a marked willingness to publish the work of young writers from outside Britain, Katherine Mansfield, T. S. Eliot, and John Crowe Ransom among others. The breadth of Plomer's readings, and the extent to which he had managed to keep up with movements in British publishing, even from so far away as Zululand, is suggested by his boldness in approaching them. They had previously operated by subscription, but had abandoned this system just before moving to Tavistock Square in 1924, where Plomer wrote to them on 15 June of that year.

Sir,

I am neither an 'A subscriber' nor a 'B subscriber' to your Press. It is not from indifference, but from poverty. From a distance I have followed your activities with interest and sympathy, because I suspect that you are nearer the heart of things than any other publishers in London.

I venture accordingly to introduce myself to you. I am young, and trading here until I can give all my time to writing. I have been at work upon a novel for some time, and although I do not claim the genius or meticulousness of Gray or Flaubert I believe that careful workmanship is a duty. I do not suppose that the book is likely to be finished for another year or two, but I ask that you will be so good as to allow me to submit it to you in the first instance.

If, when the time comes, you find yourselves unable to print my work, it is probable that it will remain in manuscript. I have no intention of throwing myself like a piece of meat to what is called the Public.

Perhaps I am not as vain as I sound.

I am

    Yours truly
      William Plomer

Please do not assume that I use green ink because I think it's clever: I can find no blue.[46]

The Woolfs responded to this letter from deepest Zululand as Monro had to the first letters from Marsh Moor: Leonard Woolf wrote, encouraging the young writer and asking to see his work when he was ready to send it.[47] Heartened by this, Plomer devoted the rest of 1924 to writing *Turbott Wolfe*, and dispatched it to England just before Christmas that year, shortly after his twenty-first birthday. Accompanying it was a letter summing up the advantages and drawbacks of his situation in two columns, in the style of double-entry book-keeping.

ASSETS

1. I do not depend on writing for my living, and I do not intend to, in case I should be obliged to write that which I should be ashamed of; i.e. my stomach is not allowed to get between me and my work.
2. Energy.
3. I desire to set myself a standard as high as yours, my dear Hogarth Press.
4. Sooner or later I shall 'come into my own'. I come to you first for assistance.

5. A tendency to satire. Is it to be encouraged?
6. I am young.

DRAWBACKS

1. I have no leisure. When I write, it is under the hardest of conditions. I write without silence, peace, light, air, or ease.
2. I lack intellectual stimuli.
3. I lack modesty.
4. I lack reticence.
5. I have no typewriter. For this I lay before you my humblest apologies, and my pencilled MS.
6. I am young.

To this queer mixture of appeal, apology, and boast, he added,

I know the book is short. I can't make it any longer. It seems to me complete.

I enclose with the MS a title-page & end-piece done by my own hand: these you might care to use if you printed the work. I also enclose a page of quotations to precede the whole. It might be as well to insert some such note as this:—

'This is a work of fiction. The characters are not intended to refer to living persons, and their opinions need not necessarily be taken for my own.'

So now I await your answer.[48]

He did not have to wait long. On 1 February 1925 Leonard Woolf wrote saying that he thought the book 'very interesting', adding that when Virginia, who was ill, had read it, he would write again. This letter, which Plomer wrote 'fills me with great joy',[49] was followed by another on 28 April 1925, agreeing to publish *Turbott Wolfe* and offering its author one-third of any profits it might realize. The rejoicing which this led to at Entumeni can be imagined. Plomer's growing conviction that he was destined to be a writer ('sooner or later I shall come into my own') had been vindicated: his repeated struggles to achieve publication had been successful, and his book would now appear under the imprint of what he thought of as the best publishers in the English-speaking world. To crown his triumph, Leonard Woolf wrote on 21 May 1925 to tell him that Harcourt Brace & Co. had made an offer to publish *Turbott Wolfe* in the United States. He was launched.

The novel's passage through the press, however, was not all plain sailing. Leonard Woolf was disturbed by the evidently autobiographical nature of the work, and repeatedly asked for assurances that there was no character in the novel who could be 'even remotely identified with a real person in S. Africa'.[50] In response Plomer made a series of minor changes, altering for instance the name of the African with whom Soper's son plays from Fumbatilé to Ndabakabani,[51] and changing 'Miss Rosa Grundso, as ugly as sin, and as good as gold' to 'the admirable Miss Rosa Grundso'.[52] He assured Woolf that if these changes were implemented 'there will not be the slightest ground for complaint of any sort'.[53] This was an optimistic assurance given the transparency of the disguise provided for Fred Pope and others, but in the event his optimism proved justified and the book provoked no libel actions. There was also one major change: Leonard Woolf objected to the length of the sermon Friston preaches at Mabel's marriage to Zachary Msomi. It occupied fifteen pages in manuscript, and Plomer after long thought[54] agreed to cut it completely. With that Leonard Woolf professed himself satisfied, and it was agreed that the book would appear in the autumn of 1925.

The one member of the Plomer household who cannot have been entirely pleased with Plomer's success was his father. Although Charles Plomer was enjoying himself running the store at Entumeni, and was making a profit, it must have been obvious to him that he could not hope to run it alone for very long, and it was clear now, even to him, that William's future did not lie in farming or trading. In 1924 Peter Plomer, then thirteen, had been brought back from England and sent to a high school in Durban, perhaps to save money on English school fees, perhaps because Charles had the idea that when William left Entumeni Peter might be old enough to take his place. His elder son was to write,

I think my father, as he saw Entumeni developing, looked forward to a time when it would become an enterprise on a larger scale, and he sometimes liked to imagine that both his sons, as they grew up, would take it over and expand it, perhaps running in conjunction with it a farm and a hotel; but in the meantime he was beginning to realize that the life was too much of a strain for my mother, and that although I had put my back into the work I had not put my heart into it as well.[55]

Charles now saw this dream, his last hope of staying on in the Africa he loved, evaporating in William's success. He took it philosophically enough, though it must have been a blow: 'If you want to go to the Devil,' he said quite affably, 'you must go to the Devil in your own way.'[56] He became more and more distant towards his elder son, who responded by ignoring him. Peter Plomer, at Entumeni for his school holidays, remembered years after how at meals William and his mother would share the conversation between them, while his father sat and listened in silence.[57] Peter came to dislike his father almost as much as William did, and in the semi-autobiographical novel he wrote nearly forty years later, he characterized the father of his hero as a tyrannical religious maniac.[58]

Edythe Plomer was intelligent, observant, and imaginative, but she felt the lack of an education that would have allowed her to keep up with her brilliant son, and sometimes apologized to him for it.[59] Absence of intellectual stimulus was one of the complaints he had made to the Woolfs, and with the success of his first novel's acceptance behind him he was looking actively for greater worlds to conquer. His parents must have realized that it was only a matter of time before he would leave Entumeni. Zululand could not hold him much longer.

6. Voorslag

1925–1926

AMONG Plomer's main contributions to the running of the trading station at Entumeni, apart from serving in the store, were his buying expeditions to Durban. He would drive down to that steamy, thriving port, put up for a few days at Twine's Hotel on the Esplanade facing Durban Bay, and tour the great warehouses of the importers, buying—'for the supposed benefit of the Zulus and the modest profit of the Plomers', as he put it[1]—imitation jewellery from Czechoslovakia, American uniforms left over from the World War, tinned bully beef from Argentina, penknives from Solingen, handkerchiefs from Osaka. On these visits to civilization (or the nearest approximation to it which Natal could offer) he also got to know some of the intelligentsia of the city, much as he had in Johannesburg, by going round the art galleries and getting to meet painters, art critics, and journalists.

One of the people he met in this way was Leo François, an Alsatian painter of very limited talent who was president of the Natal Society of Artists, and who wrote art criticism for a Natal paper under the pen-name 'Vermilion'; behind this mask he had been known to praise the work of Leo François.[2] Another was the cultured and beautiful Mrs Anna von Schubert,[3] an amateur painter of the German Expressionist school[4] and an enthusiastic art collector, whose wealthy husband Paul, a German-speaking Estonian businessman, had settled temporarily in South Africa. From one or other of these acquaintances[5] Plomer heard of a young poet named Roy Campbell, who had settled in Durban, and whom he was advised to try to meet.

On his next trip to Durban, in June 1925, Plomer contacted Campbell and invited him to lunch at Twine's. Roy Campbell was twenty-four, only two years older than Plomer, but he was already famous. He had been born in Durban of a distinguished pioneering family: his ancestors had built the breakwater that made entry to Durban's difficult harbour possible, had constructed the first railway in the Colony, had helped to pioneer the growing of sugar-cane, which remained Natal's chief crop, and had produced a series of remarkable men. Campbell's own father was a brilliant doctor and educator; it was Dr Sam Campbell who had impressed Edythe Plomer, during the first of those illnesses through which her dislike of Africa manifested itself, by lending her his carriage during her convalescence in Durban in 1901. He had founded the town's technical college and had laid the foundation of what was to become the University of Natal.

Roy Campbell, in a vain effort to live up to this remarkable father, had gone to England after the war to try to enter Oxford, but had sent himself down after failing to learn enough Greek to pass Responsions. He had then drifted round Europe, married an unusually beautiful girl, Mary Garman, and settled with her in a converted cowshed in the Welsh village of Aberdaron, where he had written a long poem entitled *The Flaming Terrapin*. On the recommendation of T. E. Lawrence, it had been published by Jonathan Cape in 1924, and had received rave reviews on both sides of the Atlantic. This promising start was to lead to a series of volumes of poetry during the 1930s that made him far and away South Africa's best-known poet in English, and one of the most remarkable writers of the first half of the twentieth century.

Campbell was a striking figure. The painter Augustus John, on first meeting him in London, had at once asked him to sit for a portrait. He was powerfully built and forthright, with large, very wide-set, grey-blue eyes, and there was about him a defiant, swaggering air. In spite of his youth he was balding rapidly, and in a vain attempt to hide this he combed long sun-bleached hair across his bald spot, where it contrasted with darker curls round the side of his head.[6] Like Plomer he was tall and broad-shouldered, but he had none of Plomer's composure and feline self-assurance; instead he had a childlike naïvety and frankness that made him unable to keep a secret about himself or anyone else, and which fascinated the cautious Plomer. Campbell loved to tell hilarious boastful stories in which he figured as a heroic man of action, though no one who knew him would have taken them seriously for a moment. He was deeply emotional and expressed his emotions openly. Where Plomer was judicious and reflective, Campbell's opinions ran easily to extremes. He reacted to people he met with intense liking or hatred, and fortunately he took to Plomer at once. Something of the generous, passionate spirit of this remarkable poet

came through to Plomer, and the two were firm friends from that
first day.

This was perhaps surprising in view of the temperamental
differences that might have kept them apart. Years later, writing
of himself in the third person, Plomer was to remark upon his and
Campbell's

marked differences of racial background, temperament, & upbringing. W.P.
very English in character, sympathies, manners: R.C. not in the least
English in any way, but expansively 'Celtic' & 'Colonial'. (Imprecise terms,
these.) But—their friendship was fostered by propinquity, isolation, some
community of interest, possibly an attraction of opposites, mutual liking,
mutual (I feel sure) admiration, & youthful high spirits & playfulness.[7]

They had lunch on the wide veranda of the old hotel, overlooking
the palms of the Esplanade and the Indian Ocean beyond, and after
the meal they walked on the sand of the bay, for the tide was out,
and talked for hours, spending most of the afternoon together.[8]
Towards the end of this time Campbell's vivacious wife Mary joined
them; she liked Plomer at first sight, and even he, not susceptible
to female beauty, thought her 'a brunette of striking appearance'.[9]
They quickly found they shared many opinions—on the difficulties
of dealing with 'the older generation', on the stuffiness of South
African society, the iniquities of the colour bar,[10] the absurdity of
the pretensions of Leo François and the other members of the Natal
Society of Artists,[11] and the scandalous lack of recognition accorded
to young geniuses in Natal. Plomer had read and admired *The
Flaming Terrapin*,[12] and he told Campbell about *Turbott Wolfe*, now
being prepared for the press. He also told Campbell about the
intense difficulty he had in writing at Entumeni. Plomer struck
Campbell as 'very delicate, worn out with a life of hardship, which
has not warped his nature in any way'.[13] Campbell's response was
characteristically quick and generous: he offered Plomer a new
home and a job.

Campbell's sympathy was the more easily engaged because until
very recently he had been in an even more difficult position than
Plomer. On his return to South Africa from England he had found
himself at a loose end in Durban, where he had been disappointed
in his original hope that his father would support him while he
wrote, though he and his wife and child lived at first in the
Campbells' large family home.[14] Contemporary accounts held that

he was a voluntary prisoner in a bedroom stacked with beer bottles.[15] But in March 1925 Maurice Webb, a businessman and friend of Campbell's father, had introduced Campbell to a wealthy young sugar-planter named Lewis Reynolds,[16] who admired Campbell's work and had for some time been planning to found a literary magazine to give mental uplift to the life of Natal. Campbell had complained bitterly to Reynolds about the difficulty of working in Durban, and the ignominy of being supported by his parents; and Reynolds, after thinking it over for some weeks, asked him to edit the new magazine.[17] Campbell would have control of the literary direction, while the business side would be managed by Maurice Webb.[18] Edward Roworth, a local painter who had befriended Campbell, would be art editor. Reynolds also offered Campbell a house on his family estate, Umdoni Park, and a salary of £20 a month for his editorial services, with extra payment for any poem he published in the new magazine.[19] This generous offer Campbell accepted with alacrity, and he proposed that the journal be called *Voorslag*, Afrikaans for 'whiplash'.

Campbell, his wife, and their two-year-old daughter, Teresa, had been living in Reynolds's house for only a month at the time of the meeting with Plomer at Twine's Hotel. It was already becoming clear to Campbell that his political views and those of Reynolds did not coincide, and that there was likely to be a tussle for ultimate control of the magazine. One of those involved in the original planning, Edward Roworth, who was making his fortune by painting portraits of South African politicians, millionaires, and their houses,[20] was to write later that the original plan was for *Voorslag* to be a purely literary magazine, with no political content.[21] Campbell, on the other hand, thought of it from the start as strongly political in tone, and by August 1925 was boasting to Edward Garnett, the reader for Campbell's publisher Jonathan Cape, that he had persuaded the South African government to support it:

Its main object will be to collect the intellectual resources of the country in an effort to counteract the stultifying effects of party politics and race-difference[22] and thereby to rouse some sort of national consciousness in the people. It will be contributed to both in Afrikaans and in English and will be a good thing for the country. It will be literary, scientific, artistic and political though representing no party.[23]

Such differences of view among those involved with *Voorslag* even before the first number appeared boded ill for the future of the journal, and Campbell was no doubt keen to gather all the allies he could find for his enterprise. Plomer seemed just the man. Campbell now offered to share the £20 salary with him if he would act as 'sub-editor',[24] though quite how the money would be divided was never made clear. He also offered Plomer the use of a rondawel, a round, thatched, free-standing room some little distance from the house the Campbells were occupying at Umdoni Park.

This offer was particularly attractive to Plomer, for his father, perhaps because of worsening health, perhaps because he realized that his elder son would not stay much longer, had begun looking for a way out of his sublease of the trading station.[25] However, Plomer was not without options, for he considered travelling to England, at least for a time, when his parents went 'Home' to retire.[26] In addition Manilal Gandhi had earlier invited him to live on the settlement at Phoenix, an invitation he seriously considered taking up.[27] He was much too cautious to leap at Campbell's offer without looking first; he made a two-week visit to Umdoni Park in September 1925,[28] travelling out there by train with Campbell, who went into Durban every Tuesday to lecture to the Workers Institute.[29]

Umdoni Park, at Sezela on the coast south of Durban, was extensive and beautifully cultivated. The main house, Lynton Hall, resembled a minor English stately home in a subtropical setting, surrounded by manicured lawns, palms, and flowering trees. Campbell took Plomer up to see it, and to talk to Lewis Reynolds. Reynolds, twenty-eight years old at this time, was a pleasant, cultivated man, who had studied at Oxford and then acted as private secretary to General Smuts during the Versailles conference.[30] He had educated tastes and a great interest in fostering South African painting and literature; no doubt he too was impressed to hear of the imminent publication of *Turbott Wolfe*.

Among the amenities of Umdoni Park were a private golf course, a big salt-water swimming-pool filled by the sea, hectares of rolling subtropical forest full of buck and silver-furred vervet monkeys, a fine large house on a hill that Sir Frank Reynolds had given to the nation for the use of retired prime ministers (it was occupied by the widow of General Louis Botha at this time), and several other houses for the use of friends or guests. It was one of these that had been offered to the Campbells. Built two kilometres from Lynton

Hall on a hillside less than a hundred metres from the sea, it had no garden, but stood in a clearing in the bush. From the front door a footpath led over the railway line and down through a tunnel of bush, over deep, dry white sand to the beach. A plain wood and iron structure, panelled inside in varnished light-coloured wood, the house had a deep cool balcony on three sides, from which there were superb views of the Indian Ocean. Before the Campbells took it over the house had been occupied by Roworth, and it was still full of his furniture, books, and other possessions. A little distance from the house was the rondawel that Plomer was being offered; Roworth had used it as a studio, and it was full of his canvases and easels.[31] Plomer was much taken with it, and he got on well with Mary Campbell, at this time expecting her second child.[32] She was impressed by his perfect manners and by the way in which he tried to help her to moderate Campbell's wild swings of mood and to conserve and channel his energies. She also found him physically attractive.

Campbell proved an even more delightful and amusing companion than he had seemed at their first meeting. He and Plomer drank quantities of beer together (despite his youth, Campbell was far along the road to alcoholism), each showed the other his latest work, and they talked late into the night about what they had recently read, giving each other advice that was to enlarge the reading of both. Plomer had brought with him a camera with which he photographed the Campbells, later sending them copies of the pictures.[33] The photographs the Campbells took of him show a tall, broad-shouldered and pale young man, his hair parted near the middle of his head, vertical lines deeply marked between his eyes, perhaps showing the stress he had been through in writing *Turbott Wolfe* at speed while helping to run Entumeni.[34]

Campbell was soon describing Plomer in letters as 'My great friend, William Plomer',[35] and he was even more impressed after he had read a small part of the manuscript of *Turbott Wolfe* that Plomer had brought with him. Campbell thought it 'something very out of the ordinary' and longed to read the rest, remarking that if Plomer had managed to put much of himself into it, *Turbott Wolfe* would be worth reading.[36] He and Plomer settled down at once to write a 'manifesto' for *Voorslag*, which they hoped to persuade the magazine's newly appointed business manager, Maurice Webb, to print instead of the flyer he had prepared himself. This hope was to prove vain, and its frustration irritated Campbell. From the start Campbell had been contemptuous of Webb. The latter's sole publishing experience had been the production of a commercial directory, and Campbell used to tell a story of how Webb once found a manuscript of Bernard Shaw's being used for wrapping fish. 'That's the closest Webb ever came to literature!' Campbell would say gleefully.[37]

It was probably during this visit late in September 1925 that Plomer introduced Campbell to a twenty-year-old Afrikaner journalist working on Wodson's *Natal Advertiser*. He came of an old, noble Dutch family which had been transplanted to the Cape early in the white settlement of South Africa, and which had grown rich in land,[38] but he had already formed the ambition of making a living by writing in English. His name was Laurens van der Post.[39] Plomer's mother and his brother, Peter, had gone to the offices of the *Natal Advertiser* to consult its files, probably to check on reviews of *Turbott Wolfe*, and had met Van der Post, who, after showing them the files invited them to lunch;[40] this in turn had led the strikingly handsome young Afrikaner to a meeting with Plomer.[41] Plomer was impressed by Van der Post, later describing him as 'a young man of uncommon distinction and intelligence, who seemed to me modest yet confident, and imaginative, and who had perfect manners'.[42] He seems also to have believed that Van der Post's journalistic skills should be drawn on for *Voorslag*. He took him out to meet Campbell at Sezela.

Though Van der Post had by 1925 written little, and though he was intensely reserved and tongue-tied, Campbell recognized him at once as a fellow artist. 'You're one of us,' he told him. 'Come along.' And Van der Post, who never forgot the generosity of this unreserved instinctive act of recognition, immediately agreed to become 'Afrikaans editor' of the magazine, making it the first bilingual literary journal in South Africa. (In fact, neither Van der Post nor Plomer was ever officially appointed to the editorial board, or paid for work on the magazine.) Campbell planned to make the magazine trilingual, by including contributions in Zulu—perhaps Plomer had suggested asking John Dube for articles—but he was never to bring this plan to fruition.

Van der Post shared Campbell's and Plomer's interest in counter-acting racism. On Dingaan's Day[43] 1911, when he was six years old, he had seen his sister stop a white man from beating an African. The incident showed him that something could and should be done about injustice; it had, as he later said, 'started me on my particular road'.[44] The similarity of his political views to those of Campbell and Plomer was an added qualification for his work on the magazine, for they fully intended that it should live up to its name and 'sting the mental hindquarters . . . of the bovine citizenry of the Union', in Plomer's words.[45] After this introduction Van der Post made repeated weekend trips to Sezela to spend whole nights talking to Campbell and Plomer. The second issue of *Voorslag* was to contain Van der Post's article 'Kunsontwikkeling in Afrikaans' (The Development of Art in Afrikaans).[46]

After Plomer returned to Zululand in October 1925 he corresponded regularly with Campbell, the two men criticizing each other's poetry, swapping books they had enjoyed, and planning the first issue of *Voorslag*. Campbell gave Plomer useful advice on his verse, particularly praising a new poem, 'Birkenhead', as 'a perfect gem of a poem', and quoting one couplet that seemed to him especially effective:

> His glittering prizes were tears of salt
> His temple of fame is the family vault.[47]

For his part Plomer advised Campbell to try to avoid overcolouring his poetry with vague adjectives and references to 'silver and gold', a fault that Campbell humbly acknowledged. Campbell's letters to Edward Garnett contain occasional glimpses of Plomer at this time, and his tone is one of admiration, affection, and respect, in spite of his use of such phrases as 'counter-jumper':[48]

My great friend, William Plomer, whose book has just been published by the Hogarth Press,[49] is a counter-jumper in a native truck-store in Zululand—his book of which I have only read a very small part in manuscript seems to express a good deal of the conflict between the lower type of white and the native. The Hogarth press made him amputate about a quarter of his book, he tells me, on account of its outspokenness.[50] Whenever Plomer can get a holiday he comes and stays with us here: he is only about twenty-two. I am longing to read his novel, because he strikes me as being something very out of the ordinary. He had read the Terrapin and came and paid me a visit. I was very surprised to find such an interesting person in Durban, the home of the philistines. Since then he has stayed with us for a fortnight and is coming again soon . . . I am hoping he will soon be able to throw up his work at the store in Zululand and come and live with us. Mary and Tess [Campbell's three-year-old daughter] are very fond of him too.[51]

Plomer was still living with his parents in Zululand when *Turbott Wolfe*, long delayed by a printers' strike ('not caused', Plomer hastened to say, 'by their having to cope with this particular volume'),[52] was at last published in February 1926. It got excellent reviews in Britain and the United States. Desmond MacCarthy described it as 'So good that it kept me from looking out of a train window for nearly three hours. It must be about the best novel of the year.' 'What more could a writer ask?' said Plomer with justifiable satisfaction.[53] Richard Church called it 'a work of genius'. *The Nation* described it as 'Volcanic, disturbing, almost devastating', and the *New York World* warned its readers, 'Don't gnash your teeth. Look elsewhere for your bedtime story. This is raw meat with pepper in it.'

Plomer sent copies of the book to at least some of the originals of its characters, including Fred Pope.[54] Plomer's relations in England and other countries were also sent copies, and from his favourite uncle, Franklyn, his mother's only brother, who had now settled permanently in Spain, came what Plomer described as a sparkling letter: 'You have managed to catch an effect,' he wrote, 'where tedious people only catch malaria.'[55]

It was the reaction in South Africa, however, that had the most immediate impact on Plomer. In a letter to Leonard Woolf he described the reviews in South African papers as 'screams of rage at being what they call "touched on the raw" '.[56] The first copies of the novel reached Durban in the middle of March 1926, and the first review to appear (19 March) set the tone for most of the rest. It came in the form of a leading article in the *Natal Advertiser*, Durban's main paper, and was written by the editor, Harold Wodson, himself. The headline came straight to the point: 'A NASTY BOOK ON A NASTY SUBJECT'. And after a little sorrowful reflection on the fact that 'one nowadays can say very much what he likes about South Africa', Wodson lamented,

Gone are the great days of Olive Schreiner, of Fitzpatrick's 'Jock of the Bushveld,'[57] of Rider Haggard's vivid and inspiring romances in which white men were white and the kafir was black, but a gentleman. The modern novelist, trying to 'catch' South Africa's atmosphere, usually introduces some strain of actual or potential degeneracy into characters he toys with; as if the sight of a sunlit land, four-fifths of whose populace wears little or no clothing at all, had wrenched out of position the foundations on which conventionality rests.

There have been 'nasty' books written about South Africa in times past; but we have read none that leaves an unpleasanter taste in the mouth than 'Turbott Wolfe' ... The author, Mr. William Plomer, is said to have resided in South Africa for many years. He is, says our correspondent, to collaborate with Mr. Roy Campbell in a projected magazine soon, to give 'uplift' to the intellectual life of this country; and it must, of course, be presumed, in the meantime, that he believes what he puts in 'Turbott Wolfe' ...

From first to last the book pictures rottenness; starting from the point where the white stranger with artistic leanings outrages the sentiments of his neighbours by filling his studio with native 'models,' and treating them as though they were white people, and ending with the marriage of the royally beautiful Mabel van der Horst to the full-blooded native Zachary ...

Many thinking men have pondered the possibility of Africa going Eur-African; going coffee-coloured; and clever politicians like General Hertzog, when they take the vote from the pure native and give it to the bastard, are hastening on that day. What provokes a sense of nausea in the present volume is the unrelieved wretchedness of the entire picture ... it is a pity this silly book were [sic] ever written.

The violence of this reaction in South Africa, combined with the laudatory reviews abroad, delighted Plomer and excited the aggression of Campbell, who was always spoiling for a fight. Campbell was convinced that *Turbott Wolfe* would prove to be the best novel ever written in South Africa, and wrote to tell Plomer so:

T.W. took my breath away completely. It does not matter if people in England don't realise what it means, it will wake them up properly. I bet there was never such an orgasm before experienced by the elegant and accomplished Hogarth Press. After years of publishing Herbert Read Eliot and Graves I think their printing machines must have had a fit of D.T.s when they had to go through with this. The language is really magnificent: you handle prose like poetry—it absolutely drives: in one or two places it goes as if there were a big Cunard Turbine behind it.[58]

And later that year Campbell was to put his admiration of *Turbott Wolfe* into verse in his long satire on Natal life, *The Wayzgoose*:

> Plomer, 'twas you who, though a boy in age,
> Awoke a sleepy continent to rage,
> Who dared alone to thrash a craven race
> And hold a mirror to its dirty face.

The fact that Wodson had thrown down the gauntlet by his scornful reference to the magazine that Plomer and Campbell were going to run seemed to the two young men a challenge, and they prepared to meet it head on. They would fill what Campbell called 'the grocer's paradise'[59] with serpents.

On his first visit to Sezela, Plomer had shown the Campbells a novel which he had been writing since sending *Turbott Wolfe* off to England in December 1924. He had revised it and rewritten it six times,[60] finally recasting it as a long short-story, which he entitled 'Portraits in the Nude'. Whereas *Turbott Wolfe* had managed to describe an aspect of South African life without more than passing mention of the Afrikaners who constituted the majority of the white population, 'Portraits in the Nude' is a Schreineresque tale of an Afrikaner farming family. No doubt Plomer drew in part on his own experience of the Afrikaner farmers he had met in the Stormberg, and in part on his father's experiences during his roving years. Nowhere, however, does Plomer show his Afrikaner characters the real sympathy with which he depicts Africans in *Turbott Wolfe*; instead, like *Turbott Wolfe*, 'Portraits in the Nude' attacks white immorality, complacency, and superiority, depicting Afrikaners (and whites in general) as often brutal, lustful, and rapacious, and blacks as sensitive and long-suffering. It had one strength that *Turbott Wolfe* had lacked, one that was to become characteristic of Plomer's writing: it was in places hilariously funny. Campbell intended that 'Portraits in the Nude' would be serialized in *Voorslag*, in order to continue and extend the effect of *Turbott Wolfe*.

He was now very keen that Plomer should move in with him at Sezela and become an (unofficial) joint editor of *Voorslag*, and his invitations became pressing: 'We are longing to see you again and can put you up for good if you can only get away. I think I'll be earning from £20 to £30 a month for editing "Voorslag": so we'll live like millionaires, man!'[61] Plomer accepted, moving into what had been Roworth's studio in May 1926, two months after the birth of Campbell's second daughter, Anna. Roworth, who met Plomer for the first time now, disliked him on sight, describing him as 'a slender young man with thin, rather tight lips and primly and quietly dressed ... carrying a typewriter, a thing Roy never had'.[62] Perhaps he foresaw that Plomer would replace him as friend and confidant to Campbell; if so, he was right. However, until he could be certain that he was really welcome as a long-term visitor, Plomer was cautious; for some time after moving in with the

Campbells he continued to use his Zululand address, indicating that he had not quite committed himself to life at Sezela.[63]

The two young men now settled down to an intense period of writing, turning out articles for *Voorslag*. They also seem to have planned to write, in collaboration, a series of poems describing and satirizing the course of white settlement of southern Africa. The series was to have been called 'The Conquistadors'. It is not clear how far the work progressed or why the project was abandoned. Campbell subsequently published one poem, 'Solo and Chorus from "The Conquistador" ', in his volume *Adamastor* (1930), and Plomer kept a poem entitled 'Conquistador' which appeared years later in his *Collected Poems*. These two poems are enough to show how closely the two men were collaborating at this time. Campbell was going through one of his periodic bursts of intense creativity, during which he lived chiefly on hot tea and wrote at a furious pace, turning out several poems each night, emerging in the morning to read them to his wife and Plomer, before going to bed for much of the rest of the day. It was during these weeks that he wrote such much-anthologized poems as 'The Zebras' and 'The Sisters'.

For his part, Plomer was polishing 'Portraits in the Nude' and beginning his extraordinary story 'Ula Masondo'. If *Turbott Wolfe* had put English-speaking South Africans centre-stage, and 'Portraits in the Nude' had done the same for Afrikaners, 'Ula Masondo' concentrated almost solely on Africans. It is a remarkably prophetic, sensitive story of the migration of a young Zulu, Ula Masondo, to Johannesburg to work in the mines, and of his gradual corruption there. He eventually returns home having lost the innocence of the tribesman and having adopted the worst elements of white urban culture. If in *Turbott Wolfe* Plomer had opened one major thematic vein (love across the colour bar) that English South African writing was to follow for decades to come, in 'Ula Masondo' he had opened another. The corruption of the tribal African who goes to the white man's city to find work is a theme which was to dominate dozens of novels in both English and, later, Afrikaans.[64] If he had written nothing more than *Turbott Wolfe* and 'Ula Masondo', turned out before his twenty-third birthday, these two works alone would have given him the position of central importance he occupies in the history of South African prose.

He was troubled during this time by the reflection that in everything he wrote he was attacking the white South African

society which he thought of as his own, which had nurtured him
and which he unquestionably loved. He was in fact attacking
something of himself, and he felt the need to attempt an explanation
of his actions in a letter to Leonard Woolf:

In 'Voorslag' we are making such a direct onslaught on this vast mass
of crawling filthiness called South Africa that we shall probably end by
being popped in gaol or deported. It is a lovely country, it is my own
country, and I know it and love it, and I know the nobility of the natives
and their unsurpassable human qualities, but the whites are unspeakable.
I am a white South African myself, and a man doesn't go against his
countrymen without reason.[65]

Life at Sezela was delightful, not just because the place was
materially very comfortable, but also because of Campbell's and
Plomer's conviction that they were doing something that would be
of permanent importance to South Africa and perhaps the wider
world. They believed there was a chance that they might change
the intellectual climate of South Africa, and they saw themselves
as forerunners of the new Africa that was bound to emerge as
white attitudes changed. Nor is it possible yet to say that they were
wrong. United by a sense of the importance of what they were
doing, they wrote for much of the day and talked long into the
night;[66] on one or two occasions Mary Campbell went to bed
leaving them talking, and woke to find them still at it, the candles
burning down into their sockets, pale and unnoticed in the sun's
first rays.[67] They read voraciously: Nietzsche, Herman Melville (who
was at that time little known), D. H. Lawrence, T. S. Eliot (whose
poetry Campbell reviewed for *Voorslag*), Aldous Huxley, and others.
They spent days reading the minor eighteenth-century poets in a
fine leather-bound edition, printed in 1810, of Johnson's *Works of
the English Poets*, which Campbell had been given or lent by
Roworth.[68] Plomer introduced Campbell to the German magazine
Der Querschnitt ('Cross-section'), whose striking illustrations
Campbell used to cut out and paste on the panelling of Reynolds's
bungalow.

Van der Post would come down late on Saturday nights after his
paper had been 'put to bed', generally arriving at about midnight
and walking down the railway line from Sezela in the moonlight.
He would expect to find the household asleep, but always Campbell,
Plomer, and Mary would be there, 'still writing, talking, or reading
aloud to one another by lamp and candle-light anything of interest

they had discovered during the course of the day ... All Sunday ... at Sezela the writing, reading and this related talk went on, and I would depart on Sunday night or early Monday morning leaving them still hard at it.'[69] Van der Post compared the sense of driving energy emanating from Plomer and Campbell to a swiftly operating dynamo.

Reynolds looked after them well. Every morning a large basket of fruit, milk, and other provisions would arrive from Lynton Hall, together with frequent gifts of venison, which the Campbells' Zulu housekeeper cooked for them. The house was comfortably furnished with Roworth's antique furniture, including a fine set of high-backed marquetry chairs which they used round the dining-table and a huge Dutch four-poster bed.[70] Campbell, who if he did not talk and drink all night would often write all night, tended to sleep through the morning and emerge early in the afternoon; up to a point Plomer gradually fell in with these odd hours, though he and Mary in concert tried hard, and with some success, to moderate Campbell's drinking.[71] In the afternoons they would walk in Umdoni Park, going down to the nearby beach to swim and fish, or take particular pleasure in strolling through the forest of umdoni trees that gave the place its name. These grew in a large valley, absorbing so much water with their roots that no other tree could grow with them: 'umdoni' is Zulu for 'thirst-tree'. Smooth grass between the great trunks made the floor of the forest easy to walk on, and at intervals they came on patches of blue lobelias. Brilliantly coloured birds, sunbirds and rollers, flashed against the dark foliage, and small dark-eyed vervet monkeys peered out at the intruders; the effect was one of strange, dreamlike beauty.[72]

The few human beings they came upon during these walks seem to have resented the lordly self-confidence which Plomer in particular radiated. Once, on his way to the store at Sezela, he passed a group of whites and paid them no attention. One of them, a woman, called derisively after him, 'I am! I am!' When he told Campbell about this later, the poet was much amused, and advised him to take it as a compliment: 'The *I'm nots*', he said, 'salute the *I am*.'[73]

The first issue of *Voorslag* appeared in June 1926. Campbell and Plomer were disappointed by its appearance, and Campbell called it 'a coffee-coloured [magazine] ... which would have disgraced a tradesman's catalogue'.[74] Mary Campbell described the woodcut on the cover, by a well-known Afrikaner artist, Pierneef, as 'suitable for the tiles in a ladies' waiting-room'.[75] It has to be admitted that their expectations were probably unreasonably high; in his letters to the Woolfs, Plomer had criticized most of the leading literary journals in England and America:

We can't satisfy ourselves with The London Mercury or The Dial or The Criterion or The Adelphi or The Calendar[76] or anything. Each of them has good things sometimes but none of them is what it ought to be. The precious cocksureness of The Calendar is as bad as the self-consciousness of The Dial or the 'merry-England' air of The London Mercury. What is really wanted is a quarterly without any 'character' *as a paper*, but with nice compartments for good work of any kind. I'm simply saying what *I* should like ... I know I am annoyed not to be able to get it, and I have a sneaking idea that there must be other people who would like the same thing.[77]

If they could not 'satisfy themselves' with any of these it was too much to expect that they would be happy with *Voorslag*. Campbell blamed Webb for refusing to print the manifesto Campbell and Plomer had written for the magazine, and for inserting a bland little statement of his own in which he claimed to speak for the other editors. Towards the end of June, shortly after the first issue had appeared, Campbell wrote Webb what Mary Campbell described as 'a horrid stinger of a letter', telling him that he knew as much about literature as a turnip.[78]

If Campbell and Plomer were unhappy with the first issue of *Voorslag*, the same can be said for some of the subscribers to the magazine. Though South African newspapers greeted it with deference and caution at first,[79] there were soon rumblings in the Press.[80] Webb's introductory manifesto mentioned the concern that had been expressed at *Voorslag*'s name, and tried to assure readers that 'in Politics *Voorslag* has no party. It offers an open platform for the consideration of social and political questions free from party or racial prejudice.'[81] But the declaration of freedom from racial prejudice was itself a political stance in South Africa, and the magazine's content did nothing to reassure readers. With the exception of an article on beauty by General Smuts and one on Cézanne by Roworth, the whole of the first number was written by Campbell and Plomer, using their own names and such pen-names as Mary Ann Hughes (Campbell) and Pamela Willmore (Plomer and Campbell, though not in collaboration).[82]

Three of their contributions in particular excited comment. There was an impassioned defence of *Turbott Wolfe* by Campbell, rounding on those who had condemned the novel, and beginning, 'Literary criticism in South Africa is either in its infancy or in its dotage.'[83] There was the first section of 'Portraits in the Nude', which Natalians seemed to find just as offensive as *Turbott Wolfe*. Nor were other South Africans much better pleased: 'It makes somewhat gloomy reading,' commented the Johannesburg *Star* dryly.[84] The third article, 'Dr. Leys and the Colour Question', was a strongly favourable review by Plomer of Dr Norman Leys's book *Kenya*, a swingeing attack on British treatment of the blacks in East Africa. The book had been sent to Plomer by Leonard Woolf, its publisher, in 1925.[85] Plomer's article attracted attention by its overt reference to 'the Colour Question', and by pointing out that Leys's comments were as relevant to South Africa as to Kenya. It was chillingly prophetic, and it pulled no punches:

It seems at last that there are only two solutions of the colour problem. One is thorough economic exploitation [of black by white] (which violates all possible principles of any permanent value) and the other is complete social equality (which violates nothing but an illusion). The choice of these two alternatives would seem startling to most white South Africans, but sooner or later they will have to choose. If they choose exploitation they will sooner or later be damned and overwhelmed. If they choose equality they will sooner or later be saved ... It will be necessary to learn to recognise every man's human qualities as a contribution to the building up of an indestructible future, to judge every man by the colour of his soul and not by the colour of his skin. Otherwise the coloured races of the world will rise and take by force what is denied them now by a comparatively few muddle-headed money-grubbers.[86]

What annoyed *Voorslag*'s uneasy readers almost as much as the political content was Campbell's and Plomer's tone. 'Mocking, blasphemous, unanswerable',[87] they were challenging the conventions of 'the sleepy self-satisfaction of middle-age', goading and jeering, flaunting their youth and precocious reputations. 'We must gibe, sneer and ridicule our venerable reviewers into epileptic fits,' wrote Campbell; 'we have plenty of muck to clear out of the way before we can start the great work of reconstruction.'[88] In his first autobiography, *Broken Record*, Campbell admitted that this provocative tone was probably the result of the coolness between himself and his father, Dr Sam Campbell,[89] and though Plomer never admitted it in his writing, his motivation was in part similar enough.

Voorslag's concentration on both the 'colour question' and the 'generation gap' came to a head in one of the articles Campbell wrote for the second issue, which appeared in July 1926: 'Fetish Worship in South Africa'. In it he asserted that white South Africa was as unthinking and as wrong in its acceptance of the values of 'Western Civilization' as the Africans were in worshipping their animist fetishes. 'I repeat that as a race we are unconscious,' he wrote, in a phrase which suggests the influence of D. H. Lawrence, whose work he and Plomer were reading avidly at this time.[90] 'There is only the race-mind, the mob-soul.'[91] And the white fetish he attacks most bitterly is the colour bar: 'When the white people came out here they gave the native the Bible and the native in exchange gave the white man a great black fetish to worship. It is this fetish that rules the country—Colour prejudice.'[92] It was precisely this analysis of the South African situation that Plomer was illustrating in 'Portraits in the Nude', the second part of which appeared in *Voorslag*'s second issue.

The two men wrote as young, conscious, enlightened artists addressing a middle-aged, prejudiced mob. The 'mob', predictably enough, was irritated by this attack on all its values, religious, political, social, and financial. Many Natalians regarded *Voorslag*'s urging them to 'jump the mean little fences' of the colour bar as dangerous revolutionary talk. Even the illustrations in *Voorslag* must have seemed to them to have political, and perhaps sexual, implications: the second issue included a reproduction of a painting by Anna von Schubert of the head of an African girl; *Voorslag*'s concentration on the 'colour question' was thoroughgoing.[93]

Lewis Reynolds, who had already sunk £1,000 into the magazine, became alarmed. He did not want to see the publication which he was widely known to be financing, and for which he had secured the support of the country's leaders, turned into a mouthpiece for Campbell's and Plomer's revolutionary views. He wrongly believed that Plomer's influence on Campbell had altered *Voorslag*'s intended course as a literary journal, turning it into political channels. In addition, Reynolds himself had political ambitions: he was intending to stand for Parliament in his father's old seat, South Coast.[94] He could not afford a political controversy.

The final crisis was not long in coming. Campbell had been irritated by the appearance of the first issue of *Voorslag*, and in particular by Webb's manifesto. The second issue was to bring him to the boil, a process that never required much extra heat. When the novelist Sarah Gertrude Millin, whose reputation was at that time at its height, wrote a patronizing article about the first issue, Campbell responded to her in the letter columns of the Johannesburg *Rand Daily Mail*, putting her firmly in her place and signing himself 'yours biliously'.[95] Webb, no doubt still smarting from Campbell's 'horrid stinger' to himself, then made the mistake of rebuking Campbell for this, and drew the lightning of Campbell's wrath:

If you had not put in such an apologetic little preface and if you had left at the back that list of extracts which I put there, journalists would not have dared to be so patronising. You removed this without asking my permission—damn you! Why don't you look after the business part of it and leave the literary part to me . . . You will have to change your tactics if we are going to get on together.[96]

This letter provoked the intervention of Reynolds, who asked Campbell to allow Webb control of the contents of *Voorslag*; Campbell agreed, 'on condition that he did not make a hash of the magazine'.[97] This agreement came before the production of the second issue of *Voorslag*. As if to show what he thought of the agreement, Campbell attacked Reynolds directly in the second issue, in a satirical poem entitled 'To A Young Man with Pink Eyes'.[98] It is hard to avoid the conclusion that he was now trying to force the division between himself and *Voorslag*'s financial backer into the open. Even so, it seemed that Reynolds would have been willing to overlook this direct challenge if Campbell would stick to literature.

What Reynolds and Webb could not do, however, was persuade Campbell and Plomer to dilute the expression of their political views, as the second issue made clear, and it was on this rock that *Voorslag* foundered. In later years Plomer was to sum up the split in a private letter:

Campbell wanted a freer hand than they [Reynolds, Webb, and Roworth] were prepared to give him. He wanted to *épater* the readers. He thought Reynolds & Webb timid, conventional, and provincial; they thought him wild, headstrong, and imprudent. The two totally different conceptions of the functions of the magazine proved irreconcilable. C. and I thought it should be a medium for original creative and critical writing. Reynolds &

Webb, I think, wanted it to be a dulcet dinner-bell regularly summoning old women of both sexes to a lukewarm collation of accepted ideas.[99]

Accordingly, Roworth, Reynolds, and Webb went, on Sunday morning, 25 July 1926, to make it clear to Campbell that they wanted Webb to have more control over the content of *Voorslag*. They asked Campbell to walk with them to the beach so that they could talk to him alone, away from Plomer. While Mary Campbell, Plomer, and Van der Post, alarmed, watched from a distance, they sat down on a sand-dune, Campbell squatting on his haunches like a back-veld Afrikaner farmer, bearded and truculent.[100] He had been finding his duties as editor an increasing strain: he had no organizational ability. He had hated the articles written by Smuts and Roworth for the magazine: Roworth's, he said accurately, were plagiarized word for word from French books on art. Webb, by inserting such articles, by putting in his apologetic manifesto, and by printing ill-chosen readers' letters (Campbell described one as 'a bland little chortle of admiration . . . quite beneath the dignity or the substance of *Voorslag*'),[101] as well as by allowing the printers to change his own and Plomer's manuscripts, had already irritated him. Now came this challenge. Was an artist to be overridden by a tradesman? He flared up at once. Van der Post, from a distance, saw Campbell gesticulate with his hands, in the style of a Zulu orator.[102] 'You yourself confided in me at the beginning that we must take care not to let *Voorslag* develop Webbed feet,' he told Reynolds, his voice shaking with rage. 'Now you want it to have a Webbed head. I've wasted two years of my life on *Voorslag*. You have my resignation here and now.'[103] He was as good as his word; nothing would induce him to change his mind. The third number of the magazine contained a terse introductory note: 'I have much pleasure in announcing my resignation from *Voorslag*. Roy Campbell.'

It is probable that Campbell's personality and the unbridgeable differences in outlook between Plomer and himself on the one hand and the Reynolds–Webb–Roworth side of *Voorslag*'s management on the other made the smash inevitable. The swiftness and vehemence of Campbell's response to Reynolds's and Webb's attempt to win greater control of the magazine's direction suggests that he had been looking for an opportunity to part from them. Plomer seems to have taken a detached attitude throughout; he had not been an official or paid member of the management team, and he had never thought of the rondawel as a permanent home. Even so, Campbell's decision to resign was a courageous one, for it left him once more without an income, without a settled home, and without prospects. For Plomer, unmarried and without ties, the affair was a much less serious one: 'It was a matter of total indifference to me whether *Voorslag* paid its way or not,' he wrote later.[104] His immediate reaction to the crisis was to write to Manilal Gandhi asking if there was a house at Phoenix for himself and the Campbells.[105] There was not.

Campbell, Mary, and Plomer stayed on in Reynolds's bungalow for another month, until the end of August 1926. During that month, in a brilliant burst of creativity, Campbell wrote several of his best poems—great cries of loneliness, defiance, and despair. 'The Serf', 'The Zulu Girl', 'To a Pet Cobra', 'The Making of a Poet', and 'Tristan da Cunha' were all written in these weeks, and read to Plomer as soon as they were completed.[106] The first two, with their focus on the hardships of African life, show the extent to which *Turbott Wolfe* and discussions with its creator had influenced Campbell, though Plomer perhaps tended to exaggerate the extent of his influence, as in this letter to Leonard Woolf:

I feel sure that Campbell is really capable of something great. When he came back here he was full of energy, but perhaps 'bombinans in vacuo'. I have been able to influence him in the most extraordinary way, giving his energy direction, which is exactly what it wanted. The isolation of the two of us in a bourgeois country has of course helped, and from being in daily contact with my fixed idea (the so-called 'colour question') he has been able to ally himself with me. It has been a great help to me, his coming back here, giving me a fresh and direct contact with the tendencies of modern thought. Before he came I felt like a man against a continent![107]

It was to Leonard Woolf that Plomer sent 'The Serf' and 'The Zulu Girl' on 29 July 1926, and Woolf arranged for them to be printed in the *New Statesman* and the *Nation*.[108]

'Tristan da Cunha' is the plainest illustration of the way Plomer gave Campbell 'direction'. Campbell had begun a poem called 'Kerguelen', inspired by one on the same subject by the Australian Henry Clarence Kendall,[109] but had grown dissatisfied with it after writing five stanzas. Plomer showed Campbell, on 5 August 1926, one of the letters he had received at Marsh Moor from his friend Darsie Gillie, enclosing Gillie's translation of Kuhlemann's 'Tristan d'Acunha', and Plomer now suggested that Tristan da Cunha would be a better-known, more imposing subject than Kerguelen.[110] Inspired by Gillie's translation, Campbell recast his poem between 5 and 14 August, producing one of the most magnificent and moving of his lyrics, which he read to Plomer soon after finishing it. 'Tristan da Cunha' is a profoundly moving statement of Campbell's feelings of defeat and despair at this time, and he read it so well that Plomer, carefully though he controlled his emotions, was on the verge of tears when he finished.[111]

Plomer was also the inspiration behind what is probably Campbell's best-known epigram. The two young men were discussing the writing of Sarah Gertrude Millin one evening, and Plomer, remarking that critics in Britain repeatedly praised her for the restraint of her work, quipped that this 'restraint' was like a dog-collar without a dog in it. Campbell's lines wittily and pungently applied this remark to much modern writing:

> You praise the firm restraint with which they write—
> I'm with you there, of course:
> They use the snaffle and the curb all right,
> But where's the bloody horse?

With Campbell's resignation from *Voorslag*, they were now under pressure to leave Reynolds's bungalow. Roworth, whose initial dislike of Plomer had grown steadily, and who thought that Plomer exercised a malignant, sinister influence on Campbell,[112] was keen to reoccupy the bungalow, since he was now having to rent a house at Pennington, near Sezela. Before long he persuaded Lewis Reynolds to give them notice to quit. The Campbells talked of returning to England, and Plomer intended to go with them.[113] It would take time, however, to gather the money for this trip, and there remained the question of a place to live for the moment. Though Van der Post had a small flat, in which he offered to put up the Campbells and Plomer temporarily,[114] the only reasonable move was to Campbell's parents' house. Campbell's father had died on 12 March 1926, and his mother, worn out with nursing the dying man, had gone abroad; their big house at 28 Musgrave Road was standing empty. Campbell, his family, and Plomer moved there on 29 August 1926.

Whereas Van der Post had prudently retained his post on Wodson's paper, Campbell and Plomer now had no means of support; it was clear that they would have to cast about for employment. Campbell proposed starting a new magazine of their own, in direct competition with *Voorslag*, which Lewis Reynolds intended to keep going.[115] The title Campbell came up with for his new journal, *Boomslang*, was even more threatening than *Voorslag*, a boomslang being a highly poisonous tree-snake.

Now came a surprising development. Van der Post was a considerable athlete, and in May 1926 he had captained a Natal provincial hockey team on a tour of the Transvaal. There, in Pretoria, he had intervened to save two Japanese journalists from being thrown out of a coffee shop by a woman crying in Afrikaans, 'I won't have niggers in this place! Get out!'[116] Van der Post befriended the Japanese, Shirakawa of the *Osaka-Ashi* and Hisatomi of the *Osaka-Mainichi*, two of the leading newspapers in Japan.[117] They were unable to repay his kindness before leaving South Africa, but they telegraphed a steamship company in Osaka, their home city, and asked that contact be maintained with Van der Post.

The Japanese were at this time trying to increase their trade with Africa, and in August 1926 one of the first Japanese ships to open the South African run,[118] the *Canada Maru*, of the Osaka Shosen Kaisha (Osaka Mercantile Company), docked in Durban. Her captain, Katsue Mori, asked Van der Post to call on him on 25 August 1926, gave the young journalist dinner on board, and then bowled him over by inviting him to visit Japan for a fortnight, at the shipping line's expense. Van der Post refused with reluctance, feeling (he was to say later) that he should not leave Plomer and the Campbells at this difficult time.[119]

When he told Plomer and the Campbells about the invitation the next day, Plomer exclaimed, 'But surely you weren't such a fool as to say no?' and Campbell added, 'My God, Laurie, haven't you any imagination?'[120] Van der Post, chastened and hurt, now asked Plomer and Campbell if they would come to Japan too if the Japanese captain could be persuaded to take them. Campbell was too depressed and ill to consider a trip that would mean leaving behind Mary and his two daughters, but even years later Van der Post could remember the deep delighted laugh with which Plomer greeted the idea: 'Can a duck swim?' he replied.[121] He had doubts only because going would mean leaving Campbell, who was now suffering from various neurasthenic ailments, but Campbell urged him to make the trip.[122]

Van der Post went back to the *Canada Maru* and put the idea to

Captain Mori. He harped on Plomer's international reputation as a writer, praising *Turbott Wolfe*, and telling Mori that Plomer would provide much better publicity for the Osaka Shosen Kaisha than Van der Post alone could do. Mori agreed to take Plomer too, on condition that he should be able to pass as the representative of a reputable newspaper. This Van der Post was able to arrange without much difficulty: Desmond Young, editor of the *Natal Witness*, the one Natal paper that had praised *Voorslag* unreservedly, agreed to appoint Plomer as its 'special correspondent in Japan and the Far East'.[123] On 30 August 1926 Van der Post took Plomer to meet Mori, and the two men liked each other at first sight; Plomer had to make up his mind fast, for Mori planned to sail in three days' time. He knew that if he accepted he would never be content with a mere fortnight in Japan; he also knew that if he refused, such a chance would not come again.[124] He accepted then and there.

His parents took the news philosophically; they were in any case about to sell Entumeni and return to England, while Peter Plomer, now fifteen, was shortly to decide to take himself off to America, his parents paying his fare to New York.[125] During the next two days things moved fast. There was a scramble to find suitable tropical clothes and as much money as Plomer could scrape together. It was not much; according to Campbell, he eventually sailed with thirty shillings in his pocket, and he got his passport only just in time.[126] Van der Post gave him a suit, Campbell wrote him a letter of introduction to the poet Edmund Blunden, whom Campbell had known briefly at Oxford and who they knew to be living in Japan,[127] there was a large farewell dinner at the Musgrave Road house, attended by the surviving members of the Campbell clan,[128] and in a whirl of goodbyes and vague promises that they would meet Roy and Mary Campbell again, perhaps in South Africa, perhaps in England, Plomer and Van der Post sailed on the *Canada Maru* on Thursday, 2 September 1926. Van der Post intended to come straight back to his post on the *Advertiser*, but for Plomer this was a voyage into a mysterious future. As the *Canada Maru* slipped out of Durban harbour, past the breakwater that Campbell's ancestor had built half a century before, and began to heave as it felt the first lazy surges of the Indian Ocean, Plomer was not to know that he would never live in South Africa again. But he would probably not have been daunted had he been granted a glimpse of the future. He felt ready for anything.

7. Japan
1926–1929

BY 1926 Japan, after a period of consolidation following the Great War, was beginning to look for ways to expand its influence in the world, in part through increased foreign trade, in part through an extension of military and political power abroad. Japan had had an alliance with Britain since 1905, had participated in the war on the Allied side, expelling the Germans from the Chinese city of Kiaochow, and had taken part in the Versailles peace negotiations, where it unsuccessfully pressed for the acceptance of the principle of racial equality; this diplomatic defeat, which the Japanese naturally saw in part as a slur against themselves, rankled.

British political ideals were fashionable in Japan at this time, and Britain itself, near the zenith of its power, was much admired and emulated. In 1921 Crown Prince Hirohito toured Britain, being cordially received by the royal family and cheered by the British public; the following year the Prince of Wales made a return visit to Japan, with similar success. Japanese trade, which had previously concentrated on links with other Far Eastern countries and with the United States, now began reaching out actively to parts of the British Empire that it had left largely untapped before. Among these were British territories in Africa, in particular Kenya and South Africa. Japanese imperial ambitions may have played some role too: having annexed Korea in 1910, the Japanese were looking further afield. China, sliding rapidly into chaos, held obvious attractions, but the Japanese also cast an interested eye on Africa; in particular Ethiopia, with a government nominally independent but as solid as a soap-bubble, caught the attention of such Japanese politicians as Baron Shidehara.[1]

The Japanese at this time knew little of Africa at first hand, and one of their first moves was to dispatch journalists to gather information: Shirakawa and Hisatomi, the two journalists whom Van der Post had met and befriended, were on one of these intelligence-gathering expeditions. The pioneering voyage of the *Canada Maru* was the next step. Her owners, the Osaka Shosen

Kaisha line, or OSK,[2] already knew from the journalists that racial prejudice would be one of the obstacles to be faced by Japanese trying to penetrate African markets. No doubt this was as they had expected, since the powerful anti-Japanese feeling in California had already soured relationships between Japan and the United States. The Japanese feared, and with reason, that they would be treated like Africans by whites in Britain's African colonies. The captain of the *Canada Maru* had been briefed on this problem and had been ordered to do anything he could to spread awareness of Japanese civilization and the strength of Japan's claims to equality with other world powers.[3]

The OSK could hardly have chosen a more resolute or daring man for the job. Katsue Mori, born in Kyushu in 1890 into a family of the *samurai* class, had from boyhood intended to go to sea. He had hesitated between the navy and the merchant service, eventually choosing to be trained at the Koto Shosen Gakko (nautical college of the merchant marine) at Echujima in Tokyo.[4] During the First World War, like all graduates of the nautical college, he had been inducted into the reserve service of the Imperial Navy, serving in the Mediterranean and elsewhere, and rising to the rank of lieutenant-commander before joining the OSK shipping line.[5] He was a remarkable athlete who for a time held the fiercely contested title of Japanese national champion at kendo, Japanese fencing. Taller than most of his countrymen of the period, he was broad-shouldered and powerfully built. He wore his black hair cropped; a clipped moustache and rather straggly pointed beard accentuated the strength of his face, which Plomer described as 'broad and stylized ... the eyes rather far apart, the features regular, the bony structure broad without being coarse or heavy, and the maxillary muscles noticeably developed'.[6] Even in extreme old age he would exude power and authority, effortlessly taking charge of any social gathering;[7] in middle life he was a formidable figure, instantly recognizable as a natural leader of men. He gave Plomer the impression of being master of himself and of his surroundings.[8] For all that, he did not take himself over-seriously; he joked, for instance, about the thinness of his beard and how he had stood up to the managing director of the OSK, who had wanted him to remove it on the grounds that it was a poor advertisement for Japanese productivity.[9] He did everything with enormous gusto and with a *joie de vivre* that made even his less appealing habits—

such as vigorously washing his mouth out with beer after a meal—
seem inoffensive; this vivacity and his boyish playfulness instantly
appealed to Plomer and Van der Post.

In 1926 Mori was just thirty-six years old, one of the youngest
of the OSK's hundred and twenty captains. The fact that he had
advanced so fast and had been entrusted with the important task
of opening the Africa route was a demonstration of the trust he
inspired in his superiors. Though this was his first visit to Durban,
it was his second to the African continent.[10] On his first voyage he
had got no further than Mombasa, where, however, he had scored
the diplomatic coup of persuading the British governor of Kenya,
Sir Edward Grigg, to make a brief coastal trip on the *Canada Maru*.
No doubt he had hoped to do something comparable in Durban on
his second voyage, but Plomer and Van der Post were the best he
could manage. Their chief recommendations, in his eyes, were that
they were both writers, that Plomer already had an international
reputation, and that they were both opposed to the colour prejudice
that he saw as the chief enemy of Japanese trade expansion. 'I
wanted to make a success of the new line. I wanted to break South
African colour-prejudice, and I knew that Plomer had written
strongly against it,' Mori was to say nearly sixty years later.[11]
Hence his bold move in offering Plomer and Van der Post the trip
to Japan without first seeking authorization from his company; he
simply wired to his head office in Osaka, 'I AM BRINGING JOURNALIST
VAN DER POST, NOVELIST WILLIAM PLOMER, RETURNING BY CANADA
MARU. INFORM SHIRAKAWA AND SATOMI. ARRANGE DURING STAY IN
JAPAN. CAPT. MORI.' Shirakawa and Satomi, the journalists, had not
yet returned to Japan, though Mori could not have known that,
and he expected them to be able to explain to his superiors who
Van der Post was. Without this information, not surprisingly, the
OSK head office was baffled.[12]

The *Canada Maru*, though primarily a cargo ship and of only
5,000 tonnes, was equipped to carry twelve first-class passengers,
and (no doubt with the possibility of more voyages by important
British dignitaries like Sir Edward Grigg in mind) she carried a
doctor and a first-rate chef, neither of whom would be on board
any normal cargo boat.[13] It seems clear that her mission was as
much diplomatic as commercial. Plomer and Van der Post, as
honoured guests, were given the best cabin available, a large,
luxurious two-berther opening on to the boat-deck beneath the

bridge, and connected to Mori's own cabin by a shared bathroom.

The voyage to Japan took six weeks, and for both Plomer and Van der Post it was in itself a fascinating introduction to the East. Few of the officers and none of the crew spoke even broken English, and the *Canada Maru* seemed to the two young South Africans a microcosmic Japan, what Van der Post was to describe as 'a sort of Bonsai tree of the spirit transplanted into this miniature pot of its culture afloat on a foreign sea'.[14] They found it curious at first to see the crew bowing solemnly to the rising sun each morning, but soon came to take the little ceremony for granted. Van der Post, who had done a certain amount of sailing on small whalers out of Durban, was particularly impressed by the way the members of the crew all seemed to know what was expected of them, and carried out their duties quietly and efficiently, apparently without having to be told, so that the ship ran as if directed by one mind in many bodies.[15] The delicious meals were entirely Japanese, and Plomer soon got used to chopsticks and grew to enjoy dried seaweed, pickled plums, raw fish, and vinegared rice, though this food, now available in any of the world's large cities, was entirely new and alien to him at first. 'My ignorance of Japan and the Japanese was flagrant,' he wrote, adding,

One had simply grown up with this romantic, period conception of their race as 'quaint,' 'plucky,' 'clever' little people, who lived in picturesque surroundings, their women-folk dainty and petite, with names like Nanki Poo, fluttering silk fans all day and mincing about at night with paper lanterns. Later, from Loti, one had gathered that daintiness was happily united with easy virtue. I had read a few books by or about Lafcadio Hearn,[16] two or three travel books, and a couple of metallic sonnets by Heredia. These were all right as far as they went; now one must begin to learn. It appeared that it must have seemed to the interest of the Japanese to make the most of Western sentimentality about them, and that behind a barrage of cherry blossoms the militarists had built up their heavy industries and plans to expand abroad.[17]

The process of learning began on the first afternoon at sea. Plomer and Van der Post were in their cabin when a sound that Van der Post later described as resembling 'a roar of pain from a trapped lion'[18] came from the bathroom next door. 'My God, what's that?' exclaimed Plomer, 'Murder in the first degree, I presume!' It was Captain Mori, singing in the bath. The sound went on for forty-five minutes, at undiminished volume, and stopped as suddenly as it had begun. Mori presently appeared, clad in a crisply ironed kimono with the heraldic badge of his family on the sleeves, invited his two passengers to join him on the deck for a drink while they watched the sun set, and told them he had been declaiming from the Japanese classics—an exercise that benefited his internal organs and nervous system, he assured them.[19] Had they liked the performance? Van der Post was at a loss for words, but Plomer with admirable presence of mind replied, 'We found it most impressive.'[20] Plomer later produced comments of another kind when he drew for Van der Post's amusement a series of caricatures in the style of his Marsh Moor drawings, depicting Mori 'going through convolutions and contortions of muscle and limb like a Hindu Guru, compelling the movements of his body to express the metaphysical complexities of his spirit', as Van der Post was to put it.[21] Van der Post, who venerated Mori, was slightly scandalized to find Plomer laughing at their captain in this way.

Perhaps because Mori sensed and rather admired Plomer's irreverence, a quality which, although it was so un-Japanese, Mori shared in some measure, he and Plomer got on very well together. Mori read Plomer's copy of *Turbott Wolfe*, and was immensely impressed by it; he was convinced that Plomer was a genius and clearly thought himself very lucky to have secured him as a passenger, if only because, having taken the unprecedented risk of bringing his two passengers to Japan without authorization from the company (an act of daring that could easily have cost him his job),[22] it was of the utmost importance for him to 'sell' Plomer and Van der Post to his superiors. He was determined that the trip should be a success. He spared no pains to impress Plomer and Van der Post with the value of all things Japanese, and he did his best to encourage Plomer's vague plans of staying on in Japan. Early in the voyage he and Plomer began spending each morning working on a Japanese translation of *Turbott Wolfe*. Perhaps Mori thought it would be to his advantage if his superiors could read the work of the guest on whom the OSK line was spending so much money. He and Plomer grew more and more excited as the work progressed. They also grew steadily closer to each other, leaving Van der Post with a painful sense of having been frozen out of his relationship with both of them. They talked to each other in his presence, he was to write, as if he were not there.[23] Since he had known each of them longer than either had known the other, this was at first hard for him to accept.

After three days travelling up the east coast of Africa, during which Plomer suffered badly from seasickness even though the sea was calm,[24] the *Canada Maru* reached Kilindini, the port of Mombasa, on 5 September 1926.[25] While the ship was loaded with potash from Magadi in south-east Kenya, Plomer and Van der Post went ashore to explore the town. There was not much of it: Mombasa was then a sprawling, scattered place of brick walls, little dark verandas behind mosquito netting, and unpainted galvanized iron roofs that reflected the tropical sun in a glitter almost intolerable to the eye. Despite its age—it had been an Arab trading station for many centuries—the place conveyed no sense of history, and they soon returned to the *Canada Maru* feeling that the town had no more to offer their curiosity.[26] That evening they were entertained to a huge and elaborate dinner at the house of a local Japanese merchant, who had invited them at Mori's urging. 'I have never eaten a larger or better meal,' Plomer was to write, 'and course succeeded course on a Russian scale and of a French perfection: what made it unreal was that we were all acting parts not precisely defined.'[27] He was beginning to grasp the extent to which Mori regarded him as of central importance to the *Canada Maru*'s mission.

Mori had not succeeded in getting another interview with the governor of Kenya, but he was not giving up yet: he announced that he would travel by train to Nairobi to see him, and invited Plomer and Van der Post along. From the train they got a view of a wild Africa that had already largely disappeared in the south of the continent: Thomson's gazelles, zebras, and giraffes frisked and bounded over the savannah among acacias that stood stark against a background of the tropical snows of Kilimanjaro.[28] Nairobi struck Plomer as 'a sort of tropical version of a Middle Western pioneer township',[29] and the hotel in which they stayed was full of odd characters, including a woman whom Plomer described as 'a dressy but superannuated lady novelist looking round with haggard eyes for copy and a new husband'[30] and an adventuress who, dressed in cloche hat and jodhpurs and with a pistol on each hip, rode into the hotel dining-room on a chestnut mare, dismounted, and threw the reins to the nearest waiter before snatching up the wine list and taking her seat.[31] Presumably the other guests considered that among the oddest characters in the place was the young Japanese captain, with his even younger white companions, a spectacled, confident twenty-two-year-old novelist and a twenty-year-old Afrikaner journalist who, it became known, were waiting for an invitation to see the governor. They had been joined in Nairobi by an entire Japanese film crew who had ostensibly been making a film of African wildlife, though Plomer suspected that they were yet another element of the Japanese intelligence-gathering machine now focused on Africa.[32] They had attracted attention by filming Plomer, Van der Post, and Mori getting off the train from Mombasa.[33] The trio was to be observed going round the numerous Nairobi taxidermists' shops, where Mori excited surprise when he gravely announced, 'I desire some rion's whiskers.'[34]

Presently they heard that the governor was ill and unavailable for interviews, and Mori, deeply disappointed and insulted that the man whom he had entertained in his ship should refuse to see him after the long trip up from the coast, was glumly silent all the way back in the train. In Mombasa they learned that the ship's carpenter had died suddenly, and Mori determined that he should be buried, not at sea or in some cemetery for 'coloureds', but with Englishmen in a 'European' graveyard. Arranging this was not easy, and Mori had to call in the help of the editor of the local paper (whom Plomer and Van der Post had entertained on their first day in the town), as well as the local police chief, but he had his way in the end. Plomer and Van der Post, with the immaculately uniformed crew of the *Canada Maru*, stood round the grave as a hot and cross-looking Anglican priest read the Anglican burial service over the body of a Japanese peasant under the sinking tropical sun, while a distant gramophone ground out an inappropriately cheerful song.[35] Mori thought this small victory had repaid him for the trouble of the trip to Nairobi; Plomer remarked that 'he had such a mingled expression of solemnity and satisfaction on his face that he might have been burying a rich and childless uncle'.[36] He put it another way in 'Captain Maru', the poem he later wrote about Mori:

> He fought at Kilindini with a corpse for weapon.
> A flat-faced lad from snowy Echigo fell dead,
> Peasant, ship's carpenter, then body to be buried—
> But where? Not white: but our nations were allied.
> Two days of Maru, then a surplice and a bell,
> A slow bell and a surly gown, the crew in white
> Under the saw-toothed palms, a shallow grave,

Pink sunset, distant gramophone, white flowers,
Heads turned, and honour satisfied, and Maru wore
The sure smile of a victory of the will.
'And thou shalt have
None other race but mine.'

On 13 September 1926 Plomer got a telegram from Campbell who was still in Durban: 'BOOMSLANG FULL SWING CONTRIBUTIONS ABSOLUTELY ESSENTIAL PLEASE SEND ULA MASONDO AND POLLY ANDREWS. CAMPBELL.'[37] Campbell had by now given up the idea of starting another periodical, but still wanted to put out a single polemical volume in which he would hit out at all those he considered his enemies in South Africa, before leaving the place for good.[38] Plomer, who was busy preparing his short stories for a new volume that he intended to send to Leonard Woolf as soon as he reached Japan, responded to this request by copying the stories during the voyage and posting them to Durban from Kobe, but in the end Campbell decided not to use the material he sent.[39] Instead Campbell channelled his passions into writing a long polemical poem he called *The Wayzgoose*, which Cape published in 1928. By the end of the year he had followed Plomer's lead and left South Africa, for England.

The *Canada Maru* sailed from Kilindini, with the Japanese film crew on board, on 15 September 1926, and headed across the Indian Ocean to Singapore. Plomer's seasickness, far from disappearing as he grew used to the motion of the ship, seemed to worsen by the day; he found it almost intolerable to be on his feet for any length of time, and either lay on his bunk reading the contents of the large box of books he had brought with him from Durban[40] or sat in a *chaise-longue* on the deck during his mornings of translation work with Mori.[41] He spent many days on Walter Raleigh's *Shakespeare*, reading much of it aloud to Van der Post, and concentrating on the historical plays.[42] In later years he preferred to forget about the miseries of this voyage, and he makes no mention of his sickness in either of his autobiographies.

In the calm, velvety tropical evenings, under a sky rough with stars, one of the officers would play the *shakuhachi*, a bamboo flute with great purity of tone, and the long-drawn notes seemed to Plomer 'a classical lamentation, exquisite and resigned, for some irrecoverable age of primordial peace, an evocation of what the Japanese call *awaré*—which has been translated "the ah-ness of things" '.[43] On some afternoons, Mori, always keen to hone his kendo skills, would organize displays of that energetic, alarming art in an empty hold. With rice-straw mats spread out to cushion the steel floor, he would don a masked helmet and a padded jerkin with breastplates of leather, instantly being transformed into the semblance of one of his *samurai* ancestors, and with skilful swings and lightning thrusts of his two-handed sword, punctuated with barbaric yells, he would challenge and easily defeat the more agile members of his crew. That they were not merely deferring to his rank was shown when several of them subsequently beat him at judo.

Mori was not content that his two guests should simply watch from the deck; he urged them to try kendo and judo themselves. This invitation Plomer side-stepped with his usual diplomatic skill. Before they sailed from Durban he had told Van der Post that for the purposes of the newspaper articles they were supposed to be writing about the trip, they should divide the responsibilities between them: 'I shall take charge of letters and the arts,' he had said; 'you had better look after sport and music.'[44] Now, with Mori pressing them to join the fun, he pushed the reluctant Van der Post forward with the words, 'Remember, you are minister for sport and recreation.'[45] And Van der Post, feeling like a sacrifice being led out to a strange altar, was taken on to the mats to be flung about like a parcel once Mori had taught him how to fall without hurting himself too badly and, on later occasions, to be supplied with a kendo sword and padded jerkin before being mercilessly prodded and thumped, while Plomer watched from above behind his large dark glasses. After the first session he took Van der Post by the arm and in tones of great concern exclaimed, 'What a how-d'you-do! Quite, quite unbelievable. Are you sure you're all right?'[46] His dislike of sport in general extended to this new form of it in particular, and he took great care never to be inveigled on to the mats himself.

On the first night of full moon at sea, late in September, Mori organized a Japanese-style feast for the officers and his two guests, held on the starboard deck. Plomer and Van der Post were supplied with *yukata* (light cotton kimonos), much sake was consumed, and the rising of the moon was greeted with profound silence and with a request from Mori that someone compose a poem in the moon's honour. He looked pointedly at Plomer, who dodged this challenge as he had the earlier one to kendo, by excusing himself as too inexpert for so essentially Japanese an occasion, and the purser had to step in to fill the breach with a verse. After this cultural beginning, the evening rapidly became rowdier as the sake flowed. Presently Mori, excited with wine, gave a display of fencing with a naked sword, and followed this up with a Japanese war-dance performed with such vigour and fierce sincerity that both the young foreigners felt distinctly uneasy. Plomer saw the exhibition as an anticipation of the time when Japan would show the white nations that they had underestimated her military power:

Looking at his clean and muscular feet one felt that he would like to plant them on the neck of a defeated enemy. For a few minutes the atmosphere was uncomfortable; equivocal looks and remarks were exchanged by the Japanese, and we knew without a doubt that he was dancing in honour of *der Tag*. A momentary but ineffaceable impression.[47]

The same scene and the same impression occur in Plomer's poem 'Captain Maru':

> Maru in his cups does a sword-dance on the deck,
> Bare-legged, with feet as vigorous as hands,
> With a whole ocean for a private room,
> Stamps and shouts according to old rules,
> His face all flushed and big veins in his neck,
> And muscles, eyes, and anger all belong
> To a follower of Saigo, a Kumamoto tough.[48]

Van der Post tried to dispel the tension with a rendition of a Zulu war-dance that drew blood from his right foot.[49] One of the film crew then sang mournful Japanese love-songs which Plomer unkindly described (though not to the singer) as 'in the style of a cat in rut',[50] and Plomer and Van der Post, drunk enough for anything, though neither of them could sing in tune even when sober, returned the compliment with a duet of smutty Afrikaans folk-songs, followed by a Zulu solo that Plomer had learnt at Entumeni. The Japanese applauded politely, and the evening was judged a great success.

Plomer continued to fill his mornings by translating his novel with Mori, and in the course of the work he learned some Japanese, enough to be able to use the commoner expressions of politeness, in which the language is so rich, and to be able to understand slowly enunciated phrases. In the afternoons he read hour after hour, working his way through a big edition of Shakespeare's plays, and polishing some of the short stories he had written while living with the Campbells at Sezela. He also wrote occasional articles for the *Natal Witness*, most of them rather pedestrian descriptions of what he was seeing and doing during the voyage.[51]

One afternoon not long after the moon feast they entered the straits of Malacca, and through Mori's binoculars were able to see Sumatra, with purple thunderclouds hanging over the highlands from which vivid magnesium flares of lightning stabbed continually at the dense flood of jungle rolling down to the beaches. A heavy rain began to fall on the *Canada Maru*, like glass marbles splashing on the deck. Van der Post, seeing for the first time a land utterly unlike the Africa of his birth, was made uneasy by the sight, but Plomer, after a rapid look at the fertile chaos of the forest through the binoculars, turned away with a jest that put matters in perspective, but that seemed to Van der Post to be evading emotion that should have been faced: 'It's the first time, Lorenzo,' he said, 'that I've seen earth with pubic wood.'[52]

They called briefly at Singapore, evaded the dozens of pimps who competed for their attention,[53] had a drink at Raffles Hotel, and were dismayed by what they saw of the indulgence and excessive wealth of the overweight Europeans drinking in the cool there while the Chinese, Malays, and Tamils competed in the steaming streets outside.[54] They hired a car and with Mori crossed the causeway linking the island with the Malay peninsula. They drove thirty kilometres into the jungles of Johore, to lunch at a roadside stall under towering jungle trees, before being driven back to an epic Chinese banquet arranged for them by the indefatigable Mori.[55] They also went to the opera-house one night to see a Russian company perform a Spanish ballet.[56]

Off the rocky west coast of Formosa, where they could see cliffs sometimes a thousand metres high rising sheer out of the Pacific, the *Canada Maru* ran into a typhoon that forced Plomer to keep to his bunk for two days. 'What an incredible how-d'you-do,' he exclaimed to Van der Post when the wind began to die down and he was sitting up hungrily again: 'I don't think I would ever again want a repeat performance.'[57] Van der Post later came to believe that it was this dramatic, terrifying storm that persuaded Plomer never to return to Europe by sea.[58]

They anchored at Moji, a busy coaling port near the entrance to the Shimonoseki Strait, which gives access to the Inland Sea, on a lucent and perfect autumn day at the start of October 1926. Almost at once the ship was invaded by reporters eager to meet the marvellous foreign writers Mori had brought back with him. Each proffered a smile, a bow, and a card, and each requested an interview. They were particularly keen to know more about Plomer's background. Incautiously he had let slip, in a conversation with Mori during the voyage, the fact that he was related to the Arden family from which Shakespeare's mother came. This claim had very doubtful validity; it is true that his maternal great-grandmother's name was Mary Arden, but there is no evidence of any link, direct or indirect, with Shakespeare's mother.[59] Mori, however, pounced on any detail that would enhance the value of the prize he had brought to Japan, and he passed the news on to the journalists for whom he was translating Plomer's replies. They did not know much English, but they had heard of Shakespeare, and scribbled excitedly in their notebooks.[60] The next morning Mori triumphantly translated the headlines: 'DESCENDANT OF SHAKESPEARE ARRIVES IN JAPAN!' Plomer was embarrassed enough to say nothing of this later in his autobiographies, other than to refer cryptically to the newsmen's 'powers of invention'.[61]

Now began what Plomer was later to describe as the most strenuous fortnight of his life.[62] It began when he and Van der Post were welcomed ashore by a representative of the OSK line, Maseo Tajima, and by a Japanese diplomat, head of the Africa Section of the Foreign Office. They were taken on a tour of Moji, then still largely a town of traditional wooden buildings with roofs of dark-grey tile, for it was barely two generations since the guns of Commander Perry's squadron had obliged Japan to open its doors to the West. Plomer was much struck by the sight of a memorial to the Russo-Japanese War of 1904–5, in the shape of a Russian shell incongruously mounted on a pedestal in a shrine, as if to show that the lesson Perry taught had been scrupulously learned and assimilated.[63] That evening there followed a banquet in a luxurious pleasure house, preceded by a Japanese bath at which Van der Post was intensely embarrassed to find that he was expected to share a tub already occupied by several naked bathers of both sexes. Plomer managed to seem completely at his ease, however, and displayed no surprise even when he was asked whether the hair on his chest was real. The Japanese are not a hirsute people, and there was a hiss of astonished admiration from the parboiled company when he said it was.[64]

They were then dressed in elaborate kimonos by two young female attendants, who admired Plomer's appearance. Van der Post agreed:

Tall, slim and broad-shouldered as he was, the kimono sat on him with immense elegance and conferred a certain air of aristocracy upon him ... Yet there was something else, a profound nuance to the overall effect I had never observed before and even then, when first felt, I could not name beyond an intangible suggestion that a flowering dress was more welcome to his being than a man's tailored suit.[65]

Though they had come to know each other quite well at Sezela, and had shared a cabin for six weeks, Van der Post had no suspicion that Plomer was homosexually inclined. In fact, as he came gradually to realize, he knew hardly anything about Plomer's inner life, and he was later to think that he had never known anyone quite so secretive.

The dinner that followed was an even more boozy affair than the moon feast on the *Canada Maru* had been, and the accounts Plomer and Van der Post left of it differ even in such basic details as who was present.[66] They agreed, however, that there was enough sake to float a sampan,[67] that there was a geisha for each man, and that Mori, as eager to unwind after weeks at sea as he was to entertain his guests in style, laid on what Plomer rather coyly described as 'various forms of fun and games which I need not specify'.[68] It is common for writers on Japan to deny that geishas function as prostitutes of a select kind,[69] but the truth is that sexual favours are among the services these elaborately trained hostesses provide. Mori certainly seems to have hoped that Plomer would be attracted to the girl provided for him. Her name was Teruha; she was much the most attractive of the girls, and she and Mori seemed to be on terms of close friendship. She did her best to awaken Plomer's interest, but in vain. Mori, however, did not give up easily. After much singing, dancing, and cavorting, and after a photographer had recorded the scene, Mori shepherded out the other members of the party, had quilts and pillows carried in, and settled his two white guests and himself in bed with the three geishas. Plomer's account of what followed is in his most ironic and cautious style.

Mori was something of a matchmaker and had evidently primed the most attractive and intelligent of the geishas to make up to me. She was in fact pretty, gentle and quick-witted, and had none of that affected ingenuousness which often makes geishas rather boring. I think the idea was that I should fall heavily at the outset for Japanese womanhood and accordingly for Japan, but matchmaking is such a gamble, and just as people often give as presents what they themselves like rather than what the recipients want, Mori had chosen the bait he himself would have taken. All the same she was a very nice and obliging girl and may be said to have literally laid herself out to please—nor was she unsuccessful.[70]

In all his autobiographical writing, Plomer tried hard to disguise the distaste he felt for women as sexual partners, and that last ambiguous phrase is a good example of the extreme delicacy of his irony. The truth is that Teruha, from Mori's point of view and doubtless from her own, was entirely unsuccessful (though by Van der Post's account she used every art known to woman), and neither she nor Mori could decide why.[71] Years later, when Mori met Plomer's brother Peter in Japan after the Second World War, he asked him why Plomer had never married. 'Oh,' said Peter, who had little more idea than Mori, 'I expect he was too shy.'

Plomer was made nervous by the narrowness of this escape. At one of many dinners later in their trip, their hosts debated finishing off the evening at a famous local brothel. Mori, by that stage possessed of a clearer idea of what pleased his guests, opposed the idea, but seemed about to be overruled by an important Foreign Office official who had joined them for the dinner. Plomer, who could follow only the slower parts of the conversation, listened with growing alarm, became increasingly agitated, and finally hissed to Van der Post in panic, 'My God, Lorenzo, they are determined to take us to a brothel. What *shall* we do?' The virginal Van der Post stoutly assured him that they would look but not touch. As it turned out, peril was averted when the choice of amusements fell on a night-club rather than a brothel.[72] The incident shows how firmly Plomer, who had no great aversion to casual sexual liaisons, was setting in the homosexual mould.

From Moji the *Canada Maru* made its way through the Inland Sea, with its clear water and rocky islets, each decorated with a knot of pine trees, to her final port of call, Kobe. At Tarumi they passed Mori's house, from which his wife signalled to him with her largest mirror, Mori responding with a great blast on the ship's horn.[73] In Kobe there were more reporters waiting to ask them their views on everything from Japan's modernization to the labour situation in South Africa,[74] and after they had checked into a large modern hotel, sightseeing began at once with a climb up the hill behind the city to one of the innumerable shrines with which Japan is dotted.

In Osaka, Mori, feeling that his position had been much strengthened by the publicity Plomer and Van der Post had attracted, went boldly along to the head office of the OSK line to face the managing director, Mr Murata, a formidable magnate who was to become Japan's Minister of Transport in 1940. Mori apologized for having acted without prior permission, and received the icy response, 'In this company we have one hundred and twenty ships. If any other captain had done such a thing without permission I should have fired him. Tell me why you broke the rules of the company.' But the headlines, and the account Mori was able to give of Plomer's genius and his capacity for changing white racial attitudes in Africa, turned away wrath, and the interview ended with Murata telling him he had done well.[75]

Plomer and Van der Post were introduced by Mori to Murata and the directors of the OSK line, and given another elaborate dinner, complete with geishas; they were shepherded through castles, temples, and beauty spots to enjoy 'old Japan', and through textile factories, newspaper offices, and department stores to appreciate 'new Japan'.[76] Their hosts sometimes miscalculated the effect of what they showed: the lives of the factory workers in model hostels filled Plomer, he later said, 'not with admiration but with horror and pity'.[77]

From Osaka they were whirled through the mountainous main island of Honshu along a route that is still the standard guided tour for the hundreds of thousands of foreigners who flock to Japan each year. They travelled almost entirely by the rapid, efficient Japanese rail system. In Kyoto, the ancient capital of the country, they saw the Shogun's palace with its cunningly devised 'night-ingale' floor, designed to give aural warning of the approach of assassins. They were also conducted through the old imperial palace, which so few Japanese get the opportunity to visit, as well as several of the magnificent temples that serve as national headquarters of the various Japanese Buddhist sects. The garden which most struck them was the fourteenth-century abstract garden of the Zen Buddhist temple known as 'The Dragon's Repose'. With its raked gravel like a still sea lapping around the carefully placed rocks, it is designed to inspire meditation and a composure that seems totally to evade the chattering, littering legions of tourists, Japanese and foreign, who pour through it today. On an autumn evening in 1926, though, it was silent and empty except for one attendant raking the gravel, and it led Plomer to sombre thoughts. 'You know, Lorenzo,' he said with a smile, after standing long in silence, 'this garden makes me think of what Eliot said about Webster:

> Webster was much possessed by death
> And saw the skull beneath the skin;
> And breastless creatures under ground
> Leaned backward with a lipless grin.'

The remark seemed to Van der Post to be typically oblique, and to be delivered with a pretence at light-heartedness, as so often when Plomer touched on an aspect of life with which he was uncomfortable.[78]

Death, in a peculiarly Japanese guise, came closer to them the next afternoon, during a walk up a hill behind Kyoto to see the tomb of the Emperor Meiji, during whose reign (1868–1912) Japan had made such astonishing strides from feudalism into the twentieth century. The climb was steep, and when they neared the gates of the tomb they stopped for a breather, and Van der Post lit a cigarette. As he moved towards the tomb entrance with the rest of the party, the cigarette between his lips, a uniformed guard whom they had not even noticed before gave a primeval, inarticulate belly-howl of rage and moved towards them at a run, his sword flashing from the scabbard as he came. Before any of them could move, the sword streaked down in front of the terrified Van der Post's face, shearing away the cigarette and narrowly missing his lips and nose. The guard then abused him in an angry torrent of Japanese for nearly ten minutes while the whole party stood in silence, their faces pale and strained. When the abashed group was descending the hill again, Masao Tajima of the OSK told Van der Post, with a strange tone of approval, 'You see, Post-San, it was not the man but the uniform.'[79] Van der Post later saw this remark as an analysis and foreshadowing of the forces that were to sweep Japan towards the terrible fate of Hiroshima and Nagasaki, and it was in incidents such as this that the national paradox which

Plomer was to sum up in such stories as 'A Brutal Sentimentalist'
began to take shape for him.

They visited the tourist sights of Nara and Nikko, and were
driven to Isé, the centre of Japan's indigenous religion, Shintoism,
which Plomer, sceptic that he was, termed 'the national mumbo-
jumbo'.[80] Isé is in fact one of the most remarkable sights in Japan,
with its broad clear river full of golden carp which come to be fed
and hang suspended in the crystalline water as if floating in air.
They flashed through Arashiyama, Momoyama, Hiyei-san, and
Hakoné, with its wooded hills full of trailing mists, and its lovely
views of Fuji mirrored in the giant caldera Lake Ashi. Most of all
Plomer enjoyed an early morning in a boat on Lake Chuzenji: it
was a late autumn morning, and as they rowed slowly, the oars
dipping and leaving little whirlpools trailing reluctantly off the
blades, a few red and yellow leaves fell like butterflies through the
mist and floated on the clear water, through which they could see
the lake bed of coloured pebbles.[81]

But then, near the end of the fortnight, Tokyo reached out across
the Musashi plain to envelop them, a vast, nightmarish, unplanned
city in which reeking factory chimneys rise next to crowded
apartment blocks festooned with washing, and in which modern
buildings of unparalleled hideousness already, by 1926, out-
numbered traditional structures of wood. Most of the latter had
been destroyed in the catastrophic earthquake and terrible fire that
followed it on 1 September 1923, just three years before. The
Japanese, with their acceptance of disaster and readiness to
overcome it, had already largely made good the damage, but in
town planning they have wholly lost their famous aesthetic sense.
The narrow streets that the bombing of the Second World War
would finally obliterate were crammed with people walking noisily
to work in their *geta* (wooden sandals) in the morning, and
clattering wearily home in the evening, with the disciplined
movements and the queer, rapid, restricted strides that are enforced
on a walker constantly hemmed in by a moving sea of his fellows.
In this extraordinary human hive Plomer was to spend two and a
half years.

His introduction to Tokyo was of the same whirlwind character
as the rest of the tour:

Tokyo was waiting, with more reporters and photographers, more sightseeing, luncheon with a millionaire, an interview with a Cabinet Minister,

cocktails at the Imperial Hotel, and, even stranger, a gathering of the Rotary Club, not made up of bluff, back-slapping tradesmen but of formidable and silent magnates, to whom I was constrained to make a speech, which though civil was, I must confess, not free from irony.[82]

The Cabinet Minister he mentions so briefly was Baron Kijuro Shidehara, who in July 1929 was made Foreign Minister, and who even at this period was a power in the Minseito (Democratic) party. To conduct Plomer and Van der Post to an interview with him was the crowning triumph of Mori's bold gamble, and he was particularly proud to announce to Shidehara that Plomer had now decided to stay on in Japan rather than return when the *Canada Maru* set off on the trip back in a few days. Plomer would live in Japan, perhaps for a long time, perhaps for good, and Mori was confident that he would write the definitive book explaining the country to the outside world. 'Ah,' said Shidehara flatteringly, 'You will be the second Lafcadio Hearn.' 'No sir,' said Plomer, 'I shall be the first William Plomer.' Mori heard the reply with consternation. Fifty years later, recalling the incident ruefully, he added, 'Shidehara was a great man, you don't contradict such.' And then, as if with reluctant admiration, 'I was astonished!'[83]

The truth is that Plomer, who had by now read a good deal of Hearn's work about Japan, did not regard the comparison as flattering. He considered Hearn, then much the best-known of Western writers on Japan, as having ignored important aspects of Japanese culture (the drama among them) and as having tried to pass himself off as a scholar of the Japanese language, which he was not. Above all, he felt that Hearn's attempt to japanize himself, his adoption of a Japanese name, his writing of what Plomer called 'indiscriminate japanegyrics', and his exalting of Japan at the expense of the West, amounted to righting the Japanese by wronging his own race.[84] Although Plomer already greatly admired the Japanese, and intended to make a careful study of them, he was determined not to repeat the mistakes he believed Hearn had made.

Mori was convinced that Plomer would have no trouble finding some kind of job to support him in Japan, and gave him every encouragement to stay on. Plomer's decision to do so took a good deal of courage, for he was by now virtually penniless and would soon be in real need if he did not find employment. When Mori and Van der Post left on the *Canada Maru* again, at the end of October 1926, Plomer, who had accompanied them back to Kobe, said goodbye to them on board and then took the OSK launch back to the shore, waving his black hat above his head in farewell as the sun set. Van der Post had generously left with him what money he had, and had promised to wire him more from Durban in due course. He had also given Plomer a suit, and the sleeves of the too-small jacket rode up Plomer's long arms almost to the elbow as he waved, his figure lit by the level rays of the sun as the launch puttered back to the darkening quayside. 'William had never lacked courage,' Van der Post wrote later, 'but he never possessed it in greater measure than in that autumnal sunset moment of farewell.'[85]

His first priority now was to find a job, and he made his way straight back to Tokyo by train. The letter of introduction that Campbell had given him to Edmund Blunden, visiting professor of English at the Imperial University, now stood him in good stead. In 1926 Blunden was thirty years old, and had a growing reputation as a poet. He had put his experiences in the trenches in the First World War into some very fine war poems, now recognized as among the best of their kind. He had edited the work of John Clare, at that time nearly forgotten, and by the time Plomer met him had produced several volumes of verse, mainly about aspects of rural life. He had taken the position in Tokyo in 1924, succeeding another Oxford acquaintance of Campbell's, Robert Nichols.

Plomer contacted him at the Imperial University and went to see him at the Tokyo hotel in which he lived, the Kikufuji. Blunden, very small and friendly, took to Plomer at once, and without much difficulty got him a job teaching English at the Gwaikoku Go Gakko (Tokyo School of Foreign Languages). It took Plomer some little time to learn to say the school's name, which he compared to the croaking of a bronchitic frog.[86] Native speakers of English were in short supply in Tokyo, and Plomer's reputation as a writer seems to have been considered ample compensation for the fact that his spoken Japanese was very limited. The Tokyo School of Foreign Languages was, as Plomer wrote to Leonard Woolf, 'not as grand as it sounds'.[87] It was in fact a not especially exalted teachers' training college, and the pay was far from munificent, but there was also the prospect that in April he might be able to move to a better school. The Gwaikoku Go Gakko post was a toe-hold, at least, and he must have been grateful for it.

He moved into the Kikufuji hotel, and got to know Blunden well.

It is human nature to resent a benefactor, and Plomer's description of Blunden (in a letter to Leonard Woolf) shows a regrettable willingness to backbite the hand that fed him:

You will be amused to hear that I am staying in the same hotel as Blunden, who seems to me a careful scholar and a decent little man with good sense ... but his verse is too much like *The Blunden Mercury*.[88] I do not share his enthusiasms for village cricket and Leigh Hunt ... But he has been amiable to me, and he respects you, so I don't want to cut his throat ... We are horses of different colours![89]

Woolf rather agreed with this analysis of Blunden and put the caustic terms in which it was couched down to the fact that Plomer had not yet celebrated his twenty-third birthday: 'What you say is true, but "O Youth, Youth!" '[90]

On 20 November 1926 in his Tokyo hotel room, Plomer parcelled up the completed manuscript of the short stories he had written since the completion of *Turbott Wolfe* in 1924, and dispatched them to Hogarth Press for publication. The volume, *I Speak of Africa*, was published by the Woolfs in 1927; the title is an ironic allusion to the Shakespearian line 'I speak of Africa and golden joys'.[91] It contained the seminal tale 'Ula Masondo', an unexpurgated version of 'Portraits in the Nude', part of which had appeared in *Voorslag*, and a number of shorter pieces. Most of these are rather feeble, with the exception of 'Saturday, Sunday, Monday', a highly perceptive examination of relations between two sisters, one jealous of the other's sexuality. In later years Plomer was inclined to be rather apologetic when referring to *I Speak of Africa*, remarking of it that it 'has one good long story in it, and one good very short prose fiction, hardly a story. The rest is juvenilia.'[92] For all that, the book is a remarkable production for a man who was just twenty-one when he wrote the first of the pieces in it.

The stories of the volume, as one might expect from the circumstances of their original composition, showed little development in themes and concerns beyond those of work Plomer had already published while living in Africa, and their critical reception in England, though respectful, was muted. It was in the introduction that Plomer wrote in Japan, however, that he showed the extent to which he had moved on and left South Africa behind him, for ever as he thought. The introduction is a bitter attack on the country of his birth (which he describes as 'that blasted heath') and on its 'uncivilised white owners', and focuses in particular on their cultural barrenness. He claimed to have begun, together with Roy Campbell, 'the first literary movement in South Africa'; he compared South Africans' attitude to culture with 'that of a dog to a lamp-post', and he declared that artists could not live there. This introduction caused more offence in South Africa than the stories in the volume did; the Cape *Argus* called it 'unpardonable', and described it as 'the final kick, so to speak, of a man who had already left the country far behind him ... People only descend to a like depth and quality of abuse when they have cast the very dust of the country off their feet.'[93]

There is some truth to this last remark. Virtually all his life, from the moment when, at the age of five, he had been sent off to Aunt Hilda, and had been in, but not of, her husband's school, Plomer had moved through a series of situations in which he was in an anomalous, peripheral position. He was the outsider masquerading as one of the natives, but always observing them with a cool, ironic gaze. After the hardening and alienating experience of Beechmont, he viewed even his immediate family in this way, never giving them access to his inmost thoughts. During his emotional engagement with South Africa, reflected in and vital for the writing of such an incisive analysis as *Turbott Wolfe*, he had come to recognize and acknowledge that he was a South African, loving the country he criticized. But now he was moving on, spiritually as well as physically; he needed new terms in which to define himself in Japan, and being South African was no longer enough. Never had he been more clearly an outsider, for few societies on earth are so homogeneous as that of Japan, and none more subtly resists external ideas, even while it seems to welcome and adopt them. The outsider, if he is to avoid the fate that had overtaken Lafcadio Hearn, must have a very clear, confident sense of what he is. Increasingly Plomer came to think of himself, first as a South African subject of the British Empire which the Japanese so admired at this time, and then simply as an Englishman. Van der Post had seen the process beginning even on board the *Canada Maru*, when Plomer read and reread Shakespeare's history plays, as if seeking roots for his new identity.[94] When, a few months after he had begun living in Japan, he wrote to Van der Post for news of Durban, his detachment was clear: 'I shall much enjoy, and smile at (as distantly as if I was the man in the moon), any local "literary"

gossip you may send me.'[95] In a deep sense, the introduction to
I Speak of Africa was his angry farewell to South Africa.

He did not find Japan an easy country to come to grips with.
Even now, when every young Japanese has spent six years learning
English, much of the population has only the most rudimentary
grasp of the spoken language, and the foreign traveller straying off
the tourist routes without a knowledge of Japanese can find himself
facing formidable difficulties. Plomer learnt hundreds of Japanese
characters, but he never reached the stage at which he might have
been able to read a newspaper. Nor, even at the end of his stay,
could he speak the language, though he understood enough of it
to get by in everyday situations.

He had a bad time for the first few months. He spent his
twenty-third birthday on his own, having no money with which
to celebrate. He began perforce to live in the Japanese style, since
the Western-style rooms at the Kikufuji, with such amenities as
beds, were beyond his purse. Winter that year was intensely cold,
and it seemed a reflection of the gloom into which the Japanese
people had been thrown by the death, on Christmas Day 1926, of
the old emperor. His son Hirohito, who had been regent since
1921, acceded to the throne, taking the name Showa. These great
national events, which united the Japanese population, must have
made Plomer feel even more of an outsider. He soon found that his
salary at the Gwaikoku Go Gakko was not going to go far, and he
was forced to leave the Kikufuji for a cheaper hotel in which he
suffered from the cold. He found his clothes quite inadequate for
the rigours of the climate, but he had no money to buy warmer
ones. Partly in consequence, he was ill for a week and lay shivering
in his hotel room unattended. He wrote laconically to Van der Post
(who had again offered to send him money from Durban) to tell
him of his move from the Kikufuji:

I had a bad time there for various reasons—of which the chief were that
I was without friends, books, clothes or money. I was really ill between
Christmas & the New Year; the cold was intense—9° below zero—a lot of
frost & snow—the most severe cold ever recorded in Tokyo!! In the
mountains and in the north the amount of snow has been extraordinary
& even as I write there is snow a foot deep on the ground and a few flakes
are beginning to fall again.

I would of course have written sooner & oftener if I had been well. I know you will understand. ... You are a good creature, and your letter has warmed my heart. God bless you, and I send you my best wishes.[96]

Van der Post had not overrated his courage, or his need for it.

But in the New Year things began to look up. Through Blunden's kindness he had begun to get part-time work teaching English to the children of a nobleman, Marquis Hirohata, who offered him a full-time position as tutor to his children;[97] Plomer turned it down because (through Blunden, who had taken Plomer to meet Professor Sanki Ichikawa, head of the English department at the Imperial University) he had been offered a well-paid post at an expensive Tokyo School, the Tokyo Koto Gakko (Higher School). This establishment prepared students for entry to the Imperial University, and the teaching position was in the gift of Ichikawa.

With the prospect of this comfortable income to support him, he took a small house early in February 1927 in the village of Kami Nerima, then situated in quiet farming country on the flat plain an hour by electric train outside Tokyo. Nor did he take the house on his own. Again through Blunden, he had met some of the students of English at the Imperial University, and one of these, a cheerful young man named Sumida, had suggested that he should live with Plomer on this 'Sabine farm' (as Blunden had lightly called it)[98] so that each could practise the other's language. Plomer paid him a small wage for acting as a factotum.

He found young Japanese easy to get to know and like. His move from the Gwaikoku Go Gakko to the Tokyo Koto Gakko had irritated officials of the former institution, who slandered him to his former pupils; Plomer learnt of this when a group of the pupils came to him to tell him that they would believe nothing against him, and to apologize for the behaviour of their teachers.[99] Plomer was touched, for as he later wrote, 'whether I had behaved rightly or wrongly, I was a foreigner, and xenophobia was already slightly on the increase'.[100]

His teaching at the Tokyo Koto Gakko he found easy and pleasant. The school was roughly the equivalent of a Western senior or high school. Boys spent seven years in it, four as juniors and then three at the senior level; Plomer taught only the senior boys, aged from sixteen to nineteen. The curriculum had two major divisions, sciences and humanities, and humanities itself was subdivided into English, French, and German. Graduates of the humanities side went to the Imperial University to read economics, jurisprudence, or literature. The boys, some of them only four years younger than Plomer himself, were extremely bright and eager to learn; many of them went on to most distinguished careers. Among them were the nephew of Baron Shidehara and a boy named Honda, whose English was fluent because his father, a diplomat, had been posted to England. Another boy, Toru Nakagawa, himself became a diplomat, and eventually served as Japan's ambassador to the United Nations; Kyonosuke Ibe became president of the Sumitomo Bank; Tatsuro Yamamoto became a distinguished scholar of Asian history; Ryuichi Kajiki, one of the best of Plomer's pupils and a gentle and delightful companion, became an outstanding scholar of English with an international reputation, eventually holding the chair at Meisei University; Eiichi Sano also became a professor of English and in later years edited a volume of Plomer's stories for publication in Japan.[101] Not all the boys reached such heights; Shiomi Taro ended his days as a small farmer, but he was among the pupils for whom Plomer had the warmest regard, and with whom he continued to correspond until the end of his life. It must have been clear to him very early on that he was dealing with a remarkably talented group of young men, and his teaching was accordingly conscientious and inspiring. Certainly it produced results.

The textbook he used in the first year was Boswell's *Life of Johnson* in an abridged version; in the second year he used *Hamlet*. He would discuss these works with his pupils and then ask them to paraphrase passages, a task they found intensely difficult but rewarding. They thought him a good teacher, very energetic and enthusiastic, and capable of communicating his enthusiasm to his classes.[102] The fact that he was a Westerner made him an object of attention in any case; his height, his rather pale grey eyes and fair hair, his courteous self-assurance and sense of fun, all fascinated the young Japanese he taught. Nor was it only the pupils who were impressed by him. He got on well with the other masters, finding in them 'that touch of boyish innocence which often made the Japanese endearing'.[103] His beautiful handwriting attracted much attention from other staff members; the Chinese classics teacher, who took over the classes after him each week, seeing his script on the blackboard, remarked to the class that it had the beauty of true calligraphy, a comment that several of the boys never forgot.[104]

His pupils were struck, in addition, by his approachability, which was in contrast to the rest of their teachers. Far from keeping his distance, he was not only willing to talk to them in odd moments at school, but repeatedly invited them to visit him at his Nerima house. Most of them took up the invitations at one time or another, some of them several times. They were impressed to find that he lived entirely *à la japonnaise*. The house itself was typically Japanese, wooden and very small, the floors covered with *tatami* mats of rice-straw, on which he and Sumida slept at night wrapped in quilts. The rooms were divided from one another by sliding partitions of thick cardboard supported on light timber frames; these could be removed with little difficulty, so that the whole interior of the house (with the exception of the kitchen, bathroom, and toilet) could be turned into a single room for the purposes of entertainment. Like all such traditional Japanese structures it was intensely cold in winter, despite the best that could be done with inadequate and dangerous charcoal braziers. The house contained no Western possessions at all; indeed there were few possessions of any kind.[105] This, Plomer's first home of his own, was to set the pattern for all that came after it; all his life he seems to have taken pleasure in owning very little, and many of his friends would remark on the austerity of his surroundings.

One of the boys wrote to him after a first visit, thanking him for his 'warm reception', and adding,

It was interesting for me to find you accustomed to the Japanese manner of living, and seeing you live in a simple way like a man who was thoroughly acquainted with the world I couldn't help smiling. But I believe the life you are leading now will not be unpleasant for you, and because I perceived that you have something of the genuine Japanese character in your spirit—that is, the indifference about the world's affairs, the despise for social talents and a calm and self-possessed attitude.[106]

The letter, with its faintly condescending compliments, seemed to Plomer akin to an Englishman's praise of a foreigner for not behaving like a foreigner.

He was well looked after, for his neighbours, a family named Shimoju, by a coincidence turned out to be distantly connected to Mori. When they became aware of the link between Plomer and Mori, Mrs Shimoju and her daughters insisted on doing all Plomer's housework for him, even scouring his pots.[107] When Mori returned once more from Africa in February 1927, he came at once to see how Plomer was getting on, and with extreme generosity offered to support him so that he could write unimpeded. Plomer, who knew that Mori was far from rich, declined the offer.[108] Mori also carried him off to his own home at Tarumi, on the Inland Sea, urging him to stay as long as he liked, or for good.[109]

Once he had got through the initial difficult months Plomer thoroughly enjoyed Japan. His well-paid and congenial job at the Koto Gakko gave him long holidays which he spent travelling round Japan, seeing as much of the country as he could. He led a party of boys to the mountain resort of Ikénodaira in the summer of 1927, where they climbed a mountain, sleeping in a hut half-way up and watching the dawn the next morning from a stone platform at the summit. On this trip he grew close to one of his pupils in particular, a boy named Fukuzawa, the son of a farmer. They rejoiced in the thought of having escaped Tokyo's terrible summer, and wallowed in communal hot baths, of which Plomer became a connoisseur:

Nothing stimulates well-being and benevolence like a sociable hot bath, and since hot springs exist all over Japan and I spent all my holidays in travelling about the country, I passed much time in them. They are best perhaps in winter when the sun is shining on the snow, or when the plum trees are coming into blossom a few yards from one's nose, the rest of the body being under the water, and the body of a congenial companion by one's side.[110]

In that same summer of 1927 he visited Sumida's family at Hiroshima, and from a boat one evening watched a display of fireworks, which briefly left a curious domed cloud of smoke floating over the city: an ominous sight that he was to recall nearly eighteen years later, when the whole world heard of Hiroshima.[111] With Sumida he would swim from the same beach as the cadets of Etajima, the Japanese naval college, much impressed by the strenuous physical regime by which they were obliged to live, and by the magnificent physiques that resulted from it, and that attracted him greatly.

He was gaining insights to the country granted to very few visitors. Wandering in the woods near Hiroshima with Sumida, he met two Indian visitors, who gaped at the sight of a tall young white man dressed in the conical straw hat of a Japanese countryman, a light cotton kimono, and tall clogs. And an English businessman whom he met on his return to Tokyo, on hearing that he had spent the summer travelling and staying with Japanese friends, was slightly incredulous. 'I've been fifteen years in this country,' he exclaimed, 'and no Japanese family have ever asked *me* to stay with them.'[112]

That same eventful, happy summer, he travelled further afield, to the northern island of Hokkaido, a place of wild mountain and moorland, with his pupil Honda. The trip was made by train and ferry (he was very sick on the ferry, as he had been on the *Canada Maru*). Plomer compared the northern island to Siberia, Alaska, Korea, and Canada. Uncharacteristically, he kept a detailed diary of this journey, later describing the trip under the title 'Yoka Nikki', in his volume *Paper Houses*.[113] The account he gives is remarkably frank, as when he describes meeting an American he clearly disliked:

The next day I met him in the bath and dissected his character under a barrage of platitudes. I often do this when I am analysing people. It's very effective. It's also good to agree with everything said by fools or people you dislike (it comes to the same thing), then while they are trying to take umbrage you can take notes.

There, that's the worst of a diary. So many cats get out of the bag.[114]

Among the 'cats' that escape in this diary is the fact that despite his now well-established preference for members of his own sex, he continued to be attracted to women. At one point, apropos of the public baths in which both sexes mingled freely (one of the few Japanese traditions that have given way completely to Western influence), he remarked, 'I like to see Japanese women nude, especially when their hair is dressed in their own fashion, like a voluted helmet of black lacquer.'[115] And two days later, he was served breakfast in an isolated Hokkaido inn by a beautiful maid, to whom he seems to have responded, almost involuntarily, one feels, before pulling himself back with a jerk:

According to custom, she kneels to serve us, who eat off the floor. She is a country girl of this marvellous northern type, a flower of perfection. About sixteen, she hardly ever raises her eyes, is very simply dressed, has a subdued voice, her silence is tuneful, her hair not long, she hardly knows how to smile, she turns round and round in her hands a round tray of black lacquer that rests on her thighs.

'Don't stare at her so hard,' says N. [Honda.] 'You'll make her feel

uncomfortable. See, she's blushing. Nobody,' he asserts, 'has ever told her she is beautiful.'
     Then I will—
     It is time to leave.[116]

It seems possible that in his impulses, if not in practice, Plomer was still bisexual rather than homosexual. He thoroughly enjoyed sex, and liked as much of it as possible; homosexual men, among whom multiple casual, transient relationships are common, offered more activity and variety than relations with respectable women could have done, and the homosexual habit, once formed, was not easily broken—especially since Plomer saw no reason to break it. He had little experience of women, and the few stories in which he deals with heterosexual love are marked by a complete lack of engagement: 'A Surplus Woman', published in *Paper Houses*, is a good example. Plomer knew as little of the way of a man with a maid as E. M. Forster did, and as Forster does in describing what happens in the Marabar caves, or on the Lungarno, Plomer commonly takes refuge in chilly vagueness.
     There is little doubt that he and Honda had at least a brief affair (he is one of four students whom Plomer names as having been 'dear' to him),[117] nor can it be doubted that his relations with Sumida were closer than Plomer's description of him as a 'factotum' would imply. The attitude of the Japanese to homosexuality was at this period considerably more tolerant than that of (say) the English. It was semi-respectable, in part at least because of the *samurai* tradition, which, like that of Plato's Athens, did not discourage a warrior from keeping both a wife and a catamite. Indeed, a man who had been through a frenetically active homosexual phase in youth might (and apparently often did) settle down to a lifelong marriage, his friends not thinking this out of the ordinary.[118]
     Towards the end of 1927 Sumida's parents, in the way still customary in isolated areas of Japan, arranged a marriage for him; it may not have been coincidental that they took this step after getting to know Plomer over the summer, and perhaps sensing the relationship between their son and this remarkable young foreigner. Plomer decided to give up his Nerima house and take another at Higashi Nakano, which is now almost the centre of Tokyo but was then a quiet, leafy residential area. This house was a little larger than that at Nerima, but was also in the Japanese traditional style.

Plomer did not take long to find another companion; he shared this house with Morito Fukuzawa, another of his pupils.

Fukuzawa was in his early twenties, a strikingly good-looking man with the narrow, down-turned eyes that the Japanese think of as typical of their race, the full lips of the sensualist, and a flat nose which gave his face a slightly brutal cast which Plomer found very attractive. Plomer found his temperament, sceptical and hedonistic, very much to his taste.[119] The two of them lived a free and easy life, giving frequent, noisy, sake parties, entertaining a stream of other young men as weekend guests, and encouraging in each other an enjoyment of life. They employed as a cook and maid-of-all-work a young girl who shared the house with them, having become alienated from her own family.

Fukuzawa had a wide knowledge of Japanese literature, and with his guidance Plomer set about educating himself in the Japanese classics, reading very widely. Among the modern Japanese writers they read carefully together were Mori Ogai and Akutagawa Ryunosuke. They often went to the theatre, and Plomer developed a particular fondness for Bunraku (Japanese puppetry) and for the Noh, the slowest and most stylized of the three main Japanese dramatic forms.

He was becoming aware of the extent to which he needed to educate his tastes and expand his reading, and he began a course of systematic reading in English literature, which he was to continue for the rest of his life. 'Japan was my university,' he was later to say.[120] He combined his reading with long discussions with Fukuzawa and other young Japanese friends, talks that seem to have revolved around politics and religion. Communism was gaining credence among the educated young in Japan at this time, and several of his friends were *marukusu-boi* ('Marx boys'). Plomer himself, although some of his letters of this period express views that would have been considered strongly left wing at the time, inclined to a determinism of the type he had learned from Manilal Gandhi in Natal. Though he sometimes called himself a 'Christian' determinist, he rejected those of Christ's teachings that got in the way of his pleasures, particularly his homosexual activities. For all that, he was not living an existence of careless hedonism; he was trying to discipline his life, and he largely succeeded. One feels this vigorous self-control, combined with the uncertainty about his own abilities that inspired it, in some of his letters to Leonard Woolf:

I ought to tell you that I am a fanatic. I believe the modern world resolves itself quite easily, obviously, (where are all our 'problems' and 'questions'?) into a duel between Ford and Gandhi, (or shall we say between the heart and the purse?) and I am on the side of the angels, & intend to stay there.

I feel secure in the calm delirium of prophetic certainty.

Meanwhile I have almost got into shape a curious glittering smiling philosophical pseudo-novel, which has guts as well as wings.[121] As soon as it is done I shall send it to you, but I doubt if it will be done before the end of the year.

Since I was 16 I have lived in daily contact with non-Europeans, & sometimes before that, so you can see why my view of Europe is not that of a European: & I defy anybody to say that it is distorted.

I feel rather a swine for not writing oftener, but I live a strenuous emotional & physical life. For one thing I am now a wage-slave. For another, I have stopped smoking & drinking,[122] & hardly eat anything. Physical discipline is making my brain clearer & clearer: I want it to cut like a knife. I am preparing myself for an active future.[123]

He was writing hard, not just the novel he mentions in this letter; he was also polishing the poems that were to appear in *Notes for Poems*, some of which had been written as long ago as 1920. He sent the manuscript of this book to the Woolfs on 20 June 1927, and they published it at the end of that year. It was the third volume Plomer had brought out with them in two years, and he must have felt satisfied with the rate at which he was working.

At the same time as sending *Notes for Poems* to London, he foreshadowed what he hoped would be an important book on Japan:

I am very ambitious for it, and you won't see it, I think, for at least a year. I intend it to have emotional and political world-significance: because I intend it to influence Japan emotionally and politically. Do I set myself too great a task? I think not, because some people are beginning here to respond to my personal moral influence, and I am full of passion.

And he added a confident postscript:

I have just examined carefully the works of Lafcadio Hearn, who wrote a lot about this country. He was an intelligent, industrious & tender-hearted journalist, but he had a definitely second-rate mind—it was neither wide enough, nor properly sharpened. It is not only in Japan, but elsewhere (esp: America) where he is esteemed out of all proportion to his merits. The reason is simply that he is one of the few writing outsiders who have had any real comprehension of Japanese character—this he certainly had to some extent—but he was afraid of the future. His future is my present, so I have a job to do.[124]

He was later to analyse and excuse his bumptiousness on the grounds that 'I was much alone when younger, & by bolstering up my self-esteem I must have often given the impression of arrogance, boastfulness & conceit: & of that I am ashamed.'[125]

It is true that he was very isolated at this time, at least from friends who could have criticized his work knowledgeably; he had not found another Roy Campbell to serve this vital role for him. He was not entirely without the company of intelligent Europeans, however; apart from Blunden, whom he still saw often, and who was kind enough to read some of the poems of *Notes for Poems* and urge him to publish them, he had for a time the pleasant company of Anna von Schubert, whom he had known in Durban, and who arrived in Japan with her husband in August 1927. Small and beautiful, she was very much attracted to Plomer, as she had earlier been attracted to Campbell; 'emotionally unemployed' was to be Van der Post's comment on her years later.[126] Plomer liked her painting, and thought her a woman of the rarest intelligence and sensibility. 'I had long felt the want of the society of civilized European women,' he was to write, 'and here was one who was a civilization in herself.'[127]

With her and Fukuzawa in July 1928, he revisited Lake Chuzenji, the summer resort that then, as now, was much favoured by foreigners intent on escaping the humidity and heat of Tokyo. Where he and Van der Post had enjoyed their early morning row two years before, he now found the lake so full of yachts of wealthy foreigners that a swimmer had to keep a keen look-out to avoid being brained by them. His fine poem 'At Lake Chuzenji' captures the beauty of the setting and his sense of its being disturbed by the restlessness of the foreign community. It also preserves a brief memory of Anna von Schubert, and of Plomer himself, his presence at the resort with her causing gossip:

> 'The best July resort in the whole Far East'
> So he was told, the stout Bombay Greek
> Watching the water, clear and still as aspic.
>
> The yacht race this morning looks like yesterday,
> White isosceles triangles on parallels sliding
> Passing and repassing, he wonders to what end.

V within V behind a motor boat
The splay waves spread and waver, a German lady swims,
Down comes the rain and voices interpenetrate.

'We ought to go and see that beastly waterfall.'
'Who is this young man that follows her round?'
'Three hearts.' 'And you?' 'I pass.' 'What's yours?'

A sudden yearning for an evening with geisha
Cruises along his hardening arteries,
But sadly he turns his broad back on the lake,

Resigned to missing intimacy with Japanese joys,
To no longer being young, and to not being free
From his wife, his daughter, his hotel, or propriety.

Increasingly, like the alienated 'Bombay Greek', he felt more in tune with Japanese than with his fellow Westerners, noticing, when he met other Europeans, their almost grotesque irregularity of feature, their size, their ill-natured expressions, even their smell. He took pleasure in the belief that his high cheek-bones and slightly hooded eyes made him look rather Japanese.[128] This belief was largely illusory, for his fair hair and his height ensured that he was prodigiously stared at, particularly when naked in the public baths. Try though he did to mingle with the Japanese population, these differences and the fact that he never learned to speak the language with any fluency combined to isolate him effectively. Several times in his letters to his parents he mentioned that it was months since he had spoken to a European, but he was also to admit that he was never quite at ease among his Japanese friends. He had always to speak slowly and clearly, avoiding colloquialisms, so that they could understand his English; he could never say what he really thought of Japan for fear of giving offence; he could never, in fact, be at ease and simply be himself. From this need for continual self-discipline developed that reserve, that sense of watchful self-containment and secrecy, that was so noticeable in his manner for the rest of his life. The seeds of it lay in his childhood, and had been planted in the terrible sense of rejection he felt at being sent to Beechmont, but it was his experience in Japan that brought the growth to maturity. Only among his few European friends in Japan could he feel at home, and none of them was really close to him.

Though the community of European writers in Tokyo was very small, he found another poet-friend in the shape of Sherard Vines.[129] A witty, learned man, Vines had probably been introduced to Plomer by Blunden.[130] Though his work has now been largely forgotten, Plomer thought him a poet of distinction; his writing is marked by neo-metaphysical conceits and the piling up of recondite detail. It was Vines who, on his return to Europe in June 1928, carried with him the first of Plomer's Japanese writing to be published, *Paper Houses*, which Hogarth Press brought out in 1929, and which Plomer dedicated to Vines.

These stories cast a very clear eye on Japan and the Japanese, and several of them are marked by the determinism that Plomer had firmly embraced. 'The things that happen to us, including our deaths, are not merely the appropriate but the inevitable things,'[131] he was to write looking back on this time, and many of the stories in *Paper Houses* clearly reflect this belief. Partly as a result, several of the stories contain what would normally be thought of as far-fetched coincidences, but Plomer treats them in a way that makes them, to use his words, appropriate and inevitable. Perhaps the most outstanding of these stories is 'Nakamura', the action of which is entirely dependent on a series of coincidences. It is, in addition, strikingly Japanese, being modelled on the psychological studies of Akutagawa Ryunosuke, which Plomer had read with Fukuzawa,[132] though it also reflects the influence of Maupassant, Chekhov, and Bunin.[133] One seminal scholar of the influence of Japan on writing in English has commented of Plomer that 'his is perhaps the only fiction which reads like a splendid translation from a modern Japanese novelist ... one is moved to sigh in relief, at last, over a realistic novel with a Japanese setting.'[134]

In these stories Plomer set out to interpret his own encounter with Japan, and to analyse and describe the Japanese character. In the prefatory notes with which he began the volume, he established the objective tone in which his comments were to be couched, and sets that slight but definite distance between himself and his subject-matter that characterizes all he wrote. He also made a striking prediction:

I admit that I am an admirer of the Japanese, for I can respect and love individuals. But I disbelieve in their tendency to nationalistic paranoia and their particular politico-religious superstitions, which I believe to be more insidious and locally almighty than those of nearly all other countries,

Russia and Italy included, and which, if persisted in, will have terrible results.[135]

Given that this was written before June 1928, it is a remarkably perceptive comment, and shows how well Plomer understood the totalitarian forces already at work in Japan. It was several years before the young nationalistic army officers began their programme of assassinating moderate politicians and persecuting left-wing intellectuals (among them several of Plomer's former pupils), but the dangers were already apparent to a sensitive observer.

Among the characteristics of this slowly growing nationalistic movement was a strongly marked xenophobia, and it may have been partly his perception of this threat that made Plomer announce to Leonard Woolf, on 11 June 1928, his intention to return to Europe in the spring of 1929.[136] The impending publication of *Paper Houses* may have played its part, for that volume contained a remarkable satirical piece, 'Mother Kamchatka', in which many aspects of Japanese life are mercilessly and very amusingly attacked.[137] Among the targets are the Japanese flag (which is compared to a poached egg on a white plate), Japanese nationalism, and emperor worship; and Plomer rightly remarked that 'if this had been read and understood by some chauvinist fanatic, he might have put a violent end to me'.[138] Since the volume, soon after reaching Japan early in 1929, was translated into Japanese, the danger was real enough. Besides, he had begun to realize that if he were not to stay in Japan permanently, it would be easier to break with the country and with Fukuzawa now than wait until the ties had strengthened further. It was time to go.

He began to gather up what money he could lay his hands on for the trip to England. He was determined not to return by sea; in any case, by far the quickest way of making the trip was by the Trans-Siberian Railway. On a clear, starry night in March 1929 he boarded the regular ferry from the Inland Sea port of Shimonoseki to Fusan in Korea. As the boat backed and moved away from the brightly lit quayside, not far from where he had first stepped on to Japanese soil, Plomer and Fukuzawa shouted 'Sayonara!' to each other while the dark water widened between them. The Japanese interlude was over.

8. *England*

1929–1930

In 1946, when Plomer came to record his trip from Japan to England for a publication named *Choice*,[1] he entitled his piece 'Through Siberia in a Trance'. The 'trance' he refers to was a state of dreamy indifference which, in restrospect, he believed had fallen on him the moment he said goodbye to Fukuzawa, whom he seems sincerely to have loved, and left Japan, where he had been happy:

From that moment I went into a kind of trance. It was not simply because I missed my familiar companion and had torn myself from the life in Japan I had grown accustomed to. It was also a matter of disposition. Those who are not bent upon what is called 'getting on' fall easily into trances, into a mood that may last through a lifetime of semi-indifference, of habit fitting as comfortably as an old overcoat, of dreamy resignation: and such a state, though its causes are no doubt partly physical, is by no means incompatible with activity of body or mind.[2]

This detached state, which he hints lasted all his life, meant in the longer term that he felt himself to be without ambition, a condition that had a profound effect on his life, for it made him largely indifferent to fame, money, the respect of his peers, or any of the other motivations that drive writers to the drudgery of writing. Plomer records it without any attempt to explain its origins, and perhaps they are beyond explanation. But it seems true that throughout the 1930s at least he was content to drift wherever fate might lead him, happy to enjoy whatever life might offer in the way of pleasure, and ready to endure the rest. 'I was lazy in the 1930s, and have never really made up for it since,' he was to write to his brother nearly forty years later.[3]

The steamer docked in the Korean port of Fusan on a brilliant mid-March morning, and Plomer transferred to an express train that ran north into China before crossing the Soviet border. From the window he watched the contrasts Asia presents to the traveller, contrasts which he thought increasingly threatening:

In the new and well-equipped train Japanese businessmen in white collars, black coats and striped trousers sat about smoking, reading newspapers, and talking about stocks and shares; outside it the bare mountains of Asia, rocky and remote in the pale sunshine, glided past in silence, as if floating or changing places according to some predetermined manœuvre, and beneath them from time to time could be seen stately Korean gentlemen of leisure wearing full white robes and tiny top-hats of black gauze tied with ribbons under the chin, *as if nothing had happened*—as if there was no train, no line, no Japanese expansion, no next war germinating.[4]

Across the vast biscuit-coloured plains of Manchuria he was drawn, and the tawny grassland must have reminded him of the veld as he had seen it when he steamed out from Johannesburg on his way to Fred Pope's farm near Molteno eight years before. At Harbin, in northern China, he left the train for a day or two and made the acquaintance of some of the sad Russian exiles who no longer hoped that the Bolshevik government might be overthrown, but who lacked the will or the means to move further than this gloomy, provincial Chinese town with its demoralized cosmopolitan population, its air of instability, and its wide river, the Sungari, sliding endlessly between snowy banks, like a stream of pewter under a darkening sky. In company with an acquaintance he had made on the train, Plomer visited a brothel, where he drank Japanese beer with a young Russian prostitute and was amused to notice on her wall a postcard of a handsome Durban Zulu.

Why did he visit the brothel? Perhaps his motivation was merely the curiosity of a young man determined to see and experience as much as possible, though this scarcely accords with his account of his trance-like state. It seems more likely that he was still trying to determine what his sexual role might be, to find out in fact if he were capable of responding to a woman. Repeatedly transplanted, he had become *déraciné* and unsure of himself in a number of ways. Now that he had left Japan and Fukuzawa, would he also abandon the homosexuality that had characterized his life there? Even in Japan the question must have troubled him; much later he recorded that at one time he had seriously considered marrying a Japanese girl, though he does not name her or give any details about the affair.[5] The experience in Harbin does not seem to have been any more satisfactory than his encounter with the geisha with whom Captain Mori had tried to tempt him; years later he was to refer to the Russian girl as 'a mousy blonde', and to add (with characteristic irony), 'I felt that I was seeing life, but I would rather have seen it gayer.'[6]

A friendly Czech who spoke fluent English and Russian enabled him to talk to a few Russians during the long trip across Siberia, and he listened with interest to their enthusiastic accounts of the wonders that communism was bringing about in the Soviet Union. Plomer had read Russian literature widely in translation, and he looked forward to seeing the reality of the world he had read about:

As the landscape became flatter and slightly more populous and one saw ancient-looking villages with clusters of houses and clumps of trees round churches with gilt, onion-shaped domes, and small wooden manor houses with pillared porticos, I realized how clearly my ideas about Russia had been formed by Gogol, Tolstoy, Dostoievsky, Aksakov, Turgeniev, Chechov, Gorki, and Bunin—so formed that I seemed to *recognize* what I saw, as if returning from a long absence. Even in Moscow itself, though awed and excited, I strangely did not feel like a stranger. It was a place where I had often lived and suffered vicariously, and it was haunted by characters whom I felt I had known, whom I almost felt I had *been*. Such is the power of literature.[7]

He knew little about the Russian Revolution or communism, despite having included a Communist character in *Turbott Wolfe*. In Moscow he bought a copy of John Reed's *Ten Days that Shook the World*,[8] but found it so dull that he could not get through it. Perhaps because of his lack of political knowledge, he found the Communists he talked to wholly convincing, and full of confidence and hope in their country's future.[9] He saw nothing of Stalin's terrible purges of the peasantry, particularly the kulaks, which had begun in the previous year, and in the course of which five million peasant families were killed or transported, so that famine returned to the countryside; nor was he aware of the police apparatus that enforced order and kept consumption low so that real wages fell steadily for a decade after 1928.[10] Plomer was disposed to be sympathetic to the aims of the Communists in Russia, in part because Roy Campbell had been a strong left-winger during Plomer's association with him in 1926, and in part because many of his young Japanese friends had been influenced by Marxism of a vague, ill-informed kind. For all that, he found the Soviet Union drab, impoverished, and depressing. Bayonets glittered uncomfortably in the streets; the museums were instruments of propaganda used to inform the young about the crimes of the Czarist regime; at the Bolshoi Theatre a woman with a kerchief over her head sat in the Imperial box and gnawed an apple until the curtain went up; and when Plomer sat down to dinner in the Grand Hotel, he unfolded a table napkin woven with the crown and monogram of the Czar Nicholas II, out of which ran a cockroach.[11] He was not sorry to cross the border into Poland.

By contrast with the Soviet Union, Poland seemed prosperous, well run, and relaxed, and he was able to see a good deal of its capital city in the course of his brief stop there. His old schoolfellow from Rugby, Darsie Gillie, had been living in Warsaw for some years, knew the language well, and was glad to show Plomer the sights of the city. 'The Lazienki Palace, the Jewish quarter, a cabaret, a literary salon, the best place to drink mead or borsch, and patience with an ignoramus—he displayed them all,' Plomer wrote later.[12] From there he travelled through Berlin to Ostend, and took the ferry to Dover.

He was filled with apprehension about what he would find in England. His immediate plans were to go and live with his parents, but he had become too independent to think of their house as more than a stepping-stone. He hoped to earn a living by writing. He believed he could live on very little, but wondered whether even that little could be earned; his only contacts in the literary world were Leonard and Virginia Woolf. He thought of himself as a stateless person, rather than an Englishman returning home, and he arrived with all the fears of a refugee:

One of the effects of having left England when very young and of having been long absent was that although I came back with many pleasant memories of English people, places, and things, I came back as a displaced person. Displacement had enabled me to understand, as I could not otherwise have understood, something of the strangeness a foreigner approaching England for the first time might feel, especially if he lacked the comfortable backing of a settled political and social background, a substantial capital, and secure prospects. Such a foreigner, even if unprejudiced, might feel some apprehension about the English character and about some of the traits he might have heard attributed to it. I for my part harboured disagreeable memories of a certain English attitude to life against which I had from early childhood been in rebellion. And now that I had sometimes seen this attitude disagreeably and one might almost say indecently exposed abroad, to the detriment of our national reputation, I was even more sensitive to it and even less ready to make allowances for it.[13]

This was the mood in which he stepped on board a cross-Channel ferry early in April 1929 in a bitter north-east wind, and, gloomily contemplating the effects which a rough crossing would have on his constitution, heard an Englishwoman, 'with a figure like a cricket-bat—straight, narrow, flat in front and only slightly convex at the back',[14] remark, after a glance round the faces of her fellow passengers, 'Everybody has an expression as if they were just going to take the first fence.'[15] The woman, the weather, and the prospective seasickness made the remark particularly unpalatable to Plomer; the lady of the first fence seemed to him a sort of female Bode,[16] and his fears about England and the English increased. 'I felt as if I had returned from another planet, or from the dead,' he wrote later.[17] In this mood he landed at Dover, to be met by his mother and father. 'You've come back with a golden face,' exclaimed his mother on seeing him, and perhaps he was more Japanese than he was English at this time. But then the role of outsider was nothing new to him.

His parents had bought a small house at Pinner[18] in Middlesex, and Plomer moved in with them, though he found his father no easier to live with than he had in Natal. 'Fathers are difficult,' he was to tell Virginia Woolf. 'Mine has no interest in anything. But I don't live at Pinner for choice.'[19] The town was within easy reach of London by train, being only 25 kilometres away, and he quickly began building up a circle of acquaintances in the capital, beginning with his publishers, the Woolfs. Having corresponded with them for nearly five years, from Zululand and Japan, he first met them at a small party they gave at their rooms in Tavistock Square on Saturday, 11 May 1929, to which they had also invited Edmund Blunden, knowing that he and Plomer had met in Tokyo. Virginia Woolf's first reaction to him was one of disappointment that he seemed not at all the wild, strange young man she would have expected from his correspondence, and from what she knew of his background: 'a little rigid, I fear, & too much of a gentleman' was her first diary-note on him.[20] On the other hand, she agreed with his assessment of Blunden, describing the latter as 'little Blunden, the very image of a London house sparrow, that pecks & cheeps & is starved & dirty'; and, admiring Plomer's writing, she continued to try to plumb the depths she knew to be in him. She wrote of him to her sister,

We had William Plomer who is going to be a great novelist to dine—fresh from Japan—a very spruce and yet imaginative young man, born of parents in Pinner. I think I shall have to ask him here and bring him to Charleston to meet you. But what a mix up we are!—I pretending to be an Aunt and then a contemporary—I never know which. He says that they dont talk with much freedom in Pinner.[21]

Plomer was to describe that first evening in an article written forty years later:

What I found, in the small drawing-room which owed some of its atmosphere to decorations and paintings by Vanessa Bell, and which seemed charming and secluded, was a woman of unique physical beauty and elegance. Her beauty was derived from the fineness of her features, her tall and slender figure, beautiful hands, and graceful movements. She had nothing whatever in common with popular or period or worldly beauties, or with any kind of conventional prettiness, and made an impression of combined strength and fragility—*nervous* strength and fragility.

Neither then nor at any other time did her clothes suggest either a concern with fashion or any effort to defy it. She knew, as people used to say, how to wear her clothes, which were neither simple nor complicated. She was not given to wearing ornaments, but what she was given to was smoking, after dinner, an excellent long cheroot. The cheroots came, I think, from the Army & Navy Stores, and she sometimes gave me a bundle of them to carry away.

The conversation was no doubt mostly questions from the Woolfs and answers from me. I was so different, I suppose, from their other authors and from the Cambridge young men of my generation whom they knew, that I must have been rather a problem to solve.

People have sometimes been surprised when I have said I thought Virginia Woolf a jokey person. She was in fact easily amused and we used to exchange what seemed to us entertaining anecdotes or gossip and to laugh a good deal. Occasionally one saw her convulsed with laughter, with tears in her eyes, and at such moments one became aware that she was being watched, perhaps with a touch of anxiety, by her husband.[22]

After this first evening Plomer was often invited to parties at Tavistock Square. He presented the Woolfs with a Japanese ceramic dish for which Virginia wrote to thank him in April, and the next month he brought to the office of Hogarth Press the manuscript of his next book of verse, *The Family Tree*, which the Woolfs published later that year. It contained some of his best poems about Japan, and showed his mastery of a wide range of styles, from polished

epigrams to satirical pieces written in the jazz rhythms of Vachel
Lindsay and with the verbal inventiveness of Edith Sitwell. 'Two
Hotels' is an example:

Where stout hunters unbamboozled by the stoutest of bamboos
Suck soothing syrups up through straws or strut in patent-leather shoes,
While tourists of both sexes bandy-legged or bald as bandicoots
Hobnob with Hollywood's who's-who or dally with cheroots,
Stranger, look round: or stand and listen to the band.

Japan, they say that Kipling said, is 'not a sahib's land,'
But, si sahib requiris, circumspice in the well-planned grand
Brand new Hotel Magnificent whose highly polished floors
Reflect both millionaires and brassy pseudo-Jacobean cuspidors.
Descend with despatch to the Daimyo Dining Room—
'Takes the tired tourist back to stirring feudal days'—
Refashioned all in Burmese teak like an Aztec magnate's tomb
Well it has deserved a drunken baseball champion's praise . . .

The pergola pillars on the roof are hollow
Made of cement and steel and topped with whirring cowls
To ventilate the kitchens eighty feet below
And a corridor to the ballroom where a loud-voiced gossip prowls:
'She says they say they may go from here to San Diego
By train or aeroplane or straight across the blue—
On the fat wife of a dago seed-pearls look like small sago
But she certainly asserts he is a personage in Peru.'

During the months while his manuscript was being readied for
publication, Plomer saw the Woolfs often in London. One of Plomer's
unexpected talents particularly fascinated Virginia: his gift for
graphology. By chance she discovered that he could look for a few
moments at the handwriting of someone he had never met, and
divine from it, apparently intuitively, insights into the character of
the writer. Virginia tested him with envelopes addressed to her by
her friends, and was astonished and delighted by the amount of
detail and the accuracy of his diagnoses. (He rather feared this gift
in others, and his own carefully cultivated hand was an attempt
to avoid self-revelation. A Hungarian graphologist, shown a sample
of Plomer's script, said at once, 'He masks himself.')[23] Virginia
could not resist embarrassing Plomer, on one occasion, by handing
him an envelope from Dame Ethel Smyth, the bellicose composer,
when Dame Ethel was present. Plomer, not knowing the handwriting, was in the middle of some very uncomplimentary remarks

when a series of angry snorts from the composer stopped him in his tracks, badly ruffled. 'Was it not dangerously mischievous of V.W. to have made this situation possible?' he wrote years later.[24]

But he was to experience more of her mischief. In August 1929 the Woolfs invited him to spend a weekend at their country home, Monk's House in Rodmell. As Virginia had forewarned her sister Vanessa, he was driven from there to a party at the Bells' house, Charleston, on 19 August.[25] There he met Clive Bell and his companion Mary Hutchinson, Francis Birrell, Vanessa and her friend Duncan Grant, Edward Sackville-West and Roger Fry, and helped to celebrate Quentin Bell's[26] nineteenth birthday with fireworks.[27] Here too he saw Virginia's she-devil teasing side: he had unwisely repeated to her his claim to be related to Shakespeare's mother, Mary Arden, and Virginia introduced him to the party at Charleston by gleefully telling them that he was the direct descendant, not only of Shakespeare, but also of William Blake. Plomer was as embarrassed by this as he had been when the Japanese journalists emblazoned the story in headlines, but his attempts to explain only made matters worse, so that the whole party felt ill at ease and inclined to apologize to him later for her behaviour.[28]

Plomer, still only twenty-five and fresh from the isolation of Zululand and Japan, was delighted, and perhaps a little overwhelmed, to find himself among the remains of Bloomsbury, and he enjoyed the party in spite of this poor start. He cautiously said very little, and impressed everyone as shy and modest.[29] Clive Bell, boasting energetically of his latest romantic conquest, was too noisily heterosexual for his taste, but when Virginia questioned Plomer the next day, he tactfully would say nothing except that Clive had seemed 'inharmonious'. Virginia, having had the chance to sum him up (a process which never took her very long), had now definitely placed him among her friends, confiding to her diary that he was

A compressed inarticulate young man, thickly coated with a universal manner fit for all weather & people: tells a nice dry prim story; but has the wild eyes which I once noted in Tom [Eliot], & take to be the true index of what goes on within. Once or twice he almost cracked his crust— sitting on the stones this morning for instance.

I dont suppose you know how separate I feel myself from all my contemporaries.[30] I am afraid I was very inadequate last night (at

Charleston) ... William (he said the Mr was awkward) is notably trying to be like other people: to justify his life among natives & colonels, which has given him this composure. Beside him Julian [Bell] seemed a mere child, & Duncan [Grant] a contemporary ... He is a very self-contained independent young man, determined not to be rushed in any way, & having no money at all, he gave Nelly 5/- for a tip. I think he shows up well against the Raymonds [Raymond Mortimer[31]] & the Frankies [Francis Birrell]—is somehow solid; to their pinchbeck lustre.[32]

It is plain from these scraps of their conversation that Plomer had told Virginia Woolf of his sense of alienation from English life and his determination to become part of it, his 'trying to be like other people', which was very like his attempts to blend with the Japanese. His 'universal manner' was the mask, perfected in Japan, behind which he attempted to conceal himself, and for all the acuteness with which she pounced on occasional cracks in what she called his crust, Virginia Woolf was to try in vain to penetrate the mystery.

Through his contact with the Woolfs, Plomer rapidly made a number of intellectual friends; it was through her and Leonard that he met Lytton Strachey, Vita Sackville-West and her husband Harold Nicolson, T. S. Eliot, Maynard Keynes, Desmond MacCarthy, and Lady Ottoline Morrell.[33] Virginia told them that Plomer was going to be a great novelist, and they were keen to meet him and glad to be of help to him if they could. The links that Leonard Woolf, Desmond MacCarthy, and Eliot had with literary journals meant that Plomer began to receive requests to review books for the *Nation & Athenaeum* and the *New Statesman*, and to publish poems in the *Criterion*.

The Woolfs were not Plomer's sole resource, however, even at this early stage. Several friends from his South African past had established themselves in London, and he quickly made contact with them again. The Afrikaner painter Enslin du Plessis, whom he had last seen in Johannesburg in 1920, was now working as a journalist in the Fleet Street offices of the South African company Argus Newspapers, and Plomer went to see him as soon as he had settled into his parents' house in Pinner. Du Plessis had retained his charm, and he and Plomer renewed their friendship at once. Through Du Plessis Plomer heard that Van der Post had been living in England since 1927, that he had married, had a son, and was eking out a precarious living in journalism. Du Plessis also introduced Plomer to a close friend of Van der Post and himself, a talented Frenchman named René Janin.

Janin was the son of a famous French general and also had aristocratic French relations; through them he had secured a rather unremunerative position in a large London company that imported coffee, and he was leading a very active social life in London. In France he had lived extravagantly and had kept a mistress; but, sent to Heidelberg university, he had tried the homosexuality so common among German students and, in Stephen Spender's words, had been converted.[34] His father had for a time been the French military attaché at St Petersburg, and Janin had many friends in diplomatic circles. Elegant, sophisticated, and polyglot, he seemed to know everyone and to be invited everywhere. Strongly attracted to Van der Post at first sight, he had befriended the young Afrikaner when he came to England and had shown him around London, introducing him to his friends in the diplomatic corps, to English aristocrats, to a man who had known Proust, to Egyptians of ancient family, and to writers and painters. Virginia Woolf, who was rather taken with Janin, described him as 'a thin skinned Frog all gesture & wrinkle; a coffee merchant ex diplomat; despises society; stories of Colefax,[35] French Embassy'.[36] He was a dilettante, but a charming one: 'He enriched my life, and he was a marvellous friend to me,' Van der Post was to say years later, adding that Janin's homosexuality had eventually come between them.[37]

Van der Post returned to his small flat in Hampstead[38] one evening, having walked all the way from the city in order to save the bus fare, when the door was opened to him by Janin instead of his wife. 'Ha, mon cher Laurens!' exclaimed Janin. 'I've brought a surprise home for you tonight, you can't possibly guess who it is.' Van der Post entered to find Plomer hiding behind the door. The two embraced warmly, and after that saw each other often in London or, occasionally, in Pinner.[39] Van der Post, himself living from hand to mouth at this time, was struck by the threadbare impoverishment of the Plomers' house at Pinner; he was later to say that they were so poor as to be an embarrassment to Plomer. Van der Post rather liked Plomer's parents; he described Edythe (who was suffering from a heart condition) as 'a darling woman, very sensitive, very cultivated and very nice', while Charles struck him as 'straightforward and uncomplicated'. Having sympathy for both of them, he regretted the enmity in which they lived, and attributed Plomer's homosexuality in part to it. 'In many homosexuals I have known, their inner fragmentation or homo-sexual compulsion is rooted in this area where the father and mother live in a state of enmity . . . they have to choose sides, and when they choose the mother they seem to choose the completely feminine pattern,' he was to say.[40]

Van der Post had sensed even during the voyage with Plomer to Japan that Plomer was trying to remould himself as an Englishman, and he was soon aware that in England Plomer was doing all he could to blend with the population and to put down roots in this new soil. Shortly after their reunion in 1929, Plomer invited Van der Post to accompany him on a trip to Radwell church in Hertfordshire, where some of the Plomers had been buried in the seventeenth century. Van der Post was later to describe this visit as a return to the spirit of Plomer's ancestors in the Chinese sense, a ritual of change, 'a real return of his spirit, identification and commitment to England'.[41]

It was very shortly after this pilgrimage (which may have been one of several he made to places connected with the Plomers and the Brownes) that Plomer did an extraordinary thing: he altered the pronunciation of his surname. All his life his father pro-nounced the name to rhyme with Homer, and so did Plomer's brother Peter.[42] But Plomer passed the word round to his South African friends that from now on his surname was to rhyme with 'rumour'. He pretended to believe that the origin of the name might be 'le Plumer', meaning a *plumier*, or worker with feathers, and that this justified the pronunciation. In fact the name originally signified a plumber, and Plomer knew this well enough.[43] Why did he change the pronunciation? 'Pronounced to rhyme with Rumour, one can plume oneself on having a light touch rather than a leaden one,' he joked.[44] But it remains an odd thing to have done at the age of twenty-six. Perhaps it signified a desire to break with his past and make a new start in England; perhaps it symbolized the gulf that had grown between himself and his detested father, so that they could no longer agree even on the pronunciation of their common name. Both motivations are possible, and both would indicate the extent to which Plomer was trying to redefine himself on his return to England.

There are two other indications that the change in pronunciation was not a whim, but reflected an attempt to clarify his view of

who or what he was. In the late 1930s Plomer adopted the
pseudonym 'Robert Pagan', and used it extensively in signing work
for *Penguin New Writing*. Many writers have used pen-names, but
Plomer took his to extraordinary lengths. He fabricated and
published an elaborate biographical sketch: 'Robert Pagan is of
Scottish descent on his father's side; his mother was a Greek from
the island of Zante. He was educated in England, and has travelled
widely, first as a seaman, and later, as companion and secretary
to an invalid American millionaire. . . .'[45] Thereafter, for years, he
spoke in his letters as if Pagan were a real friend of his. Long after
the matter had ceased to be amusing, friends who knew well that
Pagan was imaginary would be told, 'Poor Bob is overworked this
week,' 'Bob is enjoying doing his latest article,' or 'I'll tell Bob
what you say.' Pagan took on a life of his own, in a way that is
reminiscent of William Sharp's Fiona Macleod.

Another curious piece of evidence regarding what one might call
Plomer's identity crisis is his fascination with Dr Gruber. Something
about Plomer's manner made people occasionally take him for a
doctor, and shortly before the war a refugee couple stopped him in
the street, crying delightedly, '*Ach! Sind sie wirklich Doktor Gruber?*'
The incident stayed in Plomer's mind, and he went over and
over the implications. What would it be like to be the unknown Dr
Gruber? Later, when he wrote a poem unlike his previous work,
he felt surprised and uneasy: 'Somebody else seemed to have written
it . . . Was I perhaps Doctor Gruber? And was Doctor Gruber
perhaps a poet?'[46] His own disturbing range of potential selves
troubled him enough to make him adopt Dr Gruber as an *alter ego*,
and when he came to write his second volume of autobiography,
eventually published as *At Home*, the working title he used was
'Doctor Gruber'. In retrospect the change of pronunciation of his
surname has considerable significance.

Among the South African friends who had to make a mental
note of the new pronunciation was Teddy Wolfe, who had settled
permanently in London and was trying, without much success, to
make a living from his painting, which Plomer now thought 'gaudy,
lively, fluent, Jewish painting—the same as ever, only a bit more
so'.[47] On 20 June 1929 Plomer took Du Plessis to see Wolfe, who
gave Du Plessis advice about painting, and proposed to paint a
large portrait of Plomer, though he did not start it until Plomer
came to live in London, and it was not finished until the end of

1929. 'It is rather like me, but not a masterpiece of a picture,' Plomer was to write of it to Van der Post on 12 November 1929, adding, 'Enslin I believe describes it as a mixture of Puck & Buddha!'[48] Du Plessis, Wolfe, Janin, and Plomer occasionally dined together, and the other three seem to have been rather in awe of Plomer, as glimpses in Du Plessis's letters to Van der Post show:

I have seen Plomer once or twice. He, Janin & Teddy Wolfe dined with me—an amusing evening partly taken up . . . by a dissecting duel between Janin and Plomer. I as usual acted as spectator & was able to see the transformation of William's features into that steel mask you told me of. He is a dangerous fellow when he begins to feel & will burn everything that bars the way to what he regards as the truth—friends as well as enemies, household gods as well as forest devils & Janin likes him or rather is immensely interested in him but is a bit suspicious of his English fanaticism. The two have little in common except intelligence & that in the case of René is catlike ready to pat or leap out and scratch, in the case of William more controlled and far more devastating when roused to action.[49]

Another South African friend much in his thoughts at this time was Roy Campbell. Campbell had come to England late in 1926, and had taken a cottage in the Sussex village of Weald, where he had met Vita Sackville-West, whose large house, Long Barn, was nearby. Vita had fallen in love with Mary Campbell, and the two had had a passionate affair, the pursuit of which was made simpler when the unsuspecting Roy Campbell had accepted Vita's offer to accommodate him and his family in her gardener's cottage. When Campbell discovered what was going on, his rage was almost insane; he threatened both Mary and Vita with violence, and then quitted Long Barn for the south of France, where Mary and his children eventually joined him when Vita grew tired of the affair.[50] Campbell was subsequently to revenge himself on the Nicolsons and their friends in his savagely amusing satire *The Georgiad*.[51] Plomer's contacts with the Woolfs and their circle increasingly put him in the camp of Campbell's enemies; he had met Vita through Virginia, and over the next few years was to grow friendly with Harold Nicolson; partly as a result, his close friendship with Campbell was never to be renewed. As early as August 1929 he was telling Virginia that he disliked Campbell's pose as a romantic he-man, instancing the way Campbell used to fly a kite from a fishing-rod at Sezela.[52] Mary Campbell visited Plomer in London in

October 1929, but though the Campbells repeatedly invited him to stay with them at Martigues, where they had settled by then ('We have a room here for your permanent, or periodical, use—as you choose'),[53] and though he repeatedly promised to come, he never went.

René Janin now took Plomer up as he had Van der Post earlier, and began introducing him to a circle of grand friends and some low-life ones. It was through him that Plomer met the orientalist Arthur Waley[54] in September 1929. Although Waley had become famous for his translations of Chinese and Japanese poetry, he had never visited the Far East, and Plomer was able to provide him with much firsthand information about contemporary conditions in those countries. After reading Plomer's poetry, Waley judged that Plomer had been much influenced by modern Japanese writers, an opinion that pleased Plomer. Waley struck him as sad-faced, sharp-witted, and greatly undervalued as a poet. Years later he remembered Waley crouching silently on the floor at some Mayfair literary party in the 1930s, and thought the situation somehow characteristic of the man.[55] The acquaintance begun in this way endured until Waley's death in 1966.

Janin provided Plomer with other interesting glimpses of London life. On 28 June 1929 the two of them went to a party given by the Baroness d'Erlanger, to hear the three Sitwells[56] declaiming Edith's work. The occasion proved embarrassing for Plomer, whose growing talent for blending with the background completely failed him:

Imagine the sensation when I appeared in ordinary clothes in the drawing room at 139 Piccadilly at 9.30!! I was the only person who was not dressed. But I didn't do it from bravado—it was a piece of pure carelessness and bad manners on my part, & I was rather ashamed of being so stupid. The people were very grand—e.g. the Laverys, Mosleys, (etc), but mostly more diamonds than brains ... The Sitwells were not terribly impressive, though Edith has a remarkable control of her voice.[57]

Janin also seems to have taken Plomer to various night-clubs, boxing- and wrestling-rings, public bath-houses, and bars where homosexuals gathered in London, and he was soon a connoisseur of such places.[58]

Early in August 1929 he was delighted to get a fan letter from E. M. Forster,[59] a writer he much admired, and about whom he had heard a good deal from Virginia Woolf. Forster, *en route* to South Africa on a tour with the British Association, had read Plomer's short story 'Ula Masondo', and wrote to tell Plomer how much he had enjoyed it. Plomer replied cordially, and on Forster's return to England the two met at one of Virginia Woolf's parties and soon became fast friends—a friendship that was to endure until Forster's death in 1970. Forster made a habit of calling on Plomer when he was in London; he found Plomer's gaiety and wit, his endless flow of amusing stories, and his capacity for friendship deeply attractive. He admired Plomer as much for his poetry as his prose, and wrote to John Lehmann, in December 1940, 'Auden & Wm. Plomer are the poets I like best.'[60] Just as important, Forster's formidable mother, Lily, preferred Plomer to any of her son's other friends. When Plomer, years later, wrote an article on Forster in which he took him to task for his shabby dress, Lily Forster exclaimed with satisfaction, 'There! You see what Mr. Plomer says. How often have I told you, Morgie dear, that you really ought to brush your coat?'[61] Forster was impressed by Plomer's frenzied boy-hunting, wittily remarking to another friend that he had made Plomer's acquaintance only because he chanced to catch him in an 'unguardeed moment'.[62] Plomer, for his part, thought Forster both wise and practical. When Plomer's mother made her will, Plomer turned to Forster for advice about the matter; when he had trouble with his homosexual friends, it was often to Forster that he confided his difficulties.

An equally significant friendship, again initiated by a fan letter, also developed in 1929. While still in Japan, Plomer had received a most enthusiastic letter from an Englishman, Anthony Butts,[63] who was then living in Sicily, and who had read *Turbott Wolfe*. He had been particularly taken, he wrote, with Plomer's analysis of relations between whites and Africans. Butts himself was strongly negrophile and was convinced that European culture was on its last legs. *Turbott Wolfe*, he fancied, tended to the same conclusions. Plomer kept in contact with him from Japan, and they arranged to meet in London in May 1929.

Anthony Butts proved to be an odd and striking figure. Although only twenty-nine he was already completely bald; he was slightly built, with a rather weak chin, very small ears, and an upturned nose; but his most remarkable features were his eyes, wide-set, very large, china-blue, and slightly hypnotic. His behaviour was

eccentric, extravagant, and self-destructive, and several people who
were themselves eccentrics (Lady Ottoline Morrell among them)
thought him an outrageous buffoon. Virginia Woolf compared him
to a jerboa, because of the way he held his hands.[64] He was
contemptuous of all authority and all conventions, and Plomer,
himself innately anarchical but careful to avoid attention, found
Butts fascinating. Plomer also liked Butts's sense of humour, and
thought his endless string of anecdotes about his remarkable family
intensely amusing. (It was characteristic of them that his mother,
Mrs Colville-Hyde, once took a lobster to the chemist to be
chloroformed.) That Butts was, in Plomer's words, 'rich, lively, and
without responsibilities or clearly defined ambitions'[65] added to his
attractiveness in Plomer's eyes. Butts had studied painting under
Sickert, who thought Butts the most gifted student he had known;
in spite of this Butts was never to make anything of his talent,
though Plomer greatly admired his work. Butts was in fact a
moneyed dilettante who painted and wrote plays with equal
enthusiasm, and whose main aim in life was to enjoy it as much
as possible; in this, Plomer was ready to join him.

During the months he lived with his parents at Pinner, Plomer
worked steadily at the novel on Japan which he had begun the
previous year in Tokyo with such high hopes, and of which parts
were eventually published as *Sado*. He had several set-backs with
this, and struggled with it as he had never had to struggle with
Turbott Wolfe. In August 1929 he destroyed 50,000 words of it,
writing gloomily to Van der Post that he hoped to preserve a short
story from the debris.[66] His correspondence reveals few details of
this decision to cut so much, but it is interesting to speculate why
a writer of such experience (he had by now published five books)[67]
should have felt he had gone so far wrong as to need to destroy
more than half a novel.

Sado was to be the first novel in which Plomer approached the
subject of homosexuality head-on; the hero, an Englishman named
Vincent Lucas, has a relationship with a Japanese named Sado
Masaji, a relationship clearly modelled on that of Plomer with
Fukuzawa. At the same time Vincent is loved by an exiled
Englishwoman, Iris Komatsu, and the novel is an examination of
his responses to his male and female friends. Nothing illustrates
more plainly than *Sado* the extent to which Plomer was at this
time trying to determine his own sexual preferences, and the novel

reaches no clear conclusion. It may not be too fanciful to suppose that his struggles to finish *Sado* reflect his personal search for identity at this time. In the novel Vincent Lucas is advised by a visiting European lady (clearly modelled on Anna von Schubert) to return to Europe. 'What's all this travelling for?' she asks him, adding 'What you've got to find is yourself, and you may just as well conduct the search at home.'⁶⁸ The writing of the novel constituted part of Plomer's search, and it was clearly not an easy one.

Early in September 1929 he thought he had finished the book (though it was to go through several transformations before publication), and promptly decided to leave his parents' house in Pinner and take a room of his own in London. He had not been happy at Pinner, which he never regarded as a 'home', either for himself or for his parents, who now gave up the house and moved to the Continent for the winter, in the hope that life in France and Spain would prove cheaper than life in England. Plomer's books were bringing in very little money (his income for the whole of 1929 was £155),⁶⁹ but he was now writing occasional reviews, and he was also producing a regular article, on any subject he chose, for the *Cape Times*, thanks to the kindness of Van der Post, who had returned to South Africa and joined the staff of that paper. It was largely the *Cape Times* income (four guineas per article)⁷⁰ that allowed him to move into 6 Pembridge Villas in Bayswater, a large, cheerful mid-Victorian house run by a pretty young woman whom Plomer in his autobiography calls Beryl Fernandez. Her name was in fact Sybil da Costa, but she also went under the name of Sybil Starr. Plomer wrote to Van der Post on 3 September 1929:

As you see, I am now in London. About 5 minutes walk from Notting Hill Gate & Hyde Park, in a good room just over an arterial road with incessant noise. Whether the racket will harden or destroy my nerves only time will show. My landlady is a jewess called Sybil Starr which strikes me as a very amusing name. She is quite sympathetic, & I think we shall get on all right. It is very expensive, but I hope to keep going—largely on the strength of your 'Cape Times' arrangement—without getting into the bankruptcy court.⁷¹

Plomer's prediction that he and his landlady would 'get on all right' proved fatally accurate. She was a lonely woman in much need of a confidant, and she found Plomer a most sympathetic listener. He soon knew a good deal about her. Sybil de Costa had a six-year-old daughter, and a furtive, dark-eyed *de facto* husband whom Plomer seldom saw but who seemed to terrify his wife. None the less she was, in Plomer's well-chosen phrase, madly in love with him. He was James Achew, an American with Red Indian blood, who for reasons of his own went by the name of James Starr. He was a violent man, whose insane jealousy of his wife's friends had caused him to assault her several times, but she refused to go to the police or to leave him. He appears to have resented any man who so much as spoke to her, and once Plomer moved into the house, Achew's passions rapidly came to a head.

At 4 a.m. on the morning of Sunday, 24 November 1929, Achew locked the door of the bedroom in which his wife lay asleep, and attacked her with a razor. She sprang from the bed, terribly wounded, and battered at the locked door; Achew followed her, and when she tried to fend him off, slashed madly at her hands, arms, and face. Her daughter, who slept in the same room, awoke in terror to see Achew drag her mother screaming to the bed, kneel on her, and cut her throat. Again the woman broke away from him, snatched up the child, and holding her to her breast like a blood-soaked shield, made for the door. This time she was able to burst out of the room and climb the stairs towards the room of a woman friend who helped her run the boarding-house, before she fell dying across her child. Achew now went looking for Plomer, but found his room empty; by a lucky chance he was away for the weekend. The murderer then tried to kill himself, but was prevented by the arrival of the police, and was taken into custody.[72]

Plomer, returning to London the next afternoon, saw handbills announcing 'SHOCKING BAYSWATER TRAGEDY', and had the unpleasant task of helping to remove the copious traces of the crime so as to spare the victim's woman friend's feelings; the bedroom resembled a shambles, and according to Virginia Woolf's account Plomer had to clean scraps of flesh from the carpet.[73] Despite this, he affected to be little moved by the death of Sybil Starr, refused Du Plessis's offer to put him up so that he could get away from what the papers took to calling 'the murder house' (for the murder had become a nine days' wonder), and even gave a party there. To this party (on 12 December, to celebrate his birthday two days before) he invited the Woolfs, Janin, Butts and his mother, Teddy Wolfe, Lilian Bowes-Lyon (a poet and cousin of the then Duchess of York and a friend of Janin), and Du Plessis, who gave a lively account of the proceedings in a letter to Van der Post, remarking with pleased surprise on Virginia's short skirts, which revealed a shapely pair of legs, and on Butts's mother, Mrs Colville-Hyde, 'with powdered hair & face, ear-rings the size of record hailstones & an enormous crimson artificial flower in her robustious bosom'.[74]

But even the liveliness of the party failed to exorcize the memory of what had happened, and Plomer's imagination went to work on the scenes. He told Virginia Woolf that murders 'were not his line as a novelist',[75] but the truth was that from childhood he had been fascinated by crimes of violence. He did not attend Achew's trial at the Old Bailey in January 1930, but he followed it carefully in the papers (*The Times* carried detailed reports). Achew was initially sentenced to death, on 17 January 1930, but was reprieved on grounds of insanity and committed to Broadmoor. Plomer continued to brood on the murder, and his broodings bore fruit two years later when he wrote his next novel, *The Case is Altered*.

He who had travelled so much in earlier years was becoming unsettled again, partly under the influence of Anthony Butts, who was always ready to fly off around the world at a moment's notice. Butts and Plomer were intimates by the end of 1929, and when Butts suggested that the two of them should pay a visit to Mexico and the West Indies with Butts paying all the costs, Plomer was ready to agree.[76] The scheme eventually fell through, but Plomer's roots in England remained very shallow.

Early in December 1929 he received flattering proof that he had made a certain impression in Japan, when he was offered the chair of English literature at the Imperial University in Tokyo. He wrote to Leonard Woolf, 'I am offered a salary of £900–£1000 a year (which is more than I've ever been offered before or am ever likely to be offered again) as well as travelling expenses both ways and the chance to make an additional £200–£300 without much effort.'[77] Though the money attracted him, he was determined not to return to Japan, which he now thought of as a part of his past that was closed for ever, and he wrote without much hesitation to decline the offer. 'What it is to be a beggar *and* a chooser!' he remarked.[78] Peter Quennell, poet, historian, and editor, took the post instead.

Early in 1930 Plomer moved from Pembridge Villas to a single room at 6 Monmouth Place, not far away and rather cheaper. He was now extremely friendly with Anthony Butts, was working in a rather desultory way on another novel (never to be finished and the subject now impossible to recover), and was increasingly giving himself up to a life of pleasure. When Roy and Mary Campbell came to London for a brief visit in February 1930, Campbell and Plomer found that they had drifted apart decisively. Plomer took Campbell to an exhibition of Wolfe's pictures, which Campbell disliked; worse, he said so in a loud voice to anyone who would listen. Plomer also took Campbell to a party at which almost every guest was homosexual, and again Campbell found himself out of place. To get his own back, Campbell, who still had no suspicion of Plomer's sexual orientation, took him to a boxing-match at the Comrades Hall in Camden Town, and was rather surprised to find that he thoroughly enjoyed the display of masculine physique and physical violence. Afterwards Plomer wrote to Van der Post:

I am sorry to say a great gulf is now fixed between Roy & me, although I hope our mutual respect is essentially undiminished. It is hard to explain all the facts of the case in a letter without causing misunderstanding. The main difficulty is that I don't share his taste for low life, & he doesn't share mine for something a little more discriminating. I saw very little of them comparatively when they were here, as they spent all their pub-crawling with people I dislike. But Roy's new book [*Adamastor*] will be out very soon, & judging from the MS which I have seen, I should say it will be pretty good.[79]

Plomer was now moving almost entirely in homosexual circles. Having familiarized himself with the gay bars of London, he made trips to other British cities with Butts or Janin to sample life there; in April 1930, for instance, he visited Cardiff, and there 'got to know some Swedish sailors and something more', as he put it in a later letter.[80]

Early in 1930 Janin put Plomer in touch with a young poet who was secretary of the university English club at Oxford, and who invited both Plomer and Virginia Woolf to lecture to it. Virginia declined, but Plomer travelled to Oxford early in March to deliver a lecture on modern Japanese literature to a small group of undergraduates. The occasion was of interest chiefly because of the friendship that resulted between Plomer and the young man who had invited him; his name was Stephen Spender.[81] Spender was at this time just twenty years old and had written very little, but he was determined to dedicate himself to a life of art. He was tall, fair-haired, and good-looking, and his naïvety, shyness, and tendency to hero-worship writers older than himself attracted Plomer to him, as did his bisexuality. Janin had previously invited Plomer and Spender to meet each other at Janin's flat, where Spender had sat in silence and listened to Plomer telling Janin of the necessity of presenting a mask to the world. Spender later wrote of Plomer, in his autobiography *World Within World*:

His clear-cut features, his smoothly brushed-back fair hair, the faintly ironical yet sparkling smile on his lips, had something of the mask, a certain impassivity imposed on most unoriental features. Through that slightly bronzed face, hewn as it were from a hard light-coloured wood, very clear blue eyes looked out at the world. During the coming years I was to see how the effect of his 'mask,' which concealed his feelings, was to give him exceptional sympathy for the difficulties of others and a capacity to ignore his own troubles or, if they were discussed, to treat them with a lightness which had the effect of objectifying them.[82]

Plomer travelled down to Oxford with Janin, and Spender in later years recalled that almost their first conversation had consisted of fascinated speculation on the part of Plomer and Janin as to whether Van der Post, with whom Janin was much infatuated, was bisexual.[83] (He was not.) Plomer stayed in Oxford for two days, and during that period saw a good deal of Spender; the two were to remain friends until Plomer's death. Through Spender Plomer met W. H. Auden[84] and Christopher Isherwood.[85]

Within a year of landing in England, then, Plomer had built up a circle of acquaintances who included most of the outstanding literary figures of the time: the established names, ranging from Virginia Woolf to E. M. Forster and T. S. Eliot, and those who were still to come to prominence, including Spender, Auden, and Isherwood. These friendships were extremely useful in providing him with reviewing work and with outlets for articles and poems; from now on he tended to publish his poetry almost as soon as he wrote it, in the *New Statesman*, the *Nation*, *Criterion*, *Life & Letters*, the *Saturday Review*, and the *New Adelphi*. He was soon getting as much reviewing work as he could cope with, and was building up a reputation as a sensitive critic. In later years he was to deny ever having belonged to a literary group, and strictly speaking this is true; but it is equally true that homosexuality was the bond between himself and many of his literary friends at this time and for the rest of his life. Years later, writing to John Lehmann about 'exclusive literary orthodoxies', he remarked:

Somebody ought to write a study of this point, noting en route how many contemp: English writers are sons of clergymen—e.g. Wystan [Auden], Cecil [Day-Lewis], Rex Warner, G. Grigson, etc etc—how many have been schoolmasters & Communists, how many still sort other writers into sheep and goats—including the orthodox Christians—Waugh, Greene, Eliot, etc. Nor are the liberal anarchists (e.g. Herbert Read) always *wholly* un-dogmatic . . .[86]

Among these cliques he does not specifically mention homosexuals, but the reference to schoolmasters and Communists carries a homosexual subtext, since for writers like Auden, Spender, and Isherwood, left-wing politics offered the chance to get close to the working class that so attracted them sexually. 'Sex with the working class of course had political connotations,' Spender was to say years later. 'It was a way in which people with left-wing sympathies could feel they were really getting in contact with the working class.'[87] Plomer was largely unconcerned about politics, but he certainly found the homosexual link a useful one in the literary world in which he now moved with increasing confidence. A brilliant literary career seemed to be before him. To all outward appearances, he had made a remarkable success of putting down roots in his readopted country, and of settling down after the energetic rovings of his youth. Appearances, however, are notoriously misleading. The gypsy years were only just beginning.

9. *Maggots in the Mushroom*
1930–1932

ON 18 May 1930 Plomer and Anthony Butts left England for what they thought would be a three months' tour of Europe. Butts's earlier scheme to tour Mexico and the Caribbean with Plomer had proved over-ambitious, in part because his habitual extravagance was putting an increasing strain on his mother's bank account, but he seems to have thought that he could afford to take Plomer to the Continent. There was no question of Plomer's paying his own way, for his total income in 1930 was only £112.[1] They stopped briefly in Paris and Bonn, where Plomer used a letter of introduction from Stephen Spender to get to know the German critic Ernst Robert Curtius, whom Plomer thought the most important judge of literature in Europe, before spending some interesting days in Berlin, then the homosexual centre of Europe. Here they were entertained by Sally Coote, a friend of Spender's brother, who showed them the conventional sights of the city, and by a friend of Janin's, Möring, who conducted them through some of the hundreds of homosexual bars and night-clubs, including one called 'The Sign of the Cross', where they witnessed an elaborate enema act which Plomer found revolting. Möring himself he described as 'a wretched whimpering little fairy'.[2] On balance though, he found what he called 'the homo side of Berlin' extremely curious and interesting.

From Berlin he and Butts travelled by rail, via Milan and Verona, to Venice, where they spent a week or two, before moving on to Athens, where they settled into a comfortable hotel. Greece had long had a particular attraction for English homosexuals. Both Plomer and Butts had learned Greek at school, and their classical education provided them with something akin to a homosexual ideology. Either might have written, 'I saw myself ... in the tradition of the Classic Greeks, surrounded and supported by all the famous homosexuals of history.'[3] Plomer was delighted with the beauty of the country and its male population, whom he found sleepy, stupid, and seductive. By 4 July 1930 Plomer was writing to Stephen Spender:

We are more or less settled in Athens for the time being, & are both working—&, I may add, playing. I can't tell you how much I like this country. The light & air are marvellous. The climate is so far ideal. I get plenty of swimming which I passionately enjoy. The sun always shines. There are more men than women, & whereas England is a land of male women, Greece is a land of female men. As far as I personally am concerned, I think I am likely to stay here a long time.[4]

One of the poems he wrote shortly after his arrival in Athens, 'The Levantine', finely expresses his determination to admire what he saw as the exhaustion and corruption of Greece:

> A mouth like old silk soft with use,
> The weak chin of a dying race,
> Eyes that know all and look at naught—
> > Disease, depravity, disgrace,
> > Are all united in that face ...
>
> With Socrates as ancestor,
> And rich Byzantium in his veins,
> What if this weakling does not work?
> > He need not even take the pains
> > To blow away his dreaming brains,
>
> But drinks his coffee, smokes and yawns
> While new-rich empires rise and fall:
> His blood is bluer than their heaven,
> > Poor, but no poorer than them all,
> > And has no principles at all.[5]

Plomer began work on an autobiographical novel to which he gave the working title 'Memoirs of an Emigrant', writing it in the mornings in a city park.[6] Much of the day, however, he spent swimming or sleeping, and seldom alone. He had always been attracted to those whom he considered his social inferiors, whether Zulus or his Japanese pupils. He and Butts had chosen Greece because, as in Berlin, it was notoriously easy to find homosexual partners there. For some weeks Plomer led an intensely active, promiscuous life, joking to Stephen Spender, 'I quite agree with your remarks about going to bed with bores. Athens is so badly lighted that it is very easy to do.'[7] Presently, however, he focused his affections on a single friend, and began a passionate affair with a good-looking blond sailor named Nicky. Spender was the only one of his English friends to be told about this at the time:

First of all, I am living with a Greek sailor who is about the best lover I have ever had. It is not simply that he is what the German lady called 'a wonderful sexer,' but he is very pretty & has the nature of an angel—a fallen one of course, a cheerful and depraved one. There is a real affection between us. Every afternoon I go swimming—never less than a mile—it is the only form of exercise I really enjoy. Every morning I sit in the ex-Royal garden with my little notebook.

   Greece exactly suits me, & all being well, I shall stay here a long time. There is less nervous strain than in any place almost that I have ever been in.[8]

'There is a real affection between us': the reserve of the words scarcely conveys the reality of Plomer's feelings for Nicky. He seems to have given all his heart to this affair, and to have had no thoughts for the future; he was happy as only human beings in love for the first time can be. In his autobiographies, while careful not to name or specify the gender of his companion ('an inhabitant of Athens with whose physical beauty I had become infatuated'), he was to give lyrical descriptions of swimming with Nicky in the Bay of Phaleron and embracing him in a sailing boat that an 'old triton' guided over the sparkling waves.[9] It was for Nicky, too, that he wrote one of his most evocative love poems, 'Three Pinks':

> Crisp hair with a faint smell like honey
> Hived by fierce bees under a fallen column in a pinewood,
> A liquor of wild oleanders in a limestone gully—
> Although it is summer there is snow on Parnassus—
> Crisp hair awoke me, brushing my cheek ...
>
>   Still half awake
> We shall get up together from the bed
> And with arms interlaced cross to the window
> (The early morning is cool and heavenly),
> Then standing mutely look out over a quiet
> Aspect of Athens, rococo houses and stucco
> With a cypress or two in the middle distance
> Like marks of exclamation at such tranquillity.
>
> We'll observe through the dry and timeless air of Attica
> In which there is no nostalgia
> The pepper-tree garden where last night by full moon
> An old woman disturbed our intimacy
> To sell us three pinks with long stems.

See now, the Acropolis is still unsunned.
Forestall dawn with yet one more kiss,
Last of the night or first of the day—
Whichever way one may chance to choose to regard it.[10]

Even now his conversion to homosexuality was far from
untroubled. This is apparent in his sensitivity to Roy Campbell's
suggestions that Plomer's Greek stay had something sinister about
it: 'I suspect you are taking a class of young English girls or boys
round ancient Greece,'[11] Campbell wrote jestingly, and was puzzled
and taken aback to receive a long, irritable reply. He was soon
apologizing to Plomer: 'We did not imagine there was any mystery
in your voyage. It was all a silly joke on our part and because you
responded we went on hammering at it, because you got so
serious.'[12] But for Plomer, deeply sensitive about the matter, it was
not a joke at all. Fearful of losing his heterosexual friends, he set
about trying to convince them that bisexuality was necessary for
many artists, and that heterosexuals were for the most part
frustrated homosexuals themselves. His letter of 11 August 1930
to Enslin du Plessis is typical of those received by several of his
friends (including Van der Post) at this time:

I hope you won't mind my saying that I hope you're not going to develop
the mania that Roy & Wyndham Lewis[13] have about homosexuality. I am
always extremely suspicious of such an attitude, which usually comes
from frustration. I have reason to know that both Roy & Lewis have
experimented with their own sex, & I cannot but feel that their present
violence is quite pathological. They both protest too much. Then very often
one feels that the 'normal' man's smoking-room stories about buggery
come from an envy of the bugger's lack of responsibility & ability to live
without a taboo he himself obeys. We've had quite enough of the he-man
stuff from empire-builders & others—it is often mildly funny, but has very
little to do with the arts. The artist who makes a song about his maleness
(or her femaleness, as the case may be) is lacking in honesty, for it is a
platitude that every artist is in a sense bi-sexual. May I say without offence
that the charm of your painting lies very much in a wholly feminine
delicacy & lightness of touch? So far from condemning it, one makes that
the basis of one's admiration for your gifts.

Don't imagine that I am taking the trouble to defend homosexuality—
for I don't consider that it needs any defence ... I only discuss the point
at length because I don't like to see you in the role of killjoy when we
have enjoyed so many jokes together; & because as a somewhat effeminate

person myself I am naturally bored by the violence and intolerance of soi-disant he-men, & am slow to believe that you can find it sympathetic.[14]

A man secure in his sexuality does not feel the need to defend it at such length and with such passion, while denying that he is defending it.

It was against this background that Plomer was trying to write his autobiographical novel. He was increasingly troubled by that sense of not belonging anywhere of which he had spoken to Virginia Woolf—'I don't suppose you know how separate I feel myself from all my contemporaries'—and, connected with this, a sense of not really knowing who he was. Major elements in his sense of alienation were his loathing of his father, the feelings of abandonment he had suffered as a child in England, his consciousness of being unalterably *déraciné* as a result of his experiences in Africa and Japan (now compounded by his Greek sojourn), and, above all, his insecurity about his sexual orientation. His uncertainty about his identity showed in such outward signs as his insistence on the importance of wearing a social mask, his careful handwriting, which he intended as a mask of his character, and even his alteration of the pronunciation of his surname: all these divisions he was now trying to work out in his new novel. Years later, in an important passage in his autobiography, he was able to analyse clearly enough what the problem had been, though even then he could not bring himself to list his sexuality among the forces that combined to paralyse his creative faculty at this time:

I had come to a point where, in my myth-making, I was impelled to try and resolve some of the conflicts and harmonize some of the contrasts of my dispersed earlier years. What happens when a child does not grow up in a settled surrounding, in a fixed home, in the bosom of its own family, and constantly surrounded by other families of the same race, class, tradition, and habits as its own? When it finds itself controlled, cherished, or ignored by various kinds of grown-ups of differing social backgrounds, beliefs, and habits? When it has been involved in a series of disjointed contacts with different worlds, like scenes from different plays made to succeed one another but not composing a single play? It is likely to have been over-stimulated and un-settled. It will have learnt in some ways too much, too soon, and too superficially. Precocious and independent in some ways, it will be backward and unsure of itself in others, because it has missed the steadying, ripening effect of a fixed environment, a single tradition, and a homogeneous society. It may resemble a plant too often transplanted, putting out what flowers it can while it can. From such a child I was still evolving, and in the fiction I was trying to compose I was being too ambitious, straining such talent as I possessed, and aiming at something beyond my scope. I had miscalculated—but did not yet know it.[15]

While Plomer was happy with Nicky, his novel seemed to him to go well, and he loved the lotus-eating life he led in Athens. He carried on an active correspondence, not only with his friends and family in England, but also with writers such as Ivan Bunin, on whom he was subsequently to write an article for the *Spectator*.[16] He thought Bunin's story *The Gentleman from San Francisco* the best short story of the century, and Bunin influenced him more than any other writer of short stories except Maupassant.[17] Plomer liked to feel that he was part of the cultural life of Europe even though living a quiet, isolated life, and he resisted suggestions that an even more distant home might be found for them. He and Butts (who was involved with a series of Greek lovers of his own, and who painted each morning while Plomer wrote) were offered a house on the island of Spetsai by Irene Hadjilazaro,[18] one of the women friends Butts had made on an earlier visit to Greece and the original of the figure Plomer was to put into his frankly homosexual short story 'Local Colour'[19] as Madame Strouthokámelos. This remarkable woman was running the Refugee Commission in Athens, and she struck Plomer as an Amazon, a Juno, the 'Dictatress of Greece', so that he told Leonard Woolf, 'If I ever write about this country I shall certainly have to make a character of her.'[20] He and Butts travelled to Spetsai, by way of Hydra, to see Irene Hadjilazaro's house, but rejected it, as Plomer wrote to Spender, because 'the garden was all rocks & spiders, our only neighbours were to be nuns, & the house was hung with autographed photos of extinct grand-duchesses, while the bookshelves were full of pamphlets on pre-war Balkan politics & novels by C. E. Montague!!!'[21]

In the middle of August, however, Athens itself quite suddenly lost its charm for them. For one thing, Butts heard from his mother that their family finances were becoming severely involved, and that she could send no more money. Since Butts was paying almost all the expenses of the trip, this meant that he and Plomer had to move out of their pleasant hotel with its fine view of the Parthenon, and even to cut down on their meals. They had heard that Corfu was cheaper than Athens, and decided to spend the remainder of their time in Greece there. In addition, Plomer heard that his mother, whom he loved more than he loved anyone else, had had an operation for cancer. Though the operation appeared to have been successful, his original intention of staying in Greece for years was now abandoned.

To add to his troubles, his passionate affair with Nicky came to a sudden and miserable end. He had loved Nicky with abandon, and had believed his love was reciprocated; but Nicky grew bored with the affair, and left Plomer for another moneyed foreigner, apparently taking with him what remained of Plomer's savings. Plomer was bitterly hurt by this treachery, and by the revelation of how he had deceived himself about Nicky.[22] It was perhaps not the first such revelation, and it was certainly not to be the last, but it seems to have hit him harder than any that came later. Nor were the betrayal and the robbery all he had to endure, for after a few weeks it became clear that he had contracted a venereal disease from Nicky. He hoped it was merely gonorrhoea. He wrote in anguish to Van der Post, who was having a hard time in Cape Town, 'God knows we are all in the same boat, and it is a leaky one. I have just been through a minor hell of my own, but I won't describe it in a letter.'[23] Ten days later, after he and Butts had moved to Corfu, he wrote, 'You may imagine (from my travels & the pompous address at the top of this letter) that I have money and ought to send you some. Actually, my dear, during our last weeks in Athens we did not have enough to eat.'[24] And though he concealed the details of these days when he came to write his autobiography, one bitter, if isolated sentence escaped him: 'If one is conscious of intense happiness, one is a fool to trust it.'[25] His confidence that homosexuality was the right, joyous course for him must have been severely jolted, and from this point on his doubts about his autobiographical novel began to grow.

He was ill throughout the time he and Butts spent in Corfu, and had a very bad time of it, writing to Van der Post that his whole existence was disorganized.[26] A year or two later he was to make the island the setting of one of his most cynical yet moving stories, 'Nausicaa', in which an impoverished young Greek gives himself to a visiting foreign homosexual on the promise that the visitor will help him find his sister who has emigrated; the visitor, whose motive is merely to fill in a few empty hours in dalliance with the handsome young man, has no intention of carrying out his promise. The story analyses the ways in which foreigners took advantage of the poverty of young Greeks. Read in context, 'Nausicaa' amounts to self-examination, and perhaps self-judgement, on Plomer's part, and it suggests that he could not bring himself to blame Nicky alone for what had happened. Its title, too, suggests a deep dissatisfaction with his life; Nausicaa, whom Odysseus met on Corfu, refreshed his soul precisely because she was femininity in a pure form, that femininity which Plomer, almost in spite of himself, found repellent. The loss of the young Greek's sister, and the way homosexuality frustrates his search for her, are clearly symbolic.

Plomer and Butts returned to England, via Milan and Paris, early in November 1930. He found his mother worn and pale though recuperating, and his father even more dominant in the marriage, and even more difficult to get on with. There was no question of Plomer's living with them again, yet he could not afford to live in London; he determined to find somewhere in the English countryside where he could live cheaply and quietly, recover his health, and finish the novel.

His choice fell on Lingen in Herefordshire, a pretty village on the Welsh border, near where he had spent the summer of 1915 with his Beechmont friend Bob Synge. Finding that he could live in a hotel there, the Royal George, for £7 a month, and that he was well looked after by the family who ran it, he spent two months in this rural retreat, from the end of November 1930 to the end of January 1931, writing hard and finishing 170,000 words of his autobiographical novel. He found he rather liked the sudden change of rhythm, climate, and surroundings enforced on him by his poverty, writing to his parents on 16 January 1931,

People of a complex nervous organization absolutely *need* variety. One must not allow money troubles or indifferent health to force one into a rut. One has to make an effort, however hard, and have even a small change of diet, society & scene. Nothing is so tonic as being forced to grapple—if only for a few hours—with new surroundings.[27]

He took long walks through the lanes and over the fields, and his health improved a little in the country air. The one poem he wrote there, 'December in Lingen', has a tranquillity that contrasts strongly with the mood of his often tormented Greek poems:

A ladder in the orchard, and a handsaw hisses
Where a small summer in bare boughs these weeks has hung,
The saw of John Davies rasping dry twigs among

To sever the mistletoe, bouquets of olive-green sprays
With pearl-berries in pairs and a promise of kisses ...

As soon as he felt that his novel was finished, he took himself off
to London to show it to the Woolfs, who passed it on to one of
their readers. The book at this stage was known as 'Memoirs of an
Emigrant', and, to judge from odd snippets of information remaining
in the files of Hogarth Press and from a BBC broadcast Plomer was
to do about it years later,[28] it dealt with Plomer's move from Africa
to Japan and thence to Europe, its theme being the dissolution of
youthful priggishness and ignorance under the powerful influence
of homosexual experience. Its hero, Plomer was later to say, 'made
the awful discovery that love, to come into being, may even need
something more than the wonderful coincidence of the time and
the place and loved one'.[29] Hogarth Press's reader thought it bad,
in part because the novel seemed to have no unity, and Plomer
ruefully agreed to rewrite it and cut it down to half its length. He
believed that his difficulties resulted from his frustrated attempts to
get to grips with what he called his 'real nature', and wrote to
Van der Post, 'I am trying to learn to conduct my life & work in
accordance with my real nature, & although I am nearer to it than
I was, I have still difficulties to surmount.'[30] To put it more plainly,
it was the problem of coming to grips with his own sexuality in a
novel that gave him his first major check as a writer, and this
problem was to dog him for years to come. Not until after the war
would he completely regain his footing, and then on quite different
ground.

With the help of a £10 advance solicited from the Hogarth Press,
he moved into a sleazy bed-sitting-room at 95 Warwick Street, near
Victoria station, and began picking up the threads of his London
life again. Lunches with T. S. Eliot and parties with the Woolfs at
Tavistock Square, where he talked too much about his book and
bored Virginia,[31] were followed by evenings with Lilian Bowes-Lyon,
whose poetry he liked and whose friendship with Janin and Van
der Post provided them with common ground, and the now usual
round of homosexual parties.

It was at this time that he met Hugh Walpole[32] at one of the
Woolfs' parties. Walpole, the most popular novelist of the day, was
an ebullient, ruddy, portly figure who had made a fortune by
turning out novels that provided an uncritical public with what it

wanted: what Plomer, in a private letter, once described as 'unflagging energy and gusto, an occasional vividness, no subtlety whatever and "stock" characters which are no characters at all— the boozy baronet and disreputable housekeeper, the bright old lady with ivory cane, the wicked cripple, faithful dog, etc etc'.[33] Virginia Woolf rather envied Walpole his popular success, and he envied her her critical success, feeling that his own books were somehow old-fashioned. Though he was forty-seven at this time, he was a great encourager of young talent. He thought Plomer 'strong, manly, and sensible', and considered that 'He should be one of the fine new figures in English Letters.'[34] Accordingly, he invited Plomer to lunch the following week in his rooms overlooking Green Park. At this lunch Plomer told him of the long novel he had just scrapped. Walpole was deeply impressed: 'Marvellous, marvellous! What courage! *I've* never had the courage to destroy anything!' Then, reflectively, 'Do you know, you make me feel just like a little girl taken to see the elephants for the first time.'[35]

Plomer was aware of Walpole's charm, but never quite grew to respect him. At times when he was particularly hard up, he envied Walpole's wealth; one finds him writing about seeing two new Renoirs in Walpole's flat, for instance, and commenting, 'As they are asking £25,000 for one now on show in London I suppose dear Hugh must be cosily in funds.'[36] His remarks about Walpole in private letters are often tinged with irony and occasionally with sarcasm, and it was perhaps Walpole[37] he had in mind when he wrote 'The Playboy of the Demi-World: 1938', which begins with the memorable joke,

> Aloft in Heavenly Mansions, Doubleyou One—
> Just Mayfair flats, but certainly sublime—
> You'll find the abode of D'Arcy Honeybunn,
> A rose-red cissy half as old as time.[38]

He was exchanging long letters with Stephen Spender at this time, letters mostly filled with sensible and good-humoured advice about the poems Spender sent him. In response to three poems Spender enclosed early in 1931, for instance, he wrote:

I don't understand the grammar of 'your body are stars.' All I know is, that my body aren't. The first two stanzas of that are rather too Carnera[39]— 'vast arms,' seven league boots, gargantuan erections, and power-station kisses. 'In a Persian Garden' would, I think, be a more suitable note ...

Of the three pieces I like best 'How strangely this sun.' It is first-rate & you're a good poet. The one about the unemployed I like personally, but I don't fancy most people would. Then I, like you, am inclined to sentimentalize over the poor. As I am one myself—i.e. poor & unemployed—I suppose it to be a form of self-pity.[40]

He had reason for self-pity in these early months of 1931, for his health, far from improving, was deteriorating, and there were some alarming symptoms. When Van der Post returned to England from the Cape in April 1931, he found Plomer looking distinctly ill, pasty, and rather overweight. He seemed, in fact, quite suddenly to have become middle-aged, though he was just twenty-eight. His mean lodgings in Pimlico, with its shifting population of down-and-nearly-outs, its pinched, underpaid secretaries and 'distressed gentlefolks' cooking their lonely evening meals on gas rings in corners of the rooms in which they slept, seemed a reflection of the impoverishment into which Britain was sliding in this second year of the Great Depression.

Van der Post spent an evening with Plomer, Butts, and Janin, dining at one of Plomer's favourite Greek restaurants, Stelios in Soho. Van der Post noticed that Plomer seemed depressed, and when they parted from Butts and Janin, he and Plomer went for what Van der Post intended to be a brief walk through the London streets. Plomer, his tongue loosened by the wine they had had with dinner and by the relief of finding himself in the company of his old friend, suddenly began to talk of the misery of his life, the misery that his cheerful confident mask usually concealed so successfully. Van der Post learned for the first time what he had never suspected before, that Plomer was a homosexual; he learned of Plomer's love for Nicky and of Nicky's betrayal; worst of all, he learned of Plomer's fear that the disease he had caught from Nicky was not gonorrhoea, but syphilis. For the whole of that night the two of them walked the streets, and Plomer talked desperately of suicide, while Van der Post tried to comfort him. 'It was the only time I really saw William completely vulnerable and exposed and finished and he didn't care who knew it—there was no pose about it,' Van der Post was to say later.[41] He also came to believe that the affair with Nicky and its aftermath constituted one of the turning-points in Plomer's life. 'William had put everything, for the first time in his life, into his love for Nicky, it was an absolute commitment. If the affair had succeeded he would have been a different William, I'm certain. But from then on there was no hope that William ever would have a real balance in his life.'[42] The opinion is of interest in part because Van der Post was one of Plomer's oldest friends, and the only one whom he told of his despair at this time.

He could not remain in these depths for long and survive, and he did survive. His symptoms responded to treatment, though it was a long time before he completely recovered his health. He set to work on his failed novel, and by May 1931 had salvaged from the wreck the entire Japanese portion, which Hogarth Press published as *Sado* that autumn. The South African, Greek, and English sections he either scrapped or retained as short stories. In addition, in June 1931, he began putting together a collection of his poems for publication by Hogarth Press as *The Fivefold Screen*. It was ready for publication in September 1931, but was delayed until early 1932 because of negotiations with an American publisher. *Sado* had a generally good press; Virginia Woolf, in inviting Plomer to dinner to meet Bonamy Dobrée[43] in October 1931, could write, 'I don't know if you like meeting admirers. You seem to have many, judging from reviews.'[44] Just one of the reviews stung him; it was by Harold Nicolson, in Oswald Mosley's paper *Action* (15 October 1931), and it accused Plomer of writing a rather feeble novel of 'inversion' without having the courage to broach its subject openly. This was so shrewd a judgement that Plomer felt compelled to reply:

If my book is, as you say, 'pretty feeble' as a novel, I can only hope to do better in future; but is it altogether fair to accuse me of a want of courage, and of having failed to 'grasp the nettles'? What nettles? You admit that I have made the homosexual theme 'abundantly plain,' and at the same time reprove me for reticence. But am I to blame because it is not possible to be so frank in this country as in France or Germany or China?[45]

Virginia herself did not like *Sado*, calling it an 'episode' rather than a novel, and Spender, now moving rapidly towards communism, thought its characters effete, and in a private letter criticized Plomer for having failed to deal with what Spender called 'real values—food, fucking, money and religion'.[46] On the whole, though, Plomer got what he coveted, the approval of those whose judgement he valued. From E. M. Forster in particular came a warm and appreciative letter, on 24 September 1931, saying, 'I have enjoyed

it, and especially appreciated the shape of the end.'[47] Plomer had
fallen short of the ambitious goal he had set himself, but on the
whole he must have looked back on 1931 with some satisfaction.

Materially too the year ended on a brighter note, for Tony Butts,
who had been in Paris painting until late in the year, returned to
England with the proposal that Plomer should join him in taking
a house; as usual he would pay the lion's share of the costs. Their
choice fell on a spacious, airy house in fashionable Palace Gate, a
large step up in the world from Pimlico. They moved there early
in December 1931. A handsome, white-painted, free-standing
structure in a very quiet street, 2 Canning Place had several
bedrooms and a large sitting-room that Butts could use as a studio;
it even had a smallish walled garden, which Butts encouraged a
thick mass of convolvulus to fill with its tangle of stems and white
flowers.

Butts had what Plomer called 'a mania for convolvulus', and
perhaps the plant seemed to him a reflection of his own life, which
was increasingly entangled and confused. He, like Plomer, was
'trying to find himself', trying to establish what he was and by
what system of values he should live. But unlike Plomer, he was
happy for the moment to live in chaos, and in fact seemed to do
all he could to increase the disorder of his life. By his bawdy,
hilarious stories, his eccentric behaviour, and his febrile hedonism,
he fended off awareness of the realities of life. Chief among the
latter was the fact that the comfortable private income upon which
his carefree existence depended was by now almost exhausted. He
and his mother had for some years been living largely on the
mortgage on their large London house, and in 1931 they were
forced to sell it to pay their debts. They put most of their fine
possessions into storage, and raised further loans on the most
valuable of these, chief among them a portrait by Holbein of their
famous ancestor, the William Butts mentioned in *Henry VIII*. During
the years of the Depression this painting appreciated so rapidly in
value that they were able to remortgage it for a larger sum each
year, and Tony Butts's spending increased to keep pace. He travelled,
gambled, drank, and lavished money on his friends. Plomer grew
increasingly troubled by this behaviour, in part because he was
one of the chief recipients of Butts's generosity: 'My God, Tony,
you'll end in the gutter if you aren't careful,' he would say. But
Butts merely laughed, 'You must admit I'll make it considerably

more decorative!'[48] He was incapable of listening. On one occasion he told Van der Post that the bankruptcy of a glass-making firm in Germany had cost him and his mother £250,000: 'So—there's another quarter of a million gone,' he remarked humorously. He was evidently sliding towards ruin, and gradually, under his influence, Plomer's own life slipped once more into disorder.

Several of their friends believed, from the facts that Butts and Plomer had travelled together on the Continent and were now sharing a house, that the two men were lovers. They were not. 'I suppose you don't imagine that we live together, or have ever done so?' Plomer had written to Spender during their 1930 stay in Greece: 'We don't, & haven't.'[49] One of the curious features of English homosexuals of the upper class at this period was that as a rule (though with notable exceptions)[50] they did not regard each other as potential lovers. Spender was to remark years later, 'It would have been almost impossible between two Englishmen of our class ... Men of the same class just didn't; it would have been impossible, or at least very unlikely.'[51] This behaviour may have originated in the English public schools in which so many of them had been educated, where a senior boy often chose a younger boy as a 'friend', and tended to avoid his equals in the school hierarchy.[52]

Certainly Plomer had always been attracted to his social inferiors, if only because this gave him control over the relationship. He could have echoed E. M. Forster, who in 1935 wrote a personal memorandum: 'I want to love a strong young man of the lower classes and be loved by him ... That is my ticket.'[53] Several of Forster's friends had very similar sexual needs, among them the writer and editor J. R. Ackerley[54] and Sebastian Sprott,[55] professor of philosophy and sociology at Nottingham. With the younger writers, Spender, Auden, and Isherwood, the impulse to choose working-class partners was reinforced by left-wing political views.

Plomer had first come across Ackerley as early as 1929, but did not get to know him well until the two were brought together by Forster. Ackerley's *Hindoo Holiday*, when it appeared later in 1932, seemed to Plomer to have links with *Sado* in the way it examined relations between Europeans and Asians. Ackerley was seven years older than Plomer, and the marks of dissipation and anxiety were already clear on his handsome face; in his piercingly blue eyes, at moments of introspection, was the tense predatory stare of the monomaniac. He was obsessed with sex and with the problem of finding and keeping the Ideal Friend. Brought up, like Forster and Plomer, largely by women, and disliking his father, he was repelled by women as sexual partners and pursued boys unremittingly. He had a particular weakness for young working-class men in uniform, ranging from guardsmen to policemen. He was almost as disgusted by effeminacy in men as he was by women themselves. And like Plomer, he was often attracted not by other homosexuals, but by heterosexuals—what he called 'normal' men.[56] Such partners, he found, were most readily procured in the large barracks of London, and in particular among His Majesty's Brigade of Guards; British soldiers during the Depression years were abominably underpaid, though the lengthening dole queues ensured that there was no shortage of recruits.

It was from Ackerley that Plomer learned the advantages of cruising the bars in Knightsbridge, Victoria, or the Edgware Road, where off-duty guardsmen in their red tunics could be found nursing the only half-pint they could afford to buy. Many of the guardsmen knew these upper-class predators well, and even had a name for them: 'twanks'. They knew what was expected of them, and were prepared to provide it for a pound, part of which they might afterwards spend on girls, who were more to their taste. 'Though generally larger than I liked,' Ackerley wrote, 'they were young, they were normal, they were working-class, they were drilled to obedience.'[57]

Plomer threw himself into this twilight world with gusto, pretending, like Ackerley, that what he got from these unwilling prostitutes was love, that (in Ackerley's words) 'the quid that usually passed between us at once ... was not a *quid pro quo*',[58] and suffering from intense depression when the pretence became unsustainable. As he wrote to his parents, 'By the way, Joe says he has never seen anyone so up and down as I am—so choppiness is evidently hereditary. He says he doesn't know how I can write, because I'm "always in an emotional storm".'[59] In later years he was to recognize that homosexual love could never satisfy him, and to explain his frantic pursuit of chimeras in terms of that inadequacy: 'It is because love is never wholly satisfying that a man without weighty ambitions or responsibilities can so easily make a cult of sex, the more because of those moments when love seems to attain perfection, as if disclosing what it once was or some day may be.'[60]

Early in 1932 he began an intense affair with a trooper in the
Royal Horse Guards, Bernard Bayes, whom he had first spotted in
a London park.[61] Bernard was a muscular, but rather plain-featured,
young man of limited education, and Plomer became deeply attached
to him. When he was not on duty in Regents Park Barracks, he
spent his time at Canning Place with Plomer, who showered him
with gifts and marks of affection. If Bernard were ill, Plomer would
quiver with alarm and rally his friends to write witty notes and
cards to the invalid to cheer him up; if he were sent into the
country on manœuvres, Plomer would either follow, putting up in
country hotels in the hope of seeing him, or mope in London until
he returned; and if he suspected that Bernard was being unfaithful
to him he would be plunged into despair for days on end, suffering
torments of jealousy.

In spite of the 'emotional storm', he was writing well during this
time. The murder of Sybil da Costa had held his imagination until
he felt he must turn it into a novel, and during the early months
of 1932, working at great speed, he wrote *The Case is Altered*,
which analyses the motivations of murderer and victim. Like his
other novels, it examines the behaviour of people at moments of
crisis; but whereas *Turbott Wolfe* had brought together black and
white, and *Sado* had done the same for European and oriental, *The
Case is Altered* brought together Britons of different classes and
backgrounds, assembled them under a single roof, and carefully
followed the resulting crisis to its terrible conclusion. Of all his
books, *The Case is Altered* had most appeal to a wide readership,
and the Woolfs recognized it as a potential bestseller from the
start.[62]

The Book Society, guided in large part by Hugh Walpole, who
was the chairman of its Selection Committee, made *The Case is
Altered* its August choice, and thereby helped to ensure its popular
success. Instead of the usual £10 advance from Hogarth Press,
Plomer received £150, and his receipts from British and American
royalties were so high that his income in 1932 reached £1,051,
nearly £900 more than the previous year. The steady fall in the
prices of goods and services at this time made the improvement in
his fortunes even greater than the figures suggest. Although he
invested little of this windfall, he was never again quite as poor as
he had been in the late twenties and early thirties.

One of the Book Society's members read the novel with particular attention and interest. He was a Harley Street physician who happened to be a second cousin of Sybil da Costa, and he promptly wrote to Plomer asking to meet him. In his autobiographies Plomer was to refer to him as 'Doctor Pood': but he was in fact Dr Norman Haire,[63] an Australian-born specialist in birth control and sexual disorders. Plomer at first politely declined the invitation, but when it was renewed in January 1935, he accepted. He had by then discovered that Haire was a 'sexologist' and that he was notoriously indiscreet; with a novelist's curiosity he questioned Haire about the habits of his patients. One of these, Haire told Plomer, was a young man who revealed that he could get satisfaction only from a partner who defecated on his face. 'Yes, I see—of course, of course,' Haire had said imperturbably. 'But don't you find it rather difficult to find anybody who is willing to join you in that?' 'Oh, very difficult,' was the answer. 'And when I *do* find anybody, of course, they're *never* my type!' Plomer felt unable to give the details in his autobiographies, but he passed them on to such friends as J. R. Ackerley, who recorded them himself. Plomer also passed on to E. M. Forster Haire's view that if Forster's novels were analysed 'they would reveal a pretty mess'.[64]

Plomer could clearly have repeated the success of *The Case is Altered*, and it would have paid him handsomely to do so. He could have turned his fascination with crimes of violence to good account, for there is no reason to think that he would not soon have developed a sizeable public following. He chose not to do so. 'Literature has its battery hens,' he was to write; 'I was a wilder fowl.'[65] He might occasionally envy Hugh Walpole his income, but he was not willing to pay the price Walpole had paid to attain it.

For all that, it may have been the awareness that novels could be made to pay, while poetry lost money, that persuaded him to abandon the writing of verse after the publication of *The Fivefold Screen* in April 1932. He had also become increasingly critical of his own poetry, moreover, and in later years was modestly to describe his poems as 'a handful of semi-precious stones, which came in for the admiration of others, but were not much in demand'.[66] To Spender, who had written criticizing one of the poems Plomer had published in a literary magazine early in 1932, he responded:

How I agree with you about my poem! The Muse & I have been dancing with tears in our eyes for some time; we have decided that it is better to part; & the appearance of *The Fivefold Screen* on Thursday probably marks the occasion. It is quite a friendly separation, & no alimony will have to be paid.[67]

Not until after the war would he produce poetry in any quantity again.[68]

For the time being, he was not writing novels either, for in July 1932, after the publication of *The Case is Altered*, he was asked to write a biography of Cecil Rhodes for the publisher Peter Davies's series of short biographies. He accepted this commission in part because he was not expected to do any original research for it, and the money would be useful. He wrote to Van der Post, who had offered to introduce him to some of those who remembered Rhodes, 'If I were writing a proper *life* I should certainly make a point of seeing Leyds, but as my book is going to be little more than an anecdotic essay & will confine me as to both time & money, I shan't even pretend to be at all thorough.'[69] *Cecil Rhodes*, published in February 1933, was a pot-boiler, more interesting for what it says about Plomer's attitude to Rhodes than for any new light it sheds on its subject. From the start, when he received the commission, Plomer had told Leonard Woolf that his intention would be 'to try & show the gentleman up in his own words & deeds',[70] and during the course of the writing, he was continually urged by Tony Butts to condemn Rhodes and all he stood for. 'I hope and think that there will be something there of the violence and intolerance of the old William of "Ula Masondo",' Butts wrote to Van der Post, adding, 'Anybody of reasonable intelligence can see both sides of a question if they want to; I rather hope that he will not want to. But I think he will let himself go.'[71] Plomer did; he missed no opportunity to condemn Rhodes for greed, egotism, lack of humanity, racism, and small-mindedness. Rhodes's struggles to overcome ill health, his triumphs over youthful poverty, his capacity for hard work, and the vision that directed the uses to which he put his money once he had made it, Plomer passed over virtually without comment, excusing himself on the grounds that 'to trace in detail the full course and implications of his financial and political life would need much greater scope than space allows'.[72] Rhodes scarcely emerges as an individual from the book. The fact is that Plomer saw Rhodes as a symbol of all that he had hated in white South Africa and of the imperialist attitudes he hated in Britain, and he treated him accordingly, from his birth into the family of a long-nosed vicar in Bishop's Stortford to his burial 'in Rhodesia, in a hole in the top of a hill'.

The writing of this book, though Plomer did not spend many months on it, was a danger sign. When a novelist takes to biography, it is often because of a feared or perceived failure of imagination in himself. He may fancy that the writing of biography will prove easier than purely creative work, particularly if he has not attempted a biography before. Plomer's struggles with his long autobiographical novel seem to have unsettled him; he had abandoned poetry for the novel, and now he temporarily abandoned the novel for biography. He had suffered a crisis of confidence, and all the signs are that he was in full retreat during these years of the mid-1930s.

One of Butts's perennial financial crises forced him to lease 2 Canning Place in September 1932 and to consider taking himself abroad again, to Fez. Plomer, who had grown tired of the disorder of life with Butts, though he retained a real affection for him, decided to find a flat of his own. On 21 September 1932 he moved to 20 Redcliffe Road, where he had the top two floors; the place was expensive, but the financial success of *The Case is Altered* made him feel he could afford it. Here he lived more quietly than he had done at Canning Place, devoting himself to reviews, entertaining friends, and pursuing young men of the working class when Bernard, who had been moved to Windsor, was not on leave.

He was seeing a good deal of Forster at this time; the two of them would spend evenings playing records together on Plomer's gramophone and dancing with Bernard Bayes and other guardsmen, or they would go to the theatre with Forster's policeman friend, Bob Buckingham, or simply have a quiet evening of companionship, enjoying what Forster once described as 'scrabble and scraps'.[73] Forster gave Plomer the manuscript of *Maurice* to read, and Plomer responded enthusiastically to it:

I can't understand anybody thinking *Maurice* ought to have a tragic ending. The happy ending seems to me in a sense the whole point of the book, and the way it is led up to is magnificent. In actual technique the book seems to me marvellous—I don't know anybody who produces so well the feeling of life without fishy realism. I think in some ways your own private magic is at its very best in this book. If I had read it when I was seventeen I should have made a better job of my life in the succeeding ten years or bust in the attempt. It would have been something to steer by.[74]

Isherwood and Spender would also call, Isherwood striking Plomer as compact and full of life. On several occasions he met Auden, whom he described as 'a most original creature with a fine brain and vivid interest in life, and a very good companion'. In September 1932 he went with Auden, Spender, and Isherwood to a new Garbo film; they found the heterosexual games of Garbo and her leading man very funny, and a woman in front of them turned round and said, 'Can't you stop sniggering for five minutes?' in a very bitter tone of voice—which made them snigger even more.[75]

He was making new friends all through this period, most of them homosexual. He read and admired a covertly homosexual novel, *Saturday Night at the Greyhound*, by a young writer who called himself 'John Hampson'. His real name was John Simpson, and Plomer subsequently made his acquaintance. He was a very small man with a Hitlerian forelock and a Habsburg chin, and he was obsessed with the colour brown, dressing from head to foot in it ('Saw Hampson Simpson, quite the brown study as usual,' Plomer would write). He painted his room brown and wrote in brown ink on brown paper, a habit that did not make his letters easy to read. In addition he kept to the most stringent diet. 'He isn't easy to feed, as he doesn't eat meat, fish, fruit or cheese, so I had to work out for him a nicely balanced diet of mushrooms, toast and sherry,' Plomer wrote to Virginia Woolf, adding, 'There is no doubt that he has a metaphorical squirrel in his workbasket.'[76] But Simpson had a wicked sense of humour, and Plomer kept up his friendship until the end of his life. Another young writer whom he tried to help at this time was an unemployed Welsh coal-miner named David Morgan, some of whose short stories Plomer persuaded Louise Theiss, editor of *Everyman*, to publish in 1933, and he took the trouble to travel to Morgan's home in Blaina to see him. They got on well, and the resulting correspondence between them lasted for years.

Then there was Nancy Cunard. Plomer had come into contact with her in 1932 through Anthony Butts, who shared Cunard's interest in and admiration for Negroes. Rich, beautiful, and bored, Nancy Cunard was a member of the millionaire shipping family, and like Butts was in revolt against her society and its culture.

This was the period when she was collecting contributions for her huge compendium *Negro*, published at her own expense, and to which Plomer agreed to contribute a poem. Tall, slim, and feline, she had called on Butts and Plomer at Canning Place on a number of occasions, sometimes bringing her black friend Henry Crowder; and shortly after Plomer's move to Redcliffe Road she dropped in on him again, as he wrote to tell John Hampson Simpson, 'The other day ... I gave a wild party by mistake, for Nancy Cunard appeared at 11.45 p.m. with three buck niggers, all four of them quite tight. They brought more drinks with them and I had to turn them out at 2.15 a.m. The blackies sang some delightful native songs, and made a tropical nucleus in a desert of wet fog.'⁷⁷ Although Plomer and Cunard were never close friends, his gift for attracting and holding affection ensured that Cunard maintained a desultory correspondence with him for years; even after she had been certified insane and was confined to a nursing home, occasional amusing letters would arrive from her, to be faithfully answered by him.

By the middle of 1933 his relationship with Bernard Bayes was running into trouble. Bernard had for some time been an increasing drain on Plomer's purse. Small gifts no longer contented him, and he began pestering Plomer to help him buy a car. Although Plomer disliked all machinery, never owned a car himself, and refused even to use a telephone if he could avoid it, he found the money to buy Bernard a small second-hand car. Not long after its purchase, Bernard, in motoring to London from Windsor on one of his leaves, went into a skid on an icy patch and crashed into an oncoming truck. By great good luck he escaped serious injury, but the car was beyond repair. Thereafter he came down from Windsor less frequently, and Plomer began making plans to buy him out of the Army so that the two of them could live together permanently. Early in 1933 he borrowed £100 from Lilian Bowes-Lyon, who was both rich and generous, and secured Bernard's release. He and Plomer then lived together for some months at 20 Redcliffe Road.

Far from improving the relationship, this move made matters worse. Bernard seems to have felt that Plomer was becoming too possessive, and in any case Bernard was increasingly attracted to a young woman he had met in London. Love with a well-known writer had real drawbacks for a working-class youth. The policeman Harry Daley, Forster's friend, was to comment bitterly that ' "love" seems hardly the right word to describe the spite and back-biting it all involved ... all that was asked was that I should give up all my former friends, acquaintances, hobbies and interests, and sit waiting at home until my lovers found time to call—and on no condition tell anyone I knew them'.[78] Rather than break immediately with Plomer, Bernard showed his dissatisfaction with the relationship by demanding more and more money. Plomer sought advice from Ackerley and Forster. The latter, who had been through at least one similar experience, replied optimistically, 'I think the fact that you have very little money to give him may straighten him automatically.'[79] But the relationship continued to deteriorate, and in May 1933, after Plomer had resisted further demands for money, Bernard announced that he was leaving Plomer and intended to live with his girl-friend. As he had been by the loss of Nicky, Plomer was hit hard.[80]

At this juncture all his previous doubts about homosexual life welled up again, and for the second time in his life he seriously considered marriage. As usual he consulted Forster, and, perhaps surprisingly, got encouragement. Forster replied that he thought it likely that Plomer could be happy with a woman ('you can get on much better with them than I can') and added that he hoped to see Plomer marry.[81] Plomer had been seeing a good deal of Lilian Bowes-Lyon, whom he respected and admired both as a woman and as a poet. She was the niece of the Earl of Strathmore and the first cousin of the Duchess of York. The too-loving attentions of her father, Francis Bowes-Lyon, had caused Lilian to flee her family home in Northumberland and to live in London, where she had published two novels under the pen-name D. J. Cotman. She had also published a number of poems over her own name in *Punch*. While Plomer and Butts were living at Canning Place, Lilian Bowes-Lyon had been a near neighbour in Courtfield Gardens, and she had been a frequent and welcome guest at Canning Place. Her aristocratic connections and her wealth were not disadvantages in Plomer's eyes. By 1933 she had become a great friend of both Plomer and Van der Post, who had settled once more in London, and was trying with Plomer's help to place his first novel, *In a Province*,[82] with a publisher. It was Lilian to whom Plomer had turned when he needed money to secure Bernard's release from the Army, and it was to her he turned now.

Van der Post first learned of what was in the wind when Plomer

came to tell him about Bernard's leaving him, and to say he now
thought he should get married. With this suggestion Van der Post
agreed, though his own marriage was by then in trouble. Plomer
then told him that he was thinking of proposing to Lilian Bowes-
Lyon. Van der Post was dumbstruck because he had been having
a passionate affair with her for some months. (Her first book of
poems, *The White Hare and Other Poems*, of 1934, was to be
dedicated 'To a Friendship', the friendship being that with Van der
Post.) Unable to see how he could tell Plomer without wounding
him deeply, Van der Post held his tongue, but warned Bowes-Lyon.
Plomer looked carefully before he leapt; he thought the matter over
for several weeks and consulted his friends again before he got to
the point of inviting Bowes-Lyon to dinner, and there proposing to
her. She turned him down.

It is impossible to know what Plomer's feelings were at this
juncture, but all the evidence suggests that he was not badly
wounded. He did not break with Bowes-Lyon, but remained a close
friend until her death. Van der Post, who was in the confidence of
both parties, believed that Plomer was neither in love with her nor
sexually attracted to her, but liked her immensely; such feelings
are not the most solid foundation for a successful marriage, as
Plomer would have known. He may even have been relieved to be
rejected.

What did rankle, however, was his belated discovery of the
intimacy between Bowes-Lyon and Van der Post, whom he had
always regarded more as a pupil and a disciple than a rival. Plomer
did not break off his friendship with Van der Post, but the old
warmth in their correspondence declined from this time until after
the war, and many of his comments about Van der Post hereafter,
in conversation with friends like Spender, were faintly tinged with
irony or condescension.[83] When he came to write his first volume
of autobiography, Plomer downplayed Van der Post's role in his
life, even when dealing with the *Voorslag* period in Natal, though
in subsequent editions he inserted a long footnote to rectify the
matter.

Another side-effect of this rejection was a harshness in some of
his comments about women, and a growing dislike of them.
Occasionally this dislike came to the surface in incidents of rudeness
to women, often strangers, rudeness that was so unlike him that
his friends were taken aback by it. On one occasion he and Van

der Post were having tea in Lyons Corner House, and were talking with animation and laughing loudly. Plomer noticed that a woman at the next table was looking at them disapprovingly, and in the middle of an anecdote he suddenly turned on her: 'That's right, my good woman, stare, stare, *stare*!' he boomed, and then without a pause swung back and took up his story where he had left off.[84] Another time he and Spender were on a bus when an inoffensive stranger settled into the seat in front of them. Plomer suddenly interrupted his conversation with Spender, and began talking in a loud voice: 'Just *look* at this horrible woman in front of us—that awful hat, that fat disgusting neck, those *furs*—ugh, the wretched creature!' He went on and on, and his victim's neck turned scarlet with embarrassment and hurt.[85] On another occasion, according to Van der Post, Plomer had been spending the weekend near Birmingham at the home of John Hampson Simpson. Simpson was employed by a family named Wilson to nurse a mentally handicapped boy, who took a tremendous liking to Plomer and pestered him all weekend, following him about crying 'Cuckoo, cuckoo' and mooing like a cow.[86] When he was leaving on Monday morning, Mrs Wilson, the boy's sister, apologized for his behaviour. 'Oh, *please* don't apologize,' said Plomer, 'it was so nice to meet a *professional* idiot after knowing so many amateurs.'[87] These incidents, so entirely out of character, can be explained only in the light of Plomer's sense of having been condemned never to know lasting happiness or a fulfilling human love. 'Life's mushroom teems with maggots,' he wrote bitterly to Van der Post.[88]

10. *Lotus Eating*
1933–1936

By the beginning of 1933 Plomer was preparing for publication those parts of his failed autobiographical novel that he had not fitted into *Sado*: the South African and Greek sections. The South African section became two superbly written, long short-stories: 'Down on the Farm', based on his experiences on Fred Pope's farm at Molteno, and 'The Child of Queen Victoria', drawn from his time in Zululand. The Greek section, much briefer, yielded two short stories: 'Local Colour', which reads like a brilliantly caught piece of experience (Plomer's and Butts's first contact with Greek homosexuals), and 'The Island: An Afternoon in the Life of Costa Zappaglou', in which he tells of the beginning of his relationship with Nicky, giving himself a rather thin Greek disguise. Together with some slighter pieces set in South Africa, Greece, and France, the stories formed the collection he called *The Child of Queen Victoria*.[1] This volume is of more than literary significance, for it marked the beginning of his long association with the publisher Jonathan Cape.

In 1932 Plomer had had a brief correspondence with the manager of the Book Society, a young man named Rupert Hart-Davis.[2] Later they met in Hugh Walpole's flat overlooking Green Park, and warmed to each other immediately. Hart-Davis subsequently invited Plomer to lunch, and they were soon meeting regularly. Tall, broad, and fair, Hart-Davis was witty in a way that perfectly complemented Plomer's own quick sense of humour; he also liked Plomer's writing, and said so. Behind the smoke that went up from his ever-present pipe and the barrage of hilarious jokes, he concealed a very shrewd mind; his literary taste and common sense were remarkable, and he was clearly a young man who was going somewhere. During subsequent meetings, Plomer met Hart-Davis's second wife, Comfort, and found he liked her as he liked few women. When, at the beginning of 1933, Hart-Davis was appointed a director of the publishing company Jonathan Cape, one of the writers he invited to publish henceforth with Cape was Plomer, who had been growing increasingly dissatisfied with Hogarth Press's lack of efficiency in promoting and advertising his books. Leonard Woolf regretted Plomer's decision to move to Jonathan Cape, but put no obstacle in the way and remained a personal friend of Plomer's. Plomer accordingly offered *The Child of Queen Victoria* to Cape. Edward Garnett, the reader who had 'discovered' Conrad, Galsworthy, D. H. Lawrence, W. H. Hudson, and Roy Campbell, wrote what in retrospect is a highly perceptive report on *The Child of Queen Victoria*:

Yes. Plomer is certainly about the most original and keenest mind of the younger generation, and he comes off as well in his short stories of Greece and France as he has done with South Africa and Japan. He is emphatically of the minority—i.e., of the section of writers, the real intelligentsia, the unconventional critical-minded literary artists whom the British Public, in general don't *like*, and therefore only buy in restricted quantities. He is a Left-winger in popularity, i.e. what D. H. Lawrence was to Hugh Walpole ... Most of these stories are really incisive sketches of manners or little character studies, with nothing behind to titillate vulgar taste. The title story is very good and the last story is excellent, though one or two, such as 'Museum Piece' are a little thin.[3]

Somerset Maugham, who was sent a copy, admired the book enough to write to Cape and say so, adding, 'Only a short story writer can know how difficult it is to write a story like "Down on the Farm". Plomer has brought it off wonderfully. Technically it is to my mind the most telling and successful of all the stories. I admired it very much indeed.'[4] The book sold slowly, however, and by October 1933, three months after publication, only eighty-seven copies had been disposed of.[5] Jonathan Cape, one of the shrewdest of publishers, perhaps feeling that two titles would help each other where one struggled, began pushing Plomer for another novel, and on 9 August 1933 Plomer was telling him, 'I think you will be interested to know that I am again working at a novel. It is much too soon to say when it is likely to be done, or whether, when it is done, I shall be pleased with it, but I feel that I am making a little progress with it.'[6] This was the book he named *The Invaders*, which Cape published in October 1934. In it he detailed the experiences of a young woman who comes to London from the country and takes various jobs, and the life of a young man who joins the Army. Plomer knew relatively little about young women, particularly of the working class, and it is perhaps not surprising that he found the book a struggle, writing to Tony Butts early in

1934, 'I have just finished my book—for the *third* time.'[7] In sketching the career of the young hero, however, he was able to display a fund of expert knowledge, for he drew largely on the experiences of Bernard Bayes; the book is in a sense a valediction to Bernard. Not surprisingly, the novel evoked mixed responses; Plomer was later to claim that 'the inside view of military life in London in peacetime caused the leading non-commissioned officer of a well-known regiment to place a copy of the book before the colonel commanding it: he deferentially suggested that it would help that officer to understand better the lives and conditions of the men under his command'.[8]

The Invaders, however, confirmed Virginia Woolf in her view that Plomer had somehow lost his punch. This feeling may lie behind the Woolfs' readiness to let Plomer go to Cape, and Virginia seems to have felt confirmed in it when she next invited Plomer to Rodmell, in August 1934, noting in her diary that she thought him aged and disillusioned, adding that he had lost charm and gained weight.[9] He had no inkling of this fall in his stocks with her, however, writing to Spender:

It was a delightful weekend. Dame Ethel Smyth put in an appearance, & broadcasted to us with great vigour—she is deaf, garrulous & an egomaniac, often very funny. She has a celluloid contraption distantly related to an ear-trumpet. A terrifying object, it is called the Loch Ness Monster. The garden was bursting with flowers, fruit, goldfish, ripe figs, red hot pokers, & a marmoset with rickets called Mitzi. Some wild swans suggested Innisfree. The Woolves were altogether delightful—I am really very fond of them.[10]

Christopher Isherwood also disliked the book, writing to tell Plomer that one of the central figures, Nigel Edge, was too dull to hold the reader's interest:

As long as he is with Tony or Chick I want to hear about him, but I must say that I rather lost interest during the South of France episodes towards the end of the book. I think I really wished that Nigel had been more like yourself, not quite so much of the heroic, quiet, controlled, Weary Willy. Couldn't you have made him a bit gay externally?[11]

It may be that Plomer had succeeded a little too well in turning himself into an Englishman; in the pursuit of balance and moderation, he had lost his South African fire, the disrespect for authority and accepted views that he had displayed to such effect in *Turbott Wolfe* and in much of his Japanese writing. The aspects of English life about which he felt strongly, such as the official attitude to homosexuality, his by now impenetrable mask prevented him from addressing openly. The result was increasing paralysis of his creative powers. Nor were the laws or even the conventions of the period to blame for his reticence; writers such as Rosamond Lehmann had dealt explicitly with homosexuality, and Plomer's publishers actually encouraged him to be more open about the matter in *The Invaders*, Rupert Hart-Davis writing that the one criticism he had of the manuscript was that Plomer had been vague about the scope of Nigel's relationship with Chick: 'You don't say, and hardly even infer, whether they went to bed together or not.'[12] But Plomer declined to expand the passage.

As a result, several critics, including Peter Quennell,[13] criticized the work for its 'ambiguity'. Plomer got qualified support for what he had chosen to do from E. M. Forster, who, interestingly, compared Plomer's vagueness with his own treatment of the Marabar caves incident in *A Passage to India*:

I don't believe Quennell's really on the spot. Perhaps I'm not either and am a bit old fashioned as regards form. What seems to [be] not satisfactory in the book is a thing which I find wrong in *A Passage to India*. I tried to show that India is an unexplainable muddle by introducing an unexplained muddle—Miss Quested's experience in the cave. When asked what happened there, *I don't know*. And you, expecting to show the untidiness of London, have left your book untidy.—Some fallacy, not a serious one, has seduced us both, some confusion between the dish and the dinner.

I'm all for these London books of yours. They seem to me about a real town.[14]

'I seem to lead rather a grasshopper-like existence at present,' Plomer wrote to Lady Ottoline Morrell in August 1933[15] from France, where he was holidaying in Toulon and Paris with Ackerley, and where a Bulgarian labourer helped him while away the time. On his return he gave up the Redcliffe Road flat, which was becoming too expensive, and moved to a small ground-floor flat at 8 Portsdown Road in Maida Vale, near the Regents Canal. It was an area of decaying late Victorian houses now divided into shabby flats, and much frequented by prostitutes who, as dusk fell, took up their stations all along the pavements, so that as Plomer quipped, 'one could hardly help knowing one's own strumpet'.[16] It was an area which, as Spender was to remark, 'almost rivals Berlin in its atmosphere of decay'.[17] Here Plomer several times entertained Ottoline Morrell ('Lady Acetylene', as Plomer called her to Stephen Spender, perhaps indicating that he thought she generated more heat than light), who showed her eccentricity by demanding to know in advance that Tony Butts would not be present. Plomer was conciliatory, having clearly had a falling-out with Butts himself in 1933:

I haven't asked Tony Butts, & won't. I can well understand what you feel about him—he is often disliked, & I have known people refuse to meet him simply because of his looks & manner. His weaknesses have been too strong for him & have turned him into a fribble—or gaby—& unfortunately he isn't a *contented* one. His better nature & better judgment & talents are all wasted, & there he is, & such a good creature in some ways, & oh how badly brought up![18]

Spender, Ackerley, and Leo Charlton were now near neighbours of his. Charlton was a retired air commodore, who had resigned from a promising career in the RAF on moral grounds, because he was unwilling to bomb civilians. Author of an interesting autobiography and editor of *The Memoirs of a Northumbrian Lady*, he was living on a small private income and leading a gay life in London with his friend Tom Whichelo. In this Plomer joined them, and presently he found a replacement for Bernard Bayes, a young married labourer named Jack Carey,[19] with whom he was intimate until 1935.

He was writing less now, being content to drift. He lived mostly on earnings from reviews (from 1933 to 1936 he was a regular reviewer of fiction for the *Spectator*, but he wrote for any other publication that would pay, ranging from the *Criterion* to *Time & Tide*), and his income fell steadily back from its peak of £1,151 in 1932 to £532 in 1933, £499 in 1934, and £386 in 1935. His drifting existence was reflected in his apparent inability to find an abiding home. From the Portsdown Road flat he moved, in September 1935, to a bed-sitting-room at 8 Norfolk Square in Bayswater, of which he said approvingly that 'it has water laid on, & an electric fire, is cleanish and plainish & not as noisy as it might be'.[20] In 1936 he took a room on the Esplanade in Dover from June to October, before returning to Norfolk Square; from May 1937 to September 1938 he had rooms at 5 Ship Street Gardens in Brighton;

and in October 1938 he went back to Maida Vale, to large rooms at 12 Randolph Crescent. His needs were modest, which was as well, for his income went mostly on young men. And wherever he was, he had few possessions, no ornaments, and virtually no books; he lived like an intending traveller impatient to leave.

His social life throughout the 1930s continued to be both varied and brilliant, and one catches glimpses of it in his correspondence with his parents, correspondence which includes some memorably vivid character sketches.[21]

At tea at Morgan Forster's yesterday I met Somerset Maugham[22] & Herbert Read.[23] In spite of remarkable qualities & gifts & a by no means unimpressive appearance he [Maugham] seems to me too worldly. He is yellowish, with an icy, flabby hand, a stutter, & the eyes of a crocodile. Read, on the other hand, is gentle & charming, with a sensitive, shrewd-in-a-nice-way, & rather Chinese face. They hated each other's guts. [1 November 1933]

Last night I went to the Woolves, who were as delightful as ever, though poor Virginia has been fainting again. I found there Count Geoffrey Potocki de Montalk, who, as you remember, was sent to gaol for writing sexy poems, or rather for trying to print them.[24] Imagine a pale dark man with a Garbo bob & rather hairy forearms, sandals & a moustache, dressed à la Richard II in a crimson tea-gown with long sleeves & a girdle, & equipped with a Cockney–New Zealand accent, describing prison as 'chokey' and considering himself the King of Poland. Really, c'est un peu fort! [11 November 1933]

Last night Stephen Spender & I went to a dinner given by a City club near St. Paul's, the guest of the evening being Mosley.[25] He made a speech, then various people asked questions, to which he replied. My strongest prejudices seemed justified. He struck me as an unscrupulous & arrogant man, unpleasantly cynical. He has the very reverse of an 'open' face, nasty small eyes & a crocodile smile. He is certainly not without energy & ability, & has a gift for quick sneering repartee and a trick of turning the laugh upon hecklers by evading or twisting their questions & being personal or irrelevantly flippant. He advised the squeamish to put cotton wool in their ears & blinkers over their eyes while he is in process of winning power, which he said would be a 'terrible' process. I am sure we have by no means heard the last of him, and as a rabid anti-socialist he is tolerated if not to some extent approved by the present government. His brain is quick in a crooked way but neither original nor forceful. His attitude to culture is merely savage, & he sneered at Dostoievsky as 'that Russian decadent,' being evidently ignorant that Dostoievsky ended up as a terrific sort of pan-Slav chauvinist, almost a sort of Fascist. A man called Grigson, who is not remarkable for civility, had the courage to tell Mosley that he was 'a blackhead on the face of civilization.'[26] [2 November 1934]

For all the interest of evenings like these, the summers he spent in Dover and Brighton suggest that London life was palling a little. In fact he had long been considering living outside the capital. For a while, when his affair with Bernard was going well, he had thought of taking a little house on the Essex coast near Bernard's parents, but Bernard left him before the plan came to fruition. He much enjoyed getting out of London on weekend visits to friends who had houses in the country—to E. M. Forster's home West Hackhurst in Surrey, for instance, or to the tiny Welsh cottage of David Morgan, of whose talent Plomer was now less sure. Morgan began to irritate him by sending him enormously long letters. 'I could paper a gazebo and choke a ha-ha with his letters,' Plomer was to write in exasperated amusement to John Lehmann,[27] '& if they were laid end to end (not that I have preserved them) they would stretch from Minsk to Pinsk. Not that they are by any means devoid of ideas—oh no, not at all—but one doesn't want Welsh rarebit by the *acre*.'[28]

A much more successful visit was the one he made to Elizabeth Bowen's[29] family home, Bowens Court in County Cork. Plomer and Bowen had met after she wrote him a fan letter at the end of 1933, complimenting him on *The Invaders*, and he had responded by inviting himself to tea with her. He thought her sensitive, wise, and charming, and found that they had several friends in common, among them Stephen Spender. The friendship begun in this way flourished until their deaths in 1973. They invited each other to parties and dinners, and they several times visited exhibitions of paintings together. Plomer was a dedicated gallery-goer, and he and Bowen shared a love of Chinese and modern European paintings. He also took her once or twice to the Caledonian Market, where they indulged their passion for seeing and handling Victorian bric-à-brac. (The Caledonian Market was one of Plomer's favourite haunts, though he bought little other than collections of Victorian and Edwardian postcards. He loved to send these to his friends, and after his death large bound albums full of them, many of the sort the Victorians would have called 'improper', were found among his papers.)

He visited Bowen in Ireland only once, between 10 and 18

September 1935, travelling by ferry from Fishguard, and very grateful to find the Irish Sea calm. Bowens Court was a large Georgian country house, very plain outside and rather bare within. It was lit by candles or paraffin lamps, and had no bathroom and only exceedingly ancient lavatories, but Bowen's hospitality was open-handed, and the food and drink were excellent. He enjoyed his week with her in spite of the dampness of his bed; the liveliness of Bowen's conversation and her determination that he should see as much as possible of Ireland kept him in a pleasant whirl of activity. He was much struck by the beauty of the country, which he had not visited before, and by the air of gloom and decay, the result of ruins that he seemed to see everywhere, writing afterwards, 'So often in Ireland the dwelling and the ruin stand side by side, though as often the ruin stands alone, a reminder of cruelty and disaster in an exquisite landscape.'[30] Ultimately he came to believe that Bowen belonged to a class, the Anglo-Irish gentry, that was already anachronistic, made up of old eccentrics still living in their walled demesnes and extravagantly built country houses, but rapidly dying out, and he wondered why she kept on her house in Ireland.[31]

Ireland is a heavenly country to visit, but might be less heavenly to live in. It is so melancholy, so full of the ghosts of feuds and famines, the clouds fly low, the trees sag under the incessant rain, and the very air seems charged and weighed down with a sense of grievance. How could one keep out the climate, how could one keep the Pope and Ulster, Mr. de Valera and Mr. J. H. Thomas, the land annuities, the censorship and the future at a proper distance, except by taking to drink, going over to Rome or London, or cutting one's throat?[32]

Another friend whose hospitality he regularly enjoyed was John Lehmann. Plomer had met him first when he began working for the Hogarth Press in 1931. He had earlier met Lehmann's beautiful sister Rosamond,[33] perhaps through René Janin; Rosamond was at this time married to the painter Wogan Philipps, and Plomer paid them occasional visits at their home, Ipsden House in the Chilterns, a comfortable and beautiful place filled with Philipps's wild, childish portraits of Rosamond. John Lehmann, with his chiselled features and startlingly blue eyes, became a very close friend. Plomer was frequently invited to spend the weekend at Fieldhead, Lehmann's mother's home, and during the years when Lehmann lived in

Austria, they corresponded frequently, exchanging hundreds of letters over the years. Plomer was confident enough of Lehmann's discretion to write him letters giving details of centres of homosexual activity in towns Lehmann planned to visit:

I hasten to send you a map of Bristol. The purple ring encloses, I think, the most useful scene of operations. Purple dots give approximate positions of centres of activity ... Daylight reconnaissance patrols recommended. I hope that ... you will be able to report 'intense activity during the night—successful raids were carried out—&c.' A curious nocturnal resort, further afield, is to be found in the basement of a Christian Science Tabernacle. I think it is called the Hot Dog.[34]

Though homosexuality continued to be a bond between Plomer and various important literary friends (once Ackerley became literary editor of the *Listener* in 1935, and Lehmann editor of *New Writing* in 1936, Plomer became and remained a regular contributor to those journals), it also lost him some friends, including, in 1933, Roy Campbell. Plomer had deplored the publication of Campbell's *The Georgiad* in 1931, with its stinging attack on Harold Nicolson and Vita Sackville-West, but the relationship had not broken until August 1933. In that year Mary Campbell had made one of her regular visits to London from the Campbells' home in Provence. As she had done in the past, she dined with Plomer, to whom she had always been attracted, and afterwards, in a taxi, embraced and kissed him. Plomer shook her off, and subsequently told Van der Post, who told another South African, Uys Krige—and Krige told Campbell. Campbell, whose rage against the Nicolsons had been caused by his sense that Mary had betrayed him, reacted with bitter hurt. It took the form of a letter to Plomer, accusing him of having tried to represent Mary as being in love with himself (Plomer), and continuing:

You have unceasingly flattered and felicitated us in your letters. Yet behind our backs ... you represent Mary as being in love with you and me being jealous ... Now I have never made any sanctimonious protestations to you. I have no respect for you as a character any more than you have. I have always said you were a fine writer but a terrible old woman. ... I am not temperamentally equipped to fox out your motives but they smell Freudian enough: and knowing your general hatred of women and marriage in particular coupled with your nancydom it points to a very different sort of triangular predicament which neither of us ever suspected ...[35]

And just as Campbell had struck out at Vita Sackville-West in verse, he now struck at Plomer in a poem entitled 'Creeping Jesus', which he published in his volume *Mithraic Emblems* (1936):

> Pale crafty eyes beneath his ginger crop,
> A fox's snout with spectacles on top—
> Eye to the keyhole, kneeling on the stair,
> We often found this latter saint at prayer,
> 'For your own sake,' he'd tell you with a sigh
> (He always did his kindness on the sly).
> He paid mere friendship with his good advice
> And swarmed with counsels as a cur with lice:
> For his friends' actions, with unerring snout,
> He'd always fox his own low motives out . . .
> . . . If we put up with him—'twas as a bug
> In his own talent (an expensive rug),
> But he abused its lovely silken floss,
> One tiny insect spoiled the whole kaross:
> The leather's perished, moulted all the hair,
> But the old bug is still established there!

In his rage Campbell seems to have forgotten the original reason for his outburst. He alludes to it in only one line, accusing Plomer of having 'slandered women he could not supplant'. In this way a friendship that had for years been close ended in a permanent rupture, one that both men later regretted. 'It is well known how difficult it is to forgive those whom one has wronged,' Plomer wrote of this quarrel years later. 'I think W.P. and R.C. wronged one another and neither made enough effort to make amends.'[36]

Campbell's jibe that Plomer's talent had 'moulted' must have stung, for Plomer was once more struggling vainly with a novel. From August 1933 to February 1935 he wrestled with it, before scrapping the 25,000 words he had written and appealing to Hart-Davis to suggest 'a book depending largely on research or fact or compilation which you think I might do well'.[37] Hart-Davis suggested another biography, this time of Ali Pasha, the eighteenth-century Albanian war-lord whom Byron mentions in *Childe Harold*, and whom Victor Hugo had called a Mohammedan Bonaparte. The subject attracted Plomer partly because he was at a loose end and partly because he had always been fascinated by murders, and Ali Pasha was a mass murderer. A painting of one of his massacres of the Suliot women and children had drawn Plomer's attention during his visit to Corfu, and the image had haunted him.[38] In writing about Ali, Plomer displayed on a large scale that willingness to portray the charm of even the most cruel of human beings that is so evident in the macabre ballads he produced later. Another of the attractions of Ali was the fact that the Albanians or Scipetars were notoriously homosexual, and Plomer is uncharacteristically open in his defence of this facet of their lives:

They were much given to homosexual practices, and were quite uninhibited about them. Parallels to this can easily be found amongst other races in various ages, living a formalized or stylized military life, keeping women in subjection or at least in the background, and having always before them as an image of perfection the young warrior: one thinks of the ancient Greeks, the Germans, the Zulus at the height of their power, the Japanese as described by Saikaku. No question of degeneracy is involved ... Nor can a hopeless moral turpitude be ascribed to them, whatever Christianity may say.[39]

Unlike his biography of Rhodes, *Ali the Lion* involved Plomer in detailed research, and he spent much time during 1935 in the reading-room of the British Museum; the result was one of his most careful and readable books, a scholarly production that drew compliments from professional historians. It was perhaps in the course of writing it that Plomer began to learn that care with facts, that willingness to verify and annotate every detail, that kept him from errors when he came to write his autobiographies. He much enjoyed writing the book, telling Spender that he was 'obsessed' with his subject, and that over Easter he had even taken the manuscript down with him to Torquay, where his parents were now living, and had there written fifty pages.[40]

By May 1935 he was able to tell Hart-Davis that 'about half of it now exists in a rough draft,'[41] but his work on reviews to earn his board and lodging prevented him from finishing it until early in 1936. It was published in March that year, and got good reviews in the *Daily Telegraph* from Harold Nicolson and in the *Morning Post* from Geoffrey Grigson, as well as in the *Spectator*, the *Times Literary Supplement*, and the *New Statesman*. The historian A. J. P. Taylor wrote in the *Guardian* that 'Mr. Plomer's name is sufficient guarantee for the force and brilliance of Ali's biography. No one could have told better the barbaric story';[42] while the professor of modern Greek at Oxford, R. M. Dawkins, called the book 'brilliantly written', and added, 'No one interested in later Greece or the Nearer East should neglect this book.'[43]

Plomer was much distracted from his task by anxiety about his mother, whose long struggle with cancer now went through another crisis. In July 1935 she had another operation, and thereafter was in and out of nursing homes until her death in 1939. Plomer was frantic with worry in the middle of 1935, and excused himself even from answering his friends' letters: 'It is no good my trying to answer it now, for I am greatly troubled at present as my mother is dangerously ill,'[44] he would write. But few of them, apart from Hart-Davis, saw through his formal understatements and realized how much his mother meant to him, and how entirely alone he felt when he thought himself about to lose her. For the moment, however, she weathered the storm, and Plomer, who made repeated dashes to Torquay to visit her and comfort his father, began to relax again at the end of 1935.

His summer in Dover (June to October 1936) he explained in his autobiography in terms of a need to get out of London, a desire to pursue his passion for swimming (one of the forms of exercise he most enjoyed in these years), or a simple need to live near the sea, which, however, he thought of as 'oppressively elemental, and a great fidget'.[45] The real attraction of the place appears only in an apparently casual reference to the fact that 'the streets, very quiet in the day-time, were filled with the inaudible *frou-frou* of kilts, as the young soldiers of the garrison made their ways to the pubs'.[46] This was the Dover of which Auden, who sampled its pleasures after hearing of them from Plomer, was to write,

> Soldiers crowd into the pubs in their pretty clothes,
> As pink and silly as girls from a high-class academy.

Plomer was soon entangled with two or three soldiers at a time, and the two or three were always changing. 'I feel a little like all three of Chekhov's three sisters this morning, for a battalion of the Seaforths are leaving Dover for manœuvres, & they have really been very good company,' he wrote to Elizabeth Bowen.[47] His accounts of the pleasures of the place drew a stream of his friends: Ackerley took rooms there for several consecutive summers, Isherwood came for a brief period, and Leo Charlton and his friend Tom Whichelo, having come once or twice, eventually moved there permanently.

Even Forster brought his mother there for some months in the summer of 1936.

During the day Plomer did little but swim and loaf, observe yachts from his windows overlooking the harbour, and watch yachtsmen ('ninnies', he called them) in the town's one good restaurant, the Café Royal. He toyed with the remains of his failed novel, and he told Hart-Davis (29 July 1936) that he was considering transforming it into a play, a drawing-room farce, but this project too came to nothing, because the further he went with it the more trivial it seemed. He was uneasily aware of being indolent, ironically contrasting his own lack of production with the pace at which friends like John and Rosamond Lehmann were writing: 'Rosamond's new book seems to be doing awfully well, & I expect you will do well with the second go of *New Writing*. I did well with some Canadian sailors last night, & am doing nicely with the harbour, in which I swim.'[48]

He was not being quite so lazy as he accused himself of being, however, for it was during these months that he prepared for publication a collection of the few poems he had written over the previous three or four years, and which Cape published as *Visiting the Caves* in the autumn of 1936. Nearly half the collection had been published previously, mostly in magazines in the past year,[49] and much of it was based on experiences Plomer had had years before. 'The Devil-Dancers' and 'Captain Maru', for instance, looked back to his voyage from South Africa to Japan, while 'Archaic Apollo' and 'Good-bye to the Island' are memories of his trip to Greece with Butts. Yet often these experiences have been worked through again in the light of his more recent thoughts and feelings. 'Captain Maru', for instance, while ostensibly an accurate portrait of Captain Mori, is clearly influenced by the growing xenophobia and aggressive nationalism in Japan, which Plomer heard about in letters from his Japanese friends, and which was to lead in 1931 to the Japanese invasion of Manchuria and the tragedies that followed it. And there was a more direct influence on the poem too. At the end of 1935 Van der Post, on a voyage back to South Africa, had written to tell Plomer of a nightmare in which he had seen Captain Mori with no back to his head,[50] an account that provided the prophetic final lines of the poem:

> And now he has appeared to someone in a dream
> Or rather a nightmare, menacing, a giant,

With no back to his head, uttering a taunt—
It is the challenge of his race, the short man scorned
Not satisfied with power, but mad for more.

Several of the poems reflected Plomer's homosexual experiences in very elliptical terms. 'John Drew' is a portrait of a young Irish tramp he had picked up in London, though no one could tell that from the poem; and 'Tattooed' reflects his friendship with a young labourer. The volume was politely received, but there is a sense of tiredness about some of the weaker pieces ('A Prison for Sale' and 'Only the Word'), and there are even unassimilated echoes of T. S. Eliot ('A Traveller's Tale' derives from 'Journey of the Magi'), of which Plomer, always his own best critic, must have been uneasily aware.

He spent the winter of 1936/7 back in his Norfolk Square rooms, which had been redecorated. In December 1936 he attended Spender's wedding reception ('a somewhat bizarre affair at which I very much enjoyed myself—largely in talking to Rosamond,' he wrote to John Lehmann),[51] and he passed Christmas in Tunbridge Wells, where his parents were now temporarily living, their ceaseless moves mirroring Plomer's own homelessness. He gave John Hampson Simpson a description of the visit in a letter of 29 December 1936:

My father was mostly in bed taking alternate mouthfuls of heroin and preserved ginger; my mother, with one foot in the grave, was, so to speak, doing a high kick with the other; and my aunt [Laura] was taking refuge from her husband, who not long ago tried to compass her destruction by means of a flying machine: she was to take lessons in stunt flying! In between whiles I walked in the forests of Lord Abergavenny with an old friend called Bill who would please you, I think, and furnish a good subject for your wicked pen.

His own writing had all but stalled; he abandoned the play, and considered producing a series of short stories or vignettes of contemporary society. The first of these was 'Ever Such a Nice Boy', a delicate, subtle study of male sexual frustration, narrated by an uneducated and uncomprehending young woman. It was not the first time Plomer had used a female narrator, for one of his best Japanese stories, 'The Sleeping Husband', is partly told by a woman, but it seems to have been with 'Ever Such a Nice Boy' that the possibilities of stressing and making use of the gulf that Plomer felt existed between men and women first came to him. He was to make extended use of the technique in writing *Museum Pieces* some years later.

At the beginning of 1937 he made his first broadcast for the BBC, having been invited to do so by Forster. He and Forster spoke on modern literature on the Empire Service, though Plomer grumbled to Elizabeth Bowen, 'Why, oh why, do people build empires? And what's the good of talking to empires unless one can tell them what one thinks of them?'[52] In spite of his inexperience in this medium, he was a success from the start as a broadcaster; his deep mellow voice and precise enunciation were well suited to radio, and he spoke easily and well even on unscripted programmes. Soon he was being invited to broadcast regularly on literary topics. A BBC internal report later described his voice as 'full, warm and genial. Middle-age. Pleasant personality', and his producer noted that he was 'Very nice to work with. A good broadcaster.'[53]

Socially, his life was busier than ever. As an example of the way he dashed about he described to Elizabeth Bowen his appointments for a single week early in 1937:

Meetings with Tony Butts and Raymond ('Know-all') Mortimer, an invitation to swim at the R.A.C., lunch at Tunbridge Wells, lunch at 'the Lehmann home' in leafy Bucks, a tour of the picture galleries with Joe [Ackerley], a card-party in a slum, and so on. How interesting life is! And I'm only just back from a visit to John (Hampson) Simpson, during which I insisted on inspecting Birmingham. My goodness, what a place, what a nation of shopkeepers, and what architecture—I never saw a worse advertisement for laissez-faire. We were very thorough, art gallery, cathedral, night-life, intellectual circles, etc.[54]

To the great events gradually pushing Europe into war Plomer paid little attention, though he was in fact very well informed for the time. His friends Isherwood and Spender, with their firsthand knowledge of Germany, gave him repeated warnings of the menace of Nazism, and as early as 1930 he had tried (and failed) to avoid passing through Mussolini's Italy on his way to and from Greece, saying he 'didn't like the politics of the place'. In general, though, he thought politics not the concern of an artist. The Spanish Civil War, when it broke out in July 1936, polarized and politicized many English men of letters, but not Plomer: apart from some casual references to friends who were in Spain, whom he hoped would not 'stop a bullet', the Spanish conflict left him unmoved.

As for the British constitutional crisis of late 1936, occasioned by
Edward VIII's determination to marry the twice-married Wallis
Simpson, Plomer regarded it as a source of good jokes. 'I shunned
the Coronation as far as possible,' he wrote to Elizabeth Bowen
(May 1937), 'but did hear that the naval rank of the Duke of
Windsor has been altered from Admiral of the Fleet to 3rd mate of
an American destroyer.'[55] Spender, who had joined the Communist
party, wrote him letters exhorting him to 'move beyond liberalism',
but he parried these effortlessly and patiently. The ballad he wrote
three years later, 'Father and Son: 1939', comes closest to a sharp
reply in the biting stanza,

> With a firm grasp of half-truths, with political short-sight
> With a belief we could disarm but at the same time fight,
> And that only the Left Wing could ever be right,
> And that Moscow, of all places, was the sole source of light:
>> Just like a young hopeful
>> Between the wars.

'I do not say my way of living was virtuous, or the best possible
for my purpose,' he wrote in retrospect, 'but the increasing tension
and despair of the world's prospects did not leave the spirit free or
the judgement calm. To be deficient in hope is un-Christian. I was
deficient in hope, and a lapsed Christian.'[56] When pressed by his
Communist friends as to what he believed in, he would reply that
he believed in art and literature. As the 1930s wore on, however,
such detachment became harder to sustain. The years of drifting
and dreaming were coming to an end.

Edythe and Charles Plomer at the time of their wedding, 1901

William Plomer (standing) with his
mother Edythe and brother John, c.1907

William Plomer as a schoolboy

Roy Campbell, Mary Campbell, and Laurens van der Post at Sezela, 1926

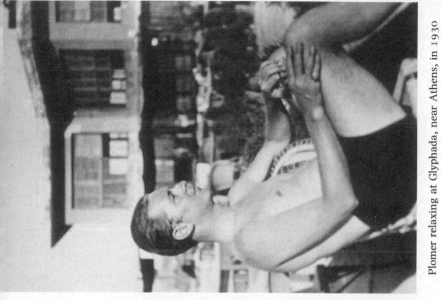

Plomer relaxing at Glyphada, near Athens, in 1930

Plomer in London, 1929

Bernard Bayes

William Plomer, Lillian Bowes-Lyon and Marjorie van der Post at Tetbury. In the front, Jan van der Post and friend.

Plomer and Virginia Woolf at Monks House, August 1934

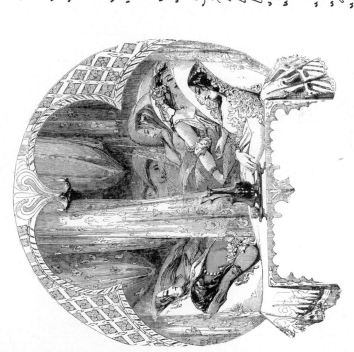

"Sleepy?"

"Mmm."

"I believe they put tranquillizers in the sherbet."

"Mmm."

"Who'd have thought that a cheap tourist night-flight by Circassian Airways could be so restful?"

"Mmm."

"It's these divine Pneumofoam Bouncispong Couchettes."

"Mmm."

"But it's a bit crowded. When I turn, you'll have to turn, so will Ayesha, so will Zuleika, Selima, Lalla Rookh, Pamela Hansford Johnson, Margharita Laski (they seem to be everywhere, those two) & the whole bunch."

"Mmm."

"Do you know whose birthday it is tomorrow?"

"Mmm."

"Aren't you going to send him a wish?"

"Mmmmm. Dear Rupert! Many, many happies!"

William Plomer's birthday card to Rupert Hart-Davis

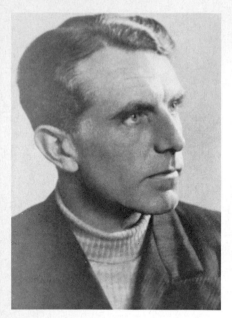

Joe Ackerley

Stephen Spender

Rupert Hart-Davis and daughter Bridget, 1935

Charles Erdmann, c. 1940

(l. to r.) Charles Erdmann, Richard Rumbold, and
William Plomer at Flansham, 1957

11. *Reader and Writer*
1937–1939

AFTER Plomer published *The Child of Queen Victoria* with Jonathan
Cape in 1933, Rupert Hart-Davis twice asked him to lunch to meet
Cape's famous reader, Edward Garnett. In appearance Garnett was
a mid-Victorian figure, dressed in a heavy, capacious suit and
peering through oval spectacles of the kind Thackeray wore, and
he had a Victorian capacity for painstaking thoroughness. He had
advised Cape since 1921, just after the firm's foundation, and had
been a major influence on the formation of Cape's list of authors.
As a detailed textual critic, a sniffer-out of talent, and an encourager
and nurturer of young writers, he had no rivals. Jonathan Cape, a
tough, hard businessman, had never really liked Garnett, but he
valued and retained him for his ability, though the two clashed
often. When Garnett died unexpectedly in February 1937, Cape set
about looking for a replacement reader at once, and Hart-Davis
suggested Plomer. Plomer, like Garnett, was distinguished in his
own right; he had published with Cape, and had built up a solid
reputation as a reviewer: he was clearly a first-rate judge of books.
It was no small compliment to be asked to replace Garnett. Jonathan
Cape agreed to give him a six-month trial, from April 1937, at a
salary of £25 a month. The association begun in this tentative way
lasted for thirty-six years.

Even in the 1930s few publishers felt competent to do without
a literary adviser, the Woolfs being exceptional in this regard. Most
publishing houses employed at least one writer to read incoming
manuscripts and to pick out the most promising for further
examination. Even Geoffrey Faber, himself a highly competent critic,
from the start of his publishing career engaged T. S. Eliot to read
for him. Plomer began working for Cape as the sole reader, though
naturally Cape took advice on specialized volumes from numerous
experts. The rhythm of the reader's work had been set by Garnett,
and Plomer carried it on without change. In essence it required
attendance at Cape's offices on only one day a week, usually
Wednesdays at lunch-time, for the regular directors' meeting. On

Wednesday morning Plomer would go to the office at 30 Bedford Square, leave with Cape's secretary his reports on the manuscripts he had read during the previous week, and hunt through the pile of manuscripts just come in, the great majority of them unsolicited. Many of these he would reject after a brief leaf-through, but a few he would put aside to take away. Usually there were two or three of these, though he might take as many as half a dozen if they were short. In company with Jonathan Cape and the other directors, Wren Howard and Rupert Hart-Davis, he would then have a meeting over lunch at a nearby restaurant, usually the Etoile in Charlotte Street. If the manuscripts under discussion warranted it, the meeting would be continued afterwards, usually in Wren Howard's room at Cape's. Both at the lunch and at the following meeting Plomer would give his recommendations verbally, and hear what decisions the directors had taken on his previous reports. In these relatively relaxed working luncheons he was able to get to know the directors and to learn the firm's business, for the decisions he was taking demanded a basic knowledge of what would or would not sell.

Like Garnett before him, Plomer found it hard to like Jonathan Cape, though he came to respect him. Born into a working-class north-country family, Cape was at this time fifty-eight years old, and the years of struggle he had undergone before establishing his firm in 1920 had reinforced a perhaps inborn determination to get a shilling's worth for a shilling. Physically he was a formidable figure, tall, with iron-grey hair and a face that in repose was forbidding, even grim. He was as insatiable a pursuer of women as Plomer was of young men; beyond their business association they had virtually nothing in common. Cape seemed just a little unconvincing, as if there were an element of masquerade about him; Plomer initially thought of him as 'an actor who had cast himself for a lifelong run in the role of an eminent London publisher'.[1] Plomer came to dislike Cape's habit of inviting him to lunch 'for a talk', and then delivering an endless monologue. Plomer might as well not have been there; one topic in Cape's soliloquy would suggest another, in what Plomer came to call 'monologue-rolling'. Cape's letters to him frequently took the same form, and he would sometimes send the best specimens on to Hart-Davis, who had suffered from them too. Yet Cape quickly came to value Plomer's judgement, and there was never a hint of friction between them. When Cape died, in 1960, Plomer delivered a generous, sincerely felt tribute to him at his memorial service, remarking that he, 'because of his faith in his staff, his affection for them, and his kindness to them, sustained them and made them not merely content, but happy, to serve him'.[2]

George Wren Howard, the firm's other founding partner, was a trim, even elegant man whose passion for neatness and precision complemented Cape's impatient energy and drive; it was Howard's attention to the details of production that made Cape's publications such models of the book-manufacturer's craft. In addition, it was he who held the purse-strings, and he was as reluctant to part with money as Jonathan Cape himself. Howard and Plomer got on well from the start, though of the three directors Plomer counted only Hart-Davis as a friend. He and Hart-Davis would kick each other under the table when the monologue began rolling, and would afterwards exchange notes on the boredom and the indifferent food, which Plomer once characterized as 'gristle pie'. The bond of sympathy between them strengthened steadily, and Plomer was soon being invited to spend enjoyable weekends with the Hart-Davis family on their farm near Henley-on-Thames.

He found the work at Cape's congenial and not so demanding as to prevent him from doing his own writing. Attendance on Wednesdays was not onerous, and he had always been a voracious reader, so that the daily labour of getting through the often ill-typed scripts was merely a chore, and not the deadly drudgery it might have been to another man. Always the task was lightened by his curiosity, and the hope, constantly renewed despite disappointments, that the next script would reveal a great, undiscovered talent. He compared the work to that of a pearl-diver prising open dull oyster-shells, hoping always for the gleam of a pearl.

After many years of experience as a reader, he was to sum up the complexities of the task like this:

The functions of a publisher's reader are not universally understood. He regularly reads a good many offerings and does not write his reports about them as a critic, in the grander sense of the word, but as a taster and adviser. It is his business to tell the publisher what sort of book he has been reading, and not merely to sum up its literary merits or faults, but to give an opinion about its prospects as a published book, either in its offered form or a revised one.

He has to take into consideration not only its matter and manner, but the author's reputation (if any), previous books, and future prospects; the readability and probable saleability of the book; its topicality or absence of topicality; its potential appeal to the supposed general reader or the specialist; the literary fashions or tendencies of the moment; the present condition of publishing; the particular status, tastes, list, prestige, and solvency of the firm whose head or heads he is advising, and various other matters.

His report is as a rule likely to be written concisely and promptly, and to be more like a snap judgment than an analytical essay. Whether the report is favourable or not, the publisher, if interested enough, may like to try it out upon one or more other readers, and perhaps to read it himself, before coming to a decision.[3]

Plomer proved to be a most conscientious reader. His reports, always handwritten in his beautiful script, were thorough, and they usually contained a clear opinion, 'Recommended', 'Not Recommended', or, if he thought the work needed further polishing before publication, 'Worth Consideration'. These recommendations were generally, though not always, followed, and the directors valued Plomer's reports because they were full and consistent enough to enable others to make an independent judgement on the basis of what he had written; even if he advised that a manuscript be rejected, his report allowed others to see whether or not a second opinion should be taken. He accused himself of having 'as many blind spots as a leopard', but in fact he had few real prejudices. One of them, oddly enough, was a deep-seated belief that no novel written in or about Canada held any interest for English readers: 'Lively, but Canadian' was his comment on a novel he had liked but advised against.[4] Another of his quirks was a willingness to reinforce adverse judgements of a work by analysis of the author's handwriting, so that in occasional reports one finds such a sentence as 'I think the author is a nut case, & his signature seems to support this theory.' But these oddities were not typical, and Cape's were ready to bear with them because the value of his advice was early recognized.

The earliest of his hundreds of reports to survive in the Cape archives, from 1 May 1937, reveals his complete confidence at an early stage in the work. He was reporting on an American thriller which seemed to him notably lacking in thrills, and of its hero, a sailor, he remarked:

His rise to the rank of captain seems too smooth & easy, & in any case he's rather a bore. So is his author—serious, heavy, much too long-winded, a writer without charm, humour, or anything that can really be called imagination. If the book were half its present length it would still be pretty dreary, & it makes the alleged glamour of the 'great days of sail' like a cold Sunday afternoon in Victorian New England.[5]

In later years this sureness of touch became steadily more marked. The reports in which he recommended publication of a book were often long (up to six pages) and thoughtful, filled with shrewd insights well expressed; they always make good, and often very amusing, reading. When advising Cape to decline a book, he could be devastatingly brief:

Harmless account of going to live at Ditchling with husband & children, with plenty of triviality, simple nature notes & bits of literary allusions. The work of an amiable & quite inoffensive nobody, it has no prospects.

A romantic-sentimental novel about Mary of Modena, the Queen of James II. It is full of chatter & twittering & smiles & kisses & eyes that fill with tears, like cisterns, & are smiled through, & people who 'shout angrily' or 'shake visibly' or 'snap with a flash of sarcasm' or 'giggle' or 'fling' themselves into chairs. And the passage of time is apt to be marked by sentences like 'Christmas came & went.' In brief, it is a typical example of its kind of low-grade, commonplace 'historical' fiction. Not up to Cape standard.

A Faber & Faber chuck-out. It couldn't be anything else but a Cape chuck-out too. Vaguely rhapsodic utterances in boneless diction about love & natural phenomena, by an author with no taste and a faulty ear.

Occasionally he condemned an offering merely by quotation:

Trivial versicles from Hemel Hempstead. Specimen:

> 'Why can't I just give my all & my lot
> I think then I would find
> Just how much I have got.'

Even more damningly, he quoted and commented,

> 'Formidable ties in different parts
> Throughout the surface of earth,
> May bring true union in body politic,
> Amidst a permanent mirth.'

A rejection slip is called for, and pretty loudly.

He was capable of recognizing new talent as soon as he saw it, and in these cases, particularly if he were dealing with poetry, he would push very hard indeed for publication. Having read the manuscript of Derek Walcott's first volume of verse, *In a Green Night: Poems 1948–1960*, Plomer reported,

Walcott is 30, and, so far as I can see, the best poet in English of his generation ... Much of the imagery of his poems is tropical or sub-tropical or Caribbean. They are not obscure and are invariably interesting, full of a pleasing sensuousness, and the work of a man with a clear intelligence, sensibility, powers of observation, and a good ear. Almost every poem has memorable lines & images, & the poems are various—retrospective, love poems, elegiac, satirical, &c.,—and the work of an original poet with a fine technique.

I have no idea how he will develop, or whether he intends only to write poetry. But I have no doubt that he would have no difficulty in finding a good publisher here, & I should like to see Cape as his publisher. I think his work, even if it doesn't at once 'pay,' would give prestige to Cape's list—in which poetry is I believe at present only represented by the dead and the middle-aged.

He also recommended publication of Ted Walker's first volume, *Fox on a Barn Door*, in 1964:

I have seen poems by this man here and there. They are not at all bad, & most have appeared in periodicals, some of distinction ... As for *quality*, he seems to me better than some who get published & have some reputation. All his poems are *about* something, about more than meets his observant eye ... It is the fashion among reviewers now to sneer at *New Yorker* contributors: I see nothing to sneer at, & something to respect, in this one.

He made mistakes, of course, and occasionally these became known, as when, in 1962, he advised against publishing Barbara Pym's *An Unsuitable Attachment* after she had published all her previous books with Cape. The most famous case was his long criticism of Malcolm Lowry's *Under the Volcano*, a criticism that Jonathan Cape sent to Lowry in 1945, provoking Lowry's masterly 15,000-word defence of his novel. Cape then published the book without alteration; Plomer was stung. After Lowry's death, when Harvey Breit and Margerie Lowry edited his letters, they proposed to print Plomer's report in its entirety. Plomer saw the volume in galleys, and objected strenuously:

I suppose somebody gave permission for this printing. But nobody asked if I minded. *I do mind.* I regard readers' reports as *confidential.* I have twice incurred odium . . . by the sending on of copies of reports by me, or parts of reports by me, to authors. Also, a good many people know that I have been a reader for Cape for 30 years or so. I don't see why *everybody* should be in a position to know what I have written *confidentially* at any time about a particular book or author.

At his insistence the report was cut from the book, and it also subsequently disappeared from Cape's files.

If Cape's sometimes disregarded his advice, it must occasionally have regretted doing so. Plomer strongly recommended that the firm publish the work of John Betjeman, for instance, and that of Vladimir Nabokov; in both cases his advice was disregarded. Among those he 'discovered' or recommended for publication very early in their careers over the coming years were, in addition to Walcott, Hughes, and Walker, Arthur Koestler, Alan Paton, John Fowles, Stevie Smith, and Ian Fleming. It is no wonder that the firm came to think highly of him, and to maintain this opinion for more than three decades.

In September 1937 he signed a contract committing him to read for Cape for another year, and raising his salary to £33. 6s. 8d. a month.[6] He was glad of the Cape position because, as he wrote to tell Elizabeth Bowen:

It provides me with what I haven't had for nearly ten years—a bare living. It's quite interesting, but of course it takes up nearly all my time, and as I still do a certain amount of reviewing I seldom have a moment. It's annoying, as I feel a novel ripening. The only thing is to take a leaf out of Balzac's book and sit up all night dressed like a monk and drinking what he called 'pure coffee.'[7]

This projected novel went very slowly, and instead of getting on with it he took himself off to what he described as 'a minute and rather bizarre flat' in Brighton, at 5 Ship Street Gardens, from May 1937 to September 1938, in spite of the fact that this move took him further from his ailing mother (his parents had now moved to a gloomy, wistaria-wrapped Victorian hotel in Cheltenham). He moved partly to enjoy the pleasures of life in a seaside town, and partly to avoid the pressures of London; the summer in Dover in 1936 had made him realize how much he disliked living in large cities. 'I've enjoyed a lot of swimming, which is much pleasanter than writing novels,' he told Bowen.[8] From Brighton he would commute to London on Wednesday mornings for the Cape meetings, an arrangement that gave him the best of both worlds, for he generally managed to see his London friends on Wednesday afternoons and evenings, returning by a late train to Brighton, laden with new manuscripts to read.

On some of his trips to Cheltenham he would call on Cecil Day-Lewis[9] who was teaching and writing poetry there while working for the creation of a socialist Britain through the Communist party, which he had joined in 1936. Plomer had met him through Spender and Auden, and came to like him in spite of thinking his poetry shallow and decorative.[10] Day-Lewis was to write that Plomer had opened his eyes to the beauties both of Cheltenham and of the surrounding countryside:

I was still insensitive to architecture, and it is deplorable that for so many years Cheltenham's beauties,—the Regency terraces and the charming 'colonial' houses—should have been lost on me. It was not until William Plomer came to stay with us that, fired by his own enthusiasm, I began to use my eyes on the elegant ironwork and stuccoed façades all round me. '*Un*stuccoed, I should call it,' William boomed as we paused before a rather tatty specimen, his deep voice rumbling slowly like an ox-waggon crossing a bridge—a voice whose resonance gives an Olympian robustness to the childish puns he occasionally makes, as when he sent me for Christmas a picture of Egyptian priestesses dancing before a god, and captioned it 'Horus with his Horus girls.' Whether in town or country, I found William a splendid companion on a walk, interested, tremendously observant, as knowledgeable about birds and wild flowers as about urban sights: his objectivity, his concern for physical detail, gave me my first direct experience of one facet of the novelist's mind.[11]

From Brighton it was also easy to see the Woolfs at Rodmell, and he began visiting them more often than he had recently, dropping in to have tea in company with T. S. Eliot, or playing bowls on the lawn with Leonard. Early in September 1937 he went to a party at which Quentin and Angelica Bell were present—'Need they be so dirty?' asked Plomer rhetorically of Elizabeth Bowen[12]— and saw another example of Virginia's ruthless teasing. The victim was a female teacher, and Virginia, stimulated by Plomer's presence, pretended to this woman that she (Virginia) was a graphologist:

Virginia tried to get hold of her letters (she had a lot in a bag) thinking it would be amusing to read them. We did get hold of one and I read it aloud. It was frightfully funny, though not meant to be. The educationist was a bit puzzled, but took it fairly well. Then Virginia tried to read a character from some handwriting on an envelope, and built up an extraordinary fantasy all about a woman with 'golden down' on her face, who was impulsive, came down to dinner in pyjamas, and kept a squirrel in her workbasket. The educationist began to look rather haughty, and finally said rather acidly, 'Are you sure it's a woman? *Perhaps* it would interest you to know that that letter is from a *MAN*. And a *MAN* who happens to be the leading authority on education *IN THE WORLD*.' And did we laugh! ... Then we played bowls and they fell into the pond, and altogether a riotous time was had by all except the educationist.[13]

When he was not travelling from Brighton to see friends, they came to see him: in a single week in September 1937, he entertained Lilian Bowes-Lyon, John Hampson Simpson, and E. M. Forster.

His correspondence, always voluminous, began to balloon at this period. Loathing the telephone, and refusing to use it unless obliged to, he was as great a letter-writer as Virginia Woolf. He tended to begin each morning with an hour or two of correspondence, dashing letters off at great speed in his clear hand, writing as easily as he talked, and with the same wit, enjoyment of life, and capacity for conveying scenes and characters that he showed in verbal anecdotes. He would fill pages with descriptions of a visit to Haworth, for instance, on a black and wintry day, with a funeral procession ascending the steep village street to the church, concluding, 'The Brontës were tremendously arty-crafty. The girls were always being busy with their needles or clever with their pencils, and as for Branwell, no wonder he went to the Black Bull.'[14] Or he would give a hilarious description of a party at the house of Forster's policeman friend Bob Buckingham, ending, 'Mrs. Buckingham senior is reported to have found me "a card". Only the joker, I expect, though it would be nice to be the Ace of Spades.'[15] Interspersed with the letters were his extraordinary postcards, many of them Victorian or Edwardian, and usually chosen with an eye to the character of the recipient. To Hart-Davis, for instance, he would often send cards of Victorian bathing belles, Japanese geishas, or Edwardian actresses posing alluringly; to John Lehmann, René Janin, or Joe Ackerley would go moustachioed Turkish wrestlers displaying their biceps, or small boys showing their buttocks. His friends looked forward to his letters and kept them; many thousands survive.

His novel meanwhile stagnated: 'I dare say it will only be a mouse, and a stale mouse, when I *am* delivered of it,' he wrote cheerfully enough.[16] He was eventually to produce 25,000 words of it before destroying them as 'not important enough for publication'. But the book he was working on with real enthusiasm during this period, and the one that would make him better known than anything he had produced so far, was not written by himself. It was *Kilvert's Diary*.

In September 1937, on one of his Wednesday forays to Cape's, Plomer had found among the pile of waiting manuscripts a packet containing two bound Victorian notebooks filled with spiky sloping script, together with a letter explaining that this was part of the diary of a Victorian clergyman, Robert Francis Kilvert, and that Kilvert's nephew, T. Perceval Smith, wondered if Cape thought it worth publishing; if so, he would send more of the volumes, of which there were twenty-two. Hart-Davis was in the room when Plomer opened the first volume, and in later years remembered Plomer wrestling for a moment with the difficult handwriting, and then groaning in mock dismay, 'Oh Lord, I'll take this away and have a look at it.' The next Wednesday he was back full of excitement: 'I think it's marvellous, send for the other twenty!' he exclaimed. At the directors' meeting that followed he argued strongly and successfully that it should be published, and also asked to edit it himself, since he did not trust anyone else to do the job.[17]

Abandoning his novel, he set to work on Kilvert's diary as soon as the other twenty volumes arrived in a cardboard suitcase. It was obvious that there was too much of the work to publish in its entirety, and Plomer determined to make a selection of about one-third of it. He began by reading the whole diary, which ran from January 1870 to March 1879, or at least as much of it as had survived, for there was an unexplained gap between September 1875 and March 1876. He found the handwriting almost illegible, but was prepared to struggle with it because the subject-matter was utterly absorbing. He had always been fascinated by the Victorian period in England, and this was a window on to that vanished world, one that offered some surprises. Kilvert's description of undressing and bathing naked on a crowded beach, for instance, modified some of the commonly accepted beliefs about the period more completely and convincingly than any scholarly book about Victorian morals could have done. In addition, much of the diary concerned the period when Francis Kilvert was curate of Clyro, in the part of the Welsh border country that Plomer had visited from Beechmont, and in which he had spent the winter of 1929 at Lingen. 'It's as good as the Caledonian Market,' he wrote enthusiastically to Bowen. 'It simply *creates* that really unknown and remote period. I showed a bit of it to Virginia [Woolf]: she was most excited. I have insisted on editing it myself ... But it's going to be a great deal of work, especially for some poor typist, who will probably be driven blind and mad.'[18]

He settled down to work on the volumes, editing them by the apparently simple process of pencilling a line in the margin to mark passages he wanted the typist at Cape to copy for him. He considered with great care what to select, however; like any diarist, Kilvert produced over time a number of passages that are very similar—descriptions of picnic outings, for example, or lyrical writing inspired by the sight of the Welsh mountains under moonlight—and of these Plomer selected what he considered the best, and omitted the others. Whether consciously or not, he tended to cut passages in which Kilvert's passionate devotion to God showed itself at length in prayers of supplication or thanksgiving, and he included almost every passage indicative of another passion, that for young girls. To an extent this was the instinct of a shrewd writer giving the public what it wanted, but it also made Kilvert more like his editor: less interested in God and more concerned with sex.

To familiarize himself with the countryside Kilvert knew so well, he visited Clyro in August 1938, staying at Crossway Farm just outside the village, and found himself in a world that seemed scarcely to have changed since the nineteenth century:

No car, no telephone, no bus, no newspaper, no wireless, no MSS. The conditions a trifle rougher than I anticipated. I eat eggs & rabbits & drink milk & perry, & take my bath under a bijou waterfall in a ferny grot. The people I am with are charming, perhaps because they are happy.

I have already been over most of Kilvert's beat. Things haven't altered much outwardly, except that there are many more houses fallen into ruin ...

The local intellectual threatens to be a bit of an incubus. He is very booksy but not very discriminating, & his attitude to culture is rather babu. 'What is your opinion of Jane Austen?' is the sort of question he asks ... One can't get away from him on foot because he is a prodigious walker: however my legs are longer than his, so I hope to triumph.[19]

The first volume of the diary was published in 1938, and it was an enormous popular success, taking Cape and even Plomer by surprise. Reviewers praised the work as a classic, and recognized Kilvert as one of the greatest English diarists, comparing him with Pepys and Evelyn—and finding other aspects of his writing comparable to Proust and Gerard Manley Hopkins. The public, increasingly alarmed at the growing tension in Europe, found Kilvert's stable, peaceful world a delightful refuge from a terrifying present, and the book sold steadily. Encouraged by the success of the first volume, Plomer set to work almost at once to produce a second, which was published in 1939, and a third, which appeared in 1940. The appearance of each volume increased the critical and popular acclaim, and the wartime tension that brought about a revival of interest in the work of Trollope ensured a huge readership for Kilvert. A Kilvert cult rapidly sprang up, and a Kilvert Society was formed, with devotees holding public readings of the diary and journeying to Clyro and Bredwardine, the nearby parish in which Kilvert had died within months of writing his final diary entry. Kilvert's delightful personality and what he himself called his power to inspire love operated as strongly through his diary as they had done during his life, and the effect was not transient; the Kilvert Society has continued to thrive since the Second World War, and now, in 1987, has more members than ever. Plomer could not have foreseen this in 1938, but even then he was known as Kilvert's discoverer and editor, and was increasingly in demand as a speaker about the diary.[20]

He also found himself sought out as a reader and adviser of other writers, for as word spread that he had taken the job at Cape, his services were increasingly called on by friends and acquaintances. In May 1938, for instance, he travelled to Uckfield to see the Oxford don Humphrey House, whom he had met through Elizabeth Bowen: House and Bowen had been lovers for a time. House wanted Plomer's advice on the book he had written about his experiences on a recent trip to India. Plomer thought what House had written insufficiently digested, too fragmented, and too impersonal, and said so.[21] He also continued to give Spender advice, though it was usually disregarded, and Spender continued to criticize Plomer's own work on the grounds that it was idealistic and insufficiently politicized. In April 1938, for instance, Plomer sent Spender a copy of 'John Drew', his fine poetic portrait of an Irish tramp in London.

Spender, though he liked the poem, thought Plomer was trying to set up kindness and a return to the primitive as answers to communism. Plomer wrote to rebut this view, arguing that he did not care to make any political point: 'My own predilections in poetry are for the sensory, pictorial & plastic rather than for the philosophical, metaphysical or political.'[22]

Through his work for Cape, Plomer met other writers, for he was now often invited to Cape's literary parties. He gave Bowen one of his vivid descriptions of such a gathering, in May 1938:

I was put on to entertain Robert Graves[23] & Laura Riding[24] (alias Gottschalk). I wonder if you know her. Her fame certainly precedes her. ... Graves looked like a seedy Roman emperor with a hangover, but obviously has charm as well as talent. Rose Macaulay, breathing purposefully in my eye, wished to know what I thought of her book about Forster. As I hadn't read it, the occasion called for as much tact as you displayed in reviewing the book, but I don't know whether it got it.

Then I was pleased to meet one or two Rising Young Authors whose works I had read. You might look out for a book called The Almond Tree by Robert Liddell. Perhaps you know him. He is a palpable slyboots, & the book, though not epoch-making, seems to me a very good piece of feminine fiction.[25]

In the summer of 1938 his mother seemed better again, and as his parents moved to a boarding-house in Worthing, Plomer left his Brighton flat for London once more, at the end of September 1938. 'I leave here for good tomorrow & am supposed to move into my new flat in Maida Vale [12 Randolph Crescent] on Monday,' he wrote to Elizabeth Bowen. 'Whether I do or not must depend on Hitler.'[26] This is one of only two references in his correspondence to the Munich crisis, or indeed to the slide towards war that had been gathering pace all through the year. In March 1938 Hitler had annexed Austria while the British and French governments stood helplessly by. There was another crisis in May 1938, when a German invasion of Czechoslovakia seemed imminent; when it did not come, the British were temporarily elated. Hitler renewed the pressure, however, and in September Neville Chamberlain met him at Berchtesgaden and again at Godesberg to try to avert a German invasion of Czechoslovakia. War seemed inevitable, and on 27 September 1938 the British Fleet was mobilized. The next day Hitler agreed to a conference in Munich, at which he obliged Chamberlain and the French Prime Minister, Daladier, to agree to

almost all his demands of the Czechs, who were not even consulted.
Chamberlain flew back to London on 30 September 1938, waving
his agreement with Hitler and proclaiming 'peace with honour' to
relieved, jubilant crowds.

Plomer was far from ignorant of the significance of these events;
his friend Harold Nicolson was now an MP and a member of the
government, and Nicolson's diary at this period was full of rage
and shame at Chamberlain's actions. Others of Plomer's friends,
among them Isherwood and Auden, considered that the fight
against fascism was lost, and were discussing leaving Europe for
the United States, a course several of them would follow the next
year. Plomer was content to leave the great events of his time to
politicians and soldiers; his own concern was with his writing, his
dying mother, and his latest lover, a military policeman. 'I am not
primarily concerned with politics at all,'[27] he told Spender.

At a time when gas masks were being issued to the population,
plans made to evacuate children from London, and trenches dug
in Green Park, Plomer was writing to Elizabeth Bowen:

An almost unpleasantly wide contact with contemporary fiction has made
more clear to me than ever what we all know perfectly well—that the
only thing that gives a novel any shape, texture, lustre, or durability is
what may bluntly be called poetry, or a poetic sense, a sense of the
momentousness of what we see and feel, of the drama in trifles and the
colour in the drab. Given this sense, the word and the phrase follow, and
the word and the phrase make literature.[28]

The gas masks were never used, the trenches have been filled in,
but Plomer's analysis is as true as when he wrote it. He was right
to confine himself to his own concerns, self-centred though those
concerns may have seemed, even to some of his friends.

His mother went through another of the crises of the terminally
ill cancer patient towards the end of 1938 and again in mid-1939;
by October 1939 he was writing to John Hampson Simpson,

You will think me a heartless faithless correspondent, but for the last year
or two I have been in a cloudy state of mind, chiefly owing to my mother's
illness, which has involved endless strain and distress for everybody
concerned, and I have hardly been anywhere, done anything, or seen
anybody. She is now thought to be dying, and is not expected to live more
than a few days.[29]

She died in Worthing on 22 October 1939, aged sixty-five, leaving

Plomer exhausted by grief and the strain of coping with his father in this extremity. It is a sign of Plomer's suffering that he did not bury his mother's cremated remains, but kept them by him for nearly a year, as if he could not bear to part with her; the ashes were not interred until August 1940, at the Streatham Park Cemetery in London.[30] But although he scarcely mentions it, this personal tragedy was, even for him, being swallowed up by, and identified with, a universal one. By the time Edythe Plomer died, Britain had already been at war for more than a month.

12. *War*

1939–1945

AT the outbreak of war Plomer was thirty-six years old, and it was not immediately clear what use he could be to Britain, since his eyesight was too poor for him to think seriously about active service. Some of his friends, not much younger than himself, joined the forces almost at once, among them Hart-Davis and Van der Post; others, like Isherwood and Auden, had seen trouble coming and had taken themselves off to the United States; still others, including Spender, Ackerley, and Lehmann, continued to live as before, waiting to see what would happen as the alarm that attended the outbreak of hostilities turned into the boredom of the phoney war. In common with millions of others, Plomer felt an upsurge of patriotism in September 1939; he registered with the War Office, listing his special qualifications, but telling Hampson Simpson, 'I have no idea whether they will ever be made use of, or whether I shall just end up as cannon fodder.'[1] The War Office seemed to have no idea either, and throughout 1940 he kept up his pre-war life, sharing his Randolph Crescent flat with his Best Friend of the moment (none lasted very long at this troubled time) and working for Cape's as before.

Editing the third and last volume of Kilvert's diary took up much of his time, and he continued to receive a large fan mail in response to the earlier volumes. Many of these letters he answered personally, and one of the acquaintances he made in this way was John Sparrow, Warden of All Souls, Oxford, who wrote to Plomer in February 1940 ('Since I can't write to Kilvert') to tell him that he thought Kilvert's prose equal to that of any other writer in English. Sparrow was a friend of Harold Nicolson, and he and Plomer had met briefly once or twice at the Nicolsons' and at the Woolfs', but it was this letter that began a correspondence that was to last for years. The two were never intimates, but Plomer would occasionally be invited to stay with Sparrow at All Souls after the war, and Sparrow's many letters make it plain that he enjoyed Plomer's humour, admired his intelligence and integrity, and liked his work.

Plomer respected Sparrow, but found that a little of his manner, alternating between dry donnishness and what Kipling called 'old-maiderie', went a long way. In his correspondence with Hart-Davis he invariably referred to Sparrow, with mock ceremony and a bow to Trollope, as 'the Warden'.

In this early period of the war, with its sense of waiting for the storm, Plomer was increasingly broadcasting for the BBC. He took part in a series entitled 'Modern Masterpieces' on such works as Joyce's *Ulysses* and Strachey's *Queen Victoria*; the speakers were very distinguished, and in addition to Plomer they included T. S. Eliot, V. S. Pritchett, and H. G. Wells. In this period too he began to work concertedly on the ballads that became his most characteristic expression. He had published the first of this type in his 1936 volume *Visiting the Caves*, the poem he called 'The Murder on the Downs', a ballad-like account of a man who strangled his girl-friend on the Sussex Downs in fine weather. Plomer's treatment of the story combines macabre humour with grim factual details:

> Jennifer, in sitting, touches
> With her hand an agaric,
> Like a bulb of rotten rubber
> Soft and thick,
>
> Screams, withdraws, and sees its colour
> Like a leper's liver,
> Leans on Bert so he can feel her
> Shiver.
>
> Over there the morning ocean,
> Frayed around the edges, sighs,
> At the same time gaily twinkles,
> Conniving with a million eyes
>
> At Bert whose free hand slowly pulls
> A rayon stocking from his coat,
> Twists it quickly, twists it neatly,
> Round her throat.
>
> 'Ah, I knew that this would happen!'
> Her last words: and not displeased
> Jennifer relaxed, still smiling
> While he squeezed.
>
> Under a sky without a cloud
> Lay the still unruffled sea,

And in the bracken like a bed
The murderee.

There is little sense of the horror or tragedy of the crime; on the contrary, the poem implies a satisfying collaboration of murderer and victim, and the lightly mocking touch suggests that the event is faintly ridiculous, perhaps even amusing. Looking back on it, Plomer was to feel that the poem summed up the mood of the whole period; the dictators were preparing to loose war on Europe and the world, and their intended victims seemed paralyzed or even half-willing collaborators in the tragedy. The rather callous tone of the poem produced an answering echo almost immediately, in Auden's ballads 'Miss Gee' and 'Victor', written in 1937,[2] and what gradually became recognized as Plomer's invention of a new type of ballad was to have a considerable influence on such different poets as Charles Causley and Frank Sargeson. Plomer recognized that he had opened a new vein in poetry: 'There is something to be said for a mine of one's own,' he wrote later, 'even if it is not very productive, and even if it does not produce quite the metal one might have expected.'[3]

'The Murder on the Downs' perhaps had a personal significance for Plomer, in that its victim is a woman. His rare moments of spleen or spite had usually been directed at women, and the death of his mother, the one woman he loved, removed a tenuous link with the female sex. Hereafter his ballads frequently picture women being murdered or drowned or dismembered, or simply being scored off by men, and always the event is seen as one suited to amusement or even satisfaction, rather than regret. In 'The Philhellene: Athens, 1930' a rich American is stripped of her fortune by a plausible handsome Greek and abandoned, half mad with grief:

Deserted, this Aspasia,
This threadbare Ophelia,
Grew dowdier and crazier,
    A solitary freak,
And in fancy-dress she lingers
With a locket in her fingers
Containing a curl from
    That xenophil Greek.

In 'The Dorking Thigh' a house-hunting couple make a horrible discovery in a new home they are being shown through:

> 'Something the workmen left, I expect,'
> The agent said, as it fell at his feet,
> Nor knew that his chance of a sale was wrecked.
> 'Good heavens, it must be a joint of meat!'
>
> Ah yes, it was meat, it was meat all right,
> A joint those three will never forget—
> For they stood alone in the Surrey night
> With the severed thigh of a plump brunette.

'A Self-made Blonde', 'The Naiad of Ostend', and 'Mews Flat Mona' all describe women dying in unpleasant circumstances. Perhaps the most striking of these ballads in context is 'The Widow's Plot', written within a month or two of Plomer's mother's death. In it an over-possessive mother who tries to keep her son from marrying, and to turn him against all other women, is killed by him— accidentally, it is true, though when accused of the crime, he terms it 'justifiable matricide'. A Freudian critic might argue that in these poems Plomer portrayed the struggle for dominance that was going on between the feminine and masculine elements in his own nature, the struggle that had largely prevented him from writing for several years.

Many of Plomer's friends thought the ballads disturbingly unlike him; they suggested a side of his personality that he had previously kept carefully hidden from almost everyone. Several friends, including Van der Post, thought the poems cruel, and said so. Plomer defended himself on the grounds that 'they reflect an age for which unpleasant would be a very mild term ... No more is being done than to offer instances of how men and women behave, or might easily behave, in or near our own lifetime.'[4]

This defence is a little thin, though one ballad directly comments on the period between the wars, and with a bitterness that is the more effective for being phrased in the jolly rhythms of an Elizabethan song. Entitled 'Father and Son: 1939', it condemned the 1930s, when the dictators were rising to power and the democracies slumbered:

On a Sunday in September other troubles had begun,
There was argument at lunch between the father and the son,
Smoke rose from Warsaw and the beef was underdone,
Nothing points to heaven now but the anti-aircraft gun:

> With a hey nonny nonny
> And a hi-de-ho.

Oh, the 'twenties and the 'thirties were not otherwise designed
Than other times when blind men into ditches led the blind
When the rich mouse ate the cheese and the poor mouse got the rind,
And man, the self-destroyer, was not lucid in his mind:
> With a hey nonny nonny
> And a hi-de-ho.

In addition to writing these ballads, he was rereading all the verse he had written, for in April 1940 John Lehmann told him that Hogarth Press, which Lehmann had rejoined after some years away, had decided to publish a selection of Plomer's poems. The changes he made in reprinting his work were relatively small, but they included changing the title of two sonnets which in *The Fivefold Screen* he had called 'Greek Love'; he now thought the latter title in bad taste, and wanted the poems called simply 'Two Sonnets'. The alteration suggests that he was growing even more circumspect in his references to homosexuality.

The cruelty his friends detected in his ballads seemed to be in the air of Europe in the first year of the war, as Nazism triumphed across the Continent. Hitler conquered Poland in less than a month, in September 1939; in April 1940 the Germans took Norway and Denmark, and in May 1940, in a brilliant campaign, invaded Belgium and Holland, struck through the Ardennes to the Channel, paralysed the French, and isolated the British Expeditionary Force. The evacuation from Dunkirk began on 27 May and ended on 3 June; the Germans entered Paris in triumph on 14 June, and by 17 June 1940 the French were suing for an armistice. Britain now stood alone, and during the next few months one invasion scare followed another.

In these circumstances Plomer decided that he could not go on living as though nothing had happened, and he must have been relieved when a call for his services came from an unexpected quarter. One of the many friends he had made in the 1930s was a young man named Ian Fleming,[5] whose brilliant brother Peter was the oldest friend of Rupert Hart-Davis. Ian Fleming, the future creator of James Bond, had greatly admired Plomer's writing, particularly *Turbott Wolfe*, which he had read as a teenager at Eton, and in 1926 had written Plomer a fan letter saying so. Plomer had received it in Japan and replied civilly, and on reaching England in 1929, he had made contact with Fleming. Fleming invited Plomer to a party at his mother's house in Cheyne Walk, and the two men had become friendly. Plomer was to admit[6] that their friendship seemed a curious one at first; the young journalist, with his passion for women and glamour, might have been expected to regard Plomer as a slightly stuffy intellectual, while Plomer could not share Fleming's love of golf, fast cars, and gambling. Each of them, however, was a great collector of characters, and each recognized the other as something quite out of the ordinary; Fleming was attracted not just by Plomer's writing, but also by his wickedly malicious wit, his flow of amusing conversation, which made him a sought-after dinner guest, and by the sense Plomer gave of really caring about other people. Plomer had impressed (and been impressed by) Fleming's formidable mother, and he became a regular guest at Fleming's parties; they were to remain close until Fleming's death in 1964.

Fleming, thirty-one in 1939, had had a rather chequered career as a foreign correspondent and stockbroker, but once war broke out he had slipped into a job that suited him perfectly: personal assistant to Rear-Admiral John Godfrey, the newly appointed Director of Naval Intelligence at the Admiralty. During the First World War the Naval Intelligence Division had been the best-organized intelligence-gathering organization of its type in the world, and Admiral Godfrey was determined to rebuild it. Working out of room 38 in the west block of the Admiralty building, he began recruiting a staff of naval officers and gifted civilians, and soon built up a remarkable body of talented men and women. Ian Fleming, with his rather swaggering air of self-assurance, his genius for organization, and his boyish passion for the mechanics of spying, was chosen to be Godfrey's personal assistant, a position that gave him power out of all proportion to his rank, which was that of reserve lieutenant. He was able to recruit his friends into the Naval Intelligence Division (NID), and one of those he chose, in July 1940, was Plomer.

NID concerned itself with all aspects of spying, collating, and interpreting the intelligence that came in, producing propaganda to discomfort the enemy, and keeping the British Navy as well informed as possible. It employed experts in every field: scientists, cryptographers, interrogators, cartographers—and writers. One of its tasks was to produce a Weekly Intelligence Report, giving a summary of the main events of the past week, listing political, technical, and military changes of which NID had become aware, and giving an interpretation of the importance or otherwise of these developments. The Report, although secret enough to be denied after 1941 to Britain's Russian allies (who tried repeatedly to secure copies of it)[7] was circulated widely to Royal Navy vessels, so that it was read by both the First Sea Lord and the lowest midshipman. In the summer of 1940 it was being edited by Simon Nowell-Smith, a bibliographer and journalist who had worked on the editorial staff of *The Times* and on the *Times Literary Supplement* before the war.[8] Plomer was appointed as Nowell-Smith's assistant, with chief responsibility for preparing the political section of the Report.

Plomer left Cape's in June 1940, and was replaced there as reader by Veronica Wedgwood.[9] Throughout the war he kept up occasional contacts with Cape's, reading and commenting on books for them at intervals, to keep his hand in; he clearly expected to return as chief reader when the war ended. These occasional reports passed through the hands of Veronica Wedgwood, who was to say that she found them a liberal education to a beginner—clear, penetrating, and careful. 'One was aware that he never skimped his reading through haste or fatigue, that he was always alert and eager to detect a potential talent. . . . In publishing history there have been readers who were his equal; I am sure there has never been one who was better.'[10]

He began his work at the Admiralty in July 1940 at a salary of £35 a month, a slight improvement on the £33 Cape had been paying him.[11] He was given the anomalous rank of 'civilian officer' on the naval staff, and rather liked this contradiction in terms, remarking wryly, 'As a fish out of water, I was in my element.'[12] He had found himself in a series of such peripheral situations ever since being sent to Aunt Hilda's school as a boy who did not belong to it, and though regular officers would sometimes make huffy remarks about not being able to stand civilians,[13] in general he got on very well with his colleagues.

Plomer and Nowell-Smith shared a table in the increasingly crowded room in which Fleming himself had a desk, room 39 on the ground floor of the Admiralty, a high-ceilinged, uncomfortable Victorian office with large iron radiators and cream-painted walls. Its windows looked out on Horse Guards Parade, where Plomer

must occasionally have recognized some old friends. The First Sea
Lord had his office immediately overhead, and on the opposite side
of the square could be seen the private entrance to 10 Downing
Street.[14] A doorway near Fleming's desk led through to Admiral
Godfrey's room, room 38, into which Godfrey (the original of 'M'
in the Bond books) summoned his subordinates by coded bursts of
the buzzer on his desk.

At the height of the war room 39 was jammed with sixteen
people: one captain, seven commanders (the rank Fleming attained
by 1942), two lieutenants, Plomer, Nowell-Smith, and four women
secretaries. The psychological pressure of working under such
conditions must have been extreme; Plomer was later to remark
that he had 'spent most of the War in a series of small enclosed
spaces, more suitable for submariners than claustrophobes'.[15] In
time, the overcrowding, overwork, and the tension of bombing told
on his nerves, but to start with he thoroughly enjoyed the job.

He would arrive each morning at the Admiralty, presenting his
pass to the marine at the entrance, and make his way down the
bustling corridors to the large black door with '39' on it in white.
Inside he would settle down at the table with Nowell-Smith and
their secretary, Marjorie Napier, and begin combing through British
and foreign newspapers, reports from the wire services, ships at
sea, diplomatic missions, and spies, any source of information the
Admiralty thought likely to be useful, and would extract from it
information about political and economic developments throughout
the world. Plomer and Nowell-Smith would call on their own
knowledge or that of the experts Godfrey and Fleming had collected
to evaluate the information, and would then select what was most
interesting and important, and condense it into a style and form
they hoped would be useful for naval officers. As Plomer later put
it, 'What we hoped was that, by doing something to dispel fogs of
ignorance and uncertainty, we should be helping them to know
better what the enemy was up to and his good and bad fortunes,
as well as those of our allies and of neutral nations, and in general
to improve visibility.'[16]

Plomer found this apparently dull task surprisingly enjoyable and
interesting. For one thing, it made him very well informed indeed
about the general course of the war, and the news he was dealing
with, after all, had immediate implications for his personal safety,
and for that of his country. In addition the task of extracting the

pith from great masses of printed material and reducing it to lucid prose was one for which much of his working life had suited him; producing his reader's reports for Cape involved precisely this task. Just once, according to Nowell-Smith, Plomer was able to enliven the stolid official prose of a report with some light verse of his own. Radio Moscow had announced that to celebrate Red Aviation Day an air-force band would parachute into Red Square playing the Red Aviation march. This ludicrous idea roused Plomer to an epigram which he entitled 'Martial Moujik':

> Angels? Or hairy-wristed nuns? Neither we understand,
> But Stalin's Rhythm Boys playing to beat the band.
> The Heavens ope: more loud the harps and trumpets play.
> 'Tis not the Judgment, but Red Aviation Day.[17]

This verse drew a tart reprimand from the First Sea Lord, and thereafter the Report confined itself to the serious business of war.[18]

Plomer found the companions with whom he shared the work 'pleasant and civilized', as he told Virginia Woolf,[19] though they never became his close friends. In 1941 Plomer and Nowell-Smith were joined by the bookseller Dudley Massey, and the three of them used to spend their lunch-hours together, in one of the cheap little restaurants of which Plomer was a connoisseur. The hunt for a good one became harder as the war progressed and the quality of food in Britain declined. Nowell-Smith preserved some lines Plomer scribbled in 1942:

> Ah, that ingenious Ministry of Food!
> It may be clever, but it is not good
> To turn potatoes into jam, and dine
> On offal, oats and home-made cabbage wine.
> What do I do when I am told to try
> A groundsel salad, or a toadstool pie?
> I fast for victory. It is not nice
> To take the Ministry of Food's advice.[20]

He and the others always worked on Sundays ('days of least interruption', Nowell-Smith was to say),[21] taking days off in mid-week instead, and in the course of their Sunday searches for a new restaurant, perhaps one in which Plomer had heard real mayonnaise was still to be had, Plomer would point out to Nowell-Smith the odd details that he alone seemed to notice: houses with ridiculous names (he collected them, and delighted in finding

'Ye Kumfy Nook' or 'Emoh Ruo'), or the statue of Clive of India which Plomer, because of a slip of the chisel on the plinth, always called 'Olive'. Nowell-Smith and Massey noticed, as Day-Lewis, Spender, and others had before them, that a walk in company with Plomer, even down a street they thought they knew well, was an apparently endless series of revelations.[22]

They noticed too, with curiosity, the way Plomer chose to keep different aspects of his life separate. He told his pre-war friends virtually nothing about what he was doing in the Admiralty, and he concealed from Nowell-Smith and Massey his life outside office hours. This was not merely a matter of keeping his low-life friends away from the grander ones, though to some extent it originated in that. One afternoon Nowell-Smith mentioned to Plomer that he was going to a play that evening. 'Which one?' asked Plomer, and on being told, he said genially, 'Enjoy it!' He did not add that he would be there himself, and Nowell-Smith was therefore surprised to see Plomer in the theatre foyer that night with Edith and Osbert Sitwell. He did not approach them, but the next morning when Plomer arrived in room 39 Nowell-Smith hinted that he had seen him 'with your socialite friends'. Plomer merely smiled, shrugged, and kept his privacy.

On another occasion in 1940 Nowell-Smith got a tiny glimpse into another aspect of Plomer's life, when the two of them went for Sunday lunch to the Garrick Restaurant in Charing Cross. As they hung up their coats inside the door Plomer spotted Hugh Walpole dining alone, and was thrown into an uncharacteristic dither. In 1940 Walpole had written to Plomer, accusing him of 'neglecting old friends', and 'passing from circle to circle', ignoring the last circle he had moved through, and though Plomer had defended himself ('I haven't got a circle, and if I neglect old friends it's because I'm not in a position to entertain them'),[23] a coolness had grown up between them. 'What shall I do?' he muttered to Nowell-Smith, who knew nothing of this estrangement, 'Do I talk to him or don't I?' In the event he went boldly up to Walpole's table, and was soon exchanging cheerful banter with him: the ill feeling was forgotten.[24]

His own writing stopped completely in the first months of his work at the Admiralty: 'I emerge from my maritime duties feeling like a boiled owl or steamed cod,' he told Hart-Davis.[25] Presently he began getting on top of the work and his writing picked up gradually again. In 1940 John Lehmann had begun editing *Penguin New Writing*, a paperback book-magazine published by Penguin Books. Plomer's contribution to the distinguished first number, which included new writing by George Orwell, Christopher Isherwood, V. S. Pritchett, and others, was a description of his visit to Elizabeth Bowen, 'Notes on a Visit to Ireland'. He soon became a regular contributor to the magazine, furnishing ballads under his own name or lightly amusing articles under the pen-name 'Robert Pagan', which he invented in November 1940.

He had a brief period of leave in September 1940 and took refuge in Worthing from the blitz, which had begun in earnest with the bombing of London on 7 September; from then until 3 November 1940 London was raided every night. Plomer stayed in Worthing with his father, who had rented a small house there, and who had become slightly eccentric after the death of Edythe; Plomer wrote Virginia Woolf a lively description of the two of them, father and son, sitting in the conservatory, Plomer eating mulberries and correcting the proofs of the third and last volume of *Kilvert's Diary*, his seventy-year-old father wearing a black skull-cap, doing a piece of tapestry in *gros point*, and reciting Schiller.[26] Charles Plomer now seemed to his son to be 'bursting with ill health and good works'; he had become a pious evangelical Christian, who, though very poor himself, spent much of his time persuading wealthy friends to help refugees and victims of the bombing. Plomer was impressed in spite of his tendency to laugh; as he wrote to Hart-Davis, who was now a captain in the Coldstream Guards,

There's even a poster on the front gate saying 'God's the Boy, pray on!' or words to that effect, and churchwardens and people keep popping in. I do wish he was Very High Church, but no, there is a decided taint of evangelicalism. However, the good works really do work, and he gets money out of the prosperous for the benefit of the indigent, re-trousers the blind, and makes the lame walk—if they think they can get something for nothing.[27]

Back in London after this period of leave, he went round to Mecklenburgh Square, where the Woolfs had leased number 39 since August 1939, to have tea with Virginia, only to find, as he later wrote to tell her, 'The square roped off, ingress forbidden, and a gap in the eastern side with a heap of débris. Also, delayed action bombs were thought to be lurking in the vicinity.'[28] Fortunately the Woolfs had decided to stay at Rodmell that weekend. Plomer himself must often have wished that, like them and such friends as E. M. Forster, he could decamp to a country home, for he was experiencing some near misses, or *'demi-vierges'* as he translated the phrase for an enquiring French acquaintance. He described the scene outside his own flat to Virginia Woolf:

The next house but one to this was set on fire last night, & there are sundry hummings, whistlings & poppings every night. There is also quite a tidy battle going on at the moment and I can see the bursts of anti-aircraft fire over my left shoulder. It all seems rather primitive.

I do hope Rodmell is peaceful, as it ought to be in September, with misty mornings and brilliant days, & the zinnias glowing, as usual, in their usual place.[29]

But even the bombing, which reached a peak of intensity towards the end of September, provided him with some amusement, and a few days later he was writing to tell her one of the slightly malicious stories she so much enjoyed:

One is really getting quite bored with ruins. They look so much better trimmed with ivy and owls. And these bombs that take so long to go off, they're really more tiresome than the ones that go off at once. What a funny life. In peace time I like an orderly world, & if I want disorder, I can provide it myself ...

A woman whom I used to dislike when I was a child made vast quantities of jam & accumulated them. She was in the habit of taking refuge in the larder where the jam was stored. The other day her house was bombed & she emerged dressed from head to foot, yes, hatted & shod as well, in blackcurrant jam, with bits of glass here & there like spangles. I'm simply delighted![30]

In October, for some weeks, NID was moved from the Admiralty to underground offices in Cricklewood, but once it became clear that the worst of the blitz had passed for the moment, Plomer and the others returned to room 39. In 1943 they were to be moved again, to the aptly named Sanctuary Buildings in Great Smith Street, Westminster, before returning finally to the Admiralty.

The death of his mother and the fact that he himself, like thousands of other Londoners, faced death every day made Plomer increasingly aware of his own mortality and inclined to draw up some sort of account of his life. The work he was doing in looking through his poems for republication by Hogarth Press—*Selected Poems* appeared in November 1940—made him review his writing career, and there are other signs that he was considering both past and future in a way that is unusual for an unmarried man in his thirties. He made a will at this time, calling on the advice of E. M. Forster, who had also advised Edythe Plomer on her will, and who was one of her executors (Plomer himself was the other). More important, he was considering writing an autobiography. During one of his lunch-hour strolls through the streets in October 1940, he was suddenly sprayed with machine-gun bullets from a German plane that was gone before he could react. 'The aim was poor,' he told John Lehmann dryly,[31] but it made him realize that he should like to leave a record of his life. He saw little chance of getting the freedom to write before the end of the war, however, telling Lehmann, 'I am virtually a prisoner. So far as lust & literature are considered, I am really a sort of Unexploded Bomb.'[32]

He exaggerated, for in both lust and literature he was finding occasional opportunities to explode. The notion that he was a prisoner, sitting behind the solid walls of the Admiralty building, acutely aware through his work of the perilous position of Britain at this time, raising his eyes to a sky streaked with con-trails and feeling that his nerves were beginning to give way, found expression in one of his finest poems of this period, 'The Prisoner':

> Every morning the prisoner hears
> Calls to action and words of warning:
> They fall not on deaf but indifferent ears.
>
> Free speech, fresh air are denied him now,
> Are not for one who is growing thin
> Between four walls of Roman thickness.
> From his cell he sees the meetings begin,
> The vehement lock on the orator's brow
> And the listeners warped by want and sickness ...
>
> While flights of bombers streak his patch of sky,
> While speakers rant and save the world with books,
> While at the front the first battalions die,
> Over the edge of thought itself he looks,
> Tiptoe along a knife-edge he slowly travels,
> Hears the storm roaring, the serpent hiss,
> And the frail rope he hangs by, twisting, unravels,
> As he steps so lightly over the abyss.

There is a clear expression in this last image of his sense that he was losing touch with reality; he was desperately tired, as almost every Londoner was in these days and nights of constant alarms and sudden death.

In the midst of so much danger and destruction, it is curious, if natural, that the deaths of two friends from his pre-war life, neither death the direct result of the bombing, should have stirred him more deeply than all the violence around him. The first was that of Virginia Woolf, who drowned herself in March 1941 by filling her pockets with stones and walking into a river. Plomer, with T. S. Eliot, Vita Sackville-West, and others, wrote 'a sort of obituary' of her for Cyril Connolly's magazine *Horizon*, but it expresses little of the deep feeling of loss he experienced when he heard the news. To Hart-Davis he wrote, with characteristic understatement, 'I was very fond of her, you know.'[33]

The other death was that of Anthony Butts, who committed suicide in May 1941 after a long struggle with cancer. In spite of his indifference to Plomer's warnings, he had avoided the gutter, but only just; there are rare references in Plomer's letters of 1940 to 'Tony Butts, seedy and needy, poor dear'.[34] By the outbreak of war he and his mother had been reduced to shabby rented lodgings and a restricted diet. Butts had for some time been in poor health, but though his friends told him he was visibly wasting away, he made light of their warnings, and, distrusting doctors, failed to get medical attention. When, in 1939, he discovered that he had inoperable cancer, he tried repeatedly but half-heartedly to kill himself with drug overdoses. The last of these attempts led to his being incarcerated in a gloomy London nursing home, where Plomer visited him several times. Each time Butts was thinner and more depressed, though he put on a brave face for Plomer, cracking jokes about his suicide attempts and telling his ribald and unlikely stories.

As much as the death of his mother, Butts's decline seemed to symbolize for Plomer the destruction of everything he held dear. Butts had epitomized the qualities of generosity, gaiety in the face of adversity, and a determination to live the life he chose no matter what the cost, which Plomer thought typical of the highest aspects of English civilization, and which he envied in part because he lacked the courage (or foolhardiness) to live like that himself. As the casualties of the bombing increased and the pressure on hospital beds grew, Butts came to feel that the best thing he could do for his country was to rid it of himself. Although deadly ill, he left the nursing home for a large London hotel, and soon after moving into it, one night at the end of May 1941,[35] scribbled a brief note to Plomer, smashed a window in his room, and threw himself four floors to the street below, dying instantly. Almost his only possession, which he left to Plomer, was a badly muddled autograph manuscript filled with hilarious anecdotes about his family, which Plomer had repeatedly urged him to write down.

Plomer was deeply shocked by Butts's death. In later years several of his friends were to say that his relationship with Butts was the most important he ever had, in emotional and intellectual terms. That distinction belongs to his love for his mother, but the degree to which Butts was important to him is shown by the literary tributes he paid Butts. The first of these was one of his most accomplished and moving poems, 'In a Bombed House: An Elegy in Memory of Anthony Butts', which he completed in October 1941 and printed privately (at the urging and expense of Butts's mother) the next year.[36] It opens with images of the disorder that Plomer had always associated with Butts, and that seemed now to have affected the whole world:

> The raid is over and the feverish night
> (War's a debauch for which our heirs must pay),
> A chair is smashed, the floor is strewn with glass,
>   Each fragment bright with day:
>
> Not this nor any other day will bring
> That dear familiar (quizzical, urbane)
> Who found life wonderful, acquitting man
>   As guilty but insane.
>
> He was a true eccentric, understood
> Nothing of money but the joys it brings,
> Loved the bright fuss of worldly luxury
>   And bold imaginings:
>
> Selecting words, or colours with a brush,
> Sometimes he caught a strangely clear effect,
> Like the chance images of passing life
>   That lonely lakes reflect.

.   .   .   .

But he was an exile in his own country
As many noble Englishmen have been:
The glowing eye grew coldly critical
   Of the unhappy mean,

Distasteful of a duller England where
Suburban civilization ruled at last
A people tamed to obey the *comme il faut*,
   Untrue to their great past.

.   .   .   .

Over the world he went—in search of what?
Beauty and truth, perhaps, that shop-soiled pair
Of vague ideals, asked more of life, perhaps,
   Than life can spare.

A dilettante with a watchful eye,
Who served the world because he could admire,
Negroes he loved, and next to Negroes, paint
   Which warmed him like a fire;

Europe he loved, a Europe of his own,
And saw it fall into a fierce decline,
And in his vitals too the rot set in—
   He was part of the design.

.   .   .   .

As in a waste of seas the cruising shark
Follows a raft, and never turns aside,
Death followed him. But love was following too,
   Was with him when he died.

Many elements in this tribute to Butts could apply just as well to
Plomer himself, particularly the references to Butts's quizzical
urbanity, his gift with words, his sense of being exiled in his own
country, his travelling in search of a reason for being, and his
realization that the moral rot that had set in all over Europe gnawed
at his own vitals too. The elegy for Butts was a lament for all that
Butts and Plomer had shared.

Another source of sadness was the terrible decline of Lilian
Bowes-Lyon, who had for years been suffering from diabetes and
Buerger's disease. Gangrene had set in shortly before the war, and
during the war years she suffered a series of amputations, first of

her toes, then her feet, then her legs below the knee, then below the hip. For years she endured intense pain, facing the inevitable with great courage, and continuing to write poetry from her bed. She welcomed her friends to a succession of nursing homes, greeting them always with apparently unforced cheerfulness, and she occupied herself with works of charity for those she thought less fortunate than herself—though such a group could scarcely have existed. 'With your strong will and warm heart you will go on mastering, as you have done this many a year, the physical enemy,' Plomer wrote to her encouragingly in January 1941,[37] but her continued decline and terrible sufferings affected him more each time he saw her, as he continued faithfully to do.

Because he knew more than the public about the losses to Allied shipping from the U-boat packs and the extent of the bombing of coastal towns, he was more aware of the perils Britain faced throughout this dark year. In part because he had consciously adopted Britain as his homeland, he was intensely patriotic, and hated to think of the diminution of British power and prestige. 'William had a terrible war,' Spender was to say later. 'He knew a lot of what was going on, and took it much to heart.'[38] In spite of that, he tried to take a philosophical attitude to the physical ruin all around him. In January 1941 he wrote to John Hampson Simpson:

The other day I went down to the City, soon after that fire-Blitz night, to look at the damage. There is something singularly *un*moving about a lot of burnt-out commercial establishments. Here and there I felt an aesthetic emotion at the sight of some Victorian façade with nothing behind it but daylight, looking like gigantic stone lace, or like something in a drawing by Piranesi. Once I laughed, at a notice saying TEAS on a door leading into a mountain of smoking débris. Once I felt philosophical, noticing outside St. Paul's those stumps, so carefully preserved, of the old St. Paul's that was burnt down in 1666 ... Well, John, it's a long war that has no turning. Good luck to us all.[39]

Luck was needed, for on Sunday morning 11 May 1941, Maida Vale was heavily bombed, and Plomer woke with a jerk as his windows blew in. During a lull in the raid his near neighbour Joe Ackerley came round to see how he was, and while the two of them were talking, Ackerley's own flat took a direct hit and was destroyed. He moved in with Plomer until he could find alternative accommodation. 'I am open to the elements, unwounded, and without gas,' Plomer wrote to John Lehmann, 'but still in situ, if not in statu quo.'[40] He did not remain *in situ*. The damage to his flat proved worse than he had at first thought, and because his front door had been blown in, he was burgled the next day, losing his clothes, two clocks, and other valuables. Accordingly he decided to leave, and though it took him months to find alternative rooms, on 6 November 1941 he moved into a first-floor flat at 29 Linden Gardens, a quiet leafy cul-de-sac of handsome white-painted mid-Victorian houses in Notting Hill Gate. This flat consisted of two rather dark rooms that had been subdivided out of a larger apartment, and which were higher than they were wide; there was also a kitchen alcove and a small bathroom. In this modest dwelling, devoid of ornament and containing scarcely any books,[41] Plomer was to spend the next twelve years. The Admiralty obliged him to install a telephone, an instrument he had always avoided. He did his best to conceal the fact that the hated intruder was in his flat, confiding his ex-directory number to very few people, among them Hart-Davis; but not even they were encouraged to ring him, except in emergencies, on what he memorably called 'the nasty little black vulcanite public convenience'.[42]

He was now coping more comfortably with his Admiralty job, though there were frantic periods early in 1942 when Nowell-Smith was ill with jaundice and Massey had influenza. But with the cessation of night bombing Plomer was less tired, and his writing began to pick up again. He was now writing regularly for *Penguin New Writing*, mostly under his own name, though 'Bob Pagan' gained life steadily in his often ribald correspondence with Lehmann:

Bob P. has just sent me an airgraph letter from the Muddle East [sic]. He says he is entirely taken up with 'operations'—as he is in the R.A.M.C. [i.e., the medical corps], I'm not quite sure what this means, but it is likely to be an elastic term with him: if there is one quality which his intimates agree in attributing to him, it is his elasticity.[43]

More important, he found the energy and time in September 1942 to begin the autobiography he had been contemplating since the start of the war. Hart-Davis was among the first to hear about it:

Quant à moi, I feel like a contemp. old half calf, spine a little worn, needs re-backing, joints cracked, very rare, but quite cheerful ... The main news is that I am writing a book of a somewhat autobiographical nature, &

hope to have finished a rough draft by the end of the year. It ain't boring to write or to read, but I don't know yet whether I shall print it.[44]

He wrote it rapidly and happily, and though he said it was to be mostly about places and things and about people other than himself, it was, like all his longer writing, an attempt to define what he was. Nearly a third of the book focused on his ancestors, suggesting the degree to which he wanted to portray himself as rooted in England; the rest of it dealt largely with Africa and Japan, and though he called it *Double Lives*, it might just as well have been entitled *Triple Lives*, or even *Multiple Lives*.

He worked at it with the care of a good biographer, checking every fact against his own letters, diary notes, and other contemporary documents, and, for the chapters on his ancestry, doing careful research into dates and genealogies. Scarcely a fact in it can be faulted. On the other hand, he committed many sins of omission: the reality of relations between his parents or between himself and his father are glossed over in the diplomatic phrases of which he had become a master in his work at Cape's. Nor could any reader ignorant of Plomer's true nature have guessed from *Double Lives* that its author was a homosexual, or that he was ever anything but contented with his lot.

Just as striking and curious is the fact that he played down or simply failed to mention several of the friends who had helped him at crucial points in his career: for example, there is no mention of Teddy Wolfe, and in the account of the *Voorslag* period and the voyage to Japan, Van der Post's and Campbell's roles are minimized. At this time (1942) Van der Post had been reported missing in action in the Far East (he had in fact been captured by the Japanese), while Campbell was serving as a coast-watcher with the British Army in East Africa, and was continuing to attack Plomer in verse for having avoided active service. Campbell's poem 'Talking Bronco', without mentioning Plomer by name, referred to a biographical note in *Penguin New Writing*, in which Lehmann had spoken of Plomer's work in the Admiralty as 'of national importance'. It is no wonder Plomer underplayed Campbell's influence on him when Campbell at this very time was penning a portrait of his former friend

> ... in the Admiralty, licking stamps,
> To wear an uniform with golden clamps

Out of his job some aged clerk to Jew
Who thrice as well as he the work could do—
Which Yesmann praises in his 'Emu Series'
(That Woolworthiser of ideas and theories)
As 'work of national importance'—(Queries!)[45]

Double Lives was published by Cape in October 1943, and it was very well received. 'Yes, William's autobiography is splendid,' E. M. Forster agreed with Christopher Isherwood,[46] and by April 1944 Forster was writing to Plomer that he was so fired by its success that he had begun an autobiographical sketch of his own.[47] At the end of 1943, just three months after publication, the entire edition had been sold, and Plomer was able to remark complacently to Hart-Davis, 'The book went off with a bang, didn't it. Rather crazy fan-mail.'[48]

He took occasional snatches of leave from the Admiralty during 1943, staying with Forster for a few days and with Rosamond Lehmann for nearly a week—'although, poor dear, she wasn't in the rudest of health', he told her brother.[49] He also spent some days with new friends, John and Myfanwy Piper, in their home Fawley Bottom at Henley-on-Thames. He had met the Pipers through Hart-Davis, whose near neighbours they were,[50] and Plomer had found them a delightful couple. John Piper was a gifted painter, designer, and poet, and Myfanwy was a writer. Plomer thought them both talented and charming.

In September 1944 he spent a weekend with Edith and Osbert Sitwell at Renishaw Hall near Sheffield. He had known them both since 1929, and he had met them at irregular intervals since at literary gatherings; but this seems to have been his first visit to Renishaw, a huge and gloomy place set on a coalfield, so that the air smelt faintly of smoke, and the clashing of shunting coal-trains kept guests awake at night. Edith had grown more eccentric with the death of her eccentric father the previous year; her toques and her huge ear-rings set off her strong features, while her sweeping skirts and fingers laden with massive rhinestones expressed her colourful personality and attracted attention as they were designed to do.

Plomer did not find his stay particularly restful, though the weather was perfect and he was able to wallow with Edith in an ornamental pool in the garden.[51] The Sitwells, though they were living in luxury and safety from bombing, seem to have spent much of their time complaining to him: about the old man who could not be prevented from making long speeches under their windows, about the gardener's dog that had barked for seven hours without stopping, about a local clergyman who suffered from loneliness and to counteract it invited Osbert to come to tea whenever he liked, about the bell-ringers who *would* practise, and about the strangers who insisted on sending them poems in shoals from all over England. 'I hope you will return before very long,' Edith wrote after he had returned to London, where V1 'doodle-bugs' had now begun to fall, 'although I must say it would be purely to *our* advantage. At the moment life is one long hell.'[52] In spite of this visit he saw the Sitwells more often in London from now on, usually meeting Edith for lunch at the Sesame Club in Grosvenor Street.

The flying bombs, when they first appeared, were something of a curiosity, though the novelty wore off with a bang. Plomer read a newspaper report of one that had fallen near Shearn's vegetarian restaurant, discomfiting the diners by depositing on one table fragments of a horse that had been standing in the Tottenham Court Road. The macabre incident amused Plomer, and inspired his ballad 'The Flying Bum: 1944', which ends,

> 'Hark, I hear an air-raid warning!'
> 'Take no notice, let 'em come.'
> 'Who'll say grace?' 'Another walnut?'
> 'Listen, what's that distant hum?'
> 'Bomb or no bomb,' stated Minnie,
> 'Lips unsoiled by beef or beer
> We shall use to greet our Maker
> When he sounds the great All-Clear.'
>
> When the flying bomb exploded
> Minnie's wig flew off her pate,
> Half a curtain, like a tippet,
> Wrapped itself round bony Kate,
> Plaster landed on Louisa,
> Tom fell headlong on the floor,
> And a spurt of lukewarm custard
> Lathered Mr. Croaker's jaw.
>
> All were spared by glass and splinters
> But, the loud explosion past,
> Greater was the shock impending
> Even than the shock of blast—

Blast we veterans know as freakish
Gave this feast its final course,
Planted bang upon the table
A lightly roasted rump of horse.

A new friend he met through Lehmann at this time was the Greek essayist and poet Demetrios Capetanakis, who was living in London and who had made the acquaintance of both Lehmann and Forster. Plomer first met him at one of Lehmann's parties, in 1941, and during the next three years got to know him well and to like him. Capetanakis was small and slightly built (Plomer once called him 'the John Hampson Simpson of Greece, or shall I say the Yanni Hampsonopoulos Simpsonakis'),⁵³ but his luminous intelligence and dark flashing eyes seemed to Plomer to give him a double brightness, and his translations of his own and other poems from the Greek were inspired. He died after a lingering illness in the spring of 1944, another on the lengthening list of Plomer's dead friends. 'That little black fire', Plomer wrote gloomily to Lehmann, 'was bound to consume itself.'⁵⁴ And in a later letter he added, 'A real poet is lost, yes, and an English poet. The growth of his sympathy with England & the English would have borne much fruit if he had lived.'⁵⁵

Plomer continued to broadcast for the BBC throughout the war, mostly on literary topics. George Orwell, working for the Indian section, invited him to talk about Forster's novels, but he declined on the grounds that he had nothing new to say about them. He spoke, however, on a variety of other subjects, ranging from *Kilvert's Diary* to Virginia Woolf. 'I contrive', he told Hart-Davis, 'to do bits of reviewing & broadcasting (to India, but does that peninsula listen?) to boil the pot, which always has a hole in it.'⁵⁶ Through this work, which, as he implies, brought a welcome addition to his income (the BBC paid £5 for a thousand-word script) he met a talks producer named John Morris, who worked for the Far Eastern section. Morris, athletic and enquiring, had been a professional soldier before the war, and had travelled widely in south-east Asia and climbed in the Himalayas. In India he had fallen in love with his batman, and had realized that he was a homosexual; this discovery had persuaded him to resign his commission and return to England, where he presently found a post at the BBC. He was a burly, round-faced, jovial man, and he and Plomer struck up a friendship that, like all Plomer's friendships except that with Campbell, proved lasting, and which over the years became increasingly close.

It was in 1943 that Plomer's almost frenzied sexual promiscuity received a sudden check. Since the mid-1930s he had had no regular partner, but had taken his pleasures where he could find them, and he found them almost everywhere, especially in barracks, dockyards, and police stations. As a matter of habit he would go out in the evenings, usually alone, to 'cruise' the pubs and clubs frequented by his kind. His friend Ackerley was to record having had relations with 'several hundred young men, mostly of the lower orders and often clad in uniforms of one sort or another,'[57] and the number of Plomer's partners is not likely to have been lower. Often no words were spoken in these encounters: contact would be made by a single, long, meaningful look directly into the other's eyes, and the act that followed would commonly take only a matter of minutes. A station or restaurant toilet, a quiet bus shelter, even a darkened doorway would do: 'William wouldn't take somebody home if he could find a blacked-out park,' John Lehmann was to say.[58] One of Plomer's poems, 'A Casual Encounter', well expresses the lovelessness of these contacts:

> ... Cliff walls of warehouses;
> no thoroughfare; at the end a hurrying
> river, dragonish; steel gates locked;
> emptiness. Whatever they said
> was said gently, was not written down,
> not recorded. Neither had need
> even to know the other's name.

Plomer intended this poem to be read as a tribute to homosexual love, as he showed in dedicating it to Forster's friend Cavafy,[59] but all the images surrounding the encounter are expressive of barrenness, futility, menace, and confinement.

The fact that London was now full of uniforms might have seemed to Plomer's advantage, but in practice it was a situation that contained hidden dangers. Before the war the professional working-class soldiers knew the rules, knew what the twank expected, and either provided it or not. Though homosexuality was a criminal offence,[60] there was virtually no danger that a soldier who objected to being solicited would call a policeman. The thousands of Allied conscripts who now thronged the streets were a different matter, however, and early in 1943 Plomer made a bad mistake. He had been strolling around Paddington station, made eye-contact with a sailor who looked his type, and thought he detected a positive response; but when he approached the other and made his intentions unmistakably clear, the sailor seized him, called a passing military policeman, and laid a charge against Plomer. In peacetime he might have blustered his way through, or smoothed over the difficulty with money; as a last resort he could have given a false name. But the National Registration Card which every citizen was obliged to carry in wartime made that impossible, and the result was what Lehmann was later to describe dryly as 'a mess with the naval authorities'.[61]

Somehow Plomer managed to get the matter hushed up: even his closest homosexual friends, Forster, Lehmann, and Ackerley, never learned how. The likelihood is that he persuaded Ian Fleming to intervene on his behalf. Fleming was a born 'fixer'; he had great loyalty to those whom he had recruited to the Naval Intelligence Division; and he had power quite disproportionate to his rank. Hushing up a matter like this before it had gone too far and had rendered a valued member of NID useless to the Division would have been well within his capacity. Admiral Godfrey provided Plomer with a certificate of reference asserting that during the period of his work for Naval Intelligence, 'he has conducted himself to my entire satisfaction',[62] and the matter was quietly dropped.

But Plomer had had a bad fright. He had always been an intensely private man who kept his various groups of friends in watertight compartments, metaphorically speaking; the idea of being tried and convicted for homosexuality, with the likelihood of a prison term to serve, the loss of his Admiralty position, the likely loss of his position at Cape's, all these were almost certainly outweighed by his horror of the publicity, the fear of examination of his letters and diary notes in court, the shame of his father and brother, and the feelings of his respectable friends. His caution and secrecy, always marked, now became almost obsessive, and even in letters to such friends as Lehmann and Forster, his references to homosexuality and his jokes about sex ceased abruptly, never to be resumed. It seems to have been at this time that he went carefully through the letters he had kept, destroying the correspondence of his homosexual friends; the pre-1944 letters to him of Ackerley, Spender, Isherwood, and Lehmann have been lost, and those of

Forster he weeded meticulously. The letters of heterosexual friends like Hart-Davis and Van der Post survived. From now on he was much less sexually adventurous. He seems to have confined himself to old friends rather than seeking new ones, and he was on the look-out for a permanent companion.

Years later he came to think of this crisis as the beginning of the stability he enjoyed after the war, and near the end of his life he told his favourite niece Billie, 'I don't think I began to get balanced until I was about 40.'[63] At the time, however, he felt that he had only just avoided a disaster. The strain of his narrow escape, and of the war generally, was beginning to tell on his nerves by the end of 1943. He described himself as suffering from *tedium belli*, and his doctor told him the problem was 'hyper-thyroidism' and put him on a diet (no meat, alcohol, or coffee). But the truth seems to be that the pressure of recent events had brought him to the brink of a nervous breakdown. 'A sudden noise would produce an uncontrollable fit of trembling,' he was to write. 'A cup of coffee or a few pages of Balzac shook me to the roots of my being and seemed to fill the brain with blue sparks. Acutely pleasurable excitement alternated with its opposite, and a natural irritability began to verge upon mania, as if the body itself had developed a neurosis.'[64] He spent some weeks in bed, telling his friends that he had influenza, and the rest did him good, though he hated the diet: 'Think of me sucking a cold parsnip these winter evenings & washing it down with a glass of cold water,'[65] he wrote humorously to Hart-Davis.

Once he returned to work in earnest, however, he soon felt ill again. The doodle-bugs seemed even harder on the nerves than manned bombers had been, or perhaps it was merely that after four years of war he was worn out. In common with the rest of London's population, he seemed always to have one ear cocked for that menacing drone in the sky, and when the motor began to cough and then fell silent, the long pause before the explosion came was like a subtle psychological torture. By November 1944, a year after his hyperthyroidism had been diagnosed and treated, his symptoms had changed, but he felt no better: 'I feel as if I were going to give birth to a hedgehog,' he grumbled to John Lehmann.[66] Even the progress of the war, which made Allied victory now only a matter of time, gave him little pleasure, for he still had sympathy for the Japanese. 'I take a black view of the Japanese war,' he wrote to Hart-Davis; 'I'm inclined to think they'll never give in &

will have to be killed one by one—I do hope I'm wrong.'[67] Depressed, nervous to the point of breakdown, and very lonely, he was in need of someone to share his life and help him cope with the strains to which he was subjected. It was in these circumstances that he met Charles Erdmann.

Erdmann had been born in London in 1909 of immigrant parents, his father being German and his mother Polish. Friedrich Erdmann, his father, had moved to England before the turn of the century in the belief that he could make a better living there than in Germany; anti-German riots at the start of the Great War drove him back to Germany, where young Charles was educated and trained as a pastry-cook. He disliked the trade, however, and worked instead as a commercial traveller, selling watches and clocks. Late in 1938, at the urging of his father, he left Germany for England, where he hoped his English birth would assure him of sanctuary from the Nazis; he crossed the Bodensee into Switzerland, where he was interned for some months before repeated appeals to the British Embassy gained him access to Britain in August 1939. Here he was again interned until his claims to English birth could be verified. He then spent the early years of the war in a series of casual jobs, working as a pastry-cook for Sainsbury's and as a waiter in one of several small restaurants in Soho. He was stockily built and completely bald even in his early thirties; his English was badly fractured, and he never learned to write the language with ease. His heavy central European accent meant that he was occasionally assailed as a 'bloody German' in wartime London, just as his father had been twenty years before, but like others of that large population of East End Jews who scraped a bare living during the war, he congratulated himself on having escaped the fate of his fellows on the Continent. His brother, he was to learn after the war, was among the many Jews and Gentiles who died at Auschwitz.

Charles Erdmann first met Plomer in June 1944 in a small Hungarian restaurant in Dean Street, where Erdmann was working as a cloakroom attendant. Plomer had come in for a meal, handed his coat to Erdmann, and exchanged a friendly word with him; a gleam of recognition had passed between them. They had not seen each other for some months after that; Erdmann's room was wrecked by a VI, and he went to Torquay to work as a wine waiter until the flying-bomb attacks had eased. He returned to a job in a Greek restaurant, the Akropolis in Percy Street; here he was paid nothing, slept in the cellar, and was expected to live on the tips he received. And here he met Plomer for the second time, and was at once recognized and greeted. Again friendly words were exchanged, and Erdmann took the opportunity to tell Plomer how hard a time he was having. As Erdmann remembered it years later, Plomer responded with an invitation to move into the Linden Gardens flat with him: 'Look, Mr Erdmann, as you're out of work here and down on your luck, why don't you come and look after me?'[68] It was partly an act of charity, but Plomer's motives were not unmixed.

In the event, Charles Erdmann proved an ideal combination of factotum and companion. He was greatly insulted, in later years, if anyone took him for a servant; the truth was that he was never paid, but that he returned Plomer's kindness by doing the housework and attending to all Plomer's needs, somewhat as Fukuzawa had done in Japan. It is true that he was in no sense Plomer's intellectual equal; asked about Plomer's poetry, he replied, 'Oh, William dear was always at his desk, writing, writing, writing. I don't know.'[69] But he was quiet and cheerful, had a puckish sense of humour, and was an excellent cook. Above all, he quickly came to love Plomer devotedly. Plomer had probably envisaged that the arrangement might last a few months, perhaps a year at most; as late as March 1946 he was still referring to Erdmann as 'my temporary co-denizen'. But Erdmann, once he had moved in, stayed for twenty-nine years, and he greatly simplified Plomer's day-to-day problems.

In part to take his mind off the last year of the war, in part as a tribute to his dead friend Tony Butts, Plomer towards the end of 1944 began to prepare for publication the manuscript of reminiscences that Butts had left him. He soon found that the task involved not so much editing as entirely recasting the book, telling Hart-Davis that he had had to 'cut and polish and largely rewrite a MS left by poor Tony Butts. I'm too near it to judge of its merits, but Jonathan [Cape] seems to like it.'[70] Cape published the work, under the title *Curious Relations*, in the autumn of 1945, giving the author's name as 'William D'Arfey'. In his introduction Plomer wrote that the manuscript had been a first draft, rough, fragmentary, and episodic, and that the theme, though expressed as a grotesque fiction, was a serious one—'that a society economically secure but lacking in adaptability may become corrupt, fantastic and moribund'. What he did not say was that this theme had found its most vivid exemplar in Tony Butts himself. The book sold well, perhaps because, like *Kilvert's Diary*, it offered a war-weary public a glimpse of a more leisured, peaceful, and prosperous world, and by the end of 1945 it had earned Plomer £316.

Beginning in March 1945, he agreed to read and comment on the contents of each edition of John Lehmann's *New Writing* as it appeared, with an eye to helping Lehmann keep up the standard of the magazine. In addition Lehmann would send him occasional manuscripts to read before they were accepted or rejected, and would also tap him for advice on new writers worth trying. Plomer was writing less for Lehmann himself at this time: 'Poor old Bob Pagan is looking fat, nervy & war-weary,' he told Lehmann, adding, 'I doubt if there is much hope of his doing his stuff. He is *tired*.'[71] In company with Lehmann he dined with the American writer Edmund Wilson[72] late in April 1945; Plomer had recently read Wilson's *Notebook of Night*, which he thought contained one exquisite piece of prose and one very funny poem. Wilson had a reputation for irascibility, but Plomer found him both genial and communicative.[73]

Peace in Europe, when it came on 8 May 1945, found Plomer little more cheerful than he had been at the outbreak of war. 'I hope you celebrated this half-peace by peaceful Thames-side,' he wrote to Lehmann.[74] As he had been before the war, he was better informed than much of the British population, for, apart from his intelligence work, he was in contact with one of his second cousins, Richard Rumbold,[75] who had recently come back from an extensive tour of Germany as a correspondent for *News of the World*. Rumbold brought terrible accounts of the destruction in Germany, the demoralization of the population, and of Russian aggression and ill-treatment of British prisoners. Plomer came to believe that, far from relaxing into peace, Britain should be preparing for another extended war, with Russia this time, and he viewed the prospect with gloomy resignation. For him a more important event than the 'half-peace' was the publication of the ballads he had been writing at odd intervals during the war: Cape brought them out in a volume entitled *The Dorking Thigh* in May 1945. Edith Sitwell was among the friends to whom he sent copies, and she was enthusiastic about them:

The impact of the book was immediate. These poems are quite unlike anything else, and Osbert was right when he said to me that no one but you could have written them,—in spite of the fact that in active life you are the exact opposite of remorseless, I find them really terrifying, but at the same time they make me laugh till I cry.[76]

The general election followed in July 1945, and the leftward swing that swept Churchill from power took many people's minds off the continuing war with Japan. Plomer, however, followed its course carefully, and was much struck by the newspaper descriptions of the nuclear bombing of Hiroshima and Nagasaki in August 1945. In particular, an eyewitness description of the mushroom cloud that had risen above Hiroshima brought vividly to his mind the strangely shaped cloud he had seen over the city during the firework display in 1927. He had always been deeply superstitious, and he came to believe that the sight had been a forewarning. It was from this germ that his eerie story 'Thy Neighbour's Creed' sprang. More than any of his other writings it showed the degree to which, even at this time of general vengefulness towards the Japanese, he felt little but compassion for them.

The end of the war found him, like everyone else, trying to get his bearings in the strange new world that had come into being; in particular, he wondered how the experience of war could be transmuted into art, so that force and grace might be combined. These reflections emerged in his response to Edith Sitwell's sending him her new volume of poems, *The Song of the Cold*. The opening of his letter must at first have seemed to her oddly irrelevant:

My dear Edith,
    The large room at the Victoria & Albert which is at present hung half with Picassos & half with Matisses produces a strange effect. The Picassos are full of sombre power & quite without charm or grace or pathos; the Matisses are all grace and charm, and there seems nothing that they have in common with the Picassos except immense accomplishment, i.e. technical skill. And yet in older masters—a Titian, a Rembrandt—the force and grace combine: so I found myself asking whether perhaps in this age it might not be impossible to combine force & grace in one man's work, in one work of art; and, if this were true, whether perhaps the violence of this age, the wars, the immense revolution and upheaval, might not have produced a fatal, if temporary, dichotomy in human nature, so that the artist must either give himself to a matching of colours & the pursuit of a sensuous perfection (like Matisse) or create myths of terror, hate and violence (like Picasso).

The reason for this lecturette is that I have much in mind your poetry & the way it has developed, & the arduous thought & feeling that have gone to the making of it; & that I think *The Song of the Cold* shows that that dichotomy I suddenly feared need not exist, for the book contains, so to speak, affinities with Matisse and Picasso ... In the longer poems you have written in these last years the two elements (if that is the word) are fused and blent, and I take this to be a great artistic triumph over the terrible shock which it is to everybody to be living, to have lived, through these times.[77]

It was to the problem of finding new modes of expression in his own work, of discovering new outlets for his abilities, that Plomer turned at the end of 1945. He had himself blended sensuality and myths of violence in his wartime ballads; now he looked for some more extended way of doing the same in prose. The result was to be the best of his novels.

13. *Picking up the Threads*
1945–1951

THE post-war world was a great disappointment to many of those who imagined that peace would bring a return to what they had known before 1939. Plomer had had no such idle hopes, but he found adjustment to his new life painful all the same. The Admiralty released him in December 1945, and after taking a month's leave, he returned to Jonathan Cape—but not, as he had expected, as chief reader. That position had been taken earlier in 1945 by Daniel George Bunting, an anthologist who wrote under the name Daniel George. Fifty-six at this time, he had had a varied career as a librarian, inventor, gas-appliance salesman, and engineer, but he was a widely read man with an apparently instinctive feel for books that were, or could be made, saleable. Plump, dapper, and affable, he had one great advantage in Jonathan Cape's eyes: he was willing to work full-time, which neither Plomer nor Garnett before him had consented to do, though Cape had pressed them each in turn. According to Nowell-Smith,[1] Plomer was disappointed to find himself partially superseded by Daniel George; but if so, he swallowed his disappointment quickly and grew to respect his fellow-reader, though he was at first saddened by his scorn for contemporary poetry. 'How right you were about Bunting,' he told Hart-Davis, 'the more I see him the more I like him.'[2] However, Plomer's new salary was not particularly warming; he was offered £34 a month, just one pound more than he had been earning six years before. 'Jonathan Cape's name was not exactly a byword for spendthrift exuberance,' he wrote with pardonable acidity years later.[3]

A greater disappointment was his discovery that Hart-Davis was leaving the firm. After demobilization Hart-Davis had suggested to Jonathan Cape and Wren Howard that his share of the managing directors' bonus be increased to one-fifth, and Cape had turned him down flat.[4] It was a decision Cape must have come to regret; Hart-Davis sold his 1,000 Cape shares, and started his own firm in partnership with David Garnett. Hart-Davis had been a major part of the editorial inspiration at Cape's, and the firm went through some thin years after he left.[5] No one at Cape's could have missed him more than Plomer, for whom he had been a sympathetic presence and a powerful seconder of Plomer's arguments for new editorial directions. They continued to lunch together frequently in London, and Hart-Davis drew on Plomer's memories of Hugh Walpole, whose biography Hart-Davis was writing; but Plomer felt keenly that Hart-Davis had left a gap at Cape's. No one ever took his place in this regard, and the firm seemed a chillier place to Plomer in consequence.

One good result of these developments was that Plomer devoted himself more to his own work than he might otherwise have done. His slow output of poetry continued, and he also shouldered an increasingly heavy load of broadcasts for the BBC, accompanying them with a steady stream of polite letters asking for better payment for his work. This dignified haggling shows in part that he was increasingly concerned about money: his income in 1946 totalled £1,121, of which only £408 came from his Cape salary, the rest being earned from published poems, reviews, and his BBC work. In addition he agreed to write several introductions to other authors' books. Before the war he had introduced L. M. Nesbitt's *Gold Fever* (1936) and Bradford Smith's *To the Mountain* (1936), and had edited the diary of Ichikawa Haruko under the title *A Japanese Lady in Europe* (1937). He now agreed to a request from Graham Greene to introduce a reprint of his old friend John Hampson Simpson's novel *Saturday Night at the Greyhound*, and he wrote an introduction to Melville's *Billy Budd* for John Lehmann (1946). Plomer had loved Melville's work since being introduced to it by Campbell at Sezela in 1926; *Billy Budd* was the third Melville volume for which he had provided an introduction.[6]

He was thinking of starting another novel in 1946, and began taking notes for it, chiefly fragments of conversations he overheard. During a stay in a Richmond nursing home for a haemorrhoids operation in June 1946, he met Lord Berners, who was there for a rest-cure, and who invited him to his house Faringdon in Berkshire, in August 1946. One of Plomer's fellow guests there was Mrs Marie Belloc-Lowndes, the novelist sister of Hilaire Belloc, who had once commanded respect, but who was now something of a figure of fun. 'Poor Marie,' Lord Berners quoted Pamela Glenconner as saying, 'she reminds me of a seagull over some harbour, screaming for garbage.' The remark appealed to Plomer, and he noted it down for possible future use.[7] He had taken Ackerley to lunch with Mrs Belloc-Lowndes some months previously, for she had admired Ackerley's *Hindoo Holiday* and expressed the wish to meet him. At this lunch it emerged that she had known Hugh Walpole, who had put her into *Fortitude* as Mrs Launce; so Plomer put her in touch with Hart-Davis in the hope that she would help with his biography. The odd fragments of Mrs Belloc-Lowndes's conversation that Plomer recorded show his ability to pick out the characteristic phrase. Disjointed though they are, they give a surprisingly clear view of one aspect of the woman who uttered them:

'When she told me, I almost *fainted* with interest.'
'Of course *she* didn't say anything, but I knew.'
'There can be no harm in saying it now.'
'He was very charming, everybody liked him, but of course he was illegitimate.'
'I *know* it is true, because he told me in the *strictest* confidence.'[8]

Even in these random observations one learns something about Plomer's attitude to women, as well as about Mrs Belloc-Lowndes. What he chooses to record of her conversation shows her as a malicious, fluff-headed gossip, too unintelligent to know or care how much she is giving away about herself.

He made and kept very few women friends in these years. Lilian Bowes-Lyon died in July 1949, and until then her slow decline continued inexorably; the circulation of her arms became affected, and in the last year of her life it was feared that gangrene might destroy her hands as it had earlier consumed her legs. Plomer was the last person to see her alive, and he had had the satisfaction of getting her to agree to the publication of her *Collected Poems*, a copy of which he was able to put into her hands a few months before she died.

Edith Sitwell he saw at rarer intervals now, and many of her letters were outcries of horror at Lilian's latest operation.[9] She was also beginning to meet some of Plomer's other friends (seldom through the agency of Plomer, who continued to keep his friends apart as far as he could), and the results of these meetings were unpredictable. In December 1947 Ian Fleming introduced himself to Edith Sitwell at a luncheon in London when Osbert was awarded the *Sunday Times Prize* for his writing. She treated Fleming with coolness, later telling Plomer, 'I thought at first, from his manner with her, that he was Lady Cunard's social secretary, but realized afterwards that she would scarcely have employed him in that capacity.'[10] To break the ice, Fleming had told Sitwell that he knew Plomer, and that he was 'very amused' to see that Plomer had listed Sitwell's *Shadow of Cain* among his favourite books in an article in *Horizon*. Sitwell was enraged by his use of the word 'amused': 'He ran no immediate risk in saying this,' she wrote acidly to Plomer, 'as we were both guests at a luncheon party given in honour of Osbert.'[11] Plomer promised to talk to Fleming about it, and his diplomacy was eventually to bring Fleming and Sitwell together amicably, in June 1948, at a luncheon also attended by T. S. Eliot, Lehmann, and Maurice Bowra, the scholar and wit.[12]

The third of his women friends in this post-war period was Sybil, Marchioness of Cholmondeley. The sister of Sir Philip Sassoon, she was beautiful and wealthy; during the war she had enlisted as a Wren and had worked in the Admiralty, where she and Plomer had come to know each other, though it was not until after the war that they became friendly through Ian Fleming, who had known Lady Cholmondeley well for years.[13] She admired Plomer's poetry and thought him the most sympathetic and amusing of human beings. He valued her friendship, enjoyed being invited to her large London house in Kensington Palace Gardens (not far from Linden Gardens, his own street), and found that her enthusiasm for good literature might be used to help sales of Cape books. 'Lady Cholmondeley is a woman with a great many important "contacts",' he wrote to Jonathan Cape in January 1947, 'and when she likes a book she talks about it, buys it, & circulates it.' Thereafter the firm sent her occasional volumes that Plomer thought she might like.

The Cholmondeleys owned a stately home in Norfolk, Houghton Hall near King's Lynn, and from 1949 until his death in 1973, Plomer spent a week there almost every summer. This visit came to be one of the regular features of his year. The Cholmondeleys' aristocratic friends fascinated Plomer, who was a great believer in the importance of ancestry and a passionate royalist,[14] and he was delighted to meet Queen Mary at Houghton in August 1948 and to spend several hours talking to her.[15] On later visits he met the Queen Mother and Princess Margaret; he particularly liked the princess, describing her as 'immensely quick and lively, extremely pretty, likes jokes ... It was rather touching to see her with her mother, as they are obviously very fond of one another. She was very good at getting down to my level, and when I told her a not over-refined joke she seemed to enjoy it a lot.'[16]

Another regular oasis in his year, after the war, was what he liked to call 'the Kilvert Jamboree'. The Kilvert Society had its origins in a small, unorganized band of fans of *Kilvert's Diary*, whose numbers continued to grow rapidly during 1946 and 1947. Each summer after 1946 they organized a memorial service for Kilvert in Hereford Cathedral, followed by various outings to places with Kilvert connections, combined with a dinner and a talk about some aspect of the diary. Plomer had had to miss the first of these 'jamborees' in 1946 because of his operation in June of that year, but thereafter he tried to go to all of them. He was naturally an honoured guest at these occasions, particularly after the society was established on more formal lines in July 1948, chiefly as the result of the enthusiasm of a Hereford man, Sid Wright, who became the first president of the society. Plomer wrote E. M. Forster a hilarious account of the 1948 celebrations to launch the society; there was a mayoral reception, attended by Lord Chesterfield, 'overbred and seemingly under-brained', followed by a giant tea-party and a public meeting, with the Dean of Hereford in the chair. On the following day, a Sunday, they went to Bredwardine, the parish in which Kilvert had died. The dean preached an emotional sermon to a congregation that included three MPs, likening Kilvert to St Francis of Assisi. He then dedicated a seat in the churchyard to Kilvert.[17] This was to be the pattern of these Kilvert gatherings in future years. Plomer was much impressed by the general atmosphere of good feeling, as this was the first Christian service he had attended for many years. Gradually and very hesitantly he was to return to the faith of his mother, and these Kilvert gatherings were the curious route by which he made the approach. In later years he often delivered the Kilvert talk or gave an address during the memorial service.

Yet another regular feature of his post-war calendar was the Aldeburgh Festival, which began in 1948, the brain-child of Benjamin Britten[18] and his companion Peter Pears. Plomer and Britten had almost certainly met in February 1937, when Britten, just twenty-three, had produced the incidental music for Auden's and Isherwood's play *The Ascent of F6*, at the opening night of which E. M. Forster, Isherwood, John Hampson Simpson, and others of Plomer's circle had been present. Homosexuality and art were the links between these men, and they were links that naturally drew in Britten and Pears too. Britten had followed Auden and Isherwood to America before the outbreak of war, but had had second thoughts about the wisdom of this action in 1941. On his return to England, he had resumed his friendship with Forster, and gradually grew closer to Plomer. Towards the end of 1946, when he was trying to put together a list of performers for the first of what he hoped would become a series of festivals in Aldeburgh, he naturally asked Forster and Plomer to participate, and they both agreed. Forster spoke on Crabbe,[19] while Plomer delivered a talk on Edward Fitzgerald, the famous letter-writer and translator of Omar Khayyám.[20] The talk, partly because of its local interest (Fitzgerald, like Crabbe, was a Suffolk man), was judged a great success, and so was the festival. Plomer missed the next few festivals, but thereafter became a regular participant at Aldeburgh, giving talks on literary topics, or readings of his own poetry, year after year. After the first visit he was generally invited to stay with Britten and Pears during the Festival, and he became very friendly with them. Britten was a rather slight, boyish figure with an engaging smile and a sense of humour that made him a delightful companion. He was also clearly a genius, and his tumultuous energies found outlet in a constant stream of compositions, interspersed with concert trips to many parts of the world. Plomer, increasingly disinclined to travel himself and writing with greater deliberation as he aged, found Britten's dynamic working methods fascinating.

Another friendship which matured just after the war was with a man Plomer was never to see in the flesh, the New Zealand writer Frank Sargeson. Sargeson lived in the Auckland suburb of Takapuna, and during the war several of his finely crafted short stories had been published by John Lehmann in *Penguin New Writing*, where Plomer read and admired them. Plomer had also read Sargeson's volume of stories *A Man and His Wife*[21] in March 1941, and had reviewed it very favourably for Lehmann's journal. 'I think I like best the terrifying "An Affair of the Heart" ... and "The Making of a New Zealander", which seems to me a wonderful sketch of the déraciné settled in a new country, and technically very skilful,' he told Lehmann.[22] The latter had then suggested that

Plomer do an article on New Zealand writers,[23] and to facilitate this—since Plomer had responded 'I only know of three NZ writers (living), but I've no doubt you have a whole regiment of them at command'[24]—Lehmann had introduced him to Denis Glover, a New Zealand poet serving in the Navy, and had also persuaded him to write to Sargeson in Auckland. Plomer and Glover seem to have met for a meal on only two or three occasions before Glover returned to New Zealand for good, but the correspondence with Sargeson, once initiated, continued for more than thirty years, until Plomer's death in 1973. It is worth digressing briefly to follow part of the course of this correspondence, because it is only the most friendly of several such long correspondences Plomer had with friends he seldom or never saw, and it is characteristic of an attractive aspect of his personality.

Sargeson (who before 1946 had published only two volumes of his own work)[25] knew and admired Plomer chiefly as a poet, and his tone in the correspondence is at first one of marked respect, and even of gratitude for having been noticed by Plomer: 'Just lately I have seen your article in New Writing & I'm afraid I felt quite overwhelmed. I had better just say that I hope it doesn't go to my head too much. It has at any rate prompted me into sticking closer to the new group of stories. I'm trying to do the best I'm capable of in the hope I won't let you down.'[26]

From this rather cautious beginning the correspondence soon warmed, as it became obvious to Sargeson that Plomer was far from being a stuffy Establishment figure, that he and Plomer had a good deal in common, from their age and colonial births to their sense of humour, their sexual preferences, and their taste in literature, and that Plomer genuinely admired and enjoyed Sargeson's writing. Soon Plomer was expressing his opinion of his contemporaries with a freedom that is rare for him on paper:

The new editor of the Times Lit. Supp. [Stanley Morrison] is a red-hot R.C. convert (or pervert, as they used to call it) & the paper is full of the clash of rosaries & distant piddlings of holy water. Then some of the alerter writers of our generation—Evelyn Waugh, Graham Greene—are also R.C.'s by adoption. It's depressing, I think. I do so hate being preached at. And I mean to go on standing on my own feet as long as I have any feet.[27]

The vigour of Plomer's judgements increased as his confidence in Sargeson's sympathy grew, so that within a year or two Plomer was writing,

I sent you lately a copy of a new book of stories by one Angus Wilson.[28] I don't like them, & I didn't like him on the only occasion when I met him. But they are obviously very clever, and so is he, and I believe there is a fashion for him in New York, where they think he is an authentic shower-up, or disemboweller, of the remains of the English 'upper' classes or something. They seem to me the work of a hysterical misanthrope & misogynist, screaming like an ape that can't get out of its smelly cage. But I shall go on reading him, for his cleverness.[29]

Plomer seldom trusted himself enough to let fly in this way at his contemporaries in correspondence with his friends in England, and one senses a relief and a release in his letters to Sargeson at being able to say what he liked without the fear that his remarks would be passed back to anyone in England. For his part, Sargeson shared with Plomer his idiosyncratic and often very shrewd literary judgements:

I think taken all round I just don't agree with the [Henry] James revival. It pains me that he should have been what he was—and an American into the bargain. That the Americans should have produced two great things, Huckleberry Finn and Whitman's verse, and then gone all wrong afterwards, seems to me colossally disastrous—though Twain has the distinction of prototyping, with marvellous fidelity, the modern American in his little bore, Tom Sawyer.[30]

To these comments Plomer responded,

About Henry James—I must admit that I've never been a James fan—so all this reprinting leaves me cold. It is certainly being overdone. I do not believe that J. can ever be 'popular' or even widely read, but he has, and deserves, & I hope he will go on having, a small & devoted following. It is to me a mystery that a man of such extraordinary intelligence & talent should have been content with such an artificial presentation of life, so remote, as far as I know it, from 'ordinary' people & what concerns them.[31]

This kind of criticism extended to each other's work. In March 1948 Plomer wrote that he was going to read his ballads to an audience of Oxford undergraduates, but that he was doubtful as to how they would go down. Sargeson responded, on 5 April 1948:

I am sure your ballads did go over well. Do you notice many imitators yet? I'm sure you will in time—indeed, you have a poor one in me, and I send you a sample. [He enclosed a ballad entitled 'Susan,' slightly modelled on one of Plomer's poems, 'Little Susan.'] But I think they are most valuable in several respects. I think it is really tragic that so few of the poets have been able to carry along Auden's ballad line for instance. Don't you sometimes think the only hope for poetry is to find a form of verse in which it is possible to use clichés? I think Auden pointed the way, and you do too.[32]

And Sargeson increasingly discussed his own work and the difficulties he was having with it:

In writing do you find that you admire most those effects that you can't bring off yourself? One reason why I read your books is because of those brilliant pictorial effects that you are *always* bringing off. E.g. Mrs. Pincus vibrating on the back seat of her car, or the negro woman with the flying tit.[33] Actually though, it's only recently that I've realized that I may have an imagination that is much closer to a musician's than a painter's.[34]

The correspondence quickly grew friendly, with Sargeson matter-of-factly and uncomplainingly telling Plomer of his poverty, his dermatitis, and his growing loss of sight as the result of retinal haemorrhages. He was struggling with his first full-length novel.[35]

I'm afraid I've been suffering from a sort of malaise, mainly owing to the worry, I think, of trying to get the various patterns in my new book to come clear. It is always the same, though. Impatience with my own books makes me impatient with other people's—so I go back to Aristotle's Poetics, and when I've finished it I wonder what the hell is the use of papers such as the New Statesman—when it was all said B.C. and said more briefly, very clearly and better.[36]

Plomer in return gave details of his own life, hinting at his homosexuality ('When I might have been practising paternity I was barking up quite another tree'),[37] telling of his carefully cultivated devices to avoid unwanted callers ('Deny them the use of the telephone; & then I am strategically fairly well-placed on a first floor, so that it's easier for me to look out & see who they are without their seeing me'),[38] and picking out his own weaknesses as a writer: 'I have no ear for dialogue and no gift for inventing it—I only hear & remember stray remarks; I am, or have become, too "literary" to create copious natural dialogue as you do.'[39]

The flow of correspondence between London and Auckland was regular for three decades, and it was clearly sustained on each side by a genuine interest in and affection for the other. With the letters, in the years just after the war, went food parcels from Sargeson (though he could ill afford to send them), English literary journals from Plomer, and a steady stream of books and manuscripts, each sending the other whatever he had recently read, written, or published. Each must have built up a surprisingly detailed picture of the world the other inhabited, and this picture included their friends and acquaintances: Sargeson got to know about Charles Erdmann, and Plomer heard a good deal about Sargeson's friend Harry Doyle, who shared Sargeson's home for years. Few of Plomer's friends in England knew more about him than Sargeson did, and the correspondence between them is another tribute to Plomer's genius for friendship—and to Sargeson's.

By 1947 Plomer's life was more closely resembling what it had been before the war. The ceaseless round of parties he had gone to in the 1930s was picking up again; late in May 1947, for instance, he helped John Lehmann (who, like Hart-Davis, had launched his own publishing business) celebrate his fortieth birthday. Plomer thought him just a little sad: 'I think, like so many, he would have liked to be whatever corresponds nowadays to a major poet—but there aren't any Shelleys nowadays, no, nor Hardys—the time isn't made for them.'[40] He also went to a party to celebrate Thomas Mann's seventy-second birthday: 'My goodness, how I admired Buddenbrooks & Tonio Kröger & Death in Venice when I read them long ago, & how I admire them in retrospect, but somehow I don't want to read them again, & I can't say I climbed the Magic Mountain with much nimbleness.'[41]

It was at this party that he met a writer whose stories he had much admired when he read them in *New Writing*, James Stern. Stern, though Irish-born, had spent twelve months during 1925 and 1926 working on an isolated farm in Rhodesia, and this African connection combined with mutual liking for each other's work helped draw them together.[42] Stern was later to write that Plomer immediately put him at his ease:

With his clipped moustache, dark hair brushed straight back, the thick-lensed horn-rimmed spectacles, the considerate, enquiring, courteous manner, he struck me as a cross between a doctor and an army chaplain with a sense, a surprising sense, of humour . . . I don't think I have known any writer inspire affection so quickly. It was not simply charm. When William was with you he gave you, like a good doctor, all of himself. And so, unlike most good talkers, he could listen. Indeed he was such a good listener (how rare a gift!) that he seemed to know what one was thinking, before one spoke. Which can be disconcerting.[43]

After this meeting Plomer occasionally spent weekends in the home of Stern and his wife, Tania, and he was always urging Stern to write more of the perceptive short stories at which he excelled.

Another aspect of the return to normality after the war was a brief European trip which Plomer and Charles Erdmann made together in June 1947, spending most of their time in Lugano. Erdmann had relations living in Switzerland, whom he was naturally anxious to see after the war. France still showed many traces of the war, and they crossed it with considerable difficulty owing to a railway strike. Amid the ruins of Calais they fought their way on to an overcrowded bus, filled (as Plomer told Sargeson) with 'expectant mothers, bursting luggage, stuffed shirts & currency sharks & [we] were driven like refugees, through a succession of ruins and an almost deserted moonlit countryside to Paris'.[44] From there they got another bus, in which they had to sit for fourteen hours on hard kitchen chairs wedged into the aisle until they reached the Swiss border. Lugano itself delighted them:

After living for years in low gear, a social & economic revolution, & an atmosphere which combines decay, dragooning & drudgery, it was astonishing to find oneself in a country where everybody is clean & polite (if a trifle dull), where everything is efficient, where there are goods in the shops & food on the table ... We were in the Ticino, the Italian part of Switzerland, which is just like Italy without the dirt & glamour (for both of which I felt a certain hunger), & we sauntered about in the hill villages, sat in sub-Alpine hayfields smelling like expensive scent, and dawdled on the lake. It certainly took one's thoughts off. But in France I got a very gloomy impression of ruin & corruption & hopelessness, inside & out—in fact France seemed a reflection of the sort of things French writers produce nowadays, nightmarish things. I must say I like my nightmares to be a bit jollier.[45]

For all that, he had enjoyed the chance to get out of England again, and he returned to Linden Gardens feeling rested and healthier than he had been for years. He and Erdmann promptly began planning another trip to Switzerland the next year. They went in March 1948, flying both ways this time. Several of Plomer's friends, who had expected him to become bored with Erdmann, were surprised that the friendship had lasted so long: 'Quelle fidélité!' remarked Forster sardonically in a letter to his policeman friend Bob Buckingham.[46] But Erdmann suited Plomer precisely because he was not highly educated, witty, or talkative. Ackerley, in his description of the Ideal Friend, had remarked, 'I did not exclude education but did not want it, I could supply all that myself and in the loved one it had always seemed to get in the way,'[47] and Plomer would have agreed wholeheartedly.

He resumed his interrupted friendship with Laurens van der Post at the end of 1947. Van der Post, having survived more than three years as a prisoner of the Japanese, had stayed on in Java to work with Lord Mountbatten, and was only now taking up the threads of his life in London. For the first time he read Plomer's *Double Lives*, and he wrote Plomer a long letter of appreciation. Plomer responded with an invitation to lunch, at which he introduced Van der Post to John Morris, who had recently returned from a post-war visit to Japan as a correspondent for the BBC. Plomer had resumed his correspondence with several of his Japanese friends as soon as the war was over, and he, Van der Post, and Morris retained a sympathy for the Japanese, a willingness to help them get over the shame of what they had done during the war, and a keenness to see Japan join the United Nations as an equal and responsible power. In this the three of them were in a minority at this time; returned British prisoners of war had brought home with them stories of the atrocities of the Japanese against Allied prisoners, and anti-Japanese feeling was so strong that Morris, as producer of several of Plomer's radio talks on Japan, had to fight hard to prevent them from being rejected on the grounds that they were too 'soft' on the Japanese.

A new link with Japan originating in this period was the outcome of Plomer's 'discovery' of the poetry of James Kirkup, which he had read in various small magazines and had recommended to Ackerley for publication in the *Listener*. Ackerley subsequently befriended Kirkup, and invited him to meet Plomer, Forster, and Morris in Ackerley's flat in the Star and Garter Mansions in Putney, in 1948. Forster and Morris, rather quiet at first, soon loosened up, but Plomer remained almost silent and immobile, strongly reminding Kirkup of Buddha. In his autobiography, Kirkup was to describe the meeting, at which Plomer seems to have given little away:

He was of medium height, broad and stocky, with a close-fitting cap of rather crinkly pale hair, a sort of pepper-and-salt mixture of faded blond, and turning grey. His face was square and almost expressionless, though his eyes behind his horn-rimmed glasses were often twinkling with some kind of private joke. He was silent to an unusual degree, and this made me feel sympathetic towards him, because I am 'the silent type' myself and am not interested in carrying on conversations. His eyes in their pale lashes were a light blue-grey. He had a rather small mouth but nice teeth, which he seldom revealed, for he rarely smiled. Altogether he gave a pleasant impression of mysterious intelligence and unusual wit, and I sensed that his secret powers of observation and expression must be formidable.[48]

Kirkup was soon to leave Europe for Japan, where he taught and edited the magazine *Orient West*, in which he occasionally printed reviews of Plomer's books, and for which Plomer once wrote a review of Kirkup's *Refusal to Conform*. He and Plomer continued to correspond irregularly until the end of Plomer's life, and it was partly through Kirkup that Plomer managed to stay in contact with several of his former pupils in Japan, including Tamura and Taro Shiomi.

In November 1948 Plomer and Erdmann made their third post-war trip to Switzerland, this time staying at Crans-Montana, where Plomer's second cousin Richard Rumbold was undergoing treatment for schizophrenia in an expensive sanatorium. Rumbold, a very wealthy young man, was being cared for by a woman friend, Hilda Young, and the two of them joined Plomer and Erdmann in tramping up and down mountainsides through the snow or going for horse-drawn sleigh rides through the silent forests. What Plomer really enjoyed about Switzerland was the food, unrationed and much better than could be obtained in London at this time. ('Whatever you have to face,' he was to write to a friend in Switzerland, after his own return to London, 'you don't have to face an English February on an eightpenny ration of old ewe. *The Times* advocates dormice for dinner, & Harrods are selling beaver meat. It's just like the siege of Paris.'[49]) He described himself and Erdmann, on a snowy Swiss postcard to Hart-Davis, as 'rampaging up hill & down dale in bright sunshine & hurrying back to the hotel at regular intervals to guzzle'.[50]

Early in January 1949 his latest volume, a collection of short stories called *Four Countries*, was published by Cape. All the stories in this collection had been published already, some of them many years before, and with Plomer's wartime publications of his *Selected Poems* and his autobiography, it suggests the extent to which he was taking stock of his achievement, rather than pressing forward with new work at this time. *Four Countries* is remarkable chiefly for its introduction, in which Plomer summed up his own concerns better than any critic had been able to do previously:

Most of my stories reflect the age by isolating some crisis caused by a change of environment or by the sudden and sometimes startling confrontation of members of different races and classes ... The African stories all touch more or less directly upon that conflict between white and black, which was, and is, and is going to be the most important of all human concerns in many parts of Africa ... The theme of detribalization and of transition from a village community to a great town, where the individual is apt to be exploited, recurs in the Japanese stories. ... The Greek stories are concerned with the pursuit of pleasure in spheres frugal, lazy and corrupt. ... The English stories are concerned, almost inevitably, with the comedy of class distinctions.[51]

And as this summary of their themes suggests, the later stories show a progressive decline in power, and a growing tendency to concern themselves with trivialities rather than with the explosive themes of love, life, and death that were so obvious in Plomer's early work, that set in Africa and Japan. Strikingly, Plomer even at this stage of retrospection, does not mention that examination of the confusions and miseries of his sexual state which had been a major (though concealed) theme from *Turbott Wolfe* onwards.

It was not simply the pressure of work that kept Plomer from producing imaginative work in the late 1940s, for his job at Cape's was not really laborious. His many 'outside' tasks—consisting chiefly of reviewing for newspapers and weekly broadcasts for the BBC, mainly now for a programme called 'The Critics' on which he, Rose Macaulay, and others discussed newly published books, and another similar programme, 'Books and People'—were undertaken mainly to increase his income, which in these years was around £1,200 annually: £1,121 in 1946, £1,562 in 1947, and £1,289 in 1948. That he did not feel overworked is shown by the fact that when the Foreign Office offered him the post of Cultural Attaché in Tokyo at a salary of £1,155 in succession to Edmund Blunden, he turned it down without hesitation, though it would have given him free travel and accommodation and much of his time to himself.[52] He was going through a fallow period, and when John Lehmann wrote to ask him for a new poem to publish, he replied, 'I haven't written a poem for many years now,' without perceptible regret.

Late in 1949 Lehmann and Edith Sitwell, who were among the administrators of the Society of Authors Travelling Scholarship Fund, arranged for Plomer to be given a grant on condition that he spend it abroad, and he and Erdmann travelled to Italy in

October 1949. They flew to Geneva, then went by train to Milan, spent some days in Florence, then went by road to Perugia and Assisi, spent some time in Rome sightseeing ('this town is a striking illustration of the old saw that it wasn't built in a day,' he wrote to Hart-Davis),[53] and then rested for a week at Amalfi, before flying back to England from Rome.

His father, seventy-nine by the end of 1949, had become a constant worry to him. Charles Plomer had developed a cancerous ulcer under his left eye and had to have radium treatment for it. The after-effects were painful, and the old man, who all his life had been a hypochondriac, was in a state of serious alarm and despondency. Miss Barwise, the woman who had acted as his housekeeper and nurse since the death of Edythe Plomer, found him a great trial, and Plomer had to make repeated visits to Worthing to see and comfort them. Plomer's brother Peter, who changed his first name to James some time before 1929, had served with distinction in the Canadian navy and was now living outside Toronto with his beautiful second wife Frances (they had married on 5 July 1945 in London) and their children. Although they wrote regularly to Charles Plomer and sent him gifts of money, there was little James and Frances could do to help from such a distance, and most of the burden of coping with the increasingly querulous old man fell on William. He could never quite make out whether it was senility or a mild protest at being lectured that made his father occasionally end his letters 'Your loving son', before striking one thin line through 'son' and writing 'father' next to it. 'It makes me feel very old,' Plomer wrote bemusedly,[54] but he continued to visit his father regularly, none the less. He wrote to Edith Sitwell, 'I see that my destiny (I say it of course without the least bitterness) is to be a sort of district nurse rather than a man of letters.'[55]

Despite this, he was at work again on a novel by the spring of 1950, telling Jonathan Cape that he had it 'mostly on paper, in the rough',[56] but adding that he thought it would have 'no money-earning characteristics'. This was the novel he called *Museum Pieces*. He worked hard at it, completing several drafts before he was satisfied; he did not finish the work until 2 November 1951,[57] and Cape published it in 1952. Plomer's labour was justified, for *Museum Pieces* is his most accomplished novel. In essence it is the story of Tony Butts's life, told by a young female narrator. What Plomer had done in *Turbott Wolfe*, in making it possible for his hero to fall in love with another man by slipping the loved one into a dress, he did at much greater length, and with greater success, in *Museum Pieces*. The narrator, Jane Valance, is enabled to express her passionate feelings for Tony Butts (here called 'Toby D'Arfey') with a freedom that would have been impossible for Plomer had he written from the viewpoint of a man. In essence the book is a brilliant reworking of the material Plomer had already dealt with in *Curious Relations*, but it has that combination of grace and power which Plomer had told Sitwell he found in her best work. The novel has a mastery of technique, a passionate clarity, and an economy in its use of language that stamps it as the work of a writer at the height of his powers. And as in the elegy Plomer wrote for Butts, there is always the feeling in *Museum Pieces* that Plomer's defence of Butts's life is also of defence of his own:

He had independence of judgement, he had shown courage, passion, and wit; and, as his mother used to say, he would do the right thing in an emergency. He did not see life steadily or whole (who does?) but he 'saw life' and threw himself into it with appetite . . . As I looked back, that one precarious life seemed to me even in its frivolity to have had a certain grandeur, like a joke made on the scaffold by a man about to be put to death as a punishment not for what he has done or not done but for what he is.[58]

The book was a considerable critical success—'I can't complain of any lack of attention in the press,' Plomer wrote to Jonathan Cape.[59] It also earned Plomer what he valued more, the praise of discerning friends. Hart-Davis thought it 'perfectly shaped and written . . . and how wildly funny!'[60] Edith Sitwell wrote that it was 'the only event that has made my life tolerable just lately . . . What a tragic, wise, humane, and, so often, wildly funny, book!'[61]

In spite of writing less in the late 1940s, he was increasingly living the life of an established man of letters: he served on the board of the Society of Authors from 1947, was elected a Fellow of the Royal Society of Literature in 1951, and was increasingly called upon to judge entries for literary prizes. Moreover, his social life continued to be full and varied. On 19 February 1951, for instance, he wrote to Van der Post:

Since I last wrote to you I have been elected a Fellow of the Royal Society of Literature (which hardly seems to butter any parsnips); I have refused an invitation from a Russian baroness (whom I have compared in print to a camel) and who lives under the aegis of the Duchess of Kent; I have been to a party at Londonderry House to hear a very interesting broadcast by my cousin Richard [Rumbold] & his girl friend about St. Exupéry; I have met the Israeli Minister (most impressive) & his wife ... Tonight I am going to dine with Cecil Day Lewis & Jill Balcon,[62] & only this morning (what a large world it is!) I had a postcard from Rosamond [Lehmann] in the West Indies, & from two other people whom I know & whom she had met by chance. Each of them had written, 'William, are your ears burning?' I hope *your* & Ingaret's[63] ears at least tingle sometimes, because Charles & I often talk about you.[64]

Another friend whom he continued to see at rather long intervals was Benjamin Britten. On 1 January 1949 Plomer had organized a party in London to celebrate E. M. Forster's seventieth birthday, and among those whom he invited was Britten. Forster, with Eric Crozier, was by this time hard at work on the libretto of Britten's next opera, *Billy Budd*, using Lehmann's edition of the Melville story, which had an introduction by Plomer. Britten renewed his expressions of admiration for Plomer's work, and reproached him for having missed the previous Aldeburgh Festival. In spite of this, it was not until July 1951 that they met again, in Norfolk, where Britten and Pears performed at the King's Lynn Festival, to which Plomer was taken by Lady Cholmondeley. Here Britten told Plomer that he wanted to have 'a serious talk' with him in Aldeburgh the following month, when Plomer went down to stay with Van der Post, who had bought a cottage in the town. During this visit, on 10 August 1951, Britten startled Plomer with a quite unexpected suggestion: it was that the two of them should collaborate on an opera for children, and that its subject should be a Beatrix Potter story, *The Tale of Mr Tod*. Since this proposal was the beginning of a major new development of Plomer's creative talents, the description of how it came about, and what flowed from it, deserves a chapter to itself.

14. *The Librettist*
1951–1953

BY 1951 Benjamin Britten had begun to establish himself as the most outstanding English operatic composer since Purcell—which, admittedly, was not saying much, for few English composers since the seventeenth century had been attracted to the genre. Britten's first opera, *Paul Bunyan*, had been written with W. H. Auden, but had not been well received. In 1945, however, he produced *Peter Grimes*, the immediate critical and popular success of which had established him as an opera composer of note. He had followed this up with several other operatic works,[1] including *Billy Budd*, and was now looking for another subject, and for another collaborator. In one sense Plomer was a natural choice, for he was associated in Britten's mind with the talented homosexual circle from which he had already selected Auden and Forster. Still, the choice was a bold one, for Plomer knew little about music and virtually nothing about modern opera.

Britten particularly admired Plomer's grimly humorous ballads, and it may have been these that suggested to him that he and Plomer should write an opera based on Beatrix Potter's *The Tale of Mr Tod*, the most bloodthirsty of her stories for children. Plomer, after thinking the matter over with his characteristic caution, reacted enthusiastically. He had reason for caution, for he knew from Forster that Britten was not always easy to work with. Boyish in appearance he might be, but his attitude to his collaborators was one of complete dominance. If he were crossed, his eyelids would droop in a way that gave his gaze a peculiarly unsettling hooded look, and he could be both imperious and steely. Moreover, he worked at an extraordinary pace, and expected his librettists to do the same. Having secured Plomer's agreement to his suggestion on 10 August 1951, he did not waste time.

By 22 August Britten had sketched the basic plan of the opera, giving a general layout of six scenes, with suggestions as to how they might be staged. Though he and Plomer had planned to meet in Aldeburgh and work on the outline together, they were for a time prevented from doing so because Plomer's father went through another bout of real or imagined illness. It was not until late October 1951 that Plomer was able to spend two days in Aldeburgh working long hours with Britten. They made rapid progress, and by the end of the second day Britten was proclaiming his pleasure at what they had accomplished and expressing confidence that they would be able to produce 'a most alarming evening's entertainment'.[2] But they were further delayed by Britten's involvement in the final preparations for the first performance of *Billy Budd* on 1 December 1951 and by Plomer's work on *Museum Pieces*, and before they got much further they learnt that copyright problems would prevent them from using Potter's story;[3] *Mr Tod* had to be abandoned.

The experience was not wasted, however. Britten had discovered that Plomer could write fluently and well for music, and, perhaps more important, that he was among the most modest and un-egotistical of men. He was easy to work with; he was willing to consider making almost any change which Britten asked for (while preserving his own artistic integrity); and he was fast and highly reliable. Britten had not found these qualities in all his previous librettists.[4] Plomer, on the other hand, had learnt a great deal about what Britten wanted in a libretto, and had also begun learning much about modern music. He had attended the dress rehearsals of *Billy Budd* at the end of November 1951 and, through discussion with Forster and John Piper (the stage designer), had begun to get a feel for the way in which the writing of a text must be modified by the demands of performance.

Having been disappointed of *Mr Tod* the two men at once began planning another opera for children, this time on the subject of space travel, with the working title 'Tyco the Vegan'.[5] By 14 March 1952 they had mapped out its essential shape, Plomer had produced a draft of the first part of the libretto, and Britten (from Austria, where he was skiing with Peter Pears and the Earl and Countess of Harewood) was suggesting that the piece should involve audience participation along the lines of his earlier piece *The Little Sweep*, with the space-travelling children asking whether they should return to earth or not, and being advised by the audience in a song that would be rehearsed in the interval.

It was during this Austrian holiday that Lord Harewood (cousin of Queen Elizabeth II, who had come to the throne in the previous month, and a director of the Royal Opera House from 1951 to 1953) first proposed that Britten consider writing 'a big national opera' to be performed in honour of the Queen's coronation in June 1953.[6] A historical subject seemed appropriate, and after considering Henry VIII, Harewood and Britten fixed on the reign of Elizabeth I. Britten did not mention this turn of events to Plomer, however, until the beginning of May 1952. When they met in London that month, Britten told Plomer of the planned opera, mentioned that it was hoped to get royal approval for it, and asked Plomer to provide the libretto. It is clear that, having worked with Plomer on two different operas, even though neither had come to fruition, Britten had complete confidence in his abilities. Characteristically, it was Plomer who seems to have hesitated, probably because he feared the inevitable publicity, and because the very tight schedule to which they would have to work would mean putting off many other tasks; he did not agree to the scheme for several days, by which time Britten was able to assure him in a letter[7] that the Queen had given her approval. He was also able to tell Plomer that potential difficulties with financing were solvable: David Webster of the Royal Opera House had assured him that if the Treasury did not provide the money, Covent Garden would.

When the official announcement was made, there was something of a stir in British musical circles. It was at once clear that the first performance of the new opera would be a musical event of considerable importance and a high point in Britten's brilliant career.[8] The fact that the as yet unwritten work had already received royal approval was without precedent,[9] and it heightened expectations and envy among Britten's fellow composers:[10] anyone connected with the project became the object of considerable public interest.[11] There must have been some surprise, too, when it became known that Britten had chosen Plomer to write the libretto. At first sight, he seemed far from an obvious choice. He had not, as far as was known, worked with Britten before; he had never produced a libretto or indeed written anything for a musical setting; and he was almost entirely unschooled in musical technique.

In 1940, before he had written his first opera, Britten had taken the firm view that the composer is dominant in the process of collaboration with the librettist, describing the stages of composition as 'the construction [by the composer] of a scenario, discussions with a librettist, planning the musical architecture, composing preliminary sketches, and writing nearly a thousand pages of orchestral score'.[12] By 1952, however, he was willing to take some direction from a librettist, particularly in the early stages of the work, and it was Plomer who began setting the direction almost at once. On 8 May he posted Britten a copy of J. E. Neale's standard biography of Elizabeth I 'as a sort of corrective to Lytton Strachey', whose *Elizabeth and Essex* had been in Britten's mind when he first proposed the subject. And in the letter accompanying the volume, Plomer pressed for the inclusion of the scene that was to prove among the most controversial of the opera, that in which Essex bursts in on the Queen and finds her being dressed by her maids, her wig on a stand beside her, her dressing-gown ragged, the wisps of grey hair hanging round her face making her seem old, pathetic, and vulnerable.[13] He also proposed new emphases for some of the main characters: 'I begin to think we must have Burleigh & Cecil as benevolent beings, if not "heroes".'[14] Britten's reply on 11 May shows that his own ideas at this stage were vague and generalized; he wanted the opera to be clear, with 'lovely pageantry', and to be unified by a strong story about Essex and the Queen.

Plomer worked largely undirected by Britten in the earliest stages, partly because of his dislike of the telephone, partly because he had no car in which to get to Aldeburgh. At the beginning of June 1952, however, he spent a weekend with Britten and was able to write, 'I am very happy to think that we have made such a hopeful beginning with our great proceeding,' adding in the margin of his letter an early form of the refrain, based on lines written by an Elizabethan boy in one of his school-books[15] and used with such effect in the opera: 'The rose is red, the leaves are green: / Long live Elizabeth, our noble Queen!' The two men saw each other again at the Aldeburgh Festival later in June 1952 but were unable to do any work because of the flurry and bustle which Britten called 'Festivalitis'. During a meeting in the first week of July 1952, however, they agreed on details of the whole of the first scene, which Plomer polished so that Britten could take it away with him on a tour from mid-July to the end of August, during which he took part in the festivals at Aix-en-Provence, Menton, and Salzburg.

On 24 July 1952, in a long letter from Aix, Britten suggested a number of changes to the first scene that were to prove characteristic of his suggestions throughout the compositional process. As an instance of his working method the letter is interesting.[16] He made it plain from this early stage that he was not prepared to wait for Plomer to finish the libretto before beginning his own contribution to the opera; on the contrary, he intended to play an active role himself in the writing of the libretto. In his letter he made important general comments, as when he expressed a worry that Plomer's use of metre and rhyme was too regular and unconversational (too much, in fact, like Plomer's ballads, and therefore not wholly appropriate for a modern setting) and appealed for a general loosening of the metrical structure. Plomer responded on 2 August 1952: 'I am sure ... the recitative *throughout* can easily be loosened up & freed from the harness of metre and rhyme, as seems best.'[17]

In the same letter Britten also made a number of very specific requests, to almost all of which Plomer acceded promptly. Plomer had begun the opera rather too slowly for Britten's liking. Britten asked that the tournament in which Essex's rival Mountjoy triumphs should begin much earlier, so that the whole of it could be described by Essex's companion Cuffe for the audience; in the final version the very first words of the chorus announce the start of the contest, as Britten asked, and Cuffe describes the action from start to finish, very effectively. Britten also suggested that Essex have little asides expressive of tension during the tournament; in response Plomer gave Essex such lines as 'I could not bear to see / Mountjoy prevail' and 'I cannot bear his luck!'

In the first scene Raleigh sings a song contemptuous of both Essex and Mountjoy ('Both lords are younglings'), and Plomer had given them no reaction to the insults; Britten asked that Mountjoy and Essex be allowed to respond, perhaps through an aside, and Plomer duly provided one which Essex and Mountjoy share: 'I curse him for his insolence, / And some day I will hurl him down.' In the same scene Britten asked for more crowd reactions, so Plomer inserted a series of comments by the chorus. Britten even directed that Essex be called 'Robin' by the Queen (as the historical Essex had been), rightly remarking that it would introduce a note of tenderness; Plomer agreed, and the use of the pet name is one of the most effective touches conveying the Queen's feeling for her spoiled favourite.

One of the most telling scenes in the opera is that in which Elizabeth appropriates Lady Essex's too fine dress, appears in it herself, looking grotesque and ridiculous, and delivers a calculated, devastating rebuke to its owner for having tried to outshine her monarch. Plomer had originally worked in a reference to this dramatic scene in Act II, scene 2, in which Essex and his wife air their grievances against the Queen while walking in the garden of their London house. Britten objected that the reference there was out of keeping with the mood of the moment, and that in any case Lady Essex was unlikely to have been wearing the magnificent dress in the garden. Plomer's initial response (in the same letter of 2 August 1952) was polite resistance: 'I am still inclined to think that Lady Essex *ought* to stroll in the garden in her "too fine" dress. I will explain why when we meet, but I won't be obstinate about the point. We must simply search out always what is most effective and appropriate to our purpose.'[18] Ultimately, Britten's view prevailed, and as a result Plomer expanded the lines into a wholly successful scene, Act II, scene 3.[19]

Perhaps the most striking of Britten's proposals in the Aix letter was that affecting the end of the opera, which Plomer had begun to think about, but had yet to write. Plomer had apparently thought of ending the work dramatically, with the signing of Essex's death warrant. Britten now proposed that instead there should be a quiet, slow, and wholly unrealistic fade-out, the lights down except for a spotlight on the Queen, with events flowing around her timelessly, and a concluding suggestion of her death in the shape of a doctor telling her to go to bed; she would refuse, and would continue to stand gauntly and majestically, until the lights faded completely, indicating the end. 'I like *very much* your suggestions about the final scene,' Plomer replied, and he followed Britten's scheme faithfully, except that Cecil was substituted for the doctor and is the recipient of Elizabeth's famous final rebuke: 'The word "must" is not to be used to Princes! Little man, little man, you durst not have said it, but you know I must die.'

It is clear, then, that far from giving his librettist a commission and waiting to see the final result, Britten took a most active part in the initial planning, in the choice of language, and indeed in the smallest details. Nor did he hesitate to modify what Plomer had written. Generally he would try to get Plomer's agreement to changes before he made them, but if necessary he would make the change first and hope to get the approval later. On 14 September 1952, for instance, he announced in a letter to Plomer that he had had to make drastic changes to the form of Act I, scene 1. He hoped Plomer would approve, but he was going ahead in the meantime, trusting that they could sort out any difficulties later—as indeed they did.

Those who collaborated with Britten were continually astonished at the speed with which he worked. Imogen Holst, whose task during the writing of *Gloriana* was to copy out his pencilled drafts of the music as soon as they were finished, was later to write:

It was astonishing to see how strictly he could keep to his time-schedule of work. He was able to say in the middle of October 1952, when he was at the beginning of Act I of *Gloriana*, that he would have finished the second act before the end of January. In February he began work on the large orchestral score ... He worked at such a tremendous speed that I thought I should never keep pace with him. He got through more than twenty pages a day, and it seemed as if he never had to stop and think.[20]

Britten did not wait for Plomer to finish even a first draft of the whole libretto before beginning to write the music. He seems to have started the composition towards the end of August 1952, immediately on his return from Europe.

By 14 September 1952, when he wrote to Plomer, Britten had written the final section of Act I, as well as the opening up to the point where Mountjoy enters, but was having to make drastic changes to the libretto in doing so. In a letter the next day, Plomer told Britten that he had just finished drafts of Act II, scene 3, and Act III, scene 1.[21] In other words, Britten was working just three scenes behind his librettist—and at feverish speed. As an afterthought to Act I, Plomer had written the little song 'Quick music is best', given to Essex just before he sings to the Queen the famous lute-song 'Happy were he', whose words are by the historical Earl of Essex; Britten had already set 'Happy were he', but was able to produce music for 'Quick music is best' and slot it in apparently effortlessly. One of the criticisms levelled at the opera after its first performance was that it seemed fragmented, more a series of discrete scenes than a conventionally dramatic story; Plomer himself was to term it 'an anthology of linked, vivid, somewhat self-contained scenes and moments'.[22] This fragmentary quality was at least partly due to the extraordinary speed with which Britten followed in the track of his librettist, so that Plomer's afterthoughts became Britten's afterthoughts too.

Late in September 1952 Plomer first heard part of the music, when Britten played him the Prelude on the piano at Aldeburgh. 'The Prelude is ringing most spiritedly & excitingly in my ear &

bosom,' Plomer wrote on 25 September 1952; 'my untutored ear has a more precise memory than I should expect.'[23] There is no evidence, though, that the experience altered the way in which he wrote for Britten. The closest Plomer came to making suggestions about the music was in describing the mood of the songs he sent Britten: 'I hope it may lend itself to lively tempo before the elegiac mood of the Brambleberry,' he wrote on 4 September 1952 of 'Quick music is best'.[24]

On 17 October 1952 Britten wrote that he had finished, in rough form, the whole of Act I and was starting on Act II, scene 2. He was always keen to fit a boy (or better still, lots of boys) into his works,[25] and pressed Plomer to introduce at least one into the London street scene involving a ballad-singer; in order to make better sense of the presence of the boy, Plomer suggested making the ballad-singer blind. Britten thought this an excellent idea, and went on in his next letter (7 November 1952) to suggest that the tumbler Plomer had introduced to entertain the nobles at the Palace of Whitehall in Act II, scene 3, should be replaced by another boy, with blackened face, doing a morris dance.[26] Plomer, in a London nursing home for another haemorrhoid operation, did not reply immediately, but Britten went ahead and composed the music for the morris dance, writing happily that it was excellent and a complete musical contrast to what went before.

By the middle of November, while Plomer was still recuperating in St Vincent's nursing home, Britten had finished most of Act II, and was struggling with the end, the scene in which Essex is finally given his wish and commissioned to take an army into Ireland to break the power of Tyrone. Plomer had given Essex no reply to this sudden change in his fortunes, writing of him that he was 'too overcome to speak'. In a letter of 20 November,[27] Britten argued that though such a reaction might be dramatically right, in opera such rules of realism did not apply. He asked Plomer to produce a reply for Essex with a somewhat ironic and characteristic flavour, bearing in mind what had gone before it (Essex's abuse of the Queen) and what would come after it (his failure in Ireland). Plomer's response was to put into Essex's mouth a prose speech at once inflated and flat: 'Armed with the favour of our gracious Empress, I am armed like a god. My resolve and duty are my helm and sword, the hopes of my countrymen are my spurs. And so into Ireland I go, to break for ever those rebel kerns. With God's help I will have victory, and you shall have peace.'

On or about 20 November 1952, Britten finished Act II (apart from the masque scene), and on 24 November he began Act III. He was now nearing the point which Plomer had reached in the libretto before his operation and was actually writing music for songs the words of which Plomer had not yet written, an extraordinary state of affairs. On 23 November 1952 he wrote to Plomer to say that the long Essex speech—almost certainly from the end of Act II—that Plomer had just sent fitted perfectly what he had planned and even sketched in, calling it a wonderful case of thought transference.[28]

Plomer must soon have felt that Britten was breathing down his neck in a most uncomfortable way. On 30 November Britten wrote to say he was well into Act III, and he pressed Plomer hard to come and recuperate at Aldeburgh, undoubtedly in part because they could then work together on the opera.[29] Plomer did go, though not for as long as Britten wanted, and was able to finish outlining Act III, scene 3 there. Britten had by then finished scene 1 and was busy on scene 2. At the same time he was making arrangements to meet the stage designer, John Piper, and the choreographer, the gifted South African John Cranko, in Aldeburgh, and in a letter of 27 November 1952 implored Plomer to be there too. 'I may not be the best living composer,' he was to remark to Plomer, 'but I'm certainly the busiest.'[30]

Plomer spent Christmas at Aldeburgh, and also spent some days with Britten at Harewood House, near Leeds, going over the opera with Lord Harewood, who naturally had a keen interest in the work, and with at least one member of the royal family, who was in residence.[31] During this visit the libretto was finished, and Plomer was able to write to Britten, with audible relief, on 13 January 1953:

What a heavenly time that was at Harewood & how thankful I am to have been able to contribute to your progress with *Gloriana* during these last few days—and indeed all along. When obstacles have arisen, you have always charmed or reasoned them away, & it has been above all a *happiness* to be working with you & to be with you. I look forward not only to being able to help as much as I can to get *Gloriana*, so to speak, into her farthingale, but to the possibility of being able to be helpful to you in the future.

I haven't really said plainly enough how excited I am by the music or how much I admire your imagination & your resourcefulness. I think I see *Gloriana* rising like a planet (I don't mean in any Holstian sense!) in the musical sky.

Bless you, dear creature, & thank you & love from William.[32]

Exactly when Britten finished the music is harder to determine with precision, but he was able to play through the whole opera to the staff of the Royal Opera House at Covent Garden on 14 February 1953, little more than a month after the completion of the libretto.[33] Nothing more clearly illustrates the speed with which he worked. He was busy with the orchestration by 15 February and appears to have finished it by mid-March.[34]

Even after Plomer had satisfied Britten's objections to parts of the libretto, there were other changes to be made. The Lord Chamberlain's office stepped in to object to an episode in Act III, scene 2, in which a housewife pours the contents of a chamber-pot over Cuffe and his rebellious followers, and asked Plomer to substitute a basin. The objection was not made from prudishness or *lèse-majesté*, Plomer was told: 'There just happens to be a rule of long standing, and the Lord Chamberlain has had *to set his face against chamber-pots.*' Plomer, with his keen eye for a grotesque turn of phrase, repeated this one to the Queen and Prince Philip when he and Britten spent an evening with them at Orme Square on 18 May 1953 to tell them about *Gloriana* before the first performance; the joke was much enjoyed.[35]

The first night, 8 June 1953, was not a happy experience for either Plomer or Britten. Covent Garden was filled with diplomats and celebrities (including Nehru, the Queen of Tonga, and chieftains from the Gold Coast, among many others). They clearly anticipated an adulatory piece full of homage to the young Queen, and were taken aback by the representation of the first Queen Elizabeth as all too human. In addition, the deliberately quiet ending thoroughly confused and alienated the audience, which seems to have expected the opera to end in a blaze of excitement and glory.[36] When the curtain came down, there was what Plomer later called 'a mere cold sprinkling of applause', and Britten, sitting in a high box with Plomer, leaned forward hissing 'Clap, damn you! *Clap!*'[37] But he hissed in vain. Plomer put as good a face on it as he could in a letter to his brother James and his sister-in-law Frances:

It went quite well, but the audience was so largely official that it was afraid the stuffing might run out of its stuffed shirts, & was not as demonstrative as a musical audience. The Royal Family turned up in force and splendour, & I had some conversation with them in the 1st interval. (We had already had a private evening some weeks ago to explain the proceedings to the Queen & Prince Philip.) They seemed to enjoy themselves and said very nice things. He took great trouble to read the libretto & I think he now knows it better than I do. He is extremely intelligent & cheerful, & I like him very much. At the end I had to take a bow with the entire cast, the composer, the conductor, the producer, & the choreographer. It was all rather fun.[38]

At the official party which followed, there were sneering private references to the opera as 'Boriana' and 'Yawniana', and Plomer felt badly bruised by the experience when he thought back on it.

In their correspondence, Britten made it plain to Plomer that, despite the initial popular response, he considered *Gloriana* to have been a great success:

I expect that you, like me, have felt a bit kicked around over it, perhaps more than me because I'm a bit more used to the jungle. But the savagery of the wild beasts always is a shock. The fact remains that I have loved working with you, my dear, and that you've produced the most wonderful libretto, that it is impossible for me adequately to express my gratitude for. Please let us some time work together again. No hurry, just don't forget me.[39]

Nor was this mere politeness on Britten's part, for after its chilly reception *Gloriana* went on to become the box-office success of the 1953 season. In any case, even the more hostile first-night critics had largely exempted Plomer from the severe judgements they had passed on the opera, *The Times* music critic remarking approvingly that 'the librettist has provided him [Britten] with opportunity for gay, excited, capricious, and ceremonious music'.[40] There is good evidence that Britten was only waiting for the right material to present itself to continue his collaboration with Plomer. His gamble had paid off, and Plomer's versatility had been amply demonstrated.

15. *The Change of Life*
1953–1966

FOR some while Plomer had been considering moving out of London again, and in June 1953 he gathered his savings, took a bank loan, and bought a small house in Rustington, on the Sussex coast. Rustington had once been a quiet village, but it was now an increasingly suburban, built-up dormitory town. None the less, there were still large market gardens and nursery gardens interspersed among the bungalows which had mushroomed in the 1930s, and there was beautiful open country within easy reach.

Plomer had several reasons for making the move. He had for years disliked the growing crowds of London, and the hordes of tourists who had crammed into the capital for the coronation in June 1953 provided the final impetus. Always a careful guardian of his privacy, he had begun to find that too many people for his liking knew his Linden Gardens address, where he had spent longer than at any other residence in his life; even his unlisted telephone, which he had retained after the war ended, had become increasingly widely known of, despite his concealing it in a screened alcove when friends called. It was time to move again. After years of living in cramped bed-sitting-rooms he could now afford a house of his own, but not in London, where prices were much higher than on the south coast. In addition he had often thought back with something like nostalgia to the pre-war periods he had spent in Dover and Brighton, and he hoped to reproduce those happy times on a permanent basis in a house of his own. Finally, his father was now eighty-three, and, having fallen out with the woman who had looked after him for so long, had had to be moved to Hove, which was within easy reach of Rustington. Plomer and Erdmann made the move on 16 July 1953, and thereafter Plomer was able to spend one day every week with his father. 'Well, here we are—we have been a week to-day in this extremely bijou bungalette,' he wrote to Benjamin Britten. 'It is rather like having not *a* but *the* change of life, after many fusty and fussy years in London.'[1]

The new house was entirely lacking in character, an anonymous bungalow with white stuccoed walls and a red-tiled roof; the previous owners had combined their first names and called it 'Rossida', and Plomer, who delighted in such names, did not change it. Tucked away behind a hedge down a narrow lane known as Stonefields, Rossida was as good a hiding-place as any of Plomer's shifting London residences. It had a telephone, but this Plomer had pulled out 'like a tooth', as he put it, the moment he took possession. Hereafter he never had a telephone in his home, a quirk of character that was ultimately to prove fatal. There was a small, unkempt garden, which he got into order and gradually came to love, planting in it English roses and a clump of bamboo to remind him of Japan. The house was near the station, easily accessible through the narrow alley-ways locally known as 'twittens', and from which Plomer could get into London by fast train in less than an hour.

Here he reproduced the way of life he had first known at Kami Nerima, outside Tokyo: country living and city work. After a time he managed to arrange things so that he went into London only on Wednesdays and crammed his city life into that one day a week. He would attend the Cape meetings over lunch, do his recordings for the BBC in the afternoon, meet his London friends for an early dinner in the evening, and then escape to his rural retreat again. As he had done in Japan, he kept the house almost bare of ornament, though on the walls of his writing-room he hung a picture of Ali Pasha (the one he reproduced in his biography of the Albanian war-lord) and a portrait of Benjamin Britten, while on a table in the same room stood a bust of Tony Butts. For the rest, the house impressed the few friends who saw it as spartan. There was a radio, but no television; what was more surprising, Plomer kept very few books. The constant stream of books that he reviewed he sold as soon as he had read them, to supplement his income. He had come to dislike all machines, used a typewriter only on sufferance, and owned no car.

The sea was less than a kilometre away, but Plomer wrote to Hart-Davis that he had 'gone off swimming'; instead he and Erdmann delighted in long walks through the Sussex countryside. Plomer, in a tweed jacket and carrying a walking-stick, would stride along tirelessly, and on several occasions the two of them did cross-country walks of thirty kilometres or more, as if the move out of London had rejuvenated them. The change had jolted Plomer into action of a different sort, too. He was writing verse again, mostly ballads, which he turned out steadily from this period until his death. In September 1953 he was engaged in writing his remarkable ballad 'A Shot in the Park'[2] (based on an incident he came across in the diary of an Edwardian hostess, Mrs Hwfa Williams), and in the same month he sent John Lehmann a poem inspired by Rossida and its kind in Rustington, the poem he called 'The Bungalows':

> In lofty light the towers dissolve
> Of yellow elms this tranquil day,
> Crumble in leisurely showers of gold
> All Turneresque in bright decay.
>
> The elms disperse their leaves upon
> A nineteen-thirty builder's row
> Of speculative dwellings, each
> An unassuming bungalow.
>
> Like concave shells, or shades, or shields
> That guard some life or light aloof,
> Like hands that cup a flame, or keep
> Some frail and captured thing, each roof.
>
> If high-pitched hopes have gone to roost
> Where low-pitched roofs so smoothly slope
> Perhaps these autumn rays diffuse
> A deeper anodyne than hope.
>
> .   .   .   .   .   .
>
> The commonplace needs no defence,
> Dullness is in the critic's eyes,
> Without a licence life evolves
> From some dim phase its own surprise:
>
> Under these yellow-twinkling elms,
> Behind these hedges trimly shorn,
> As in a stable once, so here
> It may be born, it may be born.

The final lines were the first hint most of his friends had of his increasing attachment to Christianity, though his conversion was slow and incomplete. Religion only gradually drove out his belief in many superstitions; he continued, for instance, to believe in magic, and at least one colleague at Cape's, Philippa Harrison, was involved through him in an incident connected with black magic, the details of which she was unwilling to discuss even years later.[3] He had always believed in horoscopes, and in 1954 had a detailed one drawn up for him by a distant relation, aptly named Isobel M. Pagan.[4] Though it was as accurate as most such documents— among other things it told him, 'you may become attached to the church and rise to a high position or be in the service of some magnate,' and added that he was 'prodigal of gifts . . . children abound'!—he kept it carefully to the end of his life. He gave palmistry credit too, and kept among his papers a professionally taken photograph of his own palms. But he was changing. It was in Rustington that he first began attending the village church on Sundays, and several of his friends, notably Ackerley, found his beliefs alienating and gradually moved away from him. There was never a decisive break between them, but the warmth that had previously existed gradually cooled, and they saw each other less and less.

It has to be said that Ackerley was moving further away from every other human being too, for just after the war he gave up boys for dogs—or more precisely, a single dog. Women he had always disliked, and he had come to find children repulsive. He once asked Forster, 'How can anyone enjoy seeing a baby?'[5] This steady falling away from humanity culminated in his purchase, in the last year of the war, of an Alsatian bitch named Queenie, with which he soon became obsessed. He fussed about the animal endlessly: its food, its habits, its need for exercise, and its sex life became his chief topics of conversation, and filled his letters to Plomer and his other friends. With Queenie's acquisition Ackerley's own sex life underwent a marked change: his manic pursuit of boys stopped abruptly, and his attentions were focused entirely on the animal. Not surprisingly, those who knew him well suspected him uneasily of bestiality, and though Ackerley specifically denied this in his posthumously published autobiography *My Father and Myself*, the impression lingered. His friends disliked Queenie intensely, not least because she was neurotically possessive of Ackerley and barked hysterically while they visited him, making conversation very difficult. Ackerley's gloom deepened steadily in the post-war years, until he wore an expression of utmost misery. 'Gay?' Hart-Davis was to comment sardonically, 'Gay was the *last*

word you'd use of Joe Ackerley.'[6] Plomer's interest in and compassion for his fellows contrasted strongly with Ackerley's growing
misanthropy, and the two found they had less and less in common.
He disliked the books Ackerley wrote about Queenie, *My Dog Tulip*
and *We Think the World of You*, referring to them as 'gloomy
autobi*dog*raphy'. With Forster too, Plomer's relations gradually
cooled, though the two continued to see each other and to exchange
affectionate letters.

Rupert Hart-Davis had become and remained his closest friend;
he was one of very few people to be invited to see Rossida soon
after Plomer and Erdmann moved in. He drove over from Bognor
Regis, where he was spending a summer holiday with his family.
Having inspected the new house, he drove Plomer back to Bognor
for the day. As they passed through Littlehampton, he asked Plomer
if the place had any literary connections. 'Only one,' said Plomer,
'Mrs Henry Dudeney, whose novels are so light that you have to
hold them down to read them!'[7] Hart-Davis often had Plomer to
stay at his farm near Henley-on-Thames for weekends, and the two
also met regularly in London where Hart-Davis had a flat above
his offices in Soho Square. When Plomer read a selection of his
ballads to the Royal Society of Literature on 17 December 1953,
for instance, it was with Hart-Davis that he put up for the
night afterwards. The two men maintained a constant, warm
correspondence full of wit and affection, and invented nicknames
for many of their mutual acquaintances: Nowell-Smith was 'the
Bantam', Jonathan Cape 'the Giant Bore', Dudley Massey (a
Catholic) 'the Cardinal', Lehmann, because of a series of articles
he published on logwood in Georgia, was 'Timbertoes', and so on.
The two of them also enjoyed exchanging wimbornes, newspaper
photographs with inappropriate captions; the captions had to be
part of the original clipping, not stuck on, and finding good ones
required a keen eye for maladroit or amusing juxtapositions of
photographs and text.

Plomer continued to give Hart-Davis occasional advice about
authors who might be worth pursuing or books that might be
worth reprinting. He also advised John Lehmann on publishing
matters. Once Lehmann had launched the *London Magazine*, in
1954, Plomer joined the advisory board, and continued to serve
on it even after Lehmann relinquished direction of the magazine in
1961 to the poet and publisher Alan Ross. To an extent Plomer

read and commented on contributions in manuscript as soon as they came in, and he attended and animated each of the monthly editorial meetings,[8] but more significantly, his function was that of retrospective commentator. Each edition of the magazine would be followed, within a day or two, by a long letter from Plomer to Lehmann, going through each item published and giving shrewd, detailed comments on it, with suggestions as to how the magazine could be improved or enlivened in the future. He went so far as to criticize the reviews that appeared, when he thought them unjust. For instance, when Van der Post's book about his experiences as a prisoner of the Japanese, *A Bar of Shadow*, was abused by a reviewer in October 1954, Plomer commented indignantly:

I forgot to say that I think the review of Laurens v.d.P's book lamentable. It seems a sad example of 'knowing better' than the author. What a want of humility! I have known v.d.P. for nearly 30 years, and I think it absurd to use expressions about 'masquerading' and 'facile tricks' in writing about his work—as well as offensive. The remarkable thing about the book has been missed by this review entirely—that here is a man who was subjected to frightful cruelties & indignities by his Japanese captors and yet is capable of not hating them & of making a great imaginative effort to understand what went on inside them. Anything cheaper than the reviewer's final remark about feeling 'nostalgic (a trite cant word, anyway) for those chats in the prison-camp about Father Christmas ...'! Ugh, what ignorance and insensibility![9]

His sensitivity as a reader, combined with his tact in expressing uncomfortable truths, is well illustrated by another of the letters he sent to John Lehmann, who had asked him to comment on the autobiography Lehmann was then working on, and which was to be published as *The Whispering Gallery* in 1955. After two pages of obviously sincere compliments, Plomer began to criticize:

I suppose the chief dangers for an autobiographer are self-pity, self-justification, & self-importance. Of the first I find no trace, thank goodness: your life so far has been full, healthy, & energetic, & you have rightly made it seem so. Self-justification cannot really be avoided, since it is part of one's purpose to explain what one has been driving at, and how, and why. What looks to oneself like self-esteem (which is essential) sometimes appears to others like self-importance: it is a question to what extent one need guard against this.

What I do find a serious point is that you are often too *ecstatic*. I will explain what I mean. In my opinion you use far too much words like *exciting, fascinating, mysterious, great, big, large, enormous, thrilling, wonderful, astonishing, glorious,* &c. I say 'too much' because to use them too often is

  (i) to weaken or even nullify their effect;

  (ii) to make the reader say to himself 'He tells me such-and-such a thing was fascinating, but does he make it fascinating to me?' And so doubt creeps in.

This fault (as I see it) is most in evidence in the earlier part of the book. The words 'exciting' or 'excitement' occur on pages 15, 17, 19, 31, 38, 46, 52. [He then spends two pages going into considerable detail on such 'ecstasies', giving page references for each of them.]

I haven't been through the whole book looking for little mistakes, but I think you ought to do so, or get somebody else to do so, because here & there I have noticed the sort of mistakes that people do notice. You, of *all people*, ought not to call Chambers's *Cyclopaedia of Eng Literature* an 'encyclopaedia' (p. 9). Ely Cathedral has towers and a lantern, but *no spire* (p. 212). And I suspect that *corrios* ought to be *correos* in Costa Rica (p. 95).[10]

This is the kind of detailed criticism that even the vainest writer hopes to get from a reader. It was this combination of intelligence, tact, and the willingness to take enormous pains that made Plomer so sought-after as both reader and critic. No wonder two of the best English publishers of the period, Cape and Hart-Davis, as well as Lehmann, were glad of his services.

It was in the 1950s that Plomer made his most valuable 'discovery' as a reader for Cape's: Ian Fleming's James Bond. After the war Fleming had returned to journalism, with an influential position on the *Sunday Times*, and on Plomer's advice, Cape's sent him books he might mention favourably. Fleming had long nursed the desire to write a thriller, and he seems to have written his first at the beginning of 1951 in his small Jamaican house 'Goldeneye'. He finished it in two months, but was doubtful about letting any publisher see it, for he was deeply insecure about his own powers. Plomer was his closest friend in the publishing world, and a few years before had expressed his belief that Fleming could write a first-rate thriller if he chose. 'But', Plomer had emphasized, 'it's no good writing just one. With that sort of book, you must become regular in your habits. You must hit the nail again and again with the same hammer until it's driven into the thick head of your potential public.'[11] Fleming had given Plomer a long, thoughtful look. Having written his book, Fleming chose to make a characteristically convoluted approach to Plomer. On 12 May 1952[12] he was having lunch with Plomer at a London restaurant when he changed the course of their conversation to ask Plomer, 'How do you get cigarette smoke out of a woman once you've got it in?' Plomer, who delighted in the grotesque caprices of the human race, speculated rapidly on what he later called 'this intimate-sounding injection'. Fleming then explained that one could not use a word like 'exhales', while 'puffs it out' sounded silly to his ears. At this point Plomer looked up sharply: 'You've written a book!' And Fleming, with a great show of reluctance, admitted that he had, and consented to let Plomer read it. The work was *Casino Royale*.

Plomer was greatly impressed by it, predicting that it would have enormous sales; Daniel George, to whom he passed the manuscript, agreed. Talking Jonathan Cape round was a different matter, for he disliked all thrillers, and read this one only because of Plomer's enthusiasm. Nor were the other directors easier to convince: Wren Howard thought Fleming a 'bounder', and his son Michael thought the book revealed a sadistic, cynical brutality which he found deeply shocking.[13] But Plomer's view prevailed, and though Cape never read another of Fleming's books, he published them all, and their unparalleled success made a great deal of money for both Cape and Fleming. Years later, Plomer was to write:

Fleming's books appealed directly and almost universally to a prevalent mood of their time. There has generally been hardly more than one such author in a generation, and such an author is what a publisher needs— and needs, incidentally, if he is to allow himself to publish, for pleasure, prestige, or prospects, books on which he won't make or may lose money.[14]

Only Plomer made nothing from the venture in which he had played such a part, although he continued to read each of Fleming's books as it was written and to suggest detailed improvements and changes. His only financial reward was the sum of £500 which Fleming left him when he died in 1964, stipulating that Plomer was 'to commit some extravagance' with it.

His work for Cape's, together with his BBC broadcasts, his reviews, and the poems he published in papers and magazines as soon as he had written them, brought him in a little over £1,500 throughout the second half of the 1950s, and enabled him to pay off what he had borrowed to buy Rossida, and to add slowly to his savings. He managed this only by living very frugally, and at least one of his friends[15] thought him mean with money. To put his income in context, it is helpful to recall that in a *Horizon* survey published in 1945 his friend Elizabeth Bowen had said that a writer needed £3,500 a year.[16] Admittedly Bowen lived on rather a grand scale, and several other writers thought a little over £1,000 sufficient, but the survey had appeared nearly a decade earlier, and since then inflation had eroded the value of money.

The changes gradually taking place in Plomer, of which the move to Rustington was itself a symptom, showed also in the poetry he started writing once he moved into Rossida. The ballads he continued to produce, though he called them 'satires' when he read three of the latest on the BBC in February 1954,[17] had none of the bitterness of the poems he had written in the early days of the war. Even those that dealt, as the earlier ones had often done, with the deaths of women, did so with a compassion that is very different from the black humour so evident in the earlier work. In 'Atheling Grange: or, The Apotheosis of Lotte Nussbaum', for instance, he described the death of a lonely woman who had come to Britain as a refugee from Germany before the war and had stayed on miserably as a domestic servant, to die suddenly while gathering mushrooms. In an earlier poem the death might have been treated as a joke, and the dead woman as a joint of meat; but here, though the poem remains very funny, Lotte Nussbaum is translated into a humorous, *faux-naïf* vision of heaven, and is freed from the drudgery of life:

> '*Himmel!*' she cries. And so it is—she's right!
>   Across the new-mown lawn advance
> Her long-lost family, arrayed in white,
> Her parents leading in a lively dance
> her brothers, sisters, nieces, uncles, aunts,
> With crowns and harps—a most unearthly sight!
>
> Oh, what a welcome for Miss Nussbaum! See,
>   All's *himmelhoch* and *himmelblau!*
> Heaven is hers, and she is Heaven's now!
> She's disembodied, disencumbered, free!
> Lotte is free! ... Tomorrow Mrs. Clunch
> Will have no drudge to cook her blasted lunch.

These latest ballads achieved great success, and drew many

compliments when they were printed in the *London Magazine* or in the recently founded *Encounter*, of which Spender was co-editor. Plomer was particularly gratified to hear from Lady Cholmondeley that Princess Margaret and the Queen Mother had read them out to a party of friends, and that they had been very well received, while Lady Cholmondeley herself had read them to Winston Churchill and the Salisburys, and had set Churchill guffawing.[18]

Another element creeping into the ballads written in the mid-1950s at Rossida was a tendency, new in Plomer's work, to treat heterosexual love sympathetically. In March 1954, for instance, he told John Lehmann that he had finished 'a ballad with a Swiss theme'. This was 'Anglo-Swiss: or, a Day Among the Alps', and it described, with delicacy and warmth, a love-affair between an Englishman and a Swiss girl. It was to be followed by the most evocative and thoughtful of all his ballads, 'Bamboo', a bitter-sweet reflection on marriage that he wrote in March 1954 and described to Hart-Davis as a love-song. The emergence of this element, like his introduction of religious imagery, was symptomatic of an inner change, for Plomer was for the third time in his life, and at the age of fifty, contemplating marriage.

His choice had fallen on a widowed lady of his own age,[19] a friend of his father. His experience with Lilian Bowes-Lyon still clear in his memory, he moved with most elaborate caution. He seems to have consulted only his brother James, by letter at first, and then face to face when James was in England in December 1954. James Plomer was very hesitant about giving advice on such a matter, and in any case he and Plomer had never really been close. In the event, Plomer seems to have changed his mind, and it is not known whether he ever proposed to the widow; however it was, the idea was quietly dropped.[20] But the incident shows that once again he was reviewing his life, and was at least prepared to consider making momentous changes. There is evidence that he had ceased to be an active homosexual soon after moving to Rustington; he and Erdmann had separate rooms in Rossida, and there is no evidence that Plomer sought other lovers after the war.[21] It is clear in retrospect that the move to Rossida was in some sense what Plomer had called it: not *a* change of life, but *the* change of life.

His father was failing by the end of 1954, and had to go into a nursing home; Plomer had the unpleasant task of going through the old man's possessions and disposing of them. In this he was helped by James, who was in England on a naval training course, accompanied by his wife. Plomer was charmed by his sister-in-law Frances, and found his brother's cheerfulness a welcome relief from the gloom of their father's impending death. 'He has such a hearty laugh that I thought all the tiles would fly off Rossida like confetti,' he wrote to Hart-Davis on 29 December 1954, '& when later we went on to Hove to visit my somewhat moribund father, the old boy soon said, 'I think you'd better go now—I can't stand it—my head's going round.' I have heard of people dying of laughter, but only of *their own*.'[22] Charles Plomer died, not of laughter but of cancer, on 19 January 1955 at the age of eighty-five, after just a fortnight in the nursing home, leaving Plomer much less shaken than he had been at the death of his mother, and slightly better off financially,[23] but very tired. 'It has been a strain for me for years to bolster his morale—especially in the last year or two,' he wrote to Van der Post, '& I feel a bit tired by it all.'[24]

His latest crop of ballads was published by Cape's on 28 March 1955, under the title *A Shot in the Park*, and it increased his reputation for this form of verse that he had made his own. From the start his ballads had been written to be performed, or at least read aloud. Delivered in this way they are highly effective pieces of work, and perhaps his most characteristic productions. Like members of the group of writers known as the Movement (Philip Larkin, Kingsley Amis, D. J. Enright, and others), Plomer disliked the tendency of modern writers, particularly poets, to demand or assume a highly cultivated and even learned audience, and his ballads were a practical attempt to link up with a mass audience again. In this he was highly successful. The volume also got excellent reviews. Forster called him 'my favourite contemporary poet', and said his work was 'full of colour, feeling, distinction, character-drawing, epigram, and mischievousness'.[25] John Betjeman wrote that his poems had 'an unearthly light on them which, though very clear, is very strange';[26] while Auden remarked that Plomer had 'a first-class visual imagination'.[27]

Early in October 1955 Plomer and Erdmann flew to Switzerland for a fortnight, the fourth of their holidays there. They also visited Bavaria, where Erdmann's father was still living in a small house in Hohenschwangau. Plomer preferred Germany to Switzerland, where 'we feel the clocks too striking', he joked to Hart-Davis.[28] On the other hand, he thought the Germans a people driven by materialism, and full of self-pity and resentment: 'Being in Germany always makes me feel like an unqualified or amateur psychiatrist with several million patients in need of attention they will never get,' he was to tell Sargeson on his second visit to the country, in August 1959.[29] He was particularly impressed by the beautiful baroque and rococo churches with which that part of Germany abounds, and his fine poem 'A Church in Bavaria' was inspired by the 1959 trip. Plomer used the typographical effects of a George Herbert to convey what he had seen:

> Everything flows
>   upward over
>   chalk-white walls
>   with the ordered freedom
>   of a trellised creeper
>   wreathed and scrolled
>   in a densely choral
> anthem of ornament.
>
> Nimble angels
>   poise above
>   in attitudes,
>   huge-limbed prophets
>   banner-bearded,
>   giant apostles,
>   mitred titans
>   exemplify
> authority,
>   their garments ribbed
>   in whorls and folds,
>   corrugations
>   of pearly grace,
>   sea-shell volutions
>   turned by ages and
>   oceans of prayer ...

He did a good deal of travelling in 1956, for at the start of the year he accepted an invitation from the University of the Witwatersrand to attend a writers' conference in Johannesburg in July. Acceptance of this invitation meant turning down one from the British Council to lecture in Greece that month, but he had no hesitation in choosing the South African offer. In the years after he left South Africa in 1926 he would bristle if anyone described him as a South African; his birth there, he liked to say, was merely an accident, and he would quip, 'I once had a cat which had kittens in the oven, but no one mistook them for biscuits.' But in this, as in so many other things, a change had come over him. His interest in South Africa had revived since the war, and he did all he could in the 1940s and 1950s to help young South African writers. He had been delighted by the huge success of *Cry the Beloved Country*, the novel by Alan Paton that Plomer had highly recommended to Cape's when he first read it in manuscript; and when Paton later came to London, Plomer had made a point of meeting and welcoming him.[30] He had recommended the poems of the South African poets F. T. Prince and Roy Macnab to Lehmann, Spender, and other friends whom he thought might help them. He had even recommended to Lehmann a play by Guy Butler, who, though he gradually came to exercise a narrowing, stultifying influence on South African literature (the process was to become known as 'Butlerization'), had produced some talented work just after the war.

Plomer's interest in South Africa was partly the result of growing world attention to the political changes that had occurred there since the coming to power of a Nationalist government in 1948 and the passage of the series of laws that constituted apartheid. On 23 April 1956, as part of what he called 'a self-imposed course in African life and culture, in preparation for my excursion',[31] he went to hear a lecture in Central Hall by Trevor Huddleston,[32] one of the chief opponents of apartheid, and was much impressed by his eloquence and sincerity.

He left London by air for Johannesburg on 7 July 1956, and the next day was met by Professor Partridge, who held the chair of English at Witwatersrand University. On 9 July he spent most of the day with his father's former Zulu servant, Lucas Makoba, who was now running an autonomous African church and had become very wealthy. He picked Plomer up in a Cadillac, and swept him off to meet his family—'such a warm & friendly welcome, such real goodness, such good humour, such a large & handsome family, such dignity', Plomer wrote to Frank Sargeson.[33] His visit to South Africa received a good deal of publicity, and he was photographed shaking hands with Makoba, having tea with him, being presented with a walking-stick, and so on.[34] He found his welcome from both blacks and whites almost embarrassingly generous.

The conference started on 10 July 1956, and Plomer delivered a talk on 'South African Writers and English Readers', in which he spoke of the reaction in Britain to South African authors; his audience of more than five hundred listened with attention. He then sat through two days of talks by other writers and academics, some dull and some very amusing. One writer whose work he knew and admired, but who sat in silence throughout the conference, was Nadine Gordimer.[35] He was introduced to this reserved, beautiful woman, whose volumes *The Soft Voice of the Serpent* and *Six Feet of the Country* he had read, but her shyness at first kept them apart. She thought Plomer rather oriental in appearance, exquisitely dressed and groomed, and with perfect manners; but something about him kept her at a slight distance until a ludicrous little incident of the type Plomer was always on the look-out for brought them together.

Several of the writers, galvanized by Plomer's remarks, had complained bitterly about the difficulty of making South African subjects interesting to readers outside the country. It was at this point that Sarah Gertrude Millin intervened. The days when Plomer and Campbell had attacked her in the pages of *Voorslag* had long gone, and she had since then churned out a stream of undistinguished novels and had come to think of herself as the *grande dame* of South African letters. Flamboyantly dressed in a large velvet hat, with a huge diamanté brooch accentuating her generous bosom, she strode to the rostrum to upbraid the previous speakers. 'I think *I* might have something to add to this,' she began portentously. 'I have written forty-five books. And in this gathering *I* [patting her chest for emphasis] represent *bulk*.'[36] At this moment Gordimer caught Plomer's eye. He compressed his lips with a straight mouth, and widened his eyes behind his glasses in a way she thought irresistibly comic, and which she later came to realize was habitual with him when something grotesque or amusing struck him. In their shared but silent hilarity a spark passed between them, and after the session ended, Gordimer invited Plomer to her large Parktown house for a lunch that he thoroughly enjoyed.[37] After this meeting they were to see each other repeatedly in England, for Gordimer was a tireless traveller.

When she won the W. H. Smith Award for a book of stories in

1961, she found Plomer at the lunch in London and discovered to her surprise that he was on the jury which decided on the recipient; he had never mentioned it to her. It was at this function that Plomer told Gordimer that the time had come for her to speak out about South Africa. 'I can't,' she said, 'I'd rather die than get up and talk about politics.' Plomer gave her a talking-to: if she were going to go on living and writing in a country where political discussion was so thin, he told her, she had a duty to speak out plainly. After this she became increasingly willing to express herself publicly on South African political matters, which for years had been a major theme in her writing. Plomer seldom missed a chance to take her to dinner in London, and on one occasion he spent an entire day showing her and her husband round Brighton, avoiding such sights as the Pavilion, but showing them where he had lived in Ship Street Gardens before the war.[38] When she began publishing a stream of novels, she was aware that Plomer did not admire them as he did her short stories, but this did not come between them, and they remained friends for the rest of his life.

Once the Johannesburg conference had ended, Plomer gave an address to the Johannesburg PEN club,[39] gave radio interviews, read his ballads in public, and addressed a private club of judges, MPs, and other worthies, before being set free to see a little of the Africa he had known. On 18 July 1956 he flew to Durban ᐟ made his way by train to Eshowe, determined to revisit his old haunts in Zululand. He found Entumeni greatly changed and improved, and still in the possession of the Bishop family to whom the Plomers had sold it thirty years before. A new store had been built and stocked with such items as pink brassières, he reported in a letter to his brother James; the house was now much bigger and had electric light; and the Bishops, who greeted him with real friendliness, had planted great stands of wattle and eucalyptus, and were clearly prospering. 'It was a strange, disconcerting experience,' he wrote. 'I could not imagine how we ever went there or stayed as long as we did.'[40]

The contrast between the evident wealth of the sugar-planters in Natal and the African children dressed in sacking, begging from travellers at the railway sidings, struck him so forcibly that (as he said in a BBC broadcast after his return to Britain) they put him in mind of Russia before the emancipation of the serfs.[41] But he was too intelligent to think the problem of race relations in South

Africa a simple one, and he noticed several examples of whites and blacks bound together by habit, trust, and affection. Nor did he believe that black rule, when it came, would necessarily be more benevolent than white rule. In Johannesburg he witnessed the arrest of a black car thief by a black detective, who, taking a pair of handcuffs from his belt, beat the man systematically about the head with them before dragging him away. 'Men being absent, Africa is good,' he was to write in one of the remarkable poems the visit sparked off. The beauty of the country impressed him anew, and he was soon describing himself as 'a returning exile',[42] though what he called 'the dryness and the staring sun'[43] made him long for English clouds again. He did not get to Pietersburg or Louis Trichardt, despite his poem 'The Wild Doves at Louis Trichardt', and flew back to London on 9 August 1956. Before he left he told a news conference that apartheid was not just wicked but suicidal, and he was pleased when these remarks made headlines in the local papers.

His visit, brief though it was, had a profound effect on him. One outcome was a stream of articles and broadcasts in which he spoke, in a judicious, restrained way, about the problems the country faced. 'The effort to base what is called "White Survival"', he concluded, 'upon an assumption of White Superiority too rigid, too selfish, too false, and too much out of tune with what is going on in the rest of the world, is ... impractical.'[44] More important, Africa had spurred him to poetry, and the visit gave rise to several poems, of which one, 'A Transvaal Morning', was the most vividly observed he had written for years:

> A sudden waking when a saffron glare
> Suffused the room, and sharper than a quince
> Two bird-notes penetrated there
> Piercing the cloistral deep verandah twice.
>
> The stranger started up to face
> The sulphur sky of Africa, an infinite
> False peace, the trees in that dry place
> Like painted bones, their stillness like a threat.
>
> . . . .
>
> Again those two keen bird-notes! And the pert
> Utterer, a moss-green thrush, was there
> In the verandah-cave, alert,
> About to flit into the breathless air.

His return to Africa had sparked a return to the themes which he had treated in his poetry of the 1920s and 1930s.

After this visit he took an even keener interest in South African writing, and did what he could to advance the careers of Gordimer, Ruth Miller, Uys Krige, Jack Cope, Doris Lessing, and others, not only recommending their work to editors and publishers, but giving them attention in the anonymous reviews he wrote regularly for the *Times Literary Supplement* and the *Listener*. He also persuaded Lehmann to produce an edition of *London Magazine* entirely given over to writing from South Africa, in January 1957. The advancement of any promising writer gave him pleasure, but if that writer should also be a friend of his, the pleasure was naturally keener. He also paid tribute to such South African writers as Pauline Smith, whose short stories he had greatly admired when he first read them in Africa in the 1920s. Hearing that she was living in Dorset, ill and poor, he went to see her, in company with Roy Macnab, and the two of them presented her with an illuminated address, composed by Plomer and signed in her honour by twenty-five South African writers. It included the sentence 'We feel that by the delicacy, tenderness, and precision with which you have written of South African ways of life you have transcended the barriers of race and language and made essential humanity real.'[45] She was very moved by the visit and the tribute, but it was evident to Plomer that her physical and mental powers were not what they had been. 'One was inevitably reminded', he wrote later, 'that the flowering of her talent had been brief and beautiful, like that of some rare veld-flower.'[46] Plomer also showed his interest in South Africa by writing letters of protest against apartheid to both British and South African papers. In addition, he made a broadcast on South Africa with Trevor Huddleston, in May 1959, in which the two of them tried to draw the world's attention to what was happening in that country.

One of the South African writers whom he met in London after his visit to South Africa was the Afrikaner poet Ingrid Jonker, whom Van der Post introduced him to. Plomer was touched by her childlike vulnerability and her evidently rare talent (he was later to produce, with the help of the South African poet Jack Cope, an edition of Jonker's translated poems),[47] and he remembered their meeting vividly when, in July 1965, he heard of Jonker's suicide on a Cape beach. One line from her poem 'Ek dryf in die Wind' (I drift with the wind) haunted him as a key to her death: 'My volk het van my afgevrot' (My people have rotted away from me). The news of her death came just after he had heard of another suicide, that of the black South African writer Nat Nakasa, who had killed himself while a student at Harvard. Their deaths seemed to Plomer to sum up the reverberations of the tragedy playing itself out in South Africa, and at Van der Post's urging he wrote a poem about them, 'The Taste of the Fruit', which he sent to Van der Post on 23 August 1965. When it was published in the *Times Literary Supplement*, on 16 September 1965, it was described as a lament for South Africa. Much the most moving of Plomer's late poems, its power makes inescapable the sense that Plomer had risked impoverishing himself aesthetically by cutting himself off from South Africa, and that even a brief return to the country had enriched him:

> . . . Now he is free in
> A state with no frontiers,
> But where men are working
> To undermine frontiers,
> He is not there.
>
> 'My people,' in anguish
> She cried, 'from me have rotted
> Utterly away.' Everywhere
> She felt rejected;
> Now she is nowhere.
>
> Where men waste in prison
> For trying to be fruitful,
> The first fruit is setting
> Themselves fought for;
> He will not taste it.
>
> Her blood and his
> Fed the slow, tormented
> Tree that is destined
> To bear what will be
> Bough-bending plenty.
>
> Let those who savour
> Ripeness and sweetness,
> Let them taste and remember

Him, her, and all others
Secreted in the juices.

His return to the scenes of his African past caused him to reread his autobiography *Double Lives*. For some time he had been considering writing a sequel to it, and in April 1957 he began work, using the provisional title 'Are You Doctor Gruber?' He finished it in June 1957, and it was published in March 1958 as *At Home*, the working title having been rejected by Cape. It took the story of his life up to the war, and he found it very difficult to write, because so many of those mentioned were still alive. Not the least of his difficulties was his continued inability to write openly about his own sexuality. As a result, the book, although urbane, witty, and consistently good-humoured, has a subdued tone, as if the smiling face concealed sad secrets. His friends noticed. Lady Cholmondeley wrote to him, 'You won't give any part of yourself to the reader';[48] while Spender thought it 'a secret book without being secretive—it bristles with messages which I imagine will be unnoticed by most readers'.[49] Ackerley wrote to Plomer that he found it 'on the whole rather a sad book'.[50] For all that, it got very good reviews, and Plomer was pleased with the reaction to it. He had remarked in the book that he was not one of literature's battery hens, and when Hart-Davis's friend and future wife Ruth Simon wrote to compliment him, he responded, 'We non-battery hens, though infrequent layers, preen ourselves when we hear a cry of "Good egg!" '[51]

One of those who wrote to congratulate him was Benjamin Britten. Plomer had been corresponding intermittently with him in the years since the two of them worked on *Gloriana*, and they had also seen each other regularly, if infrequently. They met chiefly at the Aldeburgh festivals, to which Plomer remained a faithful contributor, but also through such events as the 1954 Snape Mayday Fair, at which signed copies of Plomer's books *Sado* and *Double Lives* were auctioned, and the Crabbe centenary celebrations on 24 April 1954, at which Britten asked Plomer to make a speech in tribute to Crabbe, who had been a native of Aldeburgh.

In October 1954 Britten had asked Plomer to write a libretto for another opera for children, suggesting a Greek myth as a basis. This new work was to be brief, perhaps no more than half an hour or forty-five minutes in length, and it was to fit with *The Little*

Sweep into an evening's entertainment, and to have a cast of not more than six children and five adults. He left the choice of myth to Plomer, but proposed the story of Phaeton, the youth who drove the chariot of the sun, modernized to make Phaeton a boy 'teased with borrowing his father's racing car and driving it into disaster'.[52] The two men had met to discuss the idea on 17 November 1954 at Aldeburgh and had considered the myths of Arion and Icarus as alternatives, since Britten's chief request was that the story should focus on a boy.[53] But the work did not get very far, chiefly because Charles Plomer was dying, and though on 26 January 1955 Britten suggested that they should think of the children's opera further in the spring, when the time came Britten's interests had turned in other directions, and the project seems to have been abandoned. The experience, however, had shown them some of the problems and opportunities that might arise in trying to transpose a story from a distant time and place into an English setting, the very problems which they were to face in their next collaboration.

The only other work they did together during this time was a brief 'scenelet', as Plomer called it, which, set to music by Britten, formed part of the Punch Revue devised by Vida Hope and staged at the Duke of York's Theatre in September 1955.[54] But their correspondence during this period was continuous, and their friendship warm. When Plomer read some of his ballads during the Aldeburgh Festival of 1955, Britten mentioned to him the extensive tour of the Far East he was proposing to make in the company of Peter Pears and the Prince and Princess of Hesse,[55] asking Plomer for advice on what to see and do in Japan.

As Plomer wrote later, he responded by advising Britten to experience the theatre in Japan: 'I strongly recommended the Japanese theatre in its various forms, Kabuki, Bunraku, and No—particularly the No. I remember describing a No play, enlarging upon the emotive effect of its strict stylization, and imitating some of the formal gestures used by the actors.'[56] Britten and Pears set off in the last months of 1955 on a concert tour that took them through Germany, Austria, Yugoslavia, and Turkey, before continuing through Bali and Thailand (where they joined up with the Hesses) to Japan.[57] On 11 February 1956 they saw in Tokyo their first performance of *Sumidagawa*.[58] The Prince of Hesse kept a travel diary during this trip, and in it he gave a lucid account of the action of the play, which was to form the heart of the work which Britten and Plomer would eventually call *Curlew River*:

The play ... is about the Sumida river: the ferryman is waiting in his boat, a traveller turns up and tells him about a woman who will soon be coming to the river. The woman is mad, she is looking for her lost child. Then she appears and the ferryman does not wish to take a mad person, but in the end he lets her into his boat ... The ferryman tells the story of a little boy who came this way a year ago this very day. The child was very tired for he had escaped from robbers who had held him. He crossed the river in this boat, but he died from exhaustion on the other side. The woman starts crying. It was her son. The ferryman is sorry for her and takes her to the child's grave.[59]

On 19 February 1956 Britten saw a second performance of *Sumidagawa*,[60] and the play had a profound effect on him. In May 1956, after his return to England, he wrote to Plomer asking when they could meet and talk about three Noh plays of which he had brought back translations, and which, in an expressive phrase, he said had 'caught music'.[61] And he ended significantly, 'Do you know the play *Sumidagawa*, by the way?' Plomer replied, 'It is a very great pleasure to me, and somehow not altogether a surprise, that your response to Japan was instant & strong. You see now how fortunate I was to be able to live there for a couple of years in my twenties. It struck me as a gong or bell is struck, & the vibration set up in me will last till I drop.'[62]

In their subsequent meeting, soon after these letters were exchanged, Britten asked Plomer to provide a libretto for 'an English version' of the Japanese original.[63] It is clear from his use of this phrase that what Britten had in mind was not an adaptation transposed into an English setting, but a straightforward translation of the Japanese original into English, with the retention of the Japanese setting and Japanese words and names.[64] Plomer was later to record that he had had immediate doubts:

Though honoured to be asked, I thought the project hardly possible. Neither he nor I nor anybody else would want a pastiche of a No play, a piece of *japonaiserie*, and as the original depended entirely upon its *mise en scene*, archaic music, all-male cast, and rigidly formal production down to the last detail of costume and movement, it was hardly transferable to the Western operatic stage. What was more, the language and action of the play belonged to an antique Buddhist culture and could only be properly appreciated by highly cultivated Japanese traditionalists. But like the poets

Yeats and Waley (neither of whom ever visited Japan), Britten had been enchanted by the No, as I had been enchanted before him, so what was the good of protesting?[65]

Plomer's doubts showed themselves not in protests, but in delay. His visit to South Africa in 1956 made it impossible for several months to consider *Sumidagawa* further. He was obliged to decline Britten's invitation to spend Christmas in Aldeburgh on the grounds that he had a prior engagement, and he was unable to attend the 1957 Aldeburgh Festival because of his plans to visit Germany with Erdmann. Britten, furiously busy as usual, did not press the matter.

Late in September 1958 they again had a chance to discuss it. Once more Britten seems to have suggested that the Japanese setting should be retained, and Plomer's objections now began to melt away:

As my mind begins to run on Sumida River, I feel less inclined to shy at Japanese names and place-names. It may be that some of them will be just as useful to you musically as 'Namu Amida' etc.

As you know, in Japanese all goes by syllables, and each syllable is, in theory, of equal weight, so, if Japanese words are to be sung or spoken, it is better that they should be rather formally enunciated than slurred or falsely accented. E.g. we ought to have, as nearly as possible,

Mi-ya-ko, not Miyàko
Su-mi-da, not Sumìda
Mu-sa-shi, not Musàshi.

Naturally when the words are said or sung in a quick tempo, the syllables do not always *seem* to be equally accented: so *shite*, as Ezra Pound so delicately tells us, can seem to sound like *shtay* ...

Don't let all this worry you, & unless you have strong feelings in the matter *against* my doing so, I shall proceed to make what seems judicious use of Japanese names. We can cut or alter later, as necessary.[66]

On 8 October Britten replied that he was 'very keen on as many nice evocative Japanese words as possible'. It is clear that Britten's observation, in the notes to the first edition of the libretto, that 'there was no question in any case of a pastiche from the ancient Japanese', and Plomer's remark in similar vein, 'It would have been impossible to transpose or imitate either the highly stylised Japanese production or the traditional subtleties of the *No*,'[67] were in part made with the advantage of hindsight.

With Britten's encouragement, Plomer went ahead with the work in October 1958, and only a fortnight later was writing that he had made some progress with a first draft of the libretto, a rewording of the Japanese original that he made with great speed. He told Britten that he found the language 'assuming great simplicity—as in a fairy tale or legend—and the rhythm of the language primitive or archaic'.[68] Britten, from Madeira, where he was holidaying, replied that he longed to see what Plomer was doing, and wondered whether Plomer intended to allow the appearance of the ghost of the dead boy at the end of the opera.[69] Plomer did.[70] By the first week of November 1958 the first draft of the work was complete,[71] and Plomer arranged to hand it to Britten in London on 13 November 1958.[72]

Another delay was now caused by Britten's acceptance of a commission from the corporation of Basel to write a cantata in celebration of the five-hundredth anniversary of that city's foundation, but by March 1959 Plomer had produced a second draft of the libretto, incorporating the suggestions Britten had put forward during their Christmas talks. He sent it to Britten, who responded, 'I think the Noh libretto is wonderful. I showed it to Lu Hesse[73] and he was enraptured.'[74] By 3 April 1959 Britten was writing that he had finished 'my Basel chore' and was clearing the decks for 'Sumida River', as the work was being called at this stage in their correspondence. For all that, he did not fly at the work of composing with his usual speed or energy, and it is hard to resist the sense, in going through his correspondence with Plomer, that something about the projected work was troubling him.

Up to this point, fully three years after Britten's trip to Japan, there had been no thought of transposing the Japanese story into an English setting. Nor was there any thought of performing it in a church, much less of Christianizing it, in spite of the fact that Britten had had considerable success with *Noye's Fludde*, the operatic work for church performance which was subsequently seen as a natural precursor of *Curlew River*.[75] The notion that it should be linked with another short opera strongly suggests that Britten and Plomer thought of the work as forming part of a double bill at a conventional operatic performance. Now that Britten was faced with the need to begin composing the music, however, there came a dramatic change of plan.

In the middle of April 1959 he wrote to Plomer, quite unexpectedly, beginning his letter with the words, 'I rather hope that you are feeling strong and courageous when you open this letter, my dear,' and saying that he had discussed the matter with Pears, and that they both believed the work should be given in one of the churches near Aldeburgh, perhaps Orford, and that it should be made into 'a Christian work'. He summed up the case for and against the proposed changes. The essence of his objections to the libretto Plomer had produced was that if the setting and costumes were Japanese, Britten would have to write what he called 'Japanesey' music, which he declared himself unable to produce, adding, 'I've been very worried lest the work should seem a pastiche of a Noh play, which however well done would seem false and thin.' Further, he thought the masks demanded by the Noh tradition would be 'a colossal problem' for the singers.[76]

The disadvantages of the changes he proposed, he admitted, were that the magic of the Japanese names would be lost, and that there would be no very good reason for Pears to do a female part, something which he and Britten had looked forward to. However, he partly answered his own objections by remarking that if the setting were made medieval or earlier, it would be appropriate not to use women, while the strongly artificial style of the Noh, if maintained in their production, would make it seem less odd for a woman to be played by a man. He now suggested that the setting should be 'pre-Conquest East Anglia, when there were shrines galore, or . . . Israel or South Italy', or even an indeterminate setting, identified simply as 'The Village' or 'The River'.[77]

Plomer, in spite of his natural disappointment at having had the work into which he had put so much energy altered so radically at this stage, replied good-humouredly:

I can't say that I'm astonished at your—I won't say throwing up the sponge, but setting fire to your—and indeed my—kimono. I really don't know *how* the piece could have turned into anything but a pasticcio grosso. But it is a little electrifying to have to think of transposing the story into Christian terms. Think I will, my first thought being that the missing child has come to be regarded locally as a saint (perhaps he could have been martyred) & that his grave has already become a place of pilgrimage. But I rather think that however formalized such a version might be, it might seem odd for the mother to be a man.[78]

The notion of making the child's grave a focus of local reverence was adhered to in the eventual production, but Plomer's doubts about a male singer playing the part of the Madwoman were eventually dispelled by Britten and Pears.

Britten visited Plomer in Rustington in May 1959, and the two went over the plans for the revised opera, which they were now calling simply 'The River',[79] an indication that the idea of an 'indeterminate' setting was dominant in their minds at this time. Only late in May did Plomer send a postcard to Britten, asking, 'Is there any reason why it shouldn't be called "Curlew River"?'[80] Britten, who continued to call it 'The River' in spite of this suggestion, then wrote to Plomer in August 1959, putting off further work on the piece for at least a year, giving as his reasons the fact that with the change of location from Japan to medieval England he was well behind schedule, and that since the Jubilee Hall at Aldeburgh was to be remodelled and enlarged, a big opera would be needed for the opening the following June, and ' "The River" being for a church wouldn't do, also it is scarcely Festive.'[81]

Plomer, relieved of any deadline, set about recasting the libretto entirely at his leisure, removing the Buddhist references of which Britten had said '[they] don't mean much to me',[82] and making the work a Christian one. It was not until August 1960, a full year later, that he completed the first draft of what he had now firmly named 'Curlew River'. He sent it to Britten, who responded, 'I'm much looking forward to starting on Curlew River. I'd love to talk about one or two bits fairly soon but it's thrilling that it is so beautifully and so convincingly shaped now.'[83] But Britten was as busy as ever, dashing off to Greece with the Hesses, touring Germany with Peter Pears for a series of concerts, and by January 1961 he had yet to settle to the music, saying that he was much looking forward to doing so, but that he was worried about a producer.[84]

Though it never quite disappeared from their correspondence, no urgency was expressed about working on the opera again until September 1963, when Britten decided on Colin Graham as the producer.[85] Composer and producer had a long talk late in October 1963 about the problems to be overcome in staging the opera,[86] and, after further discussions with Graham late in December, Britten wrote to Plomer suggesting changes in the libretto. He and Graham had decided that the chorus should cross the river in the boat, and therefore take up new positions around the shrine of the dead boy on the other side of the stage. He asked Plomer for some more lines for them to sing as they made the crossing, and Plomer in response wrote the song beginning 'Curlew River, smoothly flowing / Between the lands of east and west'. Britten once more threw the question of the title open, suggesting 'Crossing the River', but agreeing that the Tennysonian echo was a problem.[87]

Britten still felt the temptation to follow the Japanese original, as he made clear in a brief reference to a gift of some Japanese prints of scenes from Noh plays, which Plomer had sent him for Christmas of 1963: 'They are beauties, dangerously so because it is risky they may lead us back to Japan, already a strong influence in *The River*,' adding, 'I'm not serious because there is really no danger of a pastiche and one can always learn from an art so firm and universal, I find.'[88]

In mid-January Britten set off for Venice, where he spent a month in a *palazzo* once occupied by Byron,[89] and wrote hard. After what he described as a slow start, the result perhaps of the tiredness produced by putting on a new performance of *Billy Budd* shortly before he left London, he composed with his usual speed, and by mid-February was writing that 'after little more than a month I'm well towards the end. Apart from the usual bits that need clarifying I'm very pleased with it.'[90] He had already reached the point in the opera where the characters gather to pray at the tomb of the martyred child.[91]

In his previous collaboration with Plomer, Britten had learned that he could depend on his tolerance of alterations to the libretto. He now wrote, 'I have made my own changes and we must just work at them together at the earliest moment, and see that we are both happy,' adding, 'Oddly enough, as the work progressed, the Curlew grew in significance and my inclination is to go back to *Curlew River* as a title.'[92]

Britten returned to Aldeburgh, with the music all but completed,[93] on 23 February 1964, and Plomer visited him that same week, staying from Thursday to Saturday to hear Britten play through the music on the piano, and to go through further small points. Not until 2 April 1964, when Britten was negotiating with Faber and Faber about publication of the libretto, was the title finalized, with Britten writing to Plomer, 'I've been looking for a sub-title which will make it clear it is not an opera in the accepted sense and must be done in church. Do you like Curlew River, A Parable (I must learn how to spell it) for Church Performance?'[94] Plomer attended a preview on 7 June 1964, and wrote afterwards, 'I must just repeat how deeply impressed I was to hear & see all that you

& Peter [Pears] & Colin [Graham] have done to make what C. River has magically become . . . I hope you have now found a solution for the remaining unsolved problems. All ears & eyes, I press forward to Saturday, and send you in the meantime prolonged applause.'[95]

Plomer was if anything understating the case when he referred to the work as 'by no means an easy experiment',[96] but it was an experiment well worth making. The libretto was generously and rightly praised: *The Times* music critic said of it that it was, 'next to Mrs. Piper's *Turn of the Screw*, the finest, most skilfully designed for music that Britten has yet had',[97] while an anonymous *Times Literary Supplement* reviewer called it 'both brilliant and innovatory'.[98] Having worked their way to the new form they found for *Curlew River*, Britten and Plomer showed their satisfaction with it by using the same pattern for two more 'parables', *The Burning Fiery Furnace* (1966) and *The Prodigal Son* (1968). The experiment had paid off.

On 13 March 1961 Plomer's cousin Richard Rumbold, who had led a tormented life, travelling constantly, threw himself from a building in Taormina; the body was brought home to be buried in England. Like Anthony Butts, Rumbold had been a rich, homosexual dilettante, who seemed to have had everything in life but happiness. Again like Butts, he left a manuscript for Plomer to edit: a detailed diary, kept over twenty-nine years, recording his personal life in great detail. Harold Nicolson, who had been an intimate friend of Rumbold, went with Plomer to the funeral on 30 March 1961, and there got the impression that the Roman Catholic priest officiating had given him (Nicolson) a nasty look. In a letter to Plomer the next day he raged against the Biblical condemnation of homosexuality, and his letter well illustrates the difficulty Plomer and other homosexuals found in accepting the teachings of Christianity:

I know that in Christ's dear soul you and I are not cursed. It's all Saint Paul's fault that the tenderness of Christ's doctrine should have been turned to priggish, pedantic rage. 'We thank thee, O Lord, that in thy mercy ...' What mercy did Jehovah show to our poor old Richard? It was one long process of nagging and bullying. I came back feeling as if I had been beaten with thick wooden clubs.[99]

Plomer believed that he might make of the publication of Rumbold's diary some sort of vindication of the life his cousin had led. He took seriously the trust Rumbold had shown in him, and set about preparing the diary for publication.

He found the job intensely difficult, and struggled with it throughout 1961 and 1962. The problem was that Rumbold's writing was filled with what Plomer regarded as unbecoming self-pity and homosexual *Angst*, and with frank descriptions of his unsatisfactory love-affairs, which Plomer felt unable to publish, partly because of his own reticence and partly because these passages represented precisely that side of Rumbold which Plomer was trying to excuse or gloss over. Yet the work fascinated him, almost certainly because, like Butts's manuscript, it seemed to him as expressive of his own feelings as of those of the writer. The book, which he called *A Message in Code*, was published by Weidenfeld & Nicolson in 1964. It contained many vivid glimpses of Plomer himself. On one occasion Rumbold, waiting for Plomer in the Ritz, tried not to look sad or worried, but deliberately composed his features into 'an attitude of calm, objective appraisal of the passersby in the lounge; and, on entering, William immediately noticed it'. Another summer's day, in 1953, they were sitting in Hyde Park, and Rumbold suggested a competition: could they, as writers, think of something fresh to say about that tree? Plomer immediately noticed how, though there was no apparent breeze, its leaves were rustling. Rumbold could think of nothing. Perhaps even more revealing are the passages that ostensibly have nothing to do with Plomer but which, even after careful editing, shed interesting light on both Rumbold and Plomer:

I notice ... a kind of repugnance for females. The analyst says it is the fear of castration, or anyway the sense of my body having been damaged. Whether or not that is true I cannot say. Yet I know that the emotion is one of the deepest things I have in me ... affecting my whole life. And I feel that if I could only chain it to objective ends I could achieve something. (p. 92)

I was ... aware that if I were to become a practising Catholic, complications would ensue in my sex life. Quite clearly, Christianity was not the way. (p. 99)

Why, despite all this fun and experience, is one so fundamentally sad and unrequited? What is the unattainable yearning which nags, nags at one's heart? Is it love one wants? And if so, is it love of man or God? (p. 102)

Why is it that in heterosexuality there tends to be a fusion of the sexual and the emotional, whereas the homosexual is so often a divided being, separating his friendships from his affairs? (p. 128)

I have never had a love affair, however trivial, which did not generate endless *Angst* of one sort or another. (p. 145)

Plomer got Harold Nicolson to read the edited version carefully before publication, and he was much relieved when Nicolson approved of it. In spite of this support, he was 'in a great state of nerves' (as he told Hart-Davis on 19 May 1964) lest reviewers should react unsympathetically to the book; and he did all he could to ensure that his friends reviewed it, energetically and successfully drumming up support from Lehmann, Morris, and others.[100]

By the 1960s Plomer had become a literary figure whose reputation was widely recognized. He had in the past been content with the admiration of such friends as Forster and Virginia Woolf, but his name and even his face were becoming common property. The sales of his volumes of ballads far outstripped those of his earlier books of poetry,[101] and a series of little marks of recognition made him realize that he was gradually becoming a public figure. On 24 July 1958 he attended a ceremony in his honour at Stratford-upon-Avon, at which he was lauded as Poet of the Year at the Stratford Festival of Poetry. He was repeatedly invited to address student societies at Oxford, Cambridge, and other universities. In 1957 he was invited to revisit Japan, with a literary delegation from the British Council, but he declined. He served on the Arts Council, and on many committees awarding literary prizes, including the W. H. Smith Prize, the Duff Cooper Prize, and the Cholmondeley Award, which was instituted in 1966 by Lady Cholmondeley to encourage young, promising writers. Plomer was the chairman and prime mover of the Cholmondeley Award's panel of judges, which originally included Osbert Sitwell and Leslie Hartley. (The list of recipients of the award includes an impressive number of poets whose talent Plomer recognized very early on in their careers, including Ted Walker, Stevie Smith, Seamus Heaney, Derek Walcott, Douglas Livingstone, Charles Causley, and Philip Larkin.) In April 1959 the University of Durham gave him an honorary doctorate, which particularly pleased him, and thereafter he would sometimes half-jokingly sign himself 'William Plomer, D.Litt.'

His *Collected Poems* were published on 21 March 1960 by Cape's, and the volume allowed his remarkable poetic achievement to be seen as a whole for the first time. The critical reaction was enthusiastic—the poet Charles Causley, for instance, commented in *London Magazine* that Plomer had been a generation ahead of his time in his writing about Africa[102]—and the volume sold steadily. The University of Texas offered him a visiting professorship, which he declined.[103] He served from 1960 on a Unesco committee to further relations between East and West. He was elected president of the Kilvert Society; he won the Queen's Gold Medal for Poetry in 1963; and on 20 October 1958 *Punch* carried a caricature of him, with a rhymed comment more respectful than mocking, which began: 'Read William Plomer if you'd like a tip on / Africa, London, or the land of Nippon.' He was becoming a name.

16. *Hassocks and the Last Years*
1966–1973

PLOMER and Erdmann had been feeling for some time that Rustington was becoming too built up for comfort, and early in 1966 they began casting about for another house further inland. They had spent thirteen years in Rustington, and the changes they had seen had not been for the better: formerly quiet streets were roaring with traffic; a funeral parlour had been built next to Rossida; a garish supermarket had opened just across the road; and open countryside was less and less accessible. After long searching they found another, smaller house in Hassocks, near Brighton, closer to London and, Plomer hoped, more convenient than Rustington had become. As he wrote to his brother James,

Our intended new abode is extremely small. This is intentional. We look after ourselves & are both getting older, so things must be easy to manage. I have an arthritic knee (osteo, not rheumatoid, and an indication of one's age [sixty-two]) & have to accept the possibility of more bother later. The houselet—with a garden about as wide as the margin to this page—is away from the sea, behind the Downs, about 8 miles from Brighton & about 43 from London, which will be much more convenient for me—or so I hope.[1]

Years before, when he was a young man, he had passed the village by train with his mother, and she, looking out at the Downs and the village beneath, had remarked dreamily to him, 'I should have liked to live here, I'd have been happier.' Plomer remembered the incident, and when they were planning to move there he gaily told Erdmann, 'Hassocks is for Happiness'.[2] Hassocks was a relatively new settlement of commuters and retired people: the new house, 43 Adastra Avenue, was only eight years old, faced south, was in Plomer's words 'deliciously anonymous',[3] and was near a fine public garden and within an easy walk of the station. 'We think', wrote Plomer to Hart-Davis, 'that Adastra! Hassocks!! Sussex!!! sounds like three sneezes.'[4] He looked the place up in Nikolaus Pevsner's *The Buildings of England*, and found the description 'No church and no identity'. It moved him to a poem which he called 'No Identity', written in defence of anonymity, a poem that reveals something of the nature of his mask:

> ... *No identity* can be a desirable thing:
> To have a face with features noticed less
> Than one's range of expression, so that photographed
> It never looks twice the same, and people say
> 'But that's not you!'
> > One would like to reply:
> 'No, that's not me, because I'm incapable
> Of starting the very least personality cult.
> I have freed myself at last from being me;
> Don't think of me as chameleon or actor; if I take
> Protective colouring, it is that I mean to be
> A kind of medium, free to enjoy, well, *no identity*.'

He and Erdmann moved at the end of August 1966, and laboured to get the new house organized to their liking. 'A great struggle for some sort of order and method is going on here,' he wrote to Alan Ross, 'and one feels that it ought to be called Perardua Avenue.'[5] They found, to their dismay, that a constant, growing stream of jet aircraft passed over the house at night on their way to and from Gatwick; the noise worried Erdmann more than it did Plomer. But on balance both of them liked the new house and garden, and Erdmann set about taming the birds as he had tamed those at Rustington, training several of them to come into the kitchen and eat from his hand.[6] One of these birds, in search of food, would flutter between Plomer's eyes and whatever book he was reading at meals, for he and Erdmann were not great talkers when together.[7] He found Erdmann the most helpful of companions, but several of his friends thought Plomer consistently lonely through the latter half of his life. 'I think he was always seeking what he didn't have,' Spender was to remark after Plomer's death. 'He never found anyone to love who was on equal terms with him.'[8]

At the beginning of September 1966 Cape's published Plomer's latest collection of poems, with the title *Taste and Remember*. It was his seventh volume of poems, and his friends thought it his best: 'Your hand, ear and eye are now so sure and exact,' Hart-Davis wrote to him on 13 September 1966.[9] The reviewers were highly complimentary; typical of them was Richard Church, who compared Plomer to Matthew Arnold, and commented that Plomer did in verse what Chekhov had done in the short story: capture an irony and a poignancy that made the dark state of the world more bearable.[10] Plomer thought the poems appropriate utterances for a man of his age, and wrote, 'as a sexagenarian one is not only rather surprised to be still living, but one feels fortunate to be able to write poetry at all, & to know that it pleases persons one is pleased to please.'[11] Among those who wrote to congratulate him on the volume was the Poet Laureate John Masefield, who, when Plomer thanked him, wrote by return to thank him for thanking him. When Masefield died in 1967, several of the newspapers tipped Plomer as the next Poet Laureate, though he himself rejected the idea. 'The post is bizarre, and even if I were offered it, I can't imagine accepting it,' he wrote to James Plomer on 28 May 1967.[12] In the event he was pleased when it went to his old friend Cecil Day-Lewis.

The move to Hassocks had made him a near neighbour of Alan Ross (the new editor of the *London Magazine*, in succession to John Lehmann) and his wife Jennifer. Plomer, who continued to take a keen interest in the magazine, became a good friend of the Rosses, and frequently walked over to dine with them at Clayton, under the Downs. He had first met Ross in the Admiralty during the war, through their mutual friend Ian Fleming, and in later years they were brought together not only by *London Magazine*, but also by Ross's agreement to join Plomer and two others[13] on the committee that administered the Cholmondeley Award. Ross shared Plomer's love of odd postcards, and the two of them vied with each other in an exchange that Ross compared to two-handed bridge.[14] Another relatively close neighbour was Ian Parsons, who was now running Chatto and Windus and Hogarth Press. Parsons became joint chairman with Graham C. Greene of the merger between Chatto and Windus and Cape, and with his South African-born wife Trekkie often made Plomer welcome.

Plomer was a sought-after dinner guest, for he was capable of holding court without seeming to dominate the conversation. The deep mellow voice, which always seemed to have a chuckle in it (one friend compared it to that of a mischievous archdeacon with a sideline in African magic),[15] would deliver a series of amusing stories which, because they were so typical of his careful observation and wry sense of fun, could make the company yell with affectionate laughter. Some ridiculous event that had happened that day, a case of mistaken identity, affronted dignity, or the wrong thing being delivered to somebody's house, happenings that no one else would have noticed, formed the substance of his anecdotes, and he tended to avoid anything that might offend or hurt. John Betjeman, who had come to know him through Plomer's work for the Society of Authors, recorded a typical example of his humour. Plomer had been on a London bus when a mother and child got on and sat down next to a woman wearing an obviously expensive fur coat. The child began rubbing a sticky lolly up and down the coat, to the horror of its owner. 'Don't do that, Mavis,' said the mother. 'You'll get hairs all over it.'[16]

His capacity for apparently effortless, amusing conversation was put to good use in the many unscripted BBC programmes in which he took part, programmes of more or less spontaneous discussion of literary subjects. Less experienced broadcasters were often doubtful of their ability to keep the discussion going, and were impressed by Plomer's capacity to carry a programme on his own if need be. The poet Charles Causley,[17] who met Plomer when they served together on the Arts Council Literature Panel, told a self-depreciating story of taking part with him in a broadcast on the subject of Poets' Corner, on 19 April 1966. The two of them had wandered around Westminster Abbey before the recording session, trying to work out what they were going to say, and Causley had grown more and more nervous. He need not have worried. 'William was magnificent,' he wrote later. ' "Hello!" the recording engineer said to me cheerfully as we emerged from the studio. "I thought you'd gone home." '[18]

The first visitors to 43 Adastra Avenue were Plomer's niece Deirdre and her husband. Since the death of his father, Plomer had grown closer to his brother James, and the two of them had carried on a regular and warm correspondence. Their friendship was not disturbed even when James submitted the manuscript of a long novel to Cape's, and Plomer, asked to evaluate it, reluctantly turned it down. Deirdre was James's daughter by his first marriage; he had two other children, Billie and Jim, by his second, and Plomer took a close interest in all three, seldom forgetting their birthdays and in due course rejoicing in their marriages. When Billie produced a son, Michael, in December 1965, Plomer wrote with great pride to tell Hart-Davis that he had become a great-uncle. When his nieces and nephew came to England, they invariably visited Plomer, to his great delight; he and Billie found themselves particularly in accord. James's wife, Frances, was English-born, and she made trips to see her mother, Mrs Randall, in 1965, 1970, and 1971, each time calling on Plomer and being entertained by him. As a result, Plomer after the war built up a sense of family context which he had lacked since being sent to Beechmont nearly half a century earlier. He had always loved children, and it was a matter of abiding regret to him that he had none of his own. In his second volume of autobiography, *At Home*, he wrote a long, moving passage[19] about the education he would want to provide for his child—if he had one.

But by now he had accepted that he would never have one, and when marriage seemed once more (and for the last time) to be suggesting itself to him, he resisted it. He had for some time been corresponding with an energetic and enthusiastic South African, Zelda Friedlander, who had written to enlist his help with a memorial volume she was preparing on Olive Schreiner. At the end of 1965 she arrived in England for a three-month visit, and during this time she saw a great deal of Plomer and grew very fond of him. He took endless trouble to show her around London and the south coast, fussed about her when she went up to the north of England on her own, offered to lend her money if she needed it, took her shopping, and listened to her endless recital of the problems that seemed to dog her. But when, on 7 December 1965, she made a more direct appeal to him, as Mary Campbell had once done, he fended her gently off, and thereafter took a firmer line in the relationship. By 22 January 1966, when he wrote to Sargeson about her, he could be objective and amusing in his description:

Life has been complicated lately by a wildly energetic & enthusiastic & possessive & impulsive & temperamental & unmarried & middle-aged S. African Jewess (with literary aspirations, like *everybody* else) who has been paying her first visit to this country & is in ecstasies about everything and everybody. It's just like being intimate with a concrete-mixer, from the inside. But she is so warm-hearted & has done wonderful things, and with courage, for persons unable to help themselves, that one has to put up with the violent rotation. She is due to leave next week.[20]

Plomer and Friedlander continued to correspond, and hundreds of their letters survive; Plomer wrote a foreword for her Schreiner volume, *Until the Heart Changes*, which after many difficulties was published in South Africa, but he was careful to keep her at a correct distance after this brush with what might have been.

The rhythms of his life continued unaltered at Hassocks. He still went to London for the directors' meeting at Cape's every Wednesday, taking his completed reports with him and coming away, after discussion and lunch, with another batch of manuscripts. With the death of Jonathan Cape in February 1960, the firm had changed a good deal, and in 1965 Wren Howard had been persuaded by his son Michael to hand over control to two new joint managing directors, Tom Maschler and Graham C. Greene. Plomer had known both the new directors for some time, got on well with them, and had a particularly friendly relationship with Greene, whom he thought quite uncommonly intelligent, astute, and sympathetic. Greene did a good deal of travelling round the English-speaking world for Cape's, and Plomer showed the warmth he felt for Greene by giving him introductions to friends in various countries, ranging from Zelda Friedlander in Cape Town to James and Frances Plomer in Toronto.

Plomer confined his active social life to London, contriving to live so quietly in Hassocks that few of his neighbours knew more than his name. He was, they believed, 'something in the city—ever such a nice man'. Only one, questioned a decade after Plomer's death, knew that 'he used to write poetry, and I believe that he broadcast as well'.[21] He was known in the village chiefly for the long walks he and Erdmann took together, and for their love of jumble sales; Plomer's passion for the Caledonian Market was now satisfied closer to home. Erdmann in particular had a talent for finding bargains, which he would often resell later at a profit.

Plomer continued to contribute to the Aldeburgh Festival almost every year (in 1967, for instance, he read his ballads interpersed with guitar music played by Julian Bream), and would then go off to Wales for another Kilvert jamboree; then, a little later in the summer, would come his regular week at Houghton with Lady Cholmondeley. He was working during 1967 on the libretto of the third of Britten's 'parables for church performance', *The Prodigal Son*, their previous collaboration, *The Burning Fiery Furnace*, having been a great success. One of the subtle signs in his writing of his return to the Christianity of his childhood was his use in *The Prodigal Son* of the plainsong hymn with which each school day at St John's in Johannesburg had begun. Just as his poetry had returned to themes that had interested him during his South African days, in other aspects of life too he was returning to his origins. Even the title of *The Prodigal Son* is significant in context.

He received many invitations to read his work to student groups at universities and colleges, ranging from Oxford to Bath, Belfast, and St Andrews, and accepted all that he could fit in; his aim continued to be to give poetry as wide an audience as possible. He also accepted several invitations to writers' conferences, but only in Britain: his trip to Switzerland and Bavaria in 1959 proved to have been his last outside the British Isles, and he theorized to John Morris (who was travelling again in Asia during 1967) that having been shunted about continually as a child and a young adult, he now had a need to remain 'rooted like a cabbage'.

He played a leading role in three 'weekend poetry schools' organized by the Poetry Society in Oxford, York, and Bristol. At the York and Bristol 'schools' he met the poet William Oxley, who was to leave a vivid account of Plomer in his unpublished memoirs.[22] Plomer's ballads seemed to Oxley much the most effective poetry he heard read at these occasions, and he found Plomer's conversation unfailingly amusing and full of characteristic touches. At York in September 1969 Plomer told him, for instance, of the funeral of the Welsh poet Vernon Watkins, at which his fellow Welshman R. S. Thomas delivered the eulogy. In his dry gravelly voice, impregnated with the gloom of Welsh valleys, Thomas began with these words, delivered slowly and without any trace of humour: 'Well, we all know that Vernon was a fine man, but he was not a good poet.' When the service was done, Plomer went over to comfort Watkins's widow, who was visibly upset by Thomas's address. 'I don't know how Ronald could say such unkind things!' she remarked indignantly to Plomer 'When I think of all the times Vernon and I let him camp on our front lawn!'[23]

His friendships with Ackerley and Forster, under strain for some while, in part because of Plomer's increasing sympathy for Christianity (which Ackerley in particular interpreted as Plomer's having joined the Establishment), declined further in 1967. Seven years before, in August 1960, Forster had asked Plomer to write his biography. Plomer had agreed but had done nothing, intending to begin the work after Forster's death. On 29 April 1967, in a brief letter prompted by and dictated to Ackerley, Forster told Plomer of his intention to give the job to a young don at Kings College,

Cambridge, P. N. Furbank. Plomer was hurt, not so much by being relieved of the task (for which he had felt little real inclination), as by the alienation which he felt lay behind it. 'I feel that if Joe felt that I had neglected Morgan too much & should therefore be relieved of dealing with the material I had agreed to deal with after Morgan's death,' he wrote to John Morris, 'he should have talked to me about it candidly, instead of springing that curt letter upon me.'[24] His relations with Ackerley never recovered, and though he continued to see Forster, he was much more critical of him than in the past. Against Furbank he harboured no grudge, and gladly gave him the notes he had accumulated, together with his memories of Forster. Furbank, who felt awkward about the hand-over, was to leave an acutely perceptive glimpse of Plomer in his life of Forster:

Plomer was an ironic, rather secretive and mystery-loving man, with a collector's passion for oddities—for suburban house-names, public statues and human eccentrics. In manner he was precise and sedate, with a teasing and foxy aplomb. It was a manner at odds with his life ... There was in fact some split in him between irony and feeling, for he was at heart deeply sentimental—indeed, his friends said, he allowed sentiment to destroy his life.[25]

Ackerley died within months of the break with Plomer, leaving his literary executor Francis King the manuscript of his memoir *My Father and Myself*, which was published in 1968. Plomer thought it shockingly frank, and believed it should never have been written, much less published; reading it thoroughly depressed him.[26] It had been toned down a good deal since Ackerley first let John Morris read it, however; in its original version it had begun with the words 'My father's penis was twelve inches long.'[27]

Plomer continued to accumulate the honours appropriate to his achievements. He was made a Commander of the British Empire in the New Year's honours list in January 1968, and was pleased to have joined what he called 'the ranks of the three-letter men'.[28] Congratulations poured in from his friends. 'I know it is unfashionable to defend honours,' Van der Post wrote, 'but I've always believed in raising my hat to people I respect and I think nations are all the better for doing the same. One's only reservation being that they have not on this occasion raised it high enough.'[29] In November 1968 Plomer was elected to the presidency of the Poetry Society, a position he held for three years. It involved him in endless poetry readings, meetings, and committees, which he rather enjoyed, and exposed him to a good deal of publicity, which he disliked.

The first scholarly book devoted entirely to his work appeared in 1969, J. R. Doyle's *William Plomer*;[30] he was pleased to have a copy of it, but found it rather embarrassing and lacking in understanding, and attributed this partly to the fact that Doyle was an American. 'Somehow he makes me feel the Atlantic is rather wide,' he told John Morris.[31] Some potential honours he fought shy of; on being asked to allow his name to go forward for nomination to the chair of poetry at Oxford in 1968, for instance, he begged to be let off. There were also less conventional marks of recognition: in 1970 he received a gold medal from the Poetry Society of the Philippines ('What nonsense!' he wrote to his brother), while in November 1966 a letter informed him, to his surprise, that he had been unanimously elected a Knight of Mark Twain.

By 1969 he had reached the age when his friends began to droop and die. Britten was suffering from the heart disease that would kill him a few years later, and was soon to have major surgery for the condition; Forster no longer troubled to open the letters he received, and was to die in June 1970. Day-Lewis was weaker and quieter each time Plomer saw him, displaying great courage in his decline. Blunden, with whom Plomer had maintained his friendship ever since their first meeting in Japan in 1926, had had a stroke, had grown immensely fat, and spent much of his time over a bottle of beer in the kitchen, scarcely able to keep up a conversation, and no longer capable of reading or writing. Plomer was a popular speaker at memorial services in honour of his dead friends, and at services for other writers. He also contributed to television documentaries on some of them, taking part in BBC films on Ian Fleming, Virginia Woolf, and Kilvert in 1969 and 1970. He had delivered the address at the service for Jonathan Cape in 1960, and for Ian Fleming in 1964; he had preached on Kilvert in a London church in 1967, given the oration at the unveiling of a memorial tablet to Byron in Westminster Abbey in May 1969, and preached in Hereford Cathedral in June 1969. He came to rather enjoy these memorial services: 'the children's parties of second childhood', he wryly called them, and they inspired one of the poems he wrote at this time, 'At a Memorial Service'.

One of the friends who seemed likely to live for ever was Laurens van der Post. Since 1965, when *Turbott Wolfe* had been reprinted with a long introduction by Van der Post, he and Plomer had overcome the slight chill between them, and when others criticized Van der Post in Plomer's presence, he would defend his old friend stoutly. In 1968, at Van der Post's insistence (and expense), Plomer sat to the sculptress Frances Baruch for a portrait head; it was cast in bronze in August 1968, and Van der Post donated it to the Johannesburg Art Gallery. He also sat to the painter Robert Buhler for a pastel portrait in 1970, at Buhler's instigation.

Another evergreen was Hart-Davis, who had retired from his publishing house in 1964, and moved to a large, comfortable house, stuffed to the ceiling with books, in a beautiful north Yorkshire village. When he made his will for the second time, in January 1962, Plomer asked Hart-Davis to be his literary executor, saying he knew no one he could trust as much.[32] Hart-Davis was knighted in January 1967, and his third wife Ruth died very suddenly that same month. He married for the fourth time in June 1968, and that year, as he had done repeatedly, pressed Plomer to come and visit him. Plomer did, in October 1968. He was charmed by the distinction and sweetness of his friend's new wife, June, and charmed her in turn. Years later she remembered the odd little touches of humour that made him such an endearing guest: for instance, while he was helping to wash the dishes after a meal, he replaced a kitchen knife in its strong magnetic holder, and she heard him say reprovingly to the device, 'Don't snatch!'[33] The Hart-Davises took him to hear Hepzibah and Yehudi Menuhin playing Schubert in the tiny eighteenth-century theatre in nearby Richmond, and he thoroughly enjoyed the weekend with them.

He continued his round of social engagements, but at a slower pace now, keeping up contacts with old friends such as Leonard Woolf, with whom he corresponded steadily, and whom he saw at intervals. He attended Woolf's eighty-eighth birthday party in 1968, for instance, and thought him very alert still and laudably unself-centred. Years before Woolf had remarked to him that Virginia's diaries were 'censorious', but that her censoriousness was 'not the real Virginia', a remark that Plomer thought quite true.[34] On another occasion, in 1961, Plomer had been staying with Woolf, and noticed in the garden a stone Victorian bust of a serious-looking man. He asked who it was. 'It's James Stephen, the one who was Colonial Secretary,' said Woolf. Then after a pause he added rather scornfully, 'He looks it, doesn't he?' Another pause:

'I invariably use it to pump ship on.' The incident seemed to Plomer a belated instance of the old-fashioned and extreme anti-Victorianism of Bloomsbury.[35] He noticed too Leonard Woolf's passionate prejudice against received religion, telling Hart-Davis that the Woolfs had been profoundly shocked when T. S. Eliot, who was staying with them for a weekend in the 1930s, went to Communion on Sunday morning in the church next door to Monk's House.[36] (At Woolf's own funeral in 1969, Plomer knelt and prayed for some minutes, and then got up feeling vaguely guilty.)

In 1965, on another visit to Rodmell, Plomer was told by Woolf that when Eliot was living in Emperor's Gate ('surrounded by curates'), he sent the Woolfs a typescript of one of the *Four Quartets*, and also sent copies to Mary Hutchinson and McKnight Kauffer. He invited them all to read it critically, and then assemble to give him their opinions of it. He politely dismissed Hutchinson's and Kauffer's comments as of no interest, but in reply to Virginia's comment that too many lines ended with a present participle, had said, 'That's a *good* criticism, Virginia.' But Woolf remarked sardonically to Plomer that all the same, 'Tom only made one or two alterations.'[37]

On this same visit, in January 1965, Woolf said that he thought *A Passage to India* much the best of Forster's books, but added that 'all the business in the caves was absurd and unbelievable'. Plomer remarked that he had been rereading some of the novels, and had been struck anew by the oppressively feminine influences under which Forster had grown up, adding that he supposed growing up with a lot of old women must do a good deal to one's outlook. 'But Morgan is an old woman,' said Woolf earnestly. 'He always has been.'[38]

At the literary parties that Cape's gave Plomer continued to meet other writers. He met Patrick White for the first time in November 1967, and thought him not as brusque and lacking in social grace as he had been warned to expect. White congratulated Plomer on having written a poem he had always admired, but the title he mentioned was not known to Plomer, who felt rather awkward as a result.[39] He also met Robert Graves, whom he had last seen in the thirties. Plomer told Graves that he had lately met Wilfred Owen's brother, and spoke of the brother's autobiography. 'Homosexual!' said Graves, who was unaware that Plomer was one. 'The trouble is, he hides it. He never says Owen was homosexual. All that about "The poetry is in the pity", it's as if you or I were

looking at a battlefield covered with the bodies of beautiful girls.'
Graves had recently received the Queen's Medal for Poetry, which
Plomer had won before him. Plomer had simply been sent his medal
in the mail, but Graves (partly because of Plomer's protests) had
been given his by the Queen in person. He had examined the medal
closely, in silence, and the Queen, growing curious, had asked why.
'I wished', said Graves, quite unabashed, 'to ensure that it was real
gold.'[40] He also told Plomer that he had reminded the Queen that
she was descended from Muhammad, and suggested that she ought
to publicize the fact. 'It would make the Pakistanis in this country
so pleased,' urged Graves. 'I never thought of that,' said the Queen
with restraint.[41]

Plomer continued to make new friends too, one of them being
the poet Ted Walker. They met in January 1965, when Walker,
whose first book of verse was about to be published by Cape's (on
Plomer's recommendation), received an invitation to call at Plomer's
house. Walker, thirty at the time, was rather in awe of Plomer,
and feared being patronized; he arrived on a motorcycle in a rain
storm and knocked timidly at Plomer's door. His description of their
meeting is a good example of the response Plomer never ceased to
evoke in those who met him:

Not knowing what I'd say to introduce myself, I could only gawk when
the door was opened by an elegant, trim, white-haired man whose
demeanour suggested not so much a writer as a solicitous and considerate
doctor. Though his smile was shy, he was at once authoritative and
avuncular. '*You* are Ted *Walker*,' he informed me, 'and *I* am William
Ploomer.' How grateful I felt to him for sparing me the gaffe of calling him
Ploamer. Towels were produced, swiftly followed by hot tea and a fireside
chair. During the next hour he found out and wrote down a mass of details
about my family, my job, my interests, my seriousness as a poet. He said
he would do whatever he could to help me; he made me a gift of several
books; he was tactful, genial, courteous, charming and amusing. When I
left, though he'd revealed little about himself, I knew I had made a new
friend. In almost every respect, that first meeting set the pattern for a
friendship that was to last until his death.[42]

Plomer rather regretted now that he had not kept a regular diary
in his younger days, and began keeping a notebook in which he
recorded stray anecdotes, probably intending to use them for a third
volume of autobiography. He noted, for instance, that Osbert Sitwell
had told him at Brighton in 1965 that when the poet Arthur Waley

(an old friend of Plomer's) was staying at Renishaw, Sitwell took him out for a drive with the pianist Louis Kentner. Waley's conversation was often eccentric and halting, and Kentner, to break a long silence, asked whether Waley had ever played golf. 'Once,' said Waley. 'And did you enjoy it?' 'If I had enjoyed it,' said Waley, 'I should have played it again.' 'And did you find it difficult?' 'About as difficult as playing the flute.' The desperate Kentner never discovered how well Waley played the flute.[43]

In the same diary notebook Plomer recorded his visit to Cambridge with Morris for Forster's ninetieth birthday in January 1969:

John Morris & I stayed at the University Arms Hotel, & Bob Buckingham [Forster's policeman friend] brought Morgan to dine with us. He ate heartily, ordering himself melon, trout with vegetables, & some sort of peach melba. He chose to share our claret, which he much enjoyed. He wore no spectacles, but had no difficulty in dissecting his fish.

Later, when we were sitting in the lounge, some sort of head waiter or chasseur came up with an autograph book & invited Morgan to write his name in it. Morgan hesitated a moment & then said he would. 'Perhaps,' said the man, rather as if granting a favour, 'you would like to put your name on the same page as Mr. Maugham's.' 'No, I shouldn't,' said Morgan instantly, 'I'll put it on another page.' Slightly taken aback, the man then agreed & found another page, and Morgan signed his name ...

I noticed that the hair at the back of Morgan's head was still dark. He was alert, & said how much he liked a couple of stories I told him, notably one about Gandhi. He said, 'I like to hear interesting things, but I don't say anything interesting,' and twinkled.

I picked up Morgan's hand & kissed it as I said good-bye, & he snatched up mine and kissed it heartily.[44]

Plomer kept up his immense correspondence tirelessly; even the most trivial letter from him contained something memorable, interesting, or funny. 'I have, as usual, been rushing from pillar to post,' he once wrote, 'and if I had rushed to post first & pillar later, you would have heard from me sooner.'[45] In the middle of a rail strike he told John Morris, 'I could get to see you if only British Rail wouldn't keep letting one down by not picking one up.' He wrote to his favourite niece Billie, 'Do you know, I once went to a barber I hadn't been to before, & when I said "A little more off the back, please" he said "That's right, sir. It wouldn't do to have you looking like a poet." '[46] To the poet William Oxley, at the end of a long letter about Oxley's own verse, he wrote, 'I spoke yesterday to a man who told me he is the only living person to have seen Byron in the flesh. It was an exhumation in the 1930s & he wasn't looking his best.'[47] Describing a memorial service for Stevie Smith, he wrote to Hart-Davis, 'The cracking of genuflecting old women's knees was like a salvo of pistol shots, and the priest, in a rather brilliant address, said of S.S. "She looked like a tame kestrel dressed for a First Communion in a French village." '[48] When Michael Howard left Jonathan Cape's and set up a rest-home for authors in the Wye valley (a project with disastrous results, for both it and his marriage failed some years later, and he committed suicide), Plomer sent him a copy of a travel book about south Wales: 'I wish it were a cleaner copy, but I see Bessie gave it to Emma in 1904, and goodness knows what Emma has been doing with it since.'[49] In the middle of a bad winter, in 1972, he wrote, 'A woman has written to *The Times* to say her blood is boiling. Gracious, how lucky!'[50] And these late letters often tell more about him than any of his earlier, masked ones. Writing about hippies to his niece Billie, for instance, he remarked, 'I had many things to rebel against, but wore protective colouring instead of fancy dress. What I mean is that while apparently outwardly conforming to the societies in which I lived— in S. Africa, in Japan, & in this country—I put forward ideas that were absolutely against theirs.'[51]

He was beginning to feel rather an old buffer, and aspects of life in the late 1960s and early 1970s sometimes irritated him—not least the fuss made over the moon landing and the first heart transplant. 'A little less buggering about in space, and a little more attention to oiling the wheels of everyday life', he wrote to John Morris, 'would be far too sensible a course for the species to which, whether we like it or not, we belong.'[52] He expressed his irritation in several poems, including 'Your Heart and the Moon', 'The Red Fault Lamp', and in one of his pithiest and most biting epigrams, 'To the Moon and Back':

countdown	takeoff
moonprints	rockbox
splashdown	claptrap

When the Maltings, the large concert-hall near Aldeburgh, burnt down in the summer of 1969, Britten asked Plomer to write a poem about it, as part of the fund-raising effort to rebuild. Plomer responded with 'A Note From a Cello', which he wrote in 1970:

A blameless calm night, the people have gone.
Dark thickets of reeds feel a breath of disquiet:
Moorhens awake; fear saves the vole
About to be hooked by the soft-flying owl;
In the marshes of Snape a sluice and a pool
Make suddenly shapes of flame-coloured light.

A crackle of fire! An undeclared war,
Motiveless, strikes at those who contrived
That resonant shell, at ears that have heard
Rejoicings derived, in nights darker by far,
From far greater fires, wells deeper, deep dreams,
Granite, violets, blood, the pureness of dew.

The shell is restored. The orchestra settles.
A baton is raised. Renew what is old!
Make known what is new! From a cello the bow
Draws its hauntingest note, confiding, profound;
And immured in the bone the marrow responds
To the endless, exploring inventions of sound.

He showed considerable ability to write verse on request. Another of his most successful late poems is 'The Planes of Bedford Square', based on an anecdote told him years before by Ottoline Morrell, and written for a publishers' fair, 'The Book Bang', held in the summer of 1971. These poems and others he gathered in his tenth volume of verse, *Celebrations*, which Cape's published on 23 March 1972. It was the most successful of his volumes of serious verse, was chosen by the Poetry Book Society as its spring choice for 1972, and sold more copies than any of Plomer's earlier books of poetry. 'That sort of thing is rather encouraging when one is conscious of being ancient,' Plomer commented to his niece Billie.[53] Hart-Davis wrote to him, 'When I consider how many of our contemporaries have faded poetically—Auden declining upon clerihews, Spender showing no change or improvement, poor Cecil almost dead—I rejoice in the strength and fertility of your muse.'[54] The book was very widely reviewed, and several reviewers took the chance to sum up Plomer's achievement. The comment of Douglas Dunn in *Books & Writers* set the tone: 'He has been ruggedly individual, faithful to his inclinations, unconcerned with fashion, and his craftsmanship has always been scrupulous, his subjects interesting, his achievement considerable.'[55]

Several of the poems were meditations on death or depictions of a frightening new world in which there is no place for the ageing characters in the poems. The last of them, 'Now', focused on a lonely old woman contemplating her coming death among her precious possessions; through her Plomer seemed to be speaking about his own death, and about the poetry he would leave behind him:

> 'One hope I have, that these few pretty things
> inherited or acquired, outlasting me,
> may be cherished for what they are
> more than for what they'd fetch.
> Who, you ask, is to inherit them?
> Leaving the world, I leave them to the world.'

The success of the poems prompted the millionaire Paul Getty to invite Plomer to read them with Glenda Jackson in Getty's house at a performance for charity. 'I hear that his library is full of richly bound books *all* about oil,' Plomer wrote to his brother, 'I imagine with titles like *Oil's Well that Ends Well*, and *From Castor to Diesel*: *An Oil-Man's Odyssey*, or *First Steps in Lubrication*, and perhaps *The Well of Loneliness*.'[56] The reading, in June 1972, was highly successful and raised more than £1,000, though Getty, to Plomer's disappointment, put in only the briefest of appearances, along with the Duchess of Argyll and Zsa Zsa Gabor. Plomer thoroughly enjoyed the occasion.

During 1972 he was engaged in revising his two volumes of autobiography for publication as a single volume to be entitled *The Autobiography of William Plomer*. He had little difficulty with the first volume, *Double Lives*, but found *At Home* much more problematic. 'There are a thousand things to avoid,' he wrote to his brother James, 'and high on the list is anything like patting oneself on the back, of which I have a horror. I intend to be a little more candid than before about Charles-the-Father.'[57] However, he had no intention of being candid about either his own personal life or that of his friends, and this made the work very slow; in the event, he managed to revise only the first few chapters of *At Home* before tiring of the task.

Cecil Day-Lewis died in June 1972, not long after Plomer had made a long and tiring rail-trip to see him for the last time, taking a bottle of home-made jam as a gift. Once again the papers were filled with speculation about a successor to the Laureateship, and Plomer's name cropped up repeatedly. 'Idiotic newspapers are tipping me, like a horse, as a possible successor,' he wrote to his brother. 'I have no idea whether I shall be asked or not. If I am I shall almost certainly refuse ... I am too old, & am supposed to be doing less, not more.'[58] Plomer did not have to refuse, for the Laureateship was not offered to him; he was very pleased when another of his friends, John Betjeman, accepted it. 'The value of the post, from my point of view,' Plomer wrote to his brother, 'is that it's a public, or national, recognition of an art in which the English have done very well & are still active.'[59]

In the middle of 1972 Plomer was surprised to be asked to collaborate on a book for children with a young artist, Alan Aldridge. He had never written anything for the young before, though his ballads, with their deceptively simple lines, suggested that he might be good at it. The book, which he entitled *The Butterfly Ball and the Grasshopper's Feast*, required him to write thirty short, simple poems for illustration by Aldridge. Plomer did them rapidly, because of a pressing editorial deadline, and much enjoyed writing them; he thought Aldridge's illustrations strikingly beautiful.

No sooner had he finished this task, in December 1972, than a distant relation of his, Patrick Lowe-Holmes, presented him with a bundle of Victorian letters that had passed between two lesbians in the 1860s. On reading them, Plomer thought they would make a good book, and he edited them carefully, using the title 'Burn These Letters' because each letter from one of the women, Alice Lemon, ended with that phrase. When the task was done he took the manuscript to Cape's and showed it to Graham C. Greene, who thought it well worth publication. As an afterthought Greene asked, 'By the way, William, do you have the copyright?' Plomer swung round from the window through which he had been looking out on to Bedford Square: 'What do you mean?' he asked, 'I *own* them.' Greene was surprised that with all his publishing experience Plomer should not know that the copyright resided with the literary heirs of the writers.[60] Cape's advertised for the descendants of the two women, and located an heir of Alice Lemon living in Ireland; she asked to see Plomer's book, and when she had read it, indignantly refused to allow publication. 'Burn These Letters' had to be abandoned.[61]

At the beginning of 1973 he began preparing an enlarged edition of his *Collected Poems* for publication by Cape's to mark his seventieth birthday, which would fall on 10 December 1973, and he continued to write poetry. On 15 March 1973, for instance, he sent Lady Cholmondeley a short poem which has not since been collected, and which, he wrote to her, 'began with the reflection in a murky pond of a branch of sunlit, young, brilliantly green horse-chestnut leaves, and seems to be partly about the suggestion of a parallel with art in the idea of a transmuted image, and partly about the association of an image with memories of the dead'. He called it 'Painted on Darkness':

> A sunlit branch of four reflected roses
> Bright on the darkened window of that room,
> That locked and shuttered, memory-haunted room,
> Startles by tint and stillness, perfectly composed.
>
> Each rose transmuted, sweeter than itself,
> In pure vermilion stands out strange and new
> Against the haunted glass intensified,
> Painted on darkness, as a poem is.

Since the end of 1971 he had been suffering from chest pains when he was under physical or emotional strain—if he ran for a bus, for instance, or was tense about a poetry reading he had to give. His doctor told him that the pain was angina, and advised him to decline more often the invitations that flooded in. He did try to ease off during 1972, declining an invitation to serve a second three-year term as president of the Poetry Society, and refusing almost all invitations to visit friends or broadcast for the BBC.

By the beginning of 1973, however, he was feeling stronger, and he resumed his active life. The first copies of *The Butterfly Ball and the Grasshopper's Feast* arrived from the printers, and he began happily posting off copies to his friends; a good deal of publicity was promised for the book, whose publication would coincide closely with his seventieth birthday at the end of 1973. He seemed more energetic than ever, giving readings from *Kilvert's Diary* in a London theatre before an audience that included John Gielgud, broadcasting more frequently, writing dozens of reviews, attending the huge nocturnal musical wedding party given by the Jeremy Thorpes at Covent Garden in July 1973, attending the Aldeburgh Festival, reading to the Shakespeare Institute at Stratford, Kilverting in

Brecon, and spending a week (as a fellow guest of the Kenneth Clarks, whom he had known slightly for years, and of John Sparrow) with Sybil Cholmondeley at Houghton. It may be that he overdid things.

Shortly after his return from Houghton, on the night of Sunday, 15 September 1973, and again the next morning, he suffered coronary thromboses. Each time he was unconscious for some while, with what he described as 'a battle-ship grey face'. He wrote to Lady Cholmondeley, 'The cardiologist, having produced what looks like a diagram of a Mexican earthquake, says I mustn't leave the house before the end of October. I must then only "potter". This raises domestic problems. I think I had better give up all public appearances, and working for Cape, and settle down to the cabbage-like existence of an O.A.P.'[62] He was too sanguine.

On the evening of 19 September 1973 he wrote a number of letters, wrongly dating them 20 September, and then went to bed early. That night there was a wild storm of wind and rain, and at 3.45 a.m. on Friday, 20 September 1973, Erdmann woke at the sound of the toilet flushing. A few minutes later he heard a strangled cry: 'Help, help, Charles, call the doctor, anyone!' He ran to Plomer's room to find him choking in agony, scarcely able to breathe. Because they had no telephone Erdmann had to pull on a coat and run out into the storm to a nearby telephone booth. He found that it had been vandalized, and though he was now in his sixties, he had to run all the way to the doctor. Their own doctor was away on holiday, and the locum, who chanced to be South African, was not pleased to be woken at 4 a.m. by a gasping inarticulate man with a heavy German accent; when he made out what was wanted, the doctor refused to come, saying that he was not on duty. He said he would phone another doctor who was, but who lived five kilometres away. Erdmann ran back through pelting rain and falling branches to wait, and to do what he could for Plomer. He found him in terrible pain, still gasping for help; desperately, Erdmann made cold compresses and applied ice to Plomer's forehead, but with no effect. Presently Plomer lapsed into unconsciousness, and by the time a doctor arrived, at 4.20 a.m., it was too late for resuscitation to succeed: Plomer died within a few minutes, in Erdmann's arms.

Postscript

PLOMER was cremated in Brighton, where his parents had come for their honeymoon seventy-two years before. The funeral service was a simple Anglican ceremony attended by only a dozen people, among them Charles Erdmann, Laurens van der Post, Graham C. Greene, Ian and Trekkie Parsons, Alan and Jennifer Ross, and a few other friends. On 7 November 1973 a memorial service was held in St Martin-in-the-Fields, conducted by the vicar, the Reverend Austin Williams, and attended by several hundred people. John Sparrow read the lesson, Ecclesiastes 12 — 'Of making many books there is no end; and much study is a weariness of the flesh.' A choir sang Britten's *A Ceremony of Carols*; some of Plomer's poems were read by John Betjeman; the lute-song of the Earl of Essex from *Gloriana* was sung by Peter Pears accompanied by the harpist Osian Ellis, and there followed an address by Van der Post. 'He had the singular gift', said Van der Post, 'of being angry in a classical sense . . . a passion that does not blur, but makes vision clearer. He became the first person writing in English in South Africa to express this anger in terms of love, and so changed the imagination of a whole age in Africa.' Plomer, a connoisseur of memorial services, would have approved.

The Butterfly Ball and the Grasshopper's Feast, in part because of the publicity connected with his death, sold thousands of copies: 'Poet Dies Three Days from Fame' read a headline in the *Evening Argus*.[1] Several of Plomer's friends thought his contributions to the book embarrassing doggerel. Much more satisfactory to them was the success of the enlarged volume of his *Collected Poems*, a new one-volume edition of *Kilvert's Diary*, which he had prepared shortly before his death, and the volume of his previously uncollected prose pieces that Hart-Davis, a paragon among literary executors, edited and published as *Electric Delights*.

Plomer had left all his books and papers to Hart-Davis, who presently found a fitting home for them in the library of Durham University, which in 1959 had given Plomer an honorary doctorate. To his brother James (who flew over from Canada after Plomer's death) and to his nephew and nieces, Plomer left small bequests, but the largest bequest from his estate of £50,086 went to Charles Erdmann, who lived on alone in the Adastra Avenue house for some years before selling it and buying a smaller house in Hassocks. Here he continued to welcome, with delicious cakes and home-made jams, anyone who had known or who was interested in talking about 'William dear', whose memory he kept green. Neither in the village nor on his grave in Brighton is there any plaque or gravestone to Plomer. He needs none, for he had written his own epitaph years before, in the poem 'Another old man':

> Sometimes thinking aloud
> He went his own way.
> He was joky by nature,
> Sad, sceptical, proud.
> What he never would follow,
> Or lead, was a crowd.

Select Bibliography

WORKS BY WILLIAM PLOMER

Novels

Turbott Wolfe (Hogarth Press, London, 1925); reissued by Hogarth Press with an Introduction by Laurens van der Post in 1965.

Sado (Hogarth Press, London, 1931); published in the United States as *They Never Come Back* (Coward-McCann, New York, 1932).

The Case is Altered (Hogarth Press, London, 1932).

The Invaders (Jonathan Cape, London, 1934).

Museum Pieces (Jonathan Cape, London, 1952).

Short stories

I Speak of Africa (Hogarth Press, London, 1927).

Paper Houses (Hogarth Press, London, 1929). The Penguin paperback edition of 1943 has a new introduction, by Plomer, of some importance.

The Child of Queen Victoria (Jonathan Cape, London, 1933).

Four Countries (Jonathan Cape, London, 1949).

Curious Relations [with Anthony Butts] (Jonathan Cape, London, 1945).

A Brutal Sentimentalist and Other Stories, edited by Eiichi Sano (Kenkyusha, Tokyo, 1969).

Poetry

Notes for Poems (Hogarth Press, London, 1927).

The Family Tree (Hogarth Press, London, 1929).

The Fivefold Screen (Hogarth Press, London, 1932).

Visiting the Caves (Jonathan Cape, London, 1936).

Selected Poems (Hogarth Press, London, 1940).

In a Bombed House, 1941: Elegy in Memory of Anthony Butts (Curwen Press, London, 1942).

The Dorking Thigh and Other Satires (Jonathan Cape, London, 1945).

A Shot in the Park (Jonathan Cape, London, 1955). A larger collection of ballads, including earlier ones, was published in the United States as *Borderline Ballads* (Noonday Press, New York, 1955).

Collected Poems (Jonathan Cape, London, 1960).

A Choice of Ballads (Jonathan Cape, London, 1960).

Taste and Remember (Jonathan Cape, London, 1966).

The Planes of Bedford Square (The Bookbang, London, 1971).

Celebrations (Jonathan Cape, London, 1972).

Collected Poems (Jonathan Cape, London, 1973).

Autobiography

Double Lives: An Autobiography (Jonathan Cape, London, 1943).

At Home: Memoirs (Jonathan Cape, London, 1958).
The Autobiography of William Plomer (Jonathan Cape, London, 1975).

Biography
Cecil Rhodes (Peter Davies, London, 1933).
Ali the Lion (Jonathan Cape, London, 1936); reprinted in 1970 as *The Diamond of Jannina*.

Libretti
Gloriana: Opera in Three Acts (Boosey & Hawkes, London, 1953). Set to music by Benjamin Britten.
Curlew River: A Parable for Church Performance (Faber & Faber, London, 1964). Set to music by Benjamin Britten.
The Burning Fiery Furnace: Second Parable for Church Performance (Faber & Faber, London, 1966). Set to music by Benjamin Britten.
The Prodigal Son: Third Parable for Church Performance (Faber & Faber, London, 1968). Set to music by Benjamin Britten.

Occasional Pieces
Electric Delights, ed. Rupert Hart-Davis (Godine, Boston, 1978).

CONTRIBUTIONS BY PLOMER TO BOOKS AND PAMPHLETS

Aldridge, Alan, *The Butterfly Ball and the Grasshopper's Feast* (Jonathan Cape, London, 1973). With verses by Plomer.
'Britten's Church Operas', souvenir programme for the Festival of London, 8–20 July 1968, pp. 15, 17.
'Edward FitzGerald', in Anthony Gishford (ed.), *Tribute to Benjamin Britten on his Fiftieth Birthday* (Faber & Faber, London, 1963), pp. 126–43.
'Forster as a Friend', in Oliver Stallybrass (ed.), *Aspects of E. M. Forster* (Edward Arnold, London, 1969), pp. 99–105.
'A Friend of her Father's', in anon. (ed.), *Winter's Tales 2* (Macmillan, London, 1956), pp. 187–215.
'From an African Notebook', in Nancy Cunard (ed.), *Negro* (Wishart, London, 1934), pp. 649–51.
'The Gothic Arch [Rugby]', in Graham Greene (ed.), *The Old School* (Jonathan Cape, London, 1934), pp. 131–46.
'Lumford, Richard [Richard Rumbold]', *My Father's Son* (Jonathan Cape, London, 1949).
Murphy, R., and J. Vinson (eds), *Contemporary Poets* (St James Press, London, 1970).
Noble, J. R. (ed.), *Recollections of Virginia Woolf* (Peter Owen, London, 1972).
'On Not Answering the Telephone', in Ueno Kagetomi and Abe Daizabur (eds), *Modern Lighter Essays* (Kinseido, Tokyo, n.d.).
Orr, Peter (ed.), *The Poet Speaks* (Routledge and Kegan Paul, London, 1966).

'Preface' to Benjamin Britten's *War Requiem*, pamphlet accompanying the Decca recording (SET 252/3), 1963.

'A Recollection', in John Lehmann (ed.), *Demetrios Capetanakis: A Greek Poet in England* (John Lehmann, London, 1947), pp. 180–3.

'South African Writers and English Readers', in *Proceedings of a Conference of Writers, Publishers, Editors and University Teachers of English* (University of the Witwatersrand Press, Johannesburg, 1957), pp. 54–72.

'Through Siberia in a Trance', in W. Sansom (ed.), *Choice* (Progress Publishing, London, 1946), pp. 1–11.

'White Gloves', in Jeni Couzyn (ed.), *Twelve to Twelve* (Poets Trust, London, 1970), pp. 49–50.

PUBLICATIONS EDITED OR INTRODUCED BY PLOMER

Bosman, H. C., *Unto Dust* (Anthony Blond, London, 1963). Edited by L. Abrahams with an introduction by Plomer.

Butler, Guy, *South of the Zambesi: Poems from South Africa* (Abelard-Schuman, London, 1966). Introduction by Plomer.

Conrad, Joseph, *Victory* (Oxford University Press, Oxford, 1957). World's Classics, 561, introduction by Plomer.

Freislich, Richard, *The Last Tribal War* (Struik, Cape Town, 1964). Introduction by Plomer.

Friedlander, Zelda (ed.), *Until the Heart Changes: A Garland for Olive Schreiner* (Tafelberg, Cape Town, 1967). Introduction by Plomer.

Gissing, George, *In the Year of Jubilee* (Watergate Classics, London, 1947). Introduction by Plomer.

—— *A Life's Morning* (Home and Van Thal, London, 1947). Introduction by Plomer.

'Hampson, John [J. H. Simpson]', *Saturday Night at the Greyhound* (Eyre and Spottiswoode, London, 1950). Introduction by Plomer.

Ichikawa, Haruko, *A Japanese Lady in Europe* (Jonathan Cape, London, 1937). Edited by Plomer.

Jonker, Ingrid, *Selected Poems* (Jonathan Cape, London, 1968). Translated and introduced by Jack Cope and Plomer.

Kilvert, Francis, *Kilvert's Diary*, 3 vols (Jonathan Cape, London, 1938–40). Edited by Plomer. Abridged version in 1 vol. (1944); enlarged edition in 3 vols. (1961); illustrated selection in 1 vol. (Century Publishing, London, 1986).

—— *Collected Verse* (The Kilvert Society, Hereford, 1968). Edited by C. T. O. Prosser with an introduction by Plomer.

Laye, Camara, *The Dark Child* (Collins, London, 1955). First published as *L'Enfant Noir*, 1954. Translated by James Kirkup with an introduction by Plomer.

Macaulay, Rose, *The World My Wilderness* (Collins, London, 1968). Introduction by Plomer.

Melville, Herman, *Redburn* (Jonathan Cape, London, 1937). Introduction by Plomer.

Melville, Herman, *Selected Poems* (Hogarth Press, London, 1943). Edited by Plomer.
—— *Billy Budd* (John Lehmann, London, 1946). Edited and introduced by Plomer.
—— *White Jacket* (John Lehmann, London, 1952). Introduction by Plomer.
Nesbitt, L. M., *Gold Fever* (Jonathan Cape, London, 1936). Introduction by Plomer.
New Poems 1961 (Hutchinson, London, 1961). Edited by Plomer, A. Thwaite, and H. Corke.
Reich, Hans, *South Africa* (Hill and Wang, New York, 1961). Introduction by Plomer.
Rumbold, Richard, *A Message in Code: The Diary of Richard Rumbold (1932–1960)* (Weidenfeld & Nicolson, London, 1964). Edited by Plomer.
Smith, Bradford, *To the Mountain* (Hamish Hamilton, London, 1936). Introduction by Plomer.
Smith, Pauline, *The Little Karoo* (Jonathan Cape, London, 1950). Introduction by Plomer.
White, Eric Walter (ed.), *15 Poems for William Shakespeare* (The Trustees and Guardians of Shakespeare's Birthplace, Stratford-upon-Avon, 1964). Introduction by Patrick Garland, John Lehmann, and Plomer.

OTHER WORKS CONSULTED

Ackerley, J. R., *My Father and Myself* (Bodley Head, London, 1968).
—— *The Letters of J. R. Ackerley* (Duckworth, London, 1975). Edited by N. Braybrooke.
Akutagawa, Ryunosuke, *Kappa* (Hokuseido Press, Tokyo, 1949). Translated by Shiojiri Seiichi.
Alexander, Peter F., *Roy Campbell: A Critical Biography* (Oxford University Press, Oxford, 1982).
Allen, Walter, *Tradition and Dream: The English and American Novel from the Twenties to Our Time* (Dent, London, 1964).
Auden, W. H., *Secondary Worlds* (Faber & Faber, London, 1968).
Blythe, Ronald (ed.), *Aldeburgh Anthology* (Faber & Faber, London, 1972).
Bowen, Elizabeth (ed.), *The Faber Book of Modern Stories* (Faber & Faber, London, 1937).
Bownas, Geoffrey, and Anthony Thwaite (eds), *The Penguin Book of Japanese Verse* (Penguin, London, 1964).
Butler, Guy (ed.), *A Book of South African Verse* (Oxford University Press, London, 1959).
Campbell, Roy, *The Flaming Terrapin* (Jonathan Cape, London, 1924).
—— *The Wayzgoose* (Jonathan Cape, London, 1928).
—— *Adamastor* (Faber & Faber, London, 1930).
—— *Broken Record* (Boriswood, London, 1934).
—— *Mithraic Emblems* (Boriswood, London, 1936).
—— *Talking Bronco* (Faber & Faber, London, 1946).
—— *Collected Poems* (Bodley Head, London, 1949).

Carpenter, F. I., *Laurens van der Post* (Twayne, New York, 1969).

Connolly, Cyril, *The Modern Movement: A Discussion of 100 Key Books from England, France and America (1880–1950)* (Hamish Hamilton, London, 1965).

Cope, Jack, and Uys Krige (eds), *The Penguin Book of South African Verse* (Penguin, London, 1968).

Couperus, Louis, *The Hidden Force* (Jonathan Cape, London, 1922). First published as *De'r Stille Kracht* in 1900.

Day, Douglas, *Malcolm Lowry* (Oxford University Press, London, 1974).

Doyle, J. R., *William Plomer* (Twayne, New York, 1969).

Flint, John, *Cecil Rhodes* (Hutchinson, London, 1976).

Forster, E. M., *The Life to Come and Other Stories* (Edward Arnold, London, 1972). Edited by O. Stallybrass.

—— *Maurice* (Edward Arnold, London, 1971).

—— *Selected Letters of E. M. Forster*, vol. 2 (Collins, London, 1985). Edited by Mary Lago and P. N. Furbank.

Fraser, G. S., *The Modern Writer and His World* (André Deutsch, London, 1964).

Furbank, P. N., *E. M. Forster: A Life*, 2 vols (Secker & Warburg, London, 1977–8).

Glendinning, Victoria, *Elizabeth Bowen: Portrait of a Writer* (Weidenfeld & Nicolson, London, 1977).

Hart-Davis, Rupert, *Hugh Walpole* (Macmillan, London, 1952).

Howard, M. S., *Jonathan Cape, Publisher* (Jonathan Cape, London, 1971).

Howard, Patricia, *The Operas of Benjamin Britten* (Cresset Press, London, 1969).

Janeira, A. M., *Japanese and Western Literature: A Comparative Study* (Tuttle, Tokyo, and Rutland, Vermont, 1970).

Keene, Donald, *Japanese Literature: An Introduction for Western Readers* (John Murray, London, 1953).

Killam, G. D. (ed.), *African Writers on African Writing* (Heinemann, London, 1973).

Kirkup, James, *Frankly Speaking: Aspects of Europe and Japan* (Eichosa, Tokyo, 1965).

Lehmann, John, *The Whispering Gallery* (Longmans, London, 1955).

—— *I Am My Brother* (Longmans, London, 1960).

—— *The Ample Proposition* (Eyre and Spottiswoode, London, 1966).

Leys, Norman, *Kenya* (Hogarth Press, London, 1924).

Liddell, Robert, *A Treatise on the Novel* (Jonathan Cape, London, 1947).

Lockhart, J. G., and G. M. Woodhouse, *Rhodes* (Hodder and Stoughton, London, 1963).

Lowry, Malcolm, *Selected Letters of Malcolm Lowry* (Jonathan Cape, London, 1976). Edited by H. Breit and M. B. Lowry.

McLachlan, Donald, *Room 39: Naval Intelligence in Action, 1939–1945* (Weidenfeld & Nicolson, London, 1968).

Miller, G. M., and Howard Sergeant, *A Critical Survey of South African Poetry in English* (Balkema, Cape Town, 1957).

Millin, Sarah Gertrude, *God's Stepchildren* (Constable, London, 1924).

Miner, E. R., *The Japanese Tradition in British and American Literature* (Princeton University Press, Princeton, 1958).

Monro, Harold, *Some Contemporary Poets* (Leonard Parsons, London, 1920).

Morris, John, *The Phoenix Cup* (Cresset Press, London, 1947). Dust-jacket illustration by Plomer.

Mphahlele, Ezekiel, *The African Image* (Faber & Faber, London, 1962).

Naird, Ian, and Nikolaus Pevsner, *The Buildings of England: Sussex* (Penguin, Harmondsworth, 1965).

Paton, Alan, *Knocking on the Door: Shorter Writings* (David Philip, Cape Town, 1975). Edited by Colin Gardner.

—— 'Thoughts on Roy Campbell', *Contrast* (Cape Town), September 1975, pp. 64–78.

Pearson, John, *The Life of Ian Fleming* (Jonathan Cape, London, 1966).

Reed, Henry, *The Novel Since 1939* (Longmans for the British Council, London, 1946).

Roberts, Michael (ed.), *The Faber Book of Modern Verse* (Faber & Faber, London, 1936).

Sano, Eiichi, 'William Plomer and Captain Mori', *Eigo Seinen* ('The Rising Generation') (Tokyo), March 1974, p. 37.

Sargeson, Frank, *More Than Enough* (A. H. & A. W. Reed, Wellington, 1975).

Schreiner, Olive, *The Story of an African Farm* (T. Fisher Unwin, London, 1924).

—— *Trooper Peter Halket of Mashonaland* (T. Fisher Unwin, London, 1897).

Segal, Philip, 'Plomer and the African Scene', in Marcia Leveson (ed.), *Essays and Lectures* (David Philip, Cape Town, 1973).

Seymour-Smith, Martin, *Who's Who in Twentieth Century Literature* (Weidenfeld & Nicolson, London, 1976).

Sitwell, Edith, *Selected Letters* (Macmillan, London, 1970). Edited by John Lehmann and Derek Parker.

Smith, Pauline, *The Beadle* (Jonathan Cape, London, 1926).

Smith, R., *Lyric and Polemic: The Literary Personality of Roy Campbell* (Montreal and London, McGill–Queen's University Press, 1972).

Snyman, J. P. L., *The South African Novel in English: 1880–1930* (University of Potchefstroom Press, Potchefstroom, 1952).

Spender, Stephen, *World Within World* (Hamish Hamilton, London, 1951).

Strachey, Lytton, *Elizabeth and Essex* (Chatto & Windus, London, 1928).

Tolley, A. T., *The Poetry of the Thirties* (Gollancz, London, 1975).

Tucker, Martin, *Africa in Modern Literature* (Ungar, New York, 1967).

Van der Post, Laurens, *In a Province* (Hogarth Press, London, 1934).

—— *Venture to the Interior* (Hogarth Press, London, 1952).

—— *Yet Being Someone Other* (Hogarth Press, London, 1982).

—— *A Walk With a White Bushman* (Chatto & Windus, London, 1986).

Vines, Sherard, *The Pyramid* (Cobden-Sanderson, London, 1926).

White, Eric Walter, *Benjamin Britten: His Life and Operas*, 2nd edn., ed. John Evans (Faber & Faber, London, 1983).

Wilhelm, Peter, and James Polley (eds), *Poetry South Africa* (Ad. Donker, Johannesburg, 1976).

Williams, Basil, *Cecil Rhodes* (Constable, London, 1921).

Woolf, Virginia, *Letters of Virginia Woolf* (Hogarth Press, London, 1978). Edited by Nigel Nicolson.

—— *The Diary of Virginia Woolf*, 5 vols (Hogarth Press, London, 1980–82). Edited by A. O. Bell.

Abbreviations of Manuscript Collections

BP	The Britten–Pears Museum, Aldeburgh
Cape	The Archives of Jonathan Cape Ltd., University of Reading
DUL	Durham University Library
FP	In the possession of Mrs Frances Plomer
Hogarth	Hogarth Press Archives, University of Sussex
NELM	National English Language Museum, Grahamstown, South Africa
NZN	National Library of New Zealand (incorporating the Alexander Turnbull Library), Wellington
Opp	The Oppenheimer Collection, 44 Main Street, Johannesburg
RHD	In the possession of Sir Rupert Hart-Davis
SAL	South African Library, Cape Town
Spender	In the possession of Sir Stephen Spender
Texas	Humanities Research Center, University of Texas at Austin
WM	In the possession of Mrs Wilhelmina Mulholland

Notes

INTRODUCTION

1 Earl Miner, *The Japanese Tradition in British and American Literature*, p. 50.
2 Quoted by Simon Nowell-Smith in the Postscript to *The Autobiography of William Plomer*, p. 447.

I. ORIGINS AND CHILDHOOD

1 He was named William, because it was a family tradition, going back at least eight generations, that the eldest son took that name; Charles after his father; and Franklyn after his mother's only brother.
2 William Plomer, *Double Lives: An Autobiography*, p. 62. Plomer wrote two volumes of autobiography: *Double Lives* (1943) and *At Home* (1958). At the end of his life he was engaged in revising both volumes for republication. He largely rewrote *Double Lives*, but recast only the first few chapters of *At Home* before tiring of the task, and it was published just as he had left it, albeit with the addition of a postscript by Simon Nowell-Smith, under the title *The Autobiography of William Plomer* (1975).
3 *Double Lives*, p. 62.
4 The father of William II: see ibid., p. 11. Plomer was fascinated by his ancestry, in spite of his claim to be 'in no sense an ancestor worshipper', and readers interested in probing further into his antecedents should consult his lively autobiographies.
5 Ibid., p. 12.
6 Ibid., p. 14.
7 Especially *The Autobiography of William Plomer*, pp. 31–2. This work is referred to hereafter simply as *Autobiography*.
8 Ibid., p. 30.
9 *Double Lives*, p. 18. It has to be admitted that any number of other explanations for this childish escapade are possible; the point is, however, that Plomer, who knew his father as well as a son can know a father, thought this the reason.
10 In *Double Lives*, p. 31, Plomer records that his father was nineteen when he sailed.
11 Dr L. S. Jameson, one of Cecil Rhodes's most able lieutenants, was ordered by Rhodes to lead an armed party down from the north into the Transvaal in 1895. Rhodes and Jameson expected that the mostly British *Uitlander* settlers on the Reef gold-mines would rise at the news of Jameson's incursion and overthrow the Boer government led by Kruger, thereby delivering the Transvaal and its gold-fields into British

hands at a stroke. They fatally miscalculated the Kruger government's powers of resistance, and the failed raid proved a major step towards the precipitation of the Boer War in 1899.

12 *Double Lives*, p. 44.

13 Ibid., p. 24.

14 Ibid., p. 53.

15 *Autobiography*, p. 81.

16 *Double Lives*, pp. 68–9.

17 *Autobiography*, p. 82.

18 *Double Lives*, p. 70.

19 Ibid.

20 The main graveyard of Louis Trichardt was established later, around John Plomer's grave, which lies in one corner, surmounted by a plain, small, marble cross. The inscription reads: 'In loving memory of John, son of C. & E. Plomer, died 8 June 1908, aged 13 months.'

21 Ibid., p. 71.

22 Ibid., p. 59.

23 *Autobiography*, p. 85.

24 *Double Lives*, p. 73.

25 *Autobiography*, pp. 87–8.

26 *Double Lives*, p. 74.

27 Ibid., p. 74.

28 'Finding them [the local white women] ill-mannered and untrustworthy, she did not choose to live on terms of intimacy with them, and they attributed her aloofness to an affectation of superiority': ibid., p. 82.

29 Ibid., p. 78.

30 *Autobiography*, p. 90.

31 Ibid., pp. 90–1.

32 *Double Lives*, p. 77.

33 It was then thought that people with measles should be kept in darkened rooms for fear of eye damage. While such patients often find light painful, it is most unlikely that exposure to it could cause damage to the sight, although Plomer continued to share his mother's view of the origins of his myopia for the rest of his life. It is remotely possible that Plomer had suffered encephalitic myelitis of the optic nerve, but more likely that his sight had been weakening gradually over a long period. I am indebted to Christina McWilliam of Sydney for this information.

34 *Autobiography*, p. 92.

35 Peter Plomer changed his Christian name to James after the Second World War.

36 *Double Lives*, p. 37.

37 Plomer gave details of this house in a BBC broadcast, 'South Africa Revisited: The Wilds of Johannesburg', 28 September 1956: BBC Written Archives Centre.

38 *Autobiography*, p. 95.

39 A system still in force at St John's in the 1980s.

40 *St John's College Letter*, Easter and Lent Term, 1912, p. 6.

[41] In *Double Lives*, p. 89, Plomer mistakenly says he was 'nine or ten' at the time of this performance.

[42] *St John's College Letter*, Easter and Lent Term 1912, p. 8.

[43] *Double Lives*, p. 90.

[44] Several memoirs of the period detail the extent of homosexuality in British public schools before the war. Robert Graves has left one of the most vivid and candid accounts of it in *Goodbye to All That* (Jonathan Cape, London, 1929).

[45] *Double Lives*, p. 91, and *Autobiography*, p. 103. With the caution that characterizes all his veiled references to homosexuality, Plomer does not name Pritchard, and misleadingly describes him as a German. The clue to his identity is his having played Bottom in the school production of *A Midsummer Night's Dream*, since his name is given in the School's *Letter* of 1912.

[46] *Double Lives*, p. 91.

2. ADOLESCENCE

[1] *Double Lives*, p. 92.

[2] Interview with Sir Stephen Spender, London, 19 February 1987.

[3] *Double Lives*, pp. 92–3.

[4] *Autobiography*, p. 34, and *Double Lives*, p. 21.

[5] *Double Lives*, p. 42.

[6] Ibid., p. 45.

[7] He records it in *Autobiography*, p. 105.

[8] Ibid., p. 106.

[9] Ibid., p. 107.

[10] *Double Lives*, p. 94.

[11] *Autobiography*, p. 107.

[12] Unpublished letter, G. Leedham to Plomer, 1 August 1944: DUL.

[13] *Double Lives*, p. 95.

[14] *Autobiography*, p. 108.

[15] Unpublished letter, 1 August 1944: DUL.

[16] *Autobiography*, p. 109.

[17] Ibid., p. 128.

[18] 'Tirocinium' (lines 579–86). Cowper published this poem in *The Task* (1785). The poem is a wide-ranging attack on public schools; Cowper condemns such schools as, among other things, conducive to vice and cruelty.

[19] *Double Lives*, p. 95.

[20] Ibid., p. 99.

[21] *Autobiography*, p. 115. Emslie Horniman gave Plomer an excellent description of Van Gogh 'looking steadfastly at the plaster cast of an antique figure and then at a great pace making a strong black drawing of, say, a landscape with peasant figures in a storm. The visiting master used to be very annoyed, but I think recognized his talent. We thought him mad and were in awe of him—his work was so strange that in those days, when even Whistler was hardly accepted, few conceived

that a new school was already in being.' Unpublished letter, 30 June 1921: DUL.

22 Michael Sadler (1888–1957) later changed his name to Sadleir. In 1920 he was to become director of the publishing house Constable. His best-known novel, *Fanny by Gaslight*, was not published until 1940.

23 Sir Walter Alexander Raleigh (1861–1922) had since 1904 been the first occupant of the Chair of English Literature at Oxford. His best-known books are *Style* (1897), *Milton* (1900), and *Shakespeare* (1907).

24 *Autobiography*, p. 70.

25 Ibid., p. 16.

26 Ibid., p. 80.

27 Ibid., p. 47.

28 Ibid., p. 16.

29 *Double Lives*, pp. 106–7.

30 Ibid., p. 109.

31 Ibid., p. 108.

32 *Autobiography*, p. 121.

33 'In Memoriam', *The Meteor*, vol. 51 (1917).

34 *Autobiography*, p. 123.

35 *Rugby School Register*, vol. 4 (January 1892–September 1921) gives the address of this farm, but without naming the farmer.

36 *Double Lives*, p. 113.

37 Ibid.

38 *Autobiography*, p. 128.

3. AFRICAN ARTIST

1 *Autobiography*, p. 125.

2 Ibid., p. 135.

3 *Double Lives*, p. 114.

4 Ibid., p. 115.

5 He was to tell Laurens van der Post, on the voyage to Japan in 1929, that he had until very recently hesitated between writing and painting. Interview with Sir Laurens van der Post, Aldeburgh, 29 October 1983.

6 *Double Lives*, p. 115.

7 'I was beginning to grow up, and that does not always make for easiness between a son and his father,' Plomer wrote diplomatically while his father was still alive. *Double Lives*, p. 116.

8 *Autobiography*, p. 126.

9 Ibid., pp. 128–9.

10 *Double Lives*, p. 116.

11 Ibid., p. 118.

12 *Autobiography*, p. 128.

13 Ibid., p. 129.

14 Ibid., pp. 104–5.

15 *Double Lives*, p. 109.

16 *Autobiography*, p. 130.

17 *Double Lives*, p. 117.

18 One should be a little cautious in accepting Plomer's memories of his

reading at this period. Generally accurate in his reminiscences, he was betrayed by his memory when he claimed (*Double Lives*, p. 122, and *Autobiography*, p. 133) to have read Joyce's *Ulysses* at the age of sixteen—that is, in 1919–20. *Ulysses* was not published until 1922, by which time Plomer was nineteen and living at Entumeni.

[19] There is a good self-portrait by him in the National Portrait Gallery, London.

[20] *Autobiography*, p. 131.

[21] Ibid., p. 132.

[22] *Double Lives*, pp. 119–20.

[23] Interview with Van der Post, Aldeburgh, 29 October 1983. Van der Post was to describe the work as 'very beautiful and moving'.

[24] This, at least, is the view of Van der Post who, speaking of this series of works by Wolfe, remarked, 'I think that William was sexually attracted by black people because that was the pattern of his homosexual development subsequently. He was never in love with equals.' Interview in Aldeburgh, 29 October 1983.

[25] Unpublished statement, Roger Castle, CR, to W. H. Gardner, 31 May 1959: NELM.

[26] *Autobiography*, p. 133.

[27] The manuscripts of 'Evening in Oxfordshire' and 'Symphony' (both of which are dated 1920), together with other early poems that Plomer sent to Harold Monro, are at NELM.

[28] Plomer sent 'Symphony' to the *English Review* early in 1921, a measure of his desire to prove himself, and a measure of his self-confidence. Annotation on the MS, which he had sent Harold Monro (the poet and editor) on 4 April 1921: NELM.

[29] *The Johannian* (the St John's College magazine), Easter 1921, p. 9. Other prizes awarded were for English, Dutch, divinity, mathematics, science, and the form prize.

[30] *Double Lives*, p. 124.

[31] 'My father superstitiously believed that unless one passed examinations and gained degrees or certificates one would have no future': *Autobiography*, p. 130.

[32] 'When I left St. John's, I wanted to learn fruit farming. Oh no, I was forced to cope with a thousand Arthurs [i.e. sheep] at Molteno. Good creatures, but they weren't fruit-trees.' Unpublished letter, Plomer to James Plomer, 17 January 1970: FP.

4. THE STORMBERG

[1] *Autobiography*, p. 139.

[2] Horseham's name is given on the verso of one of Plomer's sketches from this period, now held at NELM. In Plomer's own copy of *Turbott Wolfe*, which is preserved with the rest of his library in DUL, Plomer added annotations about many of the characters in that novel, giving the names of the originals upon whom they are based. In these annotations Fotheringhay is identified as based on the Revd Mr

Heathcote, a priest Plomer came to know in Natal, but it is plain from his description of Horseham in *Double Lives* and *Autobiography* that Horseham also contributed significantly to the portrait of Fotheringhay.

3 *Turbott Wolfe*, pp. 80–1. The edition referred to throughout is the Hogarth Press reprint of 1965.

4 Ibid., p. 146.

5 Unpublished letter, Mr Stanley Pope (son of Fred Pope) to the writer, 8 April 1984.

6 It is now known as Marsh Moor Estates, still run by Mr Stanley Pope. The house Plomer knew has been replaced by a large, modern one; the 'scrubby kitchen garden' he described is now a splendid one of sweeping lawns and flowering trees, and there is a fine swimming-pool.

7 Unpublished letter, Mr Stanley Pope to the writer, 8 April 1984.

8 The photograph now at NELM, for instance, shows the house in 1923, with the veranda clearly visible. The point is worth making only because it shows a rare instance of Plomer's memory having deceived him. The house was flooded out subsequently, and had to be entirely rebuilt.

9 Ruddle appears in *Turbott Wolfe*, p. 153, as a Dutch carpenter. He is identified in Plomer's annotated copy of *Turbott Wolfe*: DUL.

10 *Double Lives*, p. 129.

11 This skill he was to put to good use with his description of Soper sowing in *Turbott Wolfe*, pp. 164–5.

12 *Double Lives*, pp. 129–30.

13 Ibid., p. 130.

14 *Autobiography*, p. 143.

15 In ibid., p. 142, he claims to have discovered the paintings. Fred Pope, however, knew every inch of the farm on which he had been born and spent his boyhood, and he almost certainly showed Plomer the paintings as a local curiosity.

16 Letter from Plomer to J. Meintjes, 24 January 1965: NELM.

17 The destruction of these drawings was one of the few details about Plomer which Stanley Pope could recall in later years; it had clearly made a great impression on his father and himself. Unpublished letter, Stanley Pope to the author, 8 April 1984.

18 Thanks to the initiative of Professor Stephen Gray of Rand Afrikaans University, who drove to Marsh Moor to collect the papers, the Pope collection is now at NELM.

19 Unpublished letter, Stanley Pope to the writer, 8 April 1984. The surviving card-design is at NELM.

20 *Double Lives*, p. 132.

21 *Turbott Wolfe*, pp. 156–7.

22 The Union of South Africa, as the country was known until it became a republic.

23 *Double Lives*, p. 130.

24 Unpublished letter, Stanley Pope to the writer, 8 April 1984.

25 Annotation in Plomer's copy of *Turbott Wolfe*: DUL.

26 *Double Lives*, p. 133.

27 It seems that his mother kept them all, but returned them to him before

the Second World War when she was dying, and that he destroyed them.

[28] Two of these letters from Emslie Horniman are preserved in DUL.

[29] *Double Lives*, p. 134.

[30] BBC broadcast, reprinted in *London Calling*, 30 May 1957, and collected in Plomer's *Electric Delights*, ed. Rupert Hart-Davis (Godine, Boston, 1978), p. 21.

[31] Unpublished statement, 16 November 1960, D. R. Gillie to Professor W. H. Gardner: NELM.

[32] Quoted by Gillie in his statement, 16 November 1960: NELM.

[33] *Double Lives*, p. 134.

[34] Unpublished letter, Stanley Pope to the writer, 8 April 1984.

[35] Monro (1879–1932) was himself a poet; his *Collected Poems*, introduced by T. S. Eliot, appeared posthumously in 1933.

[36] These were two of Monro's most widely anthologized poems.

[37] 4 April 1921: NELM.

[38] 'P.B.' was Monro's Poetry Bookshop.

[39] 9 October 1921: NELM.

[40] He was in fact nineteen years and four months. He seems to have regarded his youth and his year at Rugby as likely to weigh heavily with Monro, and he may well have been right.

[41] NELM.

[42] There are references to Monro's letter in Plomer's reply, 30 October 1922: NELM.

[43] Ibid.

[44] Plomer wrote, 'I don't remember the thing called "Death" that you speak about. I hope it was better than I suspect!' Ibid.

[45] He had visited Amanzimtoti only once, and was hesitant about using the name, asking Monro whether he should call the poem 'Contes Barbares'. Ibid.

[46] *Double Lives*, p. 129.

[47] Unpublished letter, Stanley Pope to the writer, 8 April 1984.

[48] *Double Lives*, p. 135.

[49] Ibid., p. 136.

[50] Donald Brace (Plomer's American publisher) quotes an unnamed South African paper's article on Plomer after the publication of *Turbott Wolfe*: 'His father was once a well-known civil servant but had to retire from the service owing to a nervous breakdown. In order to live he opened a store in Zululand, about 12 miles from Eshowe. Here the sick man and his wife tried to earn a living.' Unpublished letter, Donald Brace to Plomer, 6 June 1926: Hogarth.

[51] *Double Lives*, p. 138.

5. ENTUMENI

[1] *Double Lives*, p. 139.

[2] *Autobiography*, p. 154.

[3] *Double Lives*, p. 140.

4 *Autobiography*, p. 155.

5 *Double Lives*, p. 140.

6 *Autobiography*, p. 151.

7 Date taken from unpublished letter, Plomer to H. Monro, 14 January 1923 (though Plomer erroneously dated it 1922): 'I shall be in Zululand in a fortnight's time perhaps for ever': NELM.

8 *Double Lives*, p. 143.

9 *Autobiography*, p. 155.

10 Ibid., p. 162.

11 Ibid., p. 154.

12 *Double Lives*, p. 144.

13 Ibid., p. 145.

14 Ibid., p. 146.

15 These details about the Entumeni Mission are given in Plomer's annotations in his own copy of *Turbott Wolfe*: DUL.

16 *Double Lives*, p. 148.

17 Ibid.

18 'Ephemera', perhaps, or 'Anashuya and Vijaya', from Yeats's *Crossways*.

19 'I had been through a phase of emotional Anglo-Catholicism, very much as I had fancied myself at times to be a pantheist or a Buddhist, but was now, if anything, a determinist ... I was beginning to feel an increasing distaste for many of the manifestations and results of Christianity': *Double Lives*, p. 158.

20 It is this connection that confirms PQR's identity.

21 *Double Lives*, p. 149.

22 Ibid.

23 Laurens van der Post, *A Walk with a White Bushman*, p. 191.

24 He quotes Makoba's essay in some detail in *Double Lives*, pp. 152–5, though he was perhaps disappointed that it contained little of political substance.

25 *Double Lives*, p. 156.

26 Ibid., p. 157.

27 Ibid., p. 160.

28 The name is based on Tembuland, an area near the Stormberg in the Eastern Cape, but plainly it represents Zululand.

29 *Double Lives*, pp. 160–1.

30 The volume is preserved in the Plomer Collection in DUL.

31 It is not possible to name him here, but his name is given by Plomer in the annotated copy of *Turbott Wolfe*: DUL.

32 In *The Modern Movement: A Discussion of 100 Key Books from England, France and America (1880–1950)*, Cyril Connolly lists *Turbott Wolfe* as one of the 'key books' of modern literature. In *The African Image*, p. 124, Ezekiel Mphahlele praises Plomer's black characters as having 'a third dimension, as it were, unlike the two-dimensional characters in [Sarah Gertrude Millin's] *God's Stepchildren*, who are but creatures of fate'; while in an important article, 'The Novel and the Nation in South Africa', in *African Writers on African Writing* (ed. G. D. Killam), p. 47, Nadine Gordimer justly remarks that '*Turbott Wolfe* with its talk of

African nationalism and its view of Africa as a black man's country would seem the sort of novel of South African life far more likely to be written now than in the 1920s.' Walter Allen analysed and praised the novel in *Tradition and Dream: The English and American Novel from the Twenties to Our Time*, p. 198.

33 *Autobiography*, p. 166.
34 *Turbott Wolfe*, pp. 94–5.
35 It is possible that there was yet another original of the composite Mabel van der Horst. In one of Plomer's photograph albums preserved at Durham, among other photographs of the Entumeni period, is a picture of himself and a buxom young white woman standing together in front of a banana-tree; underneath the photograph Plomer has written, 'La Belle Dame sans Merci'. It is not impossible that he was attracted to, and rejected by, a 'Mabel' figure at the time he was writing *Turbott Wolfe*.
36 *Turbott Wolfe*, p. 191.
37 Ibid., p. 193.
38 Ibid., p. 136.
39 Friston remarks of her, 'I have never been jarred in the least by her extraordinary way of talking. It seems part of her.' Ibid., p. 175.
40 Ibid.
41 Ibid., p. 116.
42 'In general, it is true to say that "one feels in so many of Forster's novels a kind of transference at work, as though one were reading a different sort of story, but translated into socially acceptable terms" ': Donald Salter, 'That is my ticket', *London Magazine*, February/March 1975, p. 7.
43 *Double Lives*, pp. 161–2.
44 It has been reprinted recently as part of OUP's Twentieth Century Classics series.
45 *Turbott Wolfe*, pp. 63 ff.
46 Hogarth.
47 15 July 1924: Hogarth.
48 Hogarth.
49 Unpublished letter, 28 February 1925: Hogarth.
50 Unpublished letter, 28 April 1925: Hogarth.
51 *Turbott Wolfe*, p. 153. The name was misprinted as 'Ndebakabani' in the first and all subsequent editions.
52 Unpublished letter, 24 May 1925: Hogarth.
53 Ibid.
54 He wrote: 'I suffer very much from having no local criticism of my work, and I am obliged to admit that Friston's speech is tedious—but if you only knew the conditions under which I write! I am immediately considering how I can shorten this speech ... The final version will, I hope, be in your hands before the end of July.' Unpublished letter, Plomer to Leonard Woolf, 22 June 1925: Hogarth.
55 *Double Lives*, p. 156.
56 Ibid., pp. 163–4.

[57] Unpublished letter, Mrs Frances Plomer (James Plomer's second wife) to the writer, 10 September 1986.

[58] The novel, which he wrote under the pen-name Matt Lowe, was entitled 'The Man with Two Shadows'. It was never published, William Plomer himself recommending that it be rejected when it was submitted to Jonathan Cape's.

[59] *Double Lives*, p. 158.

6. *VOORSLAG*

[1] *Double Lives*, p. 164.

[2] 'Vermilion' is identified in an unpublished letter, Edward Roworth to W. H. Gardner, 31 January 1959: NELM.

[3] The von Schuberts, as they later became, at this time called themselves 'de Schubert'; Campbell and Plomer refer to them by this name in their correspondence during 1925–6.

[4] This at least is how Roworth characterized her style (unpublished letter to W. H. Gardner, 29 January 1959: NELM). According to Plomer, she had for a time been a pupil of Matisse: '*Voorslag* Days', *Standpunte*, Jaargang XII, Nr. 3 (May/June 1959), p. 4.

[5] In his autobiographies Plomer does not identify the mutual acquaintance of Campbell and himself, but François and Anna von Schubert are the only two people whom Campbell mentions in his first letter to Plomer after their meeting (unpublished letter, Campbell to Plomer, undated: DUL). The only other possibility is Douglas Mackeurtan, a friend of Plomer's father, whom Plomer had met in Cape Town in 1919. Plomer rather tentatively suggests him as the link with Campbell in an unpublished letter to W. H. Gardner (17 September 1958: NELM). Van der Post believes that Douglas Mackeurtan was in fact the chief link between Campbell and Plomer (letter to the writer, 16 April 1987).

[6] Roger Castle, 'Roy Campbell: The Author of the Flaming Terrapin', *South African Pictorial*, 25 April 1925, p. 11.

[7] Unpublished letter, Plomer to W. H. Gardner, 26 January 1958: NELM.

[8] Plomer, '*Voorslag* Days', *London Magazine*, vol. 6, no. 1 (July 1959.)

[9] '*Voorslag* Days', Standpunte, p. 6.

[10] Campbell had given a public lecture attacking the colour bar on 4 May 1925, well before meeting Plomer: Peter F. Alexander, *Roy Campbell: A Critical Biography*, p. 46.

[11] Campbell was strongly critical of 'our friend "Vermilion"', François's *nom de plume*. Unpublished letter to Plomer undated [July 1925]: NELM.

[12] *Autobiography*, p. 167.

[13] Unpublished letter, Campbell to Edward Garnett, 20 November 1925: Texas.

[14] Unpublished letter, Campbell to Edward Garnett, undated [June 1925]: Texas.

[15] Unpublished letter, Roger Castle to W. H. Gardner, 31 May 1958: NELM.

[16] Lewis Reynolds (1898–1940) was to become MP for the seat of South Coast late in the 1920s.

17 Unpublished letter, Roworth to W. H. Gardner, 23 January 1959: NELM.

18 Webb was described by Roworth in later years as 'a copper-bottomed liberal'; he was a pacifist and a vegetarian, and Campbell was to guy him mercilessly in his long satirical poem *The Wayzgoose*, in which Webb features as 'Polybius Jubb'.

19 Unpublished letter, Roworth to W. H. Gardner, 23 January 1959: NELM.

20 Roworth was a cheery, good-looking man much influenced by what Samuel Johnson once called 'the love of a shilling'. In 1937 he was to be appointed professor of fine arts at the University of Cape Town, a post from which he retired in 1950. Unpublished questionnaire, Roworth to W. H. Gardner, 31 January 1959: NELM. By the time Gardner drew on it, Roworth's memory had become untrustworthy, and I have discounted much of his evidence in the account that follows.

21 Unpublished letter, Roworth to W. H. Gardner, 23 January 1959: NELM.

22 By 'race-difference' Campbell almost certainly meant hostility between English- and Afrikaans-speaking South Africans, not that between black and white. He uses the term in the former sense in his poem 'A Veld Eclogue', written at this time:

> Think not that I on racial questions touch,
> For one was English and the other Dutch.

23 Unpublished letter, undated [August 1925]: Texas.

24 This is the term Campbell used in an unpublished letter to B. Holt, [27] May 1947 (NELM) to describe Plomer's position in running *Voorslag*.

25 Campbell wrote to Plomer: 'Don't hesitate to come here for good if you think your parents are selling the store. We'll give you the studio for your part of the establishment.' Unpublished letter, undated [28 December 1925]: DUL.

26 'I hope to come to England with it [i.e. a new novel] in time for you to publish it next spring.' Unpublished letter, Plomer to Leonard Woolf, 21 May 1926: Hogarth.

27 'I may be going to live for a time either with the Campbells or with Gandhi's son Manilal.' Unpublished letter, 21 March 1926, Plomer to Leonard and Virginia Woolf: Hogarth.

28 'Plomer is coming to stay in September. I hope you'll be here to meet him.' Unpublished letter, Campbell to Roworth, undated [late August 1925]: SAL.

29 Unpublished letter, Campbell to Plomer, undated [10 August 1925]: DUL.

30 Unpublished questionnaire, Roworth to W. H. Gardner, 31 January 1959: NELM.

31 Unpublished letter, Roworth to W. H. Gardner, 23 January 1959: NELM.

32 Campbell's second daughter, Anna, was born in February 1926.

33 'Mary says could you please lend us two or three of the negatives you took down here we want to send some photos home. We'll be very careful of them.' Unpublished letter, Campbell to Plomer, undated [12 October 1925]: DUL.

34 Photograph among the Hogarth papers, accompanying a letter of 1 July 1926, Plomer to Leonard Woolf.

35 Unpublished letter to Edward Garnett, 20 November 1925: Texas.

36 Ibid.

37 Interview with Van der Post, London, 4 December 1977.

38 In *Yet Being Someone Other*, Van der Post estimates his family's land-holdings (in the form of several Free State farms) at around 500,000 acres (approximately 200,000 hectares).

39 Sir Laurens Jan van der Post (1906–) was to achieve fame as a writer, farmer, soldier, and explorer; his many works of travel, anthropology, and adventure (much influenced by C. G. Jung, whose biography he wrote) include *The Lost World of the Kalahari* (1958), *The Heart of the Hunter* (1961), *A Story Like the Wind* (1972), and *A Far-Off Place* (1974).

40 Interview with Van der Post, Aldeburgh, 29 October 1983.

41 Interview with Van der Post, London, 3 December 1977.

42 *Autobiography*, p. 177.

43 Dingaan's Day (16 December) was the celebration of a victory by the Boers over the Zulus, hence the particular significance of the beating of an African by a white.

44 Interview with Van der Post, London, 3 December 1977.

45 *Autobiography*, p. 171.

46 Van der Post was later to comment that he had 'had a terrible struggle writing that article, because at that time there was no artistic development in Afrikaans!' Interview with the writer, London, 3 December 1977.

47 Unpublished letter, Campbell to Plomer, undated [12 October 1925]: DUL.

48 Campbell, who had had Communist sympathies at Oxford, was still a convinced left-winger (Roworth certainly thought him a Communist in 1925), and he was particularly contemptuous of shopkeepers of any kind.

49 Though due for publication in the autumn of 1925, it was held up by a printers' strike until early the next year. At the time he wrote (20 November 1925) Campbell had not heard of this delay.

50 This was quite untrue. Perhaps Plomer had exaggerated the fact that he had had to cut fifteen pages from the manuscript; more likely, the exaggeration was Campbell's.

51 Unpublished letter, Campbell to Garnett, 20 November 1925: Texas.

52 *Double Lives*, p. 106.

53 Ibid., p. 163.

54 Unpublished letter, Stanley Pope to the writer, 8 April 1984.

55 *Double Lives*, p. 163.

56 Unpublished letter, Plomer to Leonard Woolf, 21 May 1926: Hogarth.

57 Fitzpatrick was an Irish South African novelist, whose *Jock of the Bush-veld*, a romantic yarn about a dog, achieved immense popularity in the 1920s.

58 Unpublished letter, Campbell to Plomer, undated [10 April 1926]: DUL.

59 He used this term for Natal in particular and, more broadly, for the whole British Empire, in a public lecture he gave in Durban (4 May 1925) before meeting Plomer.

60 He gives the history of the writing of 'Portraits in the Nude' in his unpublished letter to Leonard and Virginia Woolf of 21 March 1926: Hogarth.

61 Unpublished letter, Campbell to Plomer, undated [12 October 1925]: DUL.

62 Unpublished letter, Roworth to W. H. Gardner, 23 January 1959: NELM.

63 'It is better still to write to Entumeni, which is my permanent address, though I am living here now with the Campbells.' Unpublished letter, Plomer to the Woolfs, 21 May 1926: Hogarth.

64 The best-known of these is probably Alan Paton's *Cry the Beloved Country* (1948); but their number, in both English and Afrikaans, is very large, and it would include Peter Abrams's *Mine Boy* (1946) and Frans Venter's *Swart Pelgrim* ['Black Pilgrim'] (1959). In 1963 Plomer himself was to remark with justifiable satisfaction that he had been the first to exploit the two great human situations from which so much 'South African fiction has sprung—the story of mutual sexual attraction between persons of the two different races, and the story of the innocent, indigenous African who is corrupted by the white man's big city': *Conversation with My Younger Self* (privately printed, Ewelme, 1960), p. 19.

65 Unpublished letter, Plomer to Leonard Woolf, 21 May 1926: Hogarth.

66 Interview with Mary Campbell, Portugal, 4 January 1975.

67 Interview with Mary Campbell, Portugal, 4 January 1975.

68 There was to be a rancorous dispute over these volumes when Campbell eventually quitted the bungalow, and Roworth went through Campbell's luggage to recover the books.

69 Van der Post's Introduction to Hogarth Press's 1965 edition of *Turbott Wolfe*, p. 24.

70 Unpublished letter and questionnaire, Plomer to W. H. Gardner, undated [1959]: DUL.

71 'There is nothing "naughty" about Plomer—he is almost too much the other way: he converted me to teetotalism which I must admit has improved my work by 25 per cent and he almost managed to cure me of smoking: he is an absolute Puritan though he is human enough not to be a prig and absolutely understands and pardons the vices of others—except dullness and bad writing.' Unpublished letter, Campbell to his benefactor C. J. Sibbett, a Cape advertising executive, undated [4 December 1926]: SAL.

72 Unpublished letter, Campbell to Edward Garnett, undated [late 1925]: Texas.

73 *Autobiography*, p. 174.

74 Unpublished memorandum, Campbell to Plomer, undated [August 1926]: DUL.

75 Unpublished letter, Mary Campbell to Plomer, undated [10 March 1926]: DUL.

[76] *The Calendar of Modern Letters* was a short-lived literary journal edited by Campbell's brother-in-law, Douglas Garman, during 1925–6.

[77] Unpublished letter, Plomer to the Woolfs, 21 May 1926: Hogarth.

[78] The letter has been lost, but Mary Campbell describes and summarizes it in a letter to Plomer, received by him at Entumeni on 24 June 1925: DUL.

[79] The Cape *Argus* of 2 June 1926 called some of the contributions 'notable' and likely to 'command wide appreciation'; the *Cape Times* of 15 June 1926, in an article probably written by Ruth Alexander, a literary hostess with whom Campbell and Plomer had corresponded for a while, praised the first issue of the magazine most warmly, picking out Plomer's contributions for special commendation and condemning Webb's foreword as 'meek-and-mild'; the article wished *Voorslag* 'more power to its elbow'. The Johannesburg *Star* of 14 June 1926 called *Voorslag* 'modest in appearance', but described its contents as 'a literary feast'.

[80] Most notably the attack by Sarah Gertrude Millin in the *Rand Daily Mail* on 16 June 1926.

[81] *Voorslag*, vol. 1, no. 1 (June 1926), p. 4.

[82] *Voorslag*, vol. 1, no. 1, contained two contributions by Pamela Willmore: 'The Strandloopers' (a satirical ballad by Plomer, the very first exercise in a genre he was to make his own) and a note on George Moore (by Campbell). Plomer gives details of the use of the pen-names in the early version of his article 'Voorslag Days', published in *Standpunte*, Jaargang XII, Nr. 3. Plomer also contributed to *Voorslag*, vol. 1, no. 1 a series of notes on Van Gogh as a student, which had been supplied by his uncle Emslie Horniman.

[83] Ibid., p. 39.

[84] *The Star*, 14 June 1926.

[85] Plomer's review of it was sent to Campbell in December 1925. Unpublished letter, Campbell to Plomer, undated [13 December 1925]: DUL.

[86] *Voorslag*, vol. 1, no. 1, pp. 55–6.

[87] Ibid., p. 60.

[88] Campbell's review of T. S. Eliot's poetry, ibid., p. 62.

[89] 'Quarrelling with my father made me generation-conscious: there was an enormous wave of Hogarth-Pressure, and I simply surfed it': Campbell, *Broken Record*, p. 50. The Hogarth Press was making something of a cult of youth at this time; this no doubt affected Plomer too.

[90] Interview with Van der Post, London, 3 December 1977.

[91] *Voorslag*, vol. 1, no. 2 (July 1926), p. 11.

[92] Ibid., p. 13.

[93] Ibid., p. 20.

[94] Unpublished letter, Roworth to W. H. Gardner, 23 January 1959: NELM.

[95] Mrs Millin's article 'A South African Magazine: Is *Voorslag* What It Should Be?' appeared in the *Rand Daily Mail* on 16 June 1926; Campbell's response was published in the same paper on 24 June 1926, under the title 'Poet Resents Criticism. Roy Campbell on *Voorslag*—Not Exclusive'.

[96] Published in *Voorslag*, Killie Campbell Africana Library Reprint Series,

no. 5, ed. C. Gardner and M. Chapman (University of Natal Press, Durban, 1985), pp. 49–50.

97 Unpublished memorandum, Campbell to Plomer, undated [August 1926]: DUL.

98 *Voorslag*, vol. I, no. 2, p. 62.

99 Unpublished letter to W. H. Gardner, 17 September 1958: NELM.

100 Interview with Van der Post, London, 4 December 1977.

101 Unpublished memorandum, Campbell to Plomer, undated [August 1926]: DUL.

102 Van der Post's Introduction to the 1965 edition of *Turbott Wolfe*, p. 27.

103 Ibid.

104 Plomer, 'Voorslag Days', *London Magazine*, vol. 6, no. I, p. 49.

105 Ibid.

106 Ibid., pp. 49–50.

107 Unpublished letter, 21 May 1926: Hogarth.

108 Unpublished letter, Plomer to W. H. Gardner, 17 Sept. 1958: NELM.

109 Kendall's poem is entitled 'Beyond Kerguelen'.

110 Letter from Campbell to T. S. Eliot, undated [August 1928]: published in Alexander, *Roy Campbell: A Critical Biography*, p. 63.

111 *Autobiography*, p. 176.

112 Unpublished letter, Roworth to W. H. Gardner, 23 January 1959: NELM.

113 Plomer, 'Voorslag Days', *London Magazine*, vol. 6, no. I, p. 50.

114 Interview with Van der Post, London, 2 December 1977.

115 *Voorslag* was to stumble on to a total of eleven issues, but the heart had gone out of it with the departure of Campbell and Plomer. Although its price was cut from 2s. 6d. to 1s., its circulation declined steadily, and in 1927 Reynolds ceased publication.

116 Van der Post, *Yet Being Someone Other*, p. 107.

117 Interview with Captain K. Mori, Tokyo, 3 November 1985.

118 Japanese shipping had for years called occasionally at Durban *en route* to other ports; what was new about the voyage of the *Canada Maru* was that it inaugurated a regular link between Japan and South Africa.

119 Interview with Van der Post, Aldeburgh, 29 October 1983.

120 Interview with Van der Post, London, 2 December 1977.

121 Interview with Van der Post, Aldeburgh, 29 October 1983, and Van der Post, *Yet Being Someone Other*, p. 117.

122 Unpublished letter, Campbell to C. J. Sibbett, undated [8 September 1926]: SAL. This contemporary letter makes nonsense of Campbell's later claim that Plomer and Van der Post had 'abandoned' him in South Africa to face the music about *Voorslag* alone.

123 Van der Post, *Yet Being Someone Other*, p. 118.

124 *Autobiography*, p. 178.

125 Ibid.

126 Unpublished letter, Campbell to C. J. Sibbett, undated [8 September 1926]: SAL.

127 This letter to Blunden is preserved among Plomer's papers at DUL, and it is not clear whether Plomer actually used it.

[128] Van der Post, *Yet Being Someone Other*, p. 119.

7. JAPAN

[1] Shidehara, when he met Plomer and Van der Post in Tokyo, questioned Van der Post about his African background. On hearing that he had worked in Port Natal (Durban), the distinguished Japanese remarked with great interest, 'Ah! Is that so?' A pause, a polite hiss, and then, 'You must know Abyssinia well!' There followed a stream of questions about Abyssinia, which Van der Post, who had never been there, tried to answer as best he could. The interview seemed to him objective confirmation of Japan's African ambitions. Van der Post, *Yet Being Someone Other*, pp. 249–50.

[2] The Osaka Shosen Kaisha has thrived since the war, and is now once again one of the largest cargo shipping lines in the world.

[3] Interview with Captain K. Mori, Tokyo, 3 November 1985.

[4] Information drawn from Professor Eiichi Sano's biographical note on Mori, written 1973, and from an interview with Mori, Tokyo, 3 November 1985. In *Double Lives*, p. 169, Plomer mistakenly asserts that Mori was a graduate of the Kaigun Haigakko (the Japanese naval college) at Etajima, near Hiroshima.

[5] Information drawn from Professor Eiichi Sano's biographical note on Mori.

[6] *Double Lives*, p. 169.

[7] He was ninety-five when I met him in Tokyo, a little shaky, but still strongly built, and with a personality that threw lesser dignitaries instantly into the shadows.

[8] *Double Lives*, p. 170.

[9] Ibid., and interview with Mori, Tokyo, 3 November 1985.

[10] *Double Lives*, p. 170.

[11] Interview with the writer, Tokyo, 3 November 1985.

[12] Ibid.

[13] Van der Post, *Yet Being Someone Other*, p. 115.

[14] Ibid., p. 123.

[15] Ibid., p. 152.

[16] Lafcadio Hearn (1850–1904), an American who became a naturalized Japanese, was one of the best-known writers on Japan in English. Among his books on Japan, which he tended to exalt at the expense of the West, are *Glimpses of Unfamiliar Japan* (1894), *Out of the East* (1895), and *Japan: An attempt at Interpretation* (1904).

[17] *Autobiography*, pp. 181–2.

[18] Van der Post, *Yet Being Someone Other*, p. 123.

[19] *Double Lives*, p. 177.

[20] Van der Post, *Yet Being Someone Other*, p. 123.

[21] Ibid.

[22] Interview with Mori, Tokyo, 3 November 1985.

[23] Van der Post, *Yet Being Someone Other*, p. 126.

[24] Ibid., p. 123.

25 Date taken from an unpublished letter, Plomer to Leonard Woolf, written from Mombasa, 5 September 1926: Hogarth.
26 Van der Post, *Yet Being Someone Other*, p. 136.
27 *Double Lives*, pp. 173–4.
28 Ibid., p. 174.
29 *Autobiography*, p. 182.
30 Ibid., p. 183. Plomer, with his usual tact, does not name her. The Danish writer Karen Christentze Blixen (1885–1962), as 'Isak Dinesen', was to win an international reputation with a number of books written in English. They include *Seven Gothic Tales* (1934) and *Out of Africa* (1937). She had by this time divorced her husband, Baron Bror Blixen-Finecke, with whom she had run a coffee farm.
31 *Autobiography*, p. 183.
32 *Double Lives*, p. 176.
33 Ibid.
34 *Autobiography*, p. 183.
35 *Double Lives*, p. 176.
36 Ibid.
37 Unpublished telegram, Campbell to Plomer, 13 September 1926: DUL. 'Polly Andrews' was a rather slight short story which Plomer had written at Sezela, and which Leonard Woolf and Campbell (who corrected the proofs) persuaded him to drop from *I Speak of Africa*, the volume in which the other African tales were published in 1927.
38 Unpublished letter, Mary Campbell to Plomer, 19 September [1926]: DUL.
39 'When he first read it ["Polly Andrews"] to me . . . I told him he ought to keep it. But when he sent me a copy of it I found that there was nothing in it at all.' Unpublished letter, Campbell to Leonard Woolf, undated [1927]: Hogarth.
40 Unpublished letter, Roy Campbell to C. J. Sibbett, undated [8 September 1926]: SAL. He had hoped to include among these books some on Japan, but had found when he enquired for one in the leading Durban bookshop that 'I might have asked for a book about the moon': 'An Afrikaner in Japan', *Natal Witness*, 2 October 1926, p. 20.
41 Van der Post, *Yet Being Someone Other*, p. 154.
42 Interview with Van der Post, Aldeburgh, 29 October 1983.
43 *Double Lives*, p. 177.
44 Van der Post, *Yet Being Someone Other*, p. 122.
45 Ibid., p. 131.
46 Ibid., p. 133.
47 *Double Lives*, p. 177.
48 'Saigo' was Saigo Takamori, the leader of the bloody and ineffective Satsuma Rebellion (1877) against Emperor Meiji's modernization plans. He came from Kumamoto, a town in Mori's home island, Kyushu, and this gives force to Plomer's comparison.
49 Van der Post, *Yet Being Someone Other*, p. 161.
50 *Double Lives*, p. 177.
51 They appeared in the *Natal Witness* on 2 October 1926, p. 20;

6 November 1926, p. 20; 12 February 1927, p. 21; 12 March 1927, p. 21; and 19 March 1927, p. 21.

[52] Van der Post, *Yet Being Someone Other*, pp. 165–6.

[53] *Double Lives*, p. 177.

[54] Van der Post, *Yet Being Someone Other*, p. 169.

[55] *Autobiography*, p. 185.

[56] 'An Afrikander [*sic*] in Japan', *Natal Witness*, 12 February 1927, p. 21.

[57] Van der Post, *Yet Being Someone Other*, p. 182.

[58] Ibid., p. 176.

[59] In Plomer's posthumously published *Autobiography*, pp. 61–2, he is much more cautious about the Arden connection than he seems to have been in conversation with Mori.

[60] Interview with Van der Post, Aldeburgh, 29 November 1983.

[61] *Autobiography*, p. 185.

[62] *Double Lives*, p. 178.

[63] Ibid.

[64] Van der Post, *Yet Being Someone Other*, pp. 199–200.

[65] Ibid., p. 200.

[66] According to ibid., pp. 205 ff., the only other guests were Tajima of the OSK and the young Japanese diplomat. Plomer, in *Double Lives*, p. 178 (written much nearer the time), mentions three other guests, all friends of Mori's, one of them a bull-necked tough who had a poor head for liquor and who frightened the young geishas.

[67] The phrase is Plomer's: *Double Lives*, p. 179.

[68] Ibid.

[69] Van der Post is among them: *Yet Being Someone Other*, p. 204.

[70] *Double Lives*, p. 179.

[71] Van der Post, *Yet Being Someone Other*, pp. 210–12.

[72] Ibid., p. 250.

[73] Ibid., p. 214.

[74] 'An Afrikander in Japan', *Natal Witness*, 12 February 1927, p. 21.

[75] Interview with Mori, Tokyo, 3 November 1985.

[76] *Autobiography*, pp. 187–8.

[77] *Double Lives*, p. 180.

[78] The lines are from Eliot's 'Whispers of Immortality', in *Poems*, 1920. Misquoted in Van der Post, *Yet Being Someone Other*, p. 228.

[79] Van der Post, *Yet Being Someone Other*, pp. 238–40.

[80] *Double Lives*, p. 181.

[81] Ibid.

[82] Ibid.

[83] Interview with Mori, Tokyo, 3 November 1985.

[84] Plomer, *Paper Houses*, pp. x–xii.

[85] Van der Post, *Yet Being Someone Other*, p. 254.

[86] *Double Lives*, p. 182.

[87] Unpublished letter, Plomer to Leonard Woolf, 20 November 1926: Hogarth.

[88] Blunden had frequently written for the *London Mercury*, the literary monthly run by Sir John Squire from 1919 to 1934; in its early days

it fought against Modernism, which Plomer admired, and its pages were filled with Georgian writers whom Plomer disliked, among them de la Mare, Chesterton, and Belloc.

89 Unpublished letter, Plomer to Leonard Woolf, 20 November 1926: Hogarth.

90 Unpublished letter, Woolf to Plomer, 3 January 1927: Hogarth.

91 *2 Henry IV*, v. iii. 100.

92 Unpublished letter to Zelda Friedlander, 15 April 1966: DUL.

93 Cape *Argus*, 4 February 1928. Campbell wrote from England to defend Plomer in the columns of the *Argus* (29 January 1928), but made matters worse when he described South Africa (and Durban in particular) as 'that Mecca of moronism' whose 'unbroken ignominy and dullness' had been disturbed only by the 'inexplicable phenomenon' of his own birth!

94 Interview with Van der Post, Aldeburgh, 29 October 1983.

95 Unpublished letter, Plomer to Van der Post, 25 February 1927: Opp.

96 Ibid.

97 *Double Lives*, p. 182.

98 Ibid., p. 192.

99 Plomer does not give details of the 'slander', and though it is perhaps pointless to speculate, it seems not impossible that he was thought to be becoming too intimate with some of his pupils. William Empson, who began teaching at the Imperial University shortly after Plomer left Japan, got into serious trouble with the authorities because of his homosexual activity, and the Japanese police were involved. Interview with Professor Ryuichi Kajiki, Tokyo, 3 November 1985.

100 *Double Lives*, p. 184.

101 Plomer, *A Brutal Sentimentalist and Other Stories*, ed. Eiichi Sano.

102 Interview with Kajiki, Tokyo, 3 November 1985.

103 *Autobiography*, p. 195.

104 Ibe, Nakagawa, and Kajiki all remarked on it in interviews, Tokyo, November 1985.

105 Interview with Kajiki, Tokyo, 3 November 1985.

106 Plomer quoted this letter in *Double Lives*, p. 184, without naming its writer.

107 Ibid., p. 185.

108 According to Plomer, when Mori offered to support him so that he could write without having to bother about working for money, Sumida instantly offered to forgo his own wage. Plomer turned down both offers: ibid., p. 185.

109 *Autobiography*, p. 194.

110 *Double Lives*, p. 190.

111 He put the incident into his story 'Thy Neighbour's Creed'.

112 *Double Lives*, p. 191.

113 Earl Miner, in his seminal study of English writers on Japan, remarks of 'Yoka Nikki' that it is written in the peculiarly Japanese genre, the fictionalized diary: *The Japanese Tradition in British and American*

Literature, p. 50. There is no evidence that the account is fictionalized, however.

[114] *Paper Houses*, p. 232.

[115] Ibid., p. 233.

[116] 'Yoka Nikki', in ibid., p. 249.

[117] *Double Lives*, p. 189.

[118] In an interview with Kajiki, for instance (Tokyo, 3 November 1985), the life which Morito Fukuzawa, Plomer's long-term Japanese companion, led before his happy marriage was mildly described as 'bohemian— yes, very bohemian', in a tone that carried no shade of judgement.

[119] *Autobiography*, p. 201.

[120] Ibid., p. 205.

[121] This was perhaps the germ of *Sado*, published eventually in 1931.

[122] It is hard to reconcile this comment with the accounts of drinking parties he later gave in his autobiographies; perhaps the letter expresses an intention rather than a fact.

[123] Unpublished letter, Plomer to Leonard Woolf, 5 June 1927: Hogarth.

[124] Unpublished letter, Plomer to Leonard Woolf, 20 June 1927: Hogarth.

[125] Unpublished letter, to Leonard Woolf, 11 June 1928: Hogarth.

[126] Interview with Van der Post, London, 3 December 1977.

[127] *Double Lives*, p. 192.

[128] Ibid., p. 209.

[129] Vines was writing a strikingly original book on Japan entitled *Yofuku*; his other publications included *The Pyramid* and *The Course of English Classicism*, and he was to go on to write a satirical novel about English provincial life in the late thirties, *Green to Amber*.

[130] Blunden had provided an introductory poem for Vines's first book, *The Pyramid* (1926).

[131] *Double Lives*, p. 198.

[132] *Autobiography*, pp. 217–18.

[133] Ibid., p. 213.

[134] Miner, *The Japanese Tradition in British and American Literature*, p. 50.

[135] Plomer, *Paper Houses*, pp. xiii–xiv.

[136] Unpublished letter, Plomer to Leonard Woolf, 11 June 1928: Hogarth.

[137] Miner believes the form of 'Mother Kamchatka' was influenced by Akutagawa's satirical *Kappa: The Japanese Tradition in British and American Literature*, p. 50.

[138] *Autobiography*, p. 213.

8. ENGLAND

[1] It was a volume of miscellaneous articles edited by William Sansom, published by Progress Publishing, London.

[2] Plomer's second volume of autobiography, *At Home*, p. 12.

[3] Unpublished letter, 10 July 1967: FP.

[4] *At Home*, p. 13.

[5] *Double Lives*, p. 209.

[6] *At Home*, p. 16.

[7] *Autobiography*, p. 231.

8 Reed, an American journalist, wrote an account of the Russian Revolution, of which he was an eyewitness. The book was published in England by the British Communist party in 1920, with an introduction by Lenin.

9 *At Home*, p. 22.

10 J. C. Chapman, *Real Wages in Soviet Russia Since 1928* (Cambridge, Mass., 1963), suggests at worst a fall of 39 per cent in real wages, at best one of 14 per cent.

11 *At Home*, p. 25.

12 *Autobiography*, p. 235.

13 *At Home*, p. 29.

14 Ibid., p. 28.

15 Ibid.

16 The Revd Clement Bode had been Plomer's loathed headmaster at Beechmont.

17 Preface to *Four Countries*, p. 9.

18 24 West Way, Pinner.

19 *The Diary of Virginia Woolf, Vol. III: 1925–1930*, ed. A. O. Bell, p. 242.

20 Ibid., p. 224.

21 *The Letters of Virginia Woolf, Vol. IV: 1929–1931*, ed. Nigel Nicolson, p. 43.

22 Plomer, 'Virginia Woolf', unpublished article: FP.

23 Unpublished letter, Plomer to Virginia Woolf, undated [1937]: Hogarth.

24 Plomer, 'Virginia Woolf', unpublished article: FP.

25 Plomer gives a brief description of the party and a partial guest list in an unpublished letter to Van der Post, 20 August 1929: Opp.

26 Arthur Clive Howard Bell (1881–1964), art critic and 'the Don Juan of Bloomsbury', had married Virginia Woolf's sister Vanessa in 1907. After 1914 the marriage was one in name only, for he transferred his affections to Mary Hutchinson, a first cousin of Lytton Strachey and wife of the barrister St John Hutchinson. Francis Locker Birrell (1889–1935) was a critic who wrote for the *Nation & Athenaeum* (of which Leonard Woolf was literary editor) and part-owner of a bookshop near Gordon Square. Vanessa Bell, née Stephen (1879–1961), Virginia's sister, married Clive Bell in 1907, but from 1914 until her death lived with Duncan Grant the painter, by whom she had a daughter, Angelica (b. 1918). Edward Sackville-West, fifth Lord Sackville, was an author and music critic. Roger Eliot Fry (1866–1934), Quaker art critic and indifferent painter, introduced the British public to Post-Impressionist art, and exercised great influence in the art world in England and (to a lesser extent) in France and the United States. Quentin was the younger son of Clive Bell and Vanessa, and became the biographer of Virginia Woolf.

27 Virginia Woolf to Vita Sackville-West, 18 August 1929, in *The Letters of Virginia Woolf, Vol. IV: 1929–1931*, p. 79.

28 Quentin Bell, *Virginia Woolf*, vol. 2 (Hogarth Press, London, 1972), p. 149.

29 *The Diary of Virginia Woolf, Vol. III: 1925–1930*, p. 242, n. 4.

³⁰ It is plain from the context (though not from the punctuation) that these are the reported words of Plomer.

³¹ Raymond Mortimer (1895–1980), critic, a close friend of Clive Bell and Harold Nicolson.

³² *The Diary of Virginia Woolf, Vol. IV: 1931–1935*, p. 85.

³³ Giles Lytton Strachey (1880–1932), critic and biographer, was a friend of Virginia's brother Thoby and of Leonard Woolf at Cambridge. At this time he had written *Eminent Victorians* (1918), *Queen Victoria* (1921), and *Books and Characters* (1922). Victoria Mary Sackville-West (1892–1962), novelist and poet, wife (since 1913) of Harold Nicolson, and briefly the lover of Virginia Woolf. Hogarth Press published thirteen of her books. Sir Harold Nicolson (1886–1968), diplomat and author, at this time posted to the embassy in Berlin. He had written books on Verlaine, Tennyson, and Byron. John Maynard Keynes (1883–1946), economist and Fellow of King's College, Cambridge. From 1923 he was chairman of the board of the *Nation & Athenaeum* and had been responsible for appointing Leonard Woolf as its literary editor. Charles Otto Desmond MacCarthy (1877–1952), critic and journalist; from 1920 he was literary editor of the *New Statesman*. Lady Ottoline Morrell (1873–1938), literary hostess and wife of the barrister and Liberal MP Philip Morrell. She was a generous patron of writers, pacifists, and artists, at least two of whom repaid her kindness by caricaturing her in their work: Aldous Huxley in *Crome Yellow*, and D. H. Lawrence in *Women in Love*. She had by this time sold her famous house, Garsington Manor, near Oxford, and was living in Gower Street, Bloomsbury.

³⁴ Interview with Spender, London, 19 February 1987.

³⁵ Lady Sybil Colefax, a society hostess.

³⁶ Virginia Woolf's diary, 17 March 1932.

³⁷ Interview with Van der Post, Aldeburgh, 29 October 1983.

³⁸ 23 Belsize Crescent, Hampstead.

³⁹ Interview with Van der Post, Aldeburgh, 29 October 1983.

⁴⁰ Ibid.

⁴¹ Interview with Van der Post, London, 3 December 1977.

⁴² Though Peter's change of his name to James after the Second World War is perhaps a curious reflection of what his brother had done earlier.

⁴³ Among his papers after his death was found a long, scholarly treatise on the origins of the name, drawn up by Bertrand Plummer, one of Plomer's distant relations, and now housed in DUL. On the envelope Plomer wrote, 'Proof, if proof be needed, that the Plomers began as Plumbers'.

⁴⁴ *Autobiography*, p. 12.

⁴⁵ Sent to John Lehmann, 29 November 1940, for publication in *Penguin New Writing*.

⁴⁶ *Autobiography*, p. 381.

⁴⁷ Unpublished letter, Plomer to Van der Post, 5 July 1929: Opp.

⁴⁸ This painting is now in the National Portrait Gallery.

⁴⁹ Unpublished letter, 14 August 1929: Opp.

⁵⁰ See Alexander, *Roy Campbell: A Critical Biography*, chaps. 6 and 7.

51 Published by Boriswood, London, 1931.
52 *The Diary of Virginia Woolf, Vol. III: 1925–1930*, p. 242.
53 Unpublished letter, Campbell to Plomer, 14 June 1929: Texas.
54 Arthur David Waley (1889–1966), authority on Chinese and Japanese literature and translator of many poems from both languages. His best-known work was *A Hundred and Seventy Chinese Poems* (1918), but he also translated the Japanese classic *The Tale of Genji* (1925–33). He had mastered Chinese and Japanese while working in the British Museum print-room, but declined many invitations to visit China and Japan.
55 Plomer, diary note for 28 June 1965, in notebook B10: DUL.
56 The Sitwell siblings, Dame Edith Louisa (1887–1964), Sir Francis Osbert (1892–1969), and Sacheverell (1897–), writers, outspoken opponents of the Georgian poets, supporters of Pound, Eliot, Wyndham Lewis, William Walton, and Roy Campbell, and (especially) of each other.
57 Unpublished letter to Van der Post, 29 June 1929: Opp.
58 In a few years he would be advising friends such as John Lehmann about the right places to make homosexual contacts.
59 Edward Morgan Forster (1879–1970) had at King's College, Cambridge, been a member of the Apostles, the undergraduate club to which most of the 'Bloomsberries' also belonged, and so moved on the fringes of the Bloomsbury group. Independently wealthy, he had travelled widely as a young man, in India, southern Europe, and Egypt. By the time Plomer met him, he had published the last of his novels, *A Passage to India* (1924), and had been offered a three-year fellowship at King's, where he was to spend most of the rest of his life.
60 Published in the *Selected Letters of E. M. Forster*, ed. Mary Lago and P. N. Furbank.
61 *Autobiography*, p. 303.
62 P. N. Furbank, *E. M. Forster: A Life*, vol. 1, p. 178.
63 Anthony Butts (1900–44) was a direct descendant of Sir William Butts, who is a character in Shakespeare's *Henry VIII*. His great-grandfather, Thomas Butts, had been a friend and patron of Blake, and the family owned several of Blake's former possessions. Butts's father had been born in 1870, and died during Butts's youth; his mother had remarried, and her second husband, Frederick Colville-Hyde, had ill-treated both her and her son, who came to hate him. Butts also hated his sister, Mary (1893–1937), author of several novels and a mendacious autobiography.
64 *The Diary of Virginia Woolf, Vol. IV*: see entry for 16 June 1937.
65 *At Home*, pp. 67–8.
66 Unpublished letter, 3 September 1929: Opp.
67 *Turbott Wolfe* (1925), *I Speak of Africa* (1927), *Notes for Poems* (1927), *Paper Houses* (1929), and *The Family Tree* (1929).
68 *Sado*, p. 194.
69 Unpublished memorandum of his income 1929–53: DUL.
70 It was at first slightly higher (£5?), but Desmond Young, editor of the *Cape Times*, reduced the amount on finding that the Johannesburg papers did not want to reprint Plomer's pieces.

71 Unpublished letter, Plomer to Van der Post, 3 September 1929: Opp.

72 Plomer gives a sketchy account of the events in *Double Lives*, pp. 241–3, and a much more detailed one, sticking very close to the facts, in *The Case is Altered*.

73 *The Diary of Virginia Woolf, Vol. III: 1925–1930*, p. 268.

74 Unpublished letter, du Plessis to Van der Post, 13 December 1929: Opp.

75 *The Diary of Virginia Woolf, Vol. III: 1925–1930*, p. 268.

76 Unpublished letter, Plomer to Van der Post, 12 November 1929: Opp.

77 Unpublished letter, 14 December 1929: Hogarth.

78 Unpublished letter to Van der Post, 14 January 1930: Opp.

79 Unpublished letter, 6 March 1930: Opp.

80 Unpublished letter to Van der Post, 4 September 1930: Opp.

81 Sir Stephen Harold Spender (1909–), son of a distinguished journalist, had at Oxford become friendly with W. H. Auden, Louis MacNeice, and Christopher Isherwood. In 1929 he had written only a handful of poems, none of which Plomer particularly admired.

82 Spender, *World Within World* (London, Faber & Faber paperback edition, 1977), pp. 149–50.

83 Interview with Spender, London, 19 February 1987. In *World Within World*, however, Spender says that Plomer travelled to Oxford with Anthony Butts. It is not possible from Plomer's correspondence to tell who his companion was on this Oxford trip.

84 Wystan Hugh Auden (1907–73), poet, librettist, playwright, and script-writer, had been one of Spender's friends at Oxford, together with MacNeice and Day-Lewis. Auden was at this time a schoolmaster and was almost unknown, having published his 1928 volume *Poems* privately, with Spender.

85 Christopher William Bradshaw Isherwood (1904–87), novelist and school friend of Auden. He had at this time published only his first novel, *All the Conspirators* (1928), heavily influenced by Forster and Virginia Woolf.

86 Unpublished letter, 20 September 1955: Texas.

87 Interview with Spender, 19 February 1987.

9. MAGGOTS IN THE MUSHROOM

1 Unpublished memorandum of Plomer's income 1929–53: DUL.

2 Unpublished letter to Spender, 19 August 1930: Spender.

3 The words are in fact those of J. R. Ackerley, *My Father and Myself*, p. 118.

4 Spender.

5 Plomer, *The Fivefold Screen*, p. 47.

6 He gave the title and the details of his writing in a BBC broadcast, 'An Unfinished Novel', 24 August 1956: BBC Written Archives Centre.

7 Unpublished letter, 19 August 1930: Spender.

8 20 July 1930: Spender.

9 *At Home*, p. 77.

10 *The Fivefold Screen*, p. 51.

11 Unpublished postcard, 3 September 1930: DUL.
12 Unpublished postcard, 11 October 1930: DUL.
13 Percy Wyndham Lewis (1882–1957), painter, poet, novelist, and critic, was one of the most remarkable minds of the twentieth century. Roy Campbell was his closest friend at this time. Lewis's *The Apes of God*, published only a few months before this letter from Plomer, had vigorously attacked effeminate male artists, among many other targets, and had particularly singled out Stephen Spender, who appears in the novel as 'Dan'. 'Ratner', in the novel, was based on a Jew named Rodker, whom Plomer knew slightly and liked.
14 NELM.
15 *At Home*, pp. 80–1.
16 Plomer was put in contact with Bunin by Leonard Woolf. The article appeared on 14 July 1933.
17 Introduction to *Four Countries*, pp. 10–11.
18 Plomer names her in a letter to Leonard Woolf, 1 July 1930: Hogarth.
19 Published in *The Child of Queen Victoria*.
20 Unpublished letter, 1 July 1930: Hogarth.
21 4 July 1930: Spender.
22 Interview with Van der Post, Aldeburgh, 29 October 1983.
23 Unpublished letter, 25 August 1930: Opp.
24 4 September 1930: Opp. The 'pompous address' was the Hotel d'Angleterre et Belle Venise on Corfu.
25 *At Home*, p. 81. He expressed a similar sentiment in a poem in *The Fivefold Screen*, 'Greek Love II', which alludes to his and Nicky's boating on the bay of Phaleron: 'Mated to mishap, fated to destroy, / Why do men suffer chiefly by their joy?'
26 Unpublished letter, 28 October 1930: Opp.
27 Notes, in Plomer's hand, from letters to his parents: DUL.
28 'An Unfinished Novel', 24 August 1956: BBC Written Archives Centre.
29 Ibid.
30 Unpublished letter, 21 February 1931: Opp.
31 In her diary for 2 February 1931, Virginia Woolf noted, 'William P. talked more of his new novel, the Autobiography or Experiences? of an Emigrant the other night than L. has talked of his books all his life.' And on 19 May 1931 she was describing the book as 'rather a disappointment—an Episode'.
32 Sir Hugh Seymour Walpole (1884–1941) was born in New Zealand and educated at Cambridge. The best known of his many novels were *Mr. Perrin and Mr. Traill* (1911), *The Dark Forest* (1916), and *Rogue Herries* (1930). He was at the height of his popularity at this time.
33 Unpublished letter, Plomer to John Hampson Simpson, 6 September 1932: RHD.
34 Rupert Hart-Davis, *Hugh Walpole*, p. 324.
35 Ibid., p. 43.
36 Unpublished letter to Hart-Davis, 14 May [1935]: RHD.
37 Against this opinion should be set that of Walpole's biographer, Hart-Davis, who believes that 'The Playboy of the Demi-World' is

intended as a portrait of the actor Robin de la Condamine. Unpublished note to the writer, August 1987.

[38] The allusion is to the Reverend J. W. Burgon's description of Petra: 'A rose-red city—"half as old as Time"!'

[39] Carnera was an Italian heavyweight boxer, at the height of his fame in 1930.

[40] Unpublished letter, 20 March 1931: Spender.

[41] Interview with the writer, Aldeburgh, 29 October 1983.

[42] Ibid.

[43] Bonamy Dobrée (1891–1974), distinguished literary critic and historian, had read and admired *Sado*.

[44] *The Letters of Virginia Woolf, Vol. IV: 1929–1931*, pp. 386–7.

[45] *Action*, 22 October 1931.

[46] Quoted in Plomer's reply to Spender, 22 September [1931]: Spender.

[47] *Selected Letters of E. M. Forster*, vol. 2, p. 109.

[48] Interview with Van der Post, Aldeburgh, 29 October 1983.

[49] Unpublished letter, 20 July 1930: Spender.

[50] Harold Nicolson, for instance, seems to have chosen many of his partners from his own class.

[51] Interview with the writer, London, 19 February 1987. He went on to add, however, that working-class homosexuals (such as Harry Daley, Forster's lover for years) did choose sexual partners from their own class. Daley often found himself in the situation of having to gaol his former lovers for burglary or other offences, and felt no embarrassment in doing so. Harry Daley's *This Small Cloud: A Personal Memoir* (Weidenfeld & Nicolson, London, 1986) gives much interesting background information on relations between different classes of English homosexuals.

[52] Graves gives a clear account of this pattern in *Goodbye to All That*.

[53] Quoted in 'That is my ticket: The homosexual writings of E. M. Forster', *London Magazine*, February/March 1975, p. 5.

[54] Joseph Randolph Ackerley (1896–1967) had at this time written only *Hindoo Holiday* (1932), an account of his experiences in India. It was he who interested Forster in India by telling him of the homosexual court of a Hindu ruler. From 1935 to 1959 he was literary editor of the *Listener*.

[55] W. J. H. Sprott was a friend of Maynard Keynes and Lytton Strachey. Trained at Clare College, Cambridge, he had gone to Nottingham University in 1926.

[56] These details are drawn from Ackerley's posthumously published autobiography, *My Father and Myself*.

[57] Ibid., p. 135.

[58] Ibid., p. 215.

[59] Quoted in *Autobiography*, pp. 308–9.

[60] Ibid., pp. 309–10.

[61] Interview with Van der Post, Aldeburgh, 29 October 1983.

[62] Unpublished letter, Leonard Woolf to Plomer, 8 February 1932: Hogarth.

[63] Norman Haire (1892–1952) had made a fortune from abortion clinics.

[64] Letter from Forster to Isherwood, 16 January 1935: *Selected Letters of E. M. Forster*, p. 128.

[65] *Autobiography*, p. 354.

[66] Ibid., p. 380.

[67] Unpublished letter, 18 April [1932]: Spender.

[68] His next volume of verse, *Visiting the Caves*, contained only eighteen poems, and these were probably all he produced during the previous four years.

[69] Unpublished letter, undated [July–September 1932]: Opp.

[70] Unpublished letter, 16 July 1932: Hogarth.

[71] Unpublished letter, undated [September 1932]: Opp.

[72] Plomer, *Cecil Rhodes*, p. 10.

[73] Unpublished letter to Plomer, 19 April 1940: DUL.

[74] Unpublished letter, undated [September 1932–September 1933]: King's College, Cambridge.

[75] Described in an unpublished letter, Plomer to John Hampson Simpson, 6 September 1932: RHD.

[76] Unpublished letter, 18 September 1937: Hogarth.

[77] Unpublished letter, 23 November 1932: RHD.

[78] Daley, *This Small Cloud*, p. 115.

[79] Unpublished letter, 3 April 1933: DUL.

[80] Interview with Van der Post, Aldeburgh, 29 October 1983.

[81] Unpublished letter, 5 May 1933: DUL.

[82] The novel deals with race relations in South Africa, and the title, suggested by Plomer, is from Ecclesiastes 5: 8: 'If thou seest the oppression of the poor, and violent perverting of judgement and justice in a province, marvel not at the matter; for he that is higher than the highest regardeth.'

[83] Interview with Spender, London, 19 February 1987.

[84] Interview with Van der Post, London, 3 December 1977.

[85] Interview with Spender, London, 19 February 1987.

[86] Plomer gives details of this behaviour in an unpublished letter to John Lehmann, 18 January 1936: Texas.

[87] Interview with Van der Post, London, 3 December 1977.

[88] Unpublished letter, 15 December 1932: Opp.

10. LOTUS EATING

[1] Published by Jonathan Cape, London, 1933.

[2] Sir Rupert Hart-Davis (1907–), nephew of Alfred Duff Cooper and Lady Diana Manners, was educated at Eton and Oxford, and from 1927 to 1929 was an actor. His first wife was Peggy Ashcroft, but the marriage was dissolved, and in 1933 he married Catherine Comfort Borden-Turner. In 1932 he was manager of the Book Society, and from 1933 to 1940 he was a director of Jonathan Cape Ltd. After wartime service in the Coldstream Guards he founded his own publishing firm, Rupert Hart-Davis, in 1946, remaining director until 1964. He was knighted in 1967.

[3] DUL.

4 Quoted in unpublished letter, Hart-Davis to Plomer, 23 October 1933: Cape.

5 Ibid.

6 Unpublished letter: Cape.

7 Unpublished letter: Spender.

8 *Autobiography*, p. 327.

9 *The Diary of Virginia Woolf, Vol. IV: 1931–1935*, p. 239.

10 Unpublished letter, 3 September 1934: Spender.

11 Unpublished letter, 2 October 1934: DUL. However, Isherwood seems to have had second thoughts, and later wrote that he was recommending the book to his homosexual uncle: 'I have told him to read *The Invaders* and am confident of the result. Many a Chick has left the mark of a beak upon him.' 13 October 1934: DUL.

12 Unpublished letter, 15 June 1934: Cape.

13 Writing in *New Statesman*, no. 8, 1934, p. 397.

14 28 September 1934. Published in *Selected Letters of E. M. Forster*.

15 Unpublished letter: Texas.

16 *Autobiography*, p. 318.

17 Spender, *World Within World*, p. 149.

18 Unpublished letter, undated [late February 1933]: Texas.

19 Carey is named and described in *At Home*, pp. 136–7, and is often mentioned in Plomer's correspondence with Van der Post. He had at least one child, who underwent an operation in December 1933.

20 Unpublished letter to Elizabeth Bowen, undated [October 1935]: Texas.

21 The letters to his parents were destroyed, probably by Plomer himself; these quotations are from notes he made and preserved: DUL.

22 William Somerset Maugham (1874–1965) trained as a doctor before discovering his vocation as a novelist and playwright. He produced some of the most polished short stories in the language and made a fortune from his plays. After 1926 he lived at Cap Ferrat on the French Riviera. In 1930 he had attacked Hugh Walpole in *Cakes and Ale*, pillorying him as Alroy Kear, a self-promoting writer. At the time Plomer met him he was at the height of his fame.

23 Sir Herbert Edward Read (1893–1968), imagist poet and editor at this time of the *Burlington Magazine*. He had until very recently been professor of fine art at Edinburgh University.

24 Count Geoffrey Wladislaw Vaile Potocki de Montalk, descended from a noble Polish family but born in New Zealand, had recently been sentenced to six months' imprisonment for publishing a group of obscene poems, including one dedicated 'to John Penis in the Mount of Venus'. He was on bail pending an appeal.

25 Sir Oswald Mosley (1896–1980) had left the Labour party, in which he had been a Cabinet Minister, and was now intent on seizing power with the help of his New party (formed in February 1931), backed by the Blackshirt organization.

26 Geoffrey Grigson (1905–), poet and critic, editor of the *Morning Post* and *New Verse*. Plomer called him 'the Pastor' in correspondence, because, he once explained to John Lehmann, 'he is such a preacher

and self-appointed sorter of sheep from goats'. Unpublished letter, 12 November 1955: Texas.

27 Rudolph John Frederick Lehmann (1907–), poet and editor, had been a friend of Julian Bell at Cambridge, and in 1931 began working at Hogarth Press. He was later to edit *New Writing* (1936–40), *Penguin New Writing* (1940–50), and the *London Magazine* (1954–61). Plomer was a regular contributor to each of these journals.

28 Unpublished letter, 12 July 1944: Texas.

29 Elizabeth Dorothea Cole Bowen (1899–1973), Anglo-Irish novelist. Born in Dublin, she had inherited her family home, Bowens Court, in 1930. Her best-known books up to this time included *The Hotel* (1927), *The Last September* (1929), and *The House in Paris* (1935).

30 'Notes on a Visit to Ireland', *Penguin New Writing*, vol. 1 (1940), p. 91.

31 Admittedly Bowen spent most of her time in Oxford, and was about to 'go over to London' (see quotation that follows).

32 'Notes on a Visit to Ireland', p. 93.

33 Rosamond Nina Lehmann (1901–), novelist, was already well known for her first novel, *Dusty Answer* (1927), and her second, *A Note in Music* (1930); the latter attracted attention because of its frank treatment of homosexuality.

34 Unpublished letter, Plomer to Lehmann, 7 October [1939]: Texas. The date explains the military metaphors.

35 Only an unfinished draft of this letter survives: SAL. It may never have been sent.

36 Unpublished letter, Plomer to W. H. Gardner, 26 January 1958: NELM.

37 Unpublished letter, 20 February 1935: RHD.

38 *Autobiography*, pp. 282–3.

39 Plomer, *Ali the Lion*, p. 28.

40 Unpublished letter, 3 May 1935: Spender.

41 Unpublished letter, 14 May [1935]: RHD.

42 A. J. P. Taylor, review of *Ali the Lion*, *Guardian*, 3 April 1936.

43 R. M. Dawkins, review of *Ali the Lion*, *Journal of Hellenic Studies*, 1936, pp. 120–1.

44 Unpublished letter, Plomer to Butts, 12 July [1935]: Spender.

45 *Autobiography*, p. 342.

46 Ibid., p. 343.

47 Unpublished letter, undated [June–September 1936]: Texas.

48 Unpublished letter, 31 July 1936: Texas. Rosamond's new book was *The Weather in the Streets* (1936); *New Writing* was the literary magazine John Lehmann was now editing.

49 'Another Country', 'Captain Maru', and 'The Prisoner' had appeared in the *London Mercury*, 'A Lost Face' in the *Spectator*, and 'The Barren Peartree' in the *Listener*.

50 Van der Post gives a full description of the dream in *Yet Being Someone Other*.

51 Unpublished letter, 16 December [1936]: Texas. Plomer also attended Spender's second wedding, during the war, and when Matthew Spender was born in February 1945, Plomer became his godfather.

52 Unpublished letter, 12 January 1937: Texas.
53 BBC memo, September 1945: BBC Written Archives.
54 Unpublished letter, 12 January [1937]: Texas.
55 Texas.
56 *Autobiography*, p. 317.

II. READER AND WRITER

1 Quoted in Michael S. Howard, *Jonathan Cape, Publisher*, p. 186.
2 Ibid., p. 281.
3 MS statement on Malcolm Lowry, in the possession of Simon Nowell-Smith of Headington Manor, Oxford.
4 Interview with Graham C. Greene, Sydney, 21 August 1985. Plomer's suspicion of Canadian writing is interesting, because his own brother lived there. Early in his career as a reader, he also tended to be dismissive of South African writers, and among those he advised Cape against publishing were Johannes Meintjes and Douglas Livingstone, both of whom became well known in their native land. He also consistently advised against the novels of Nadine Gordimer, though he much admired her short stories.
5 Cape.
6 Plomer's memorandum of income for 1929–53: DUL.
7 Unpublished letter, 13 September 1937: Texas.
8 Ibid.
9 Cecil Day-Lewis (1904–72), Irish-born poet, had edited *Oxford Poetry* (1927) with Auden, and had by 1937 published six volumes of verse. He was associated with the left-wing writers of the 1930s, and provided the last syllable of Roy Campbell's famous composite figure Macspaunday. He was Poet Laureate from 1968.
10 His reports on Day-Lewis's poetry for Jonathan Cape make this clear: Cape.
11 C. Day-Lewis, *The Buried Day* (Chatto & Windus, London, 1960), p. 200.
12 Unpublished letter, 13 September 1937: Texas.
13 Unpublished letter, Plomer to Bowen, 13 September 1937: Texas.
14 Unpublished letter, Plomer to John Hampson Simpson, 1 February 1937: RHD.
15 Unpublished letter to John Hampson Simpson, 28 April 1937: RHD.
16 Unpublished letter, Plomer to Bowen, 22 October 1937: Texas.
17 Interview with Hart-Davis, Marske-in-Swaledale, August 1983.
18 Unpublished letter, 22 October 1937: Texas.
19 Unpublished letter to Hart-Davis, 16 August [1938]: RHD.
20 The diary originally took up more than the twenty-two volumes that Plomer worked from; other volumes appear to have been destroyed earlier, perhaps by Kilvert's wife after his death. Plomer returned the twenty-two surviving volumes to T. Perceval Smith when he had finished editing them, in 1940, and in due course they were handed on to Smith's heir, Mrs Essex Hope. In September 1958 she gave one to

Plomer (the volume now held among the Plomer papers at DUL), and seems to have sold another, the so-called Sandford Notebook, which is now at the National Library of Wales. The other twenty she appears to have burned, an act of vandalism that can be compared only to the destruction of part of Hopkins's diary or the burning of Samuel Palmer's notebooks by his son. It has occasionally been claimed that a third original volume survived, but I have found no evidence of its existence. Plomer's letter of 18 September 1958 to Hart-Davis makes it plain that he received only one volume from Mrs Essex Hope, not two as she sometimes claimed.

21 Unpublished letter, Plomer to Bowen, 31 May [1938]: Texas.

22 Unpublished letter, 20 May [1939]: Spender.

23 Robert von Ranke Graves (1895–1987), poet, essayist, novelist, biographer, critic, and translator. He had at this time published several volumes of poetry, his autobiography, two seminal critical volumes (*Poetic Unreason and Other Studies* 1925, and *A Survey of Modernist Poetry* 1927), and the two Claudius novels (both 1934). He and Laura Riding were at the summit of the critical influence they exercised before the war.

24 Laura Riding (1901–), American poet and critic, Graves's constant companion from 1927 to 1939.

25 Unpublished letter to Bowen, 31 May [1938]: Texas.

26 Unpublished letter, 29 September 1938: Texas.

27 Unpublished letter, 29 May [1938]: Spender.

28 Unpublished letter, 6 October 1938: Texas.

29 Unpublished letter, 18 October 1939: RHD.

30 Edythe Plomer's burial certificate is among the Plomer papers: DUL.

12. WAR

1 Unpublished letter, 18 October 1939: RHD.

2 That, at least, was John Betjeman's belief, expressed in *London Magazine*, December 1973/January 1974, p. 13.

3 *Autobiography*, p. 381.

4 Ibid., p. 383.

5 Ian Lancaster Fleming (1908–64), educated at Eton and Sandhurst, journalist and stockbroker, creator of James Bond. The first Bond novel was *Casino Royale* (Cape, 1953), and it was followed by further Bond books in an unbroken stream, a novel a year, until Fleming's death. The books (including *Live and Let Die* (1954), *Diamonds are Forever* (1956), *From Russia with Love* (1963), and *Goldfinger* (1964), all published by Cape's) achieved unparalleled popular success, and many of them have been made into films.

6 John Pearson, *The Life of Ian Fleming*, Pan Books edition (1967), p. 202.

7 Donald McLachlan, *Room 39: Naval Intelligence in Action, 1939–1945*, p. 70.

8 Simon Harcourt Nowell-Smith (1909–) was to become secretary and librarian of the London Library after the war.

9 Dame Cicely Veronica Wedgwood, OM (1910–), historian; her publications before the war included *Strafford* (1935), *The Thirty Years' War* (1938), and *Oliver Cromwell* (1939).

10 Quoted in Nowell-Smith, Postscript to *Autobiography*, p. 432.

11 Plomer's memorandum of income, 1929–53: DUL.

12 *Autobiography*, p. 396.

13 Quoted in Donald McLachlan, *Room 39*, p. 67.

14 John Pearson, *The Life of Ian Fleming*, pp. 106–7.

15 Quoted in Donald McLachlan, *Room 39*, p. 70.

16 Ibid., pp. 69–70.

17 Quoted in Nowell-Smith, Postscript to *Autobiography*, p. 429.

18 Interview with Nowell-Smith, Oxford, 13 October 1983.

19 Unpublished letter, 30 September 1940: Hogarth.

20 Printed in Postscript to *Autobiography*, p. 429 n.

21 Nowell-Smith, Postscript to *Autobiography*, p. 429.

22 Interview with Nowell-Smith, Oxford, 13 October 1983.

23 Quoted in Nowell-Smith, Postscript to *Autobiography*, p. 431.

24 Interview with Simon Nowell-Smith, Oxford, 13 October 1983.

25 Unpublished letter, undated [August/September 1940]: RHD.

26 Unpublished letter, undated [September 1940]: Hogarth.

27 Unpublished letter, 18 January 1941: RHD.

28 Unpublished letter, undated [September 1940]: Hogarth.

29 Ibid.

30 Unpublished letter, 30 September 1940: Hogarth.

31 Unpublished letter, 28 October 1940: Texas.

32 Ibid.

33 Unpublished letter, undated [early May 1941]: RHD.

34 Unpublished letter to Lilian Bowes-Lyon, undated [5 June 1940]: RHD.

35 'Tony threw himself out of a window last week & was killed.' Unpublished letter, Plomer to Bowes-Lyon, 4 June 1941: RHD.

36 It was printed by the Curwen Press, 1942, in an edition of only fifty copies.

37 RHD.

38 Interview with Spender, London, 19 February 1987.

39 RHD.

40 12 May 1941: Texas.

41 Unpublished letter, Hart-Davis to the writer, 13 August 1984.

42 Unpublished letter to Hart-Davis, 12 July [1942]: RHD.

43 Unpublished letter, undated [15 August 1942]: Texas.

44 Unpublished letter, 7 November 1942: RHD.

45 Campbell, *Talking Bronco*.

46 Letter, Forster to Isherwood, 28 February 1944, in *Selected Letters of E. M. Forster*.

47 The editors of Forster's letters date the letter in which he told Plomer that he had begun his own autobiographical essay 'April 1943'. However, this date seems unlikely, since Plomer's book did not appear

until October that year. April 1944 seems more probable. Forster's piece
was 'West Hackhurst: A Surrey Ramble'.

⁴⁸ Unpublished letter, 3 December 1943: RHD.
⁴⁹ Unpublished letter, 1 October 1943: Texas.
⁵⁰ Hart-Davis lived at Bromsden Farm at Bix, near Henley-on-Thames.
⁵¹ Unpublished letter, Plomer to Hart-Davis, 8 September 1944: RHD. ·
⁵² Unpublished letter, 5 September 1944: RHD.
⁵³ Unpublished letter to John Lehmann, undated [May 1941]: Texas.
⁵⁴ Unpublished letter, undated [spring 1944]: Texas.
⁵⁵ Unpublished letter, 26 April 1944: Texas. Plomer also wrote a moving
tribute to Capetanakis, printed in *Demetrios Capetanakis: A Greek Poet in
England*, edited and published by John Lehmann in 1947.
⁵⁶ Unpublished letter, 20 February 1945: RHD.
⁵⁷ Ackerley, *My Father and Myself*, p. 110.
⁵⁸ Interview with the writer, London, 12 October 1983.
⁵⁹ Constantine Cavafy (1863–1933) was born in Alexandria of Greek
parents. Plomer never met him, but corresponded briefly with him at
the urging of Forster, who had befriended Cavafy in Alexandria in 1917.
Cavafy's poems treat homosexual themes with great frankness.
⁶⁰ Homosexual acts between consenting adults were not legitimized until
the passage of the Sexual Offences Act of 1967.
⁶¹ Interview with the writer, London, 12 October 1983.
⁶² The certificate is dated 11 February 1943: DUL.
⁶³ Unpublished letter, 20 January 1972: WM.
⁶⁴ *Autobiography*, p. 397.
⁶⁵ Unpublished letter to Hart-Davis, 31 December 1943: RHD.
⁶⁶ Unpublished letter, 11 November 1944: Texas.
⁶⁷ Unpublished letter, 28 February 1945: RHD.
⁶⁸ Interview with Charles Erdmann, Hassocks, 26 August 1983.
⁶⁹ Ibid.
⁷⁰ Unpublished letter, 20 February 1945: RHD.
⁷¹ Unpublished letter, 10 March 1945: Texas.
⁷² Edmund Wilson (1895–1972), poet, novelist, short-story writer, and
critic. His best-known book is a study of symbolist literature, *Axel's
Castle*, but he also produced plays, volumes of articles and reviews, one
novel, and a memoir.
⁷³ Unpublished letter, Plomer to John Lehmann, 1 May 1945: Texas.
⁷⁴ Unpublished letter, 14 May 1945: Texas.
⁷⁵ Richard William John Nugent Rumbold (1913–61), author of *My
Father's Son*, a book about the disastrous marriage of his parents.
Rumbold's grandfather, Charles Rumbold, had in 1863 married one of
Plomer's great-aunts, Agatha Franklyn.
⁷⁶ Unpublished letter, 1 June 1945: DUL.
⁷⁷ Unpublished letter, 10 December 1945: Texas.

13. PICKING UP THE THREADS

¹ Nowell-Smith, Postscript to *Autobiography*, p. 433.
² Unpublished letter, 2 March 1946: RHD. Plomer's affection for Daniel

George endured; when his fellow reader died in 1967, Plomer wrote an appreciative obituary of him for *The Times* (3 October 1967).

3 Michael S. Howard, *Jonathan Cape, Publisher*, p. 185.

4 Ibid., pp. 197–8.

5 Ibid., p. 198.

6 The others were *Redburn* (Cape, London, 1937) and *Selected Poems* (Hogarth Press, London, 1943). For a full list of the volumes to which Plomer provided introductions, see Select Bibliography in this volume.

7 Untitled notebook among Plomer's papers: DUL.

8 Ibid.

9 Her unpublished letter to Plomer of 20 April 1947 is an example: 'I am *aghast* at this dreadful thing about poor Miss Bowes-Lyon. It really is too terrible for any words, as you know, I have never met her, but can imagine the full tragedy from every respect. It simply isn't to be thought of.' DUL.

10 Unpublished letter, 20 December 1947: DUL.

11 Ibid.

12 Unpublished letter, Edith Sitwell to Plomer, 19 May 1948: DUL. Sir Cecil Maurice Bowra (1898–1971) was from 1938 Warden of Wadham College, Oxford, where he became renowned for his warmth and his wit; he was a Greek scholar and an influential critic.

13 Unpublished letter, Sybil Cholmondeley to Hart-Davis, 17 January 1976: RHD.

14 Characteristically, however, he was also an active mocker of royalty. Van der Post remembers several scurrilous caricatures of royalty which Plomer showed his friends at parties in the 1930s.

15 Unpublished letter, Plomer to Wren Howard, 26 August 1948: Cape.

16 Unpublished letter to Frances Plomer, 21 October 1952: FP.

17 Unpublished letter, Plomer to Forster, 21 July 1948: King's College, Cambridge.

18 Edward Benjamin Britten (1913–76), foremost English composer of his generation.

19 George Crabbe (1754–1832) was born in Aldeburgh, and worked there for years as a doctor before moving to London and beginning his remarkable career as a poet.

20 Edward Fitzgerald (1809–83) lived for the last two decades of his life in Woodbridge, and spent much time sailing with Suffolk fishermen. His best-known work is his free translation of *The Rubáiyát of Omar Khayyám* (1859).

21 Published by the Caxton Press, Christchurch, 1940.

22 Unpublished letter, Plomer to Lehmann, undated [March 1941]: Texas.

23 It was eventually to appear as 'Some Books from New Zealand', in *Penguin New Writing*, no. 17 (1943).

24 Unpublished letter, 28 June 1941: Texas.

25 *Conversation with my Uncle and Other Sketches* (Unicorn Press, Auckland, 1936) and *A Man and His Wife* (Caxton Press, Christchurch, 1940). Other work published by him during his correspondence with Plomer included *That Summer and Other Stories* (John Lehmann, London, 1946),

When the Wind Blows (Caxton Press, Christchurch, 1945), *I Saw in My Dream* (John Lehmann, London, 1949), *I For One* (Caxton Press, Christchurch, 1954), *Collected Stories, 1935–63* (Blackwood and Janet Paul, Auckland, in conjunction with MacGibbon & Kee, London, 1964), *Wrestling with the Angel, Two Plays: A Time for Sowing and The Cradle & The Egg* (Caxton Press, Christchurch, 1964), *Memoirs of a Peon* (MacGibbon & Kee, London, 1965), *The Hangover* (MacGibbon & Kee, London, 1967), and *Joy of the Worm* (MacGibbon & Kee, London, 1969).

[26] Unpublished letter, 26 January 1942: NZN.

[27] Unpublished letter, 17 November 1945: NZN.

[28] Like Plomer, Angus Frank Johnstone Wilson (1913–) was born in South Africa. At this time he worked in the Foreign Office, and had published only two volumes, *The Wrong Set* (1949) and the book Plomer now sent Sargeson, *Such Darling Dodos* (1950).

[29] Unpublished letter, 28 August 1950: NZN.

[30] Unpublished letter, Sargeson to Plomer, 30 November 1947: NZN.

[31] Unpublished letter, 20 March 1948: NZN.

[32] NZN.

[33] 'Mrs. Pincus' is a reference to one of Plomer's short stories; 'the negro woman' is a reference to an incident in his first autobiography, *Double Lives*.

[34] Unpublished letter, 1 December 1945: NZN.

[35] It would be published in 1965 as *Memoirs of a Peon*.

[36] Unpublished letter, 24 August 1946: NZN.

[37] Unpublished letter, 31 October 1946: NZN.

[38] Unpublished letter, 25 July 1949: NZN. Plomer's wish to avoid unwanted callers was not mere eccentricity or misanthropy; working at home as he did, he had a real need to defend himself from those who thought they would just pop in and save him from boredom by asking his opinion of their latest manuscript.

[39] Unpublished letter, 2 December 1949: NZN.

[40] Unpublished letter to Sargeson, 4 June 1947: NZN.

[41] Ibid.

[42] Letter from James Stern to the writer, 6 July 1987.

[43] Stern, *London Magazine*, October/November 1973, pp. 9–10.

[44] Unpublished letter, Plomer to Sargeson, 8 July 1947: NZN.

[45] Ibid.

[46] 1 March 1948. Published in *Selected Letters of E. M. Forster*.

[47] Ackerley, *My Father and Myself*, p. 125.

[48] Quoted in unpublished letter, James Kirkup to the writer, 30 November 1986.

[49] Unpublished letter, Plomer to Van der Post, 19 February 1951: Opp.

[50] Unpublished letter, 23 November 1948: RHD.

[51] Introduction to *Four Countries*, p. 10.

[52] Unpublished letter, G. E. Stockley of the Foreign Office to Plomer, 6 October 1949: DUL.

[53] Unpublished postcard, 27 October 1949: RHD.

[54] Unpublished letter to Edith Sitwell, 22 May 1951: Texas.

[55] Unpublished letter, 18 November 1949: Texas.

[56] Unpublished letter, 28 April 1950: Cape.

[57] 'Some events of 1951', unpublished diary note: DUL.

[58] *Museum Pieces*, pp. 255–6.

[59] Unpublished letter, 6 September 1952: Cape.

[60] Unpublished letter, 31 August 1952: RHD.

[61] Unpublished letter, 20 September 1952: RHD.

[62] Jill Balcon was Cecil Day-Lewis's second wife; she was (and is, 1987) a fine actress, and Plomer was a particular admirer of hers. He many times asked that she read his poetry in BBC broadcasts, and the two became good friends.

[63] Ingaret Giffard became Van der Post's second wife.

[64] Unpublished letter: Opp.

14. THE LIBRETTIST

[1] Britten's librettists (other than Auden) had been Montague Slater (*Peter Grimes*), Ronald Duncan (*The Rape of Lucretia*), Eric Crozier (*Albert Herring*, *The Little Sweep*, *Billy Budd*), and E. M. Forster (*Billy Budd*).

[2] Unpublished letter, Britten to Plomer: BP.

[3] Interview with Sir Peter Pears, Aldeburgh, October 1983.

[4] For instance, 'Slater seems to have been both resistant to change and slow in delivering agreed revisions': *Benjamin Britten: 'Peter Grimes'*, ed. Philip Brett (Cambridge, 1983), p. 60.

[5] There has been some confusion among Britten scholars as to when Britten worked on 'Tyco the Vegan' (whose title has not previously been given in the scholarly literature). For example, White states that work on it was carried out 'about 1954': *Benjamin Britten: His Life and Operas*, 2nd edn., ed. John Evans, Faber & Faber (London, 1983), p. 83. The letters make it clear that 'Tyco' was not thought of before December 1951 and was abandoned in March 1952.

[6] White, *Benjamin Britten: His Life and Operas*, p. 79.

[7] Undated, but about 7 May 1952: BP.

[8] The *Manchester Guardian* critic was to write of the opera on 11 June 1953 that it was 'an event of the first interest to the musical world at large'.

[9] See White, *Benjamin Britten: His Life and Operas*, pp. 190–1.

[10] The envy with which Britten had to contend during this period is well documented in Michael Kennedy, *Britten* (Dent, London, 1981), pp. 62–3.

[11] Plomer was pestered for interviews about his collaboration with Britten before they had even begun work, and he refused many requests from the BBC to broadcast a talk about the libretto before the opera was first performed, as his letters to the BBC reveal.

[12] Quoted in White, *Benjamin Britten: A Sketch of his Life and Works* (Boosey & Hawkes, London, 1948), p. 19.

[13] 8 May 1952: BP.

[14] Ibid.

[15] He quotes the original lines in 'Notes on the Libretto of "Gloriana" ', *Tempo*, no. 28 (1953), p. 7.

[16] DUL.

[17] BP.

[18] BP.

[19] Even with the change, the garden scene was picked out for special criticism by the *Manchester Guardian* on 11 June 1953, on the grounds that it was too tightly worked to prepare the audience for the next dramatic step.

[20] Kennedy, *Britten*, 3rd edn. (1980), p. 55.

[21] BP.

[22] Plomer, 'Let's Crab an Opera', *London Magazine*, vol. 3, no. 7 (October 1963), p. 103.

[23] BP.

[24] 'The Brambleberry' was Britten's name for the song 'Happy were he', which contains a reference to a brambleberry bush.

[25] There were occasional muted comments, even at Aldeburgh, about the homosexual undertone of Britten's works. Nigel Fortune recalls Plomer quoting the vicar of Aldeburgh as saying plaintively, 'Couldn't we have a little more sweetness and light, and less sodomy and what-have-you?' And the vicar placed a definite emphasis on 'you'. Letter, Nigel Fortune to the writer, 15 October 1985.

[26] DUL.

[27] DUL.

[28] DUL.

[29] DUL.

[30] Quoted in unpublished autobiographical note dated 9 June 1966, in notebook B10: DUL.

[31] Identified only as 'HRH' in the correspondence, but almost certainly Lord Harewood's mother, The Princess Royal. Even in their letters to one another, Plomer and Britten were extraordinarily careful in their references to royalty. This is perhaps a reflection of the feelings aroused in Britten's fellow composers by the royal approval granted to *Gloriana* and of the envy that his 'friends in high places' produced.

[32] BP.

[33] The date can be established from Britten's letter to Plomer of 11 February 1953: DUL.

[34] In a letter to Plomer of 8 March Britten says that the work will be finished 'by next Monday week'—i.e. 16 March, when he was planning to leave for a trip to Ireland.

[35] Unpublished letter, Plomer to René Janin, 21 August 1953: DUL.

[36] Writing ten years later, Plomer remarked that the audience was 'troubled by the deliberately quiet conclusion . . . some resentment was shown at Britten's not having produced a conventionally operative, popular, lush, rip-roaring sentimental drama or melodrama . . .': 'Let's Crab an Opera', pp. 101–4. The critic of *The Times* (who was generous in his praise of the libretto) had remarked of the last scene on 9 June 1953 that 'excursion into melodrama with speech intruding upon what operatic

convention demands should be sung is always extremely questionable on the fundamental grounds of the aesthetics of opera'.

[37] Plomer, unpublished autobiographical note dated October 1966, in notebook B10: DUL.

[38] Unpublished letter, 12 June 1953: FP.

[39] Unpublished letter, 20 July 1953: DUL.

[40] *The Times*, 9 June 1953, p. 2.

15. THE CHANGE OF LIFE

[1] Unpublished letter, Plomer to Britten, 23 July 1953: BP.

[2] He sent it to Lehmann on 20 October 1953, with an unpublished letter of that date: Texas.

[3] Unpublished letters to the writer from Philippa Harrison, 1987.

[4] One of Plomer's ancestors (William VII) had married a Miss Pagan, and this was one reason for his choice of the pseudonym 'Robert Pagan'.

[5] P. N. Furbank, *E. M. Forster: A Life*, vol. 2, p. 280.

[6] Interview with the writer, Marske-in-Swaledale, August 1983.

[7] Interview with Sir Rupert Hart-Davis, Marske-in-Swaledale, July 1983.

[8] John Lehmann, 'Kilvert's Chronicler', *Sunday Telegraph*, 23 September 1973.

[9] Unpublished letter, 13 November 1954: Texas.

[10] Unpublished letter, 14 September 1954: Texas.

[11] Plomer, 'Ian Fleming Remembered', *Encounter*, vol. 24, no. 1 (January 1965).

[12] John Pearson, *The Life of Ian Fleming*, Pan Books edition (1967), p. 243.

[13] Howard, *Jonathan Cape, Publisher*, p. 258.

[14] Plomer's notes on Jonathan Cape Ltd., sent to Michael Howard, 24 January 1968: Cape.

[15] Interview with Van der Post, Aldeburgh, 29 October 1983.

[16] Reprinted as 'The Cost of Letters', in C. Connolly, *Ideas and Places* (Weidenfeld & Nicolson, London, 1953).

[17] They were 'It Was All Such Fun' (not collected), 'Atheling Grange', and 'The Palmer Triplets'. Unpublished letter, Plomer to Howard Newby of the BBC, 25 January 1954: BBC Written Archives Centre.

[18] Unpublished letter, Lady Cholmondeley to Plomer, 15 February 1954: DUL.

[19] It is not possible to name her.

[20] Unpublished letter, Frances Plomer to the writer, 10 April 1987.

[21] Hart-Davis, who knew Plomer and Charles Erdmann as well as anyone did during these years, was convinced that they were not lovers in any physical sense. Charles Erdmann, questioned by the writer on this point by letter, gave no reply.

[22] Unpublished letter: RHD.

[23] Unpublished letter to Hart-Davis, 29 January 1955: RHD. The correspondence contains no details of how much Charles Plomer left, but it cannot have been much. He had lived in very straitened circumstances since the death of Edythe, having only one room in the houses in which he lodged.

24 Unpublished letter, 4 February 1955: Opp.

25 Forster, review of *A Shot in the Park*, in the *Listener*, April 1955.

26 Betjeman, review of *A Shot in the Park*, in the *Sunday Times*, April 1955.

27 Auden, review of *A Shot in the Park*, in *Poetry*, April 1955.

28 Unpublished postcard, 11 October 1955: RHD.

29 Unpublished letter, 18 August 1959: NZN.

30 Interview with Alan Paton, Natal, 22 November 1983.

31 Unpublished letter to Hart-Davis, 1 May 1956: RHD.

32 Huddleston, a member of the Anglican Community of the Resurrection (the order that ran St John's College, Johannesburg, where Plomer had spent part of his schooldays), had worked as a priest in Soweto, near Johannesburg, and had come to believe that apartheid must be destroyed by any peaceful means possible.

33 Unpublished letter, 23 October 1956: NZN.

34 Unpublished letter to James Plomer, 3 September 1956: FP.

35 Nadine Gordimer (1923–), short-story writer and novelist. She had up to this time published only *The Soft Voice of the Serpent* (1953), a collection of short stories.

36 Interview with Nadine Gordimer, Johannesburg, 1983.

37 Ibid.

38 Ibid.

39 PEN is an international association of poets, playwrights, editors, essayists, and novelists, founded in 1921 to promote international understanding and goodwill among writers and others.

40 Unpublished letter, 26 July 1956: FP.

41 Plomer, BBC talk, 'South Africa Revisited', 10 October 1956: BBC Written Archives.

42 Ibid.

43 Unpublished letter to Hart-Davis, 27 August 1956: RHD.

44 Plomer, *Sunday Times*, 2 September 1956.

45 Letter, Plomer to Ridley Beeton, 10 September 1970: NELM.

46 Ibid.

47 I. Jonker, *Selected Poems*, translated and introduced by Jack Cope and William Plomer.

48 Unpublished letter, 16 March 1958: DUL.

49 Unpublished letter to Plomer, 8 March [1958]: DUL.

50 Unpublished letter, 8 March 1958: DUL.

51 Unpublished letter, Plomer to Ruth Simon, 29 May 1958: RHD.

52 Unpublished letter, Britten to Plomer, 25 October 1954: DUL.

53 Unpublished letters, Plomer to Britten, 6 November 1954, and Britten to Plomer, 8 November 1954: BP and DUL, respectively.

54 Unpublished letter, Plomer to Britten, 14 April 1955: BP

55 Ludwig, Prince of Hesse and the Rhine (1908–68), who, with his Scots wife Margaret (daughter of the first Baron Geddes), was a patron and supporter of the Aldeburgh Festival. Britten, in company with Pears, often stayed at the Hesses' home, Schloss Wolfsgarten, near Darmstadt, West Germany.

56 Plomer's programme notes for the Festival of the City of London performance of *Curlew River* (July 1968).

57 Details of the itinerary of this tour were supplied to the writer by Pears, in an interview at Aldeburgh, 26 September 1983.

58 The title means 'Sumida River', the Sumida being the river on which Tokyo (previously Edo) was built.

59 'Ausflug Ost', in A. Gishford (ed.), *Tribute to Benjamin Britten on his Fiftieth Birthday* (Faber & Faber, London, 1963), pp. 60–1.

60 See the cover note by Britten in the published libretto of *Curlew River*. For the date of the second performance I am indebted to Mr Mervyn Cooke of King's College, Cambridge.

61 Unpublished letter, Britten to Plomer, 13 May 1956: DUL.

62 Unpublished letter, Plomer to Britten, 14 May 1956: BP.

63 Plomer's note for the Festival of the City of London performance, July 1968.

64 Britten was not aware at this stage that *Sumidagawa* had previously formed the basis of an opera in English: Clarence Raybould had used the translation made by Marie Stopes (who spent some years in Japan) as the libretto for a one-act opera performed at the Glastonbury Festival in 1913. When Plomer brought this fact to Britten's attention on 7 October 1958, he replied, 'Actually I didn't know that C. Raybould even composed. Don't let it worry us. But what a funny coincidence.' Unpublished letter, 8 October 1958: DUL.

65 Plomer's note for the Festival of the City of London performance, July 1968.

66 2 October 1958: BP.

67 Cover note to the first edition of the libretto of *The Burning Fiery Furnace*.

68 Unpublished letter, 21 October 1958: BP.

69 Unpublished letter, 29 October 1958: DUL.

70 Unpublished letter, Plomer to Britten, 4 November 1958: BP.

71 Unpublished letter, Plomer to Britten, 7 November 1958: BP.

72 Unpublished letter, Plomer to Britten, 7 November 1958: BP.

73 That is, Ludwig, Prince of Hesse and the Rhine.

74 Unpublished letter, 8 March 1959: DUL.

75 White, *Benjamin Britten, His Life and Operas*, p. 205, provides an example of this form of critics' hindsight.

76 In the first performance Pears (as the Madwoman) did wear a mask, but one covering only his eyes and nose. Traditional Noh masks are considerably larger and much more ornate than those used for *Curlew River*.

77 Unpublished letter, 15 April 1959: DUL.

78 Unpublished letter 17 April 1959: BP.

79 Unpublished letter, Britten to Plomer, 24 May 1959: DUL.

80 Unpublished postcard, Plomer to Britten, 26 May 1959: BP.

81 Unpublished letter, 17 August 1959: DUL.

82 Unpublished letter, 15 April 1959: BP.

83 Unpublished letter, 4 August 1960: DUL.

84 Unpublished letter, 1 January 1961: DUL.

85 Unpublished letter, Britten to Plomer, 24 September 1963: DUL. Graham (1931–) had been assistant producer of *The Turn of the Screw* in 1954, and had produced the première of *Noye's Fludde* in 1958.

86 Details given in unpublished letter, Britten to Plomer, 23 October 1963: DUL.

87 Unpublished letter, 4 January 1964: DUL. In fact the screens made for the first performance had 'Crossing the River' painted on their backs, so they must have been constructed at this time. I am indebted to Miss Rosamund Strode for this information.

88 Unpublished letter, 4 January 1964: DUL.

89 The Palazzo Mocenigo.

90 Unpublished letter, 15 February 1964: DUL.

91 Britten wrote, 'I'm just approaching the big moment round the tomb.' Ibid.

92 Ibid.

93 Kennedy, in *Britten*, p. 86, gives the date of completion of *Curlew River* as 2 April 1964. It is worth noting that the manuscript of the full score is dated 'Maundy Thursday, March 1964' (i.e. 26 March), probably because Britten continued to make changes up to that date. The following week (26 March to 2 April) seems to have been occupied by the work of his assistant, Imogen Holst, whose task it was to make fair copies of Britten's manuscript. On 7 March 1964 Britten had written to Plomer, '*Curlew River* is on the way to completion except the score. I know Imo has worked rapidly and well on it.' And on 2 April 1964 he again wrote to Plomer, 'It [*Curlew River*] is all now finished and the machinery is grinding away producing parts for everyone to learn. I'm fairly happy with it except for one bit which I don't think I've got quite right yet, but if I can see it more clearly after a bit of a break I could always redo it.' This unsatisfactory part, according to Miss Rosamund Strode, was 'undoubtedly the passage where the Spirit of the Boy appears; this was rewritten over and over again until the final version was at last achieved quite late on in the rehearsal stage, only days before the final performance'. Letter to the writer, 1 November 1985.

94 DUL.

95 Unpublished letter to Britten, 8 June 1964: BP.

96 Cover note for the libretto of *The Burning Fiery Furnace*.

97 *The Times*, 15 June 1964, p. 6.

98 'The Dream that is made manifest by Music', review of P. J. Smith, *The Tenth Muse*, in the *Times Literary Supplement*, 17 September 1971, p. 1123.

99 Unpublished letter, 31 January 1961: DUL.

100 In an unpublished letter to John Morris, 4 May 1964, Plomer wrote: 'I do wish it were possible for you to review the book: you would do it with special understanding ... I believe Maurice Cranston [one of Plomers's friends at the BBC] is doing it for the *Listener*: I am delighted to hear about Raleigh Trevelyan. I'm not quite sure who is doing it for the *Sunday Times*.' DUL.

101 *A Shot in the Park* (1955) had sold 1,500 copies by September 1958,

whereas an earlier volume of poems, *Visiting the Caves* (1936) had sold only 500 by that date. Unpublished letter, Wren Howard to Jonathan Cape, 15 September 1958: Cape.

[102] Charles Causley, *London Magazine*, August 1960.

[103] Unpublished letter, Plomer to Frances Plomer, 29 February 1960: FP.

16. HASSOCKS AND THE LAST YEARS

[1] Unpublished letter, 8 April 1966: FP.

[2] Quoted in Alan Ross, *London Magazine*, December 1973/January 1974, p. 6.

[3] Unpublished letter to Hart-Davis, 4 September 1966: RHD.

[4] Change-of-address card, Plomer to Hart-Davis, 25 August 1966: RHD.

[5] Unpublished letter, 4 September 1966: Texas.

[6] Charles Erdmann had become a vegetarian because he hated to think of animals being killed. On at least one occasion he wrote to the local paper appealing to people not to kill wasps, and concluding, 'A happy new year to all the wasps!': *West Sussex Gazette*, 7 January 1971.

[7] Unpublished letter, Plomer to Billie Mulholland, 16 May 1972: WM.

[8] Interview with the writer, London, 19 February 1987.

[9] RHD.

[10] Richard Church, review of *Taste and Remember*, in *Country Life*, 6 October 1966.

[11] Unpublished letter to John Lehmann, 19 September 1966: Texas.

[12] FP.

[13] L. P. Hartley and David Guest.

[14] Ross, *London Magazine*, December 1973/January 1974, p. 6.

[15] Charles Causley, in *London Magazine*, December 1973/January 1974, p. 16.

[16] Betjeman, *London Magazine*, December 1973/January 1974, p. 14.

[17] Charles Causley (1917–), a Cornish poet whose work shows the influence of the ballad tradition that Plomer had done so much to revivify, at this time had published *Farewell, Aggie Weston* (1951), *Survivor's Leave* (1953), and *Johnny Alleluia* (1961).

[18] Causley, *London Magazine*, December 1973/January 1974, p. 18.

[19] *Autobiography*, pp. 275, 277.

[20] NZN.

[21] Interview with Miss Gladys Wiles, Hassocks, 26 August 1983.

[22] I am grateful to William Oxley for the opportunity to read these.

[23] William Oxley's unpublished memoirs.

[24] Unpublished letter, 22 July 1967: RHD.

[25] Furbank, *E. M. Forster: A Life*, p. 178.

[26] Unpublished postcard, Plomer to Morris, 13 August 1968: RHD.

[27] Unpublished letter, Morris to Plomer, 7 August 1967: DUL.

[28] Unpublished letter, Plomer to John Morris, 5 January 1968: RHD.

[29] Unpublished letter, 1 January 1968: Opp.

[30] Published in the Twayne World Authors Series, New York, 1969. Plomer wrote to his brother James, 21 April 1969: 'I find the book a

bit embarrassing, partly because of the oddly distributed emphasis, the lack of knowledge or perception in some directions, etc.' FP.

31 Unpublished letter, 19 April 1969: RHD.
32 Plomer had prepared the ground carefully: as early as 1955 he seems to have hinted to Hart-Davis that he would like him to serve as his literary executor. Hart-Davis wrote to George Lyttelton on 27 November 1955: 'I am already literary executor for Hugh Walpole, Duff Cooper and Humphrey House—also *in posse* for William Plomer and others': *The Lyttelton Hart-Davis Letters* (John Murray, London, 1985), vol. 1, p. 31.
33 Interview with Lady Hart-Davis, Yorkshire, February 1987.
34 Plomer, diary note in notebook B10: DUL.
35 Ibid.
36 Unpublished letter, 3 November 1969: RHD.
37 Plomer, diary note in notebook B10: DUL.
38 Ibid.
39 Unpublished letter, Plomer to Sargeson, 11 November 1968: NZN.
40 William Oxley, unpublished memoirs, pp. 236–7: Oxley.
41 Plomer's diary note, 12 December 1968, in notebook B10: DUL.
42 E. Walker, 'About William Plomer', *London Magazine*, December 1973/ January 1974, pp. 23–4.
43 When Waley was dying in great pain, of cancer of the spine, the only book he could bear his wife to read to him was the third volume of *Kilvert's Diary*. After his death in 1966 she found he had marked one passage with a very faint pencil note: 'Like Chinese poem.' Plomer thought this a great compliment to Kilvert. Unpublished letter, Plomer to Hart-Davis, 24 December 1970: RHD.
44 Plomer's diary note in notebook B10: DUL.
45 Unpublished letter, Plomer to John Morris, 31 October 1968: RHD.
46 Unpublished letter, 31 December 1970: WM.
47 Unpublished letter, 5 August 1971: Oxley.
48 Unpublished letter, 5 April 1971: RHD.
49 Unpublished letter, 1 May 1971: DUL.
50 Unpublished letter to John Lehmann, 14 February 1972: Texas.
51 Unpublished letter, 27 July 1971: WM.
52 Unpublished letter, 2 August 1973: RHD.
53 Unpublished letter, 30 December 1971: WM.
54 Unpublished letter, 4 April 1972: RHD.
55 Douglas Dunn, *Books & Writers*, November 1962, pp. 63–4.
56 FP.
57 Unpublished letter, 28 March 1972: FP.
58 Unpublished letter, 12 June 1972: FP.
59 Unpublished letter, 26 October 1972: FP.
60 Interview with Graham C. Greene, Sydney, 21 August 1985.
61 The typescript is now in DUL.
62 Unpublished letter, 20 September 1973: DUL.

POSTSCRIPT

1 *Evening Argus*, 22 September 1973.

Index

WP = William Plomer